Architecting Data Solutions with Snowflake

Design scalable, cloud-native data platforms
for analytics, warehousing, and beyond

Pooja Kelgaonkar

bpb

www.bpbonline.com

First Edition 2025

Copyright © BPB Publications, India

ISBN: 978-93-65899-382

To View Complete
BPB Publications Catalogue
Scan the QR Code:

www.bpbonline.com

Dedicated to

My beloved husband
Mahesh
and
My daughter Anvi

About the Author

Pooja Kelgaonkar is a recognized leader in the data architecture and engineering space, and one of the esteemed **Snowflake Data Superheroes**. With nearly two decades of industry experience, she has built a reputation as a trusted expert in data modernization, distributed systems, and cloud-native data platforms. Over the course of her career, she has held key roles across diverse technology stacks, designing and implementing scalable data solutions that drive business transformation.

Currently serving as a **senior data architect at Rackspace Technology**, Pooja leads enterprise-grade data implementations with a focus on performance, scalability, and seamless integration. Her strategic guidance plays a pivotal role in enabling clients to achieve their data-driven goals through optimized architecture and modern data platform design. Beyond her professional achievements, Pooja is a passionate advocate for continuous learning and community engagement. Her thought leadership is reflected in her technical blogs on **Snowflake** and **Google Cloud Platform (GCP)**, many of which are regularly featured by Snowflake and Google in their community channels.

A frequent **public speaker**, Pooja actively participates in conferences, tech webinars, and community events, where she shares practical insights and architectural best practices. Her deep commitment to education, mentorship, and community growth underscores her mission to empower the next generation of data professionals and contribute to the ongoing evolution of the data ecosystem.

About the Reviewers

❖ **Gaurav Jain** is a passionate Telecom/IT practitioner with extensive professional experience in the domain of telecom products and services deliveries. Along with hands-on exposure of Pre-sales, AWS, VMware Open Cloud Deliveries, Architect of Products and Database Implementation, Cloud Vendor Evaluation, Cloud Policy and Cloud Economics.

He is a holder of multiple industry certifications in AWS, 5G, AI-ML.

Gaurav Jain specializes in pre-sales, delivery, architecture and preparation of various technical documents and loves working with customers on helping them in getting the most out of their problems in live networks.

He is currently working in Nokia as a senior solution architect and part of Global Service Delivery Team.

❖ **Raghvendra Maloo** is an accomplished parallel and distributed computing technology leader with over two decades of experience at renowned companies, including Microsoft, Intel, and Amazon. He possesses deep expertise in cloud computing, distributed systems, cybersecurity, data protection and compliance, touch technology, AI-based algorithm design, data storage optimization, and system software development. Additionally, he is highly skilled in team leadership and mentorship. Mr. Maloo holds seven patents and has authored numerous international publications. His work has consistently delivered impactful business results and garnered industry recognition. As a senior member of IEEE, he has also served as the program committee member and reviewer for various prestigious conferences such as ACM Cods Comad 2024, IEEE WCNC 2025, and ISEC 2025. He has been a distinguished speaker at events like the Intel Developer Forum and High-Performance Computing conferences. Currently, Raghvendra Maloo is part of the Microsoft Defender team at Microsoft Corp, USA.

❖ **Anup Sahoo** is a Cloud Technical Lead at Insight India with over 14 years of rich experience in the field of quality engineering, test automation, and DevOps. As a seasoned professional and a lifelong learner, Anup is passionate about solving real-world problems by merging deep technical expertise with cutting-edge technologies.

He is a Generative AI enthusiast and researcher, exploring how **large language models (LLMs)** and AI-driven automation can transform the future of software testing and quality engineering. As a technical author, Anup has shared his insights through technical blogs, research-backed frameworks, and a growing portfolio of practical tools that aim to make QA smarter and more adaptive.

When he's not immersed in designing intelligent test frameworks or experimenting with AI-infused pipelines, Anup channels his energy into mentoring aspiring professionals, creating impactful DevOps and automation content, and exploring nature through trekking. His curiosity-driven approach and commitment to innovation make him a driving force in both the tech and learning communities.

Acknowledgement

I wish to extend my deepest gratitude to my family for their steadfast support and encouragement throughout the development of this book. Their unwavering belief in my abilities has served as a constant source of inspiration and motivation.

I am sincerely thankful to BPB Publications for affording me the opportunity to author another book on Snowflake. I am grateful to the entire BPB team for their valuable collaboration and guidance across both editorial and technical dimensions, which greatly enriched this endeavor.

I would also like to express my profound appreciation to my mentor and Snowflake community. Their consistent encouragement and commitment to knowledge-sharing have significantly influenced my professional journey. It is a privilege to be associated with such a distinguished group dedicated to continuous learning and innovation.

Finally, to the readers whose interest and support have played an integral role in bringing this work to fruition, I extend my heartfelt thanks. Your engagement and encouragement have been truly instrumental in the realization of this project.

Preface

In the ever-evolving landscape of enterprise data, the role of the data architect and engineer has become more critical than ever. As organizations accelerate their digital transformation journeys, the demand for agile, scalable, and cost-efficient data solutions has grown exponentially. Traditional on-premise and legacy systems are giving way to modern, cloud-native platforms that support real-time analytics, governed data sharing, and cross-functional data collaboration. At the forefront of this transformation is Snowflake—a cloud-native data platform purpose-built to simplify data architecture while maximizing performance, scalability, and flexibility.

Snowflake has emerged as a cornerstone in this modern data architecture as a unified, cloud-native platform designed to support diverse workloads, enable seamless data sharing, and deliver exceptional performance at scale. This book is crafted specifically for data architects and engineers who are responsible for designing and implementing robust data solutions. Whether you are modernizing a legacy data warehouse, designing a new data lakehouse architecture, or enabling real-time data pipelines, this guide will help you understand how to leverage Snowflake's features to build enterprise-ready platforms.

This book is distinguished by its solution-oriented approach, combining reference architectures, industry-aligned best practices, recommendations, along with hands-on exercises. You will understand and learn to design scalable, secure, and resilient data platforms that align with business goals and future-ready architectures to adopt AI and ML workloads.

Prepare to navigate the future of data architecture with confidence. Whether you are aiming to accelerate your career, modernize your organization's data infrastructure, or build expertise in cloud-native data platforms, the ultimate guide to architecting data solutions with Snowflake is your strategic companion in the journey.

Chapter 1: Navigating Snowflake Account Setup and Configuration - The chapter covers the high-level concepts of Snowflake - Data on Cloud. You will learn the typical challenges of traditional data platforms and how Snowflake overcomes them with its unified features. This helps to understand the account setup and Snowflake's Organization, account, and resource hierarchy. You will learn to set up a trial account with Snowflake. This also covers the role-based access setup and implementation.

Chapter 2: Unraveling the Three-Tier Architecture - Shares Snowflake's unique three-layered architecture delivers performance, scale, elasticity, and concurrency in organizations. The three-layered architecture consists of storage, compute, and cloud services layers that are integrated to serve data needs. This also supports the scalability with independent scaling of each layer, which helps workloads scale independently, making it an ideal platform for data solutions.

Chapter 3: The Pillars of Architectural Excellence - Covers the five core pillars of distributed systems and data architecture design. This chapter helps to understand the five core principles - security, reliability, cost-effectiveness, performance, and scalability, along with their importance in architecture design implementation. This is the foundation of any data platform architecture and design.

Chapter 4: Understanding Snowflake's Security Features - Focuses on understanding and implementing Snowflake's security features. This helps to learn network policies, security setup, etc. This also covers the data protection features of Snowflake. This chapter helps to learn about time travel, failsafe, data replication, and data encryption.

Chapter 5: Implementing Data Governance - Shares the most critical pillar of the data platform design. This chapter covers data governance and implementation using Snowflake native features. This chapter focuses on implementing data security - row-level and column-level data security. You will learn dynamic masking, role-based policies, object tagging, and object-tagged policies.

Chapter 6: Evaluating and Optimizing Snowflake's Performance - Optimization is the critical pillar that focuses on the maintenance, performance, and cost-effectiveness of the data platform. This chapter focuses on understanding Snowflake's performance elements and evaluation process. You will learn to use Snowflake metadata views to compute the usage and performance of the account. This also helps to learn performance optimization techniques.

Chapter 7: Unlocking Snowflake's Cost and Performance - Cost-effectiveness is one of the architectural pillars of data platform design. This chapter focuses on understanding Snowflake's cost and components. This focuses on calculating the cost using Snowflake metadata views. This also covers the derivation of usage metrics and shares details of implementing these identified usage metrics. This also helps to learn various cost optimization techniques.

Chapter 8: Implementing Data Integrations - Data integration is one of the important aspects of platform design where you need to integrate your platform to source in as well as share data with consumer applications. This chapter focuses on consumer integration.

This helps to understand Snowflake's unique feature - data sharing. This also covers data cloning - maintaining multiple environments with optimal space. This covers the need to have data consumers and consumer models. This also helps to learn the benefits of data sharing and cloning.

Chapter 9: Designing Data Solutions - This chapter sets the foundation of data solution designing based on the data architecture pillars. This covers the most important integrations in any data applications like logging, monitoring, error handling, altering, auditing, etc. You will learn these standard practices followed in data application design.

Chapter 10: Designing Data Engineering Pipelines - Data engineering is part of the data platform design that takes care of data integrations, data transformations, data quality, data aggregations, and data readiness for consumption. This chapter focuses on designing and implementing engineering pipelines with Snowflake. This chapter helps to understand various data pipelines as per the data loads and frequency. This will also help you understand the streaming and batch use cases to design the data pipelines to ingest data to the Snowflake tables.

Chapter 11: Designing ETL and ELT with Snowflake - **Extract, Transform, and Load (ETL)** and **Extract, Load, and Transform (ELT)** are the most common patterns used for data integration and transformation. This chapter covers the two most essential approaches - ETL and ELT that are used to design the data processing layer. This also helps to understand the implementation using Snowflake native services and features. This is the foundation of upcoming data workload pattern designing.

Chapter 12: Architecting Data Warehouse - Data warehouse is one of the widely used enterprise data platform architectures. This chapter covers the data warehouse architecture and implementation with Snowflake native services and features. This helps to understand the warehouse architecture, how to design a warehouse, and share real-time use cases, and best practices to implement a data warehouse using Snowflake.

Chapter 13: Implementing Data Lake Solutions - Data Lake is the next data platform design accepted to address some of the challenges from DW design. Data Lake has its unique features and design to integrate and process data within the platform. This chapter covers designing and implementing data lake solutions with Snowflake. This covers the data lake architecture pattern and explores how this can be implemented using Snowflake services. This also shares some of the best practices and recommendations on Snowflake design.

Chapter 14: Exploring Data Mesh Design Options - Data Mesh is the emerging data platform design to overcome challenges that are brought with DW and Data lake designs. Data mesh solves the data-silos and integrates applications under one umbrella. This chapter covers designing data mesh solutions with Snowflake. This covers the data mesh architecture pattern and explains how to implement data mesh using Snowflake services. This also covers the various design approaches to implement data mesh for your data using Snowflake.

Chapter 15: Building Data Lakehouses - A Lakehouse is designed to have capabilities of both warehouses as well as data lake. This chapter covers designing data lakehouse solutions with Snowflake. This covers the data lakehouse architecture and the benefits of lake house architecture pattern. Also covers Implementation of a lakehouse use case using Snowflake services. This helps to learn iceberg integration to use iceberg tables - open table format and using it with workloads.

Chapter 16: Embracing Snowpark and Snowpark ML - Snowpark is one of the Snowflake offerings that is rich in programming support, data frames, built in libraries to support engineering as well as data science and ML needs. This chapter helps to understand Snowpark ML libraries and its use. This also helps to understand how Snowpark is different and used to design and develop engineering as well as ML pipelines. You will learn to implement ML lifecycle using Snowpark ML libraries and features.

Chapter 17: Architecting LLM Solutions with Snowflake - **Large Language Models (LLM)** are widely used these days to implement generative AI use cases. Snowflake offers a wide range of integrations and services to build applications with Snowflake. This chapter covers the most interesting offerings of Snowflake- native apps that support LLM capabilities and are used to implement most of the latest solutions with Snowflake. This helps to learn about the native apps, integrating the Open AI model with Snowpark and Streamlit to design and implement your first application with Snowflake.

Chapter 18: Unleashing Snowflake's Advanced Capabilities - Snowflake is working on enhancing the platform with the addition of a set of advanced features. Snowflake announced many features during SNOWDAY 2023. This chapter covers the latest and greatest offerings of Snowflake - Horizon and Cortex. This also helps to learn the usage of LLM functions to summarize, generate content, or translate the data on the fly. This chapter helps to learn the advanced features of Snowflake to deploy the LLM-based functionalities to improve the performance of applications or enhance application usability to derive new value adds with these LLM-based functions.

Code Bundle and Coloured Images

Please follow the link to download the
Code Bundle and the *Coloured Images* of the book:

https://rebrand.ly/h3ff8pc

The code bundle for the book is also hosted on GitHub at
https://github.com/bpbpublications/Architecting-Data-Solutions-with-Snowflake.
In case there's an update to the code, it will be updated on the existing GitHub repository.

We have code bundles from our rich catalogue of books and videos available at
https://github.com/bpbpublications. Check them out!

Errata

We take immense pride in our work at BPB Publications and follow best practices to ensure the accuracy of our content to provide with an indulging reading experience to our subscribers. Our readers are our mirrors, and we use their inputs to reflect and improve upon human errors, if any, that may have occurred during the publishing processes involved. To let us maintain the quality and help us reach out to any readers who might be having difficulties due to any unforeseen errors, please write to us at :

errata@bpbonline.com

Your support, suggestions and feedbacks are highly appreciated by the BPB Publications' Family.

Piracy

If you come across any illegal copies of our works in any form on the internet, we would be grateful if you would provide us with the location address or website name. Please contact us at business@bpbonline.com with a link to the material.

If you are interested in becoming an author

If there is a topic that you have expertise in, and you are interested in either writing or contributing to a book, please visit www.bpbonline.com. We have worked with thousands of developers and tech professionals, just like you, to help them share their insights with the global tech community. You can make a general application, apply for a specific hot topic that we are recruiting an author for, or submit your own idea.

Reviews

Please leave a review. Once you have read and used this book, why not leave a review on the site that you purchased it from? Potential readers can then see and use your unbiased opinion to make purchase decisions. We at BPB can understand what you think about our products, and our authors can see your feedback on their book. Thank you!

For more information about BPB, please visit www.bpbonline.com.

Join our Discord space

Join our Discord workspace for latest updates, offers, tech happenings around the world, new releases, and sessions with the authors:

https://discord.bpbonline.com

Table of Contents

CHAPTER 1

Navigating Snowflake Account Setup and Configuration

Introduction

Snowflake is data on cloud designed to implement data platforms with features like scalability, performance and cost efficiency, isolated compute and storage, and excellent integrations. You can get started with Snowflake by signing up for a trial version. You can get started with this chapter, which covers the high-level concepts of Snowflake. You will learn Snowflake's unified features and get introduced to the three-layered architecture of Snowflake. You will be able to understand the account setup, Snowflake's Organization account, and resource hiera rchy. You will also learn to set up a trial account with Snowflake. This chapter also covers the role-based access setup and implementation.

Structure

This chapter consists of the following topics:

- Data on cloud
- Account and organization setup
- Setting up accounts
- Access control setup
- Access control with RBAC

Objectives

By the end of this chapter, you will be able to understand the need for a Snowflake data platform over traditional or enterprise platforms. You will also be able to set up a trial account for yourself. This trial account will be used to perform various exercises throughout this book.

Data on cloud

Snowflake is a data platform built from scratch on the cloud. This does not leverage any existing database technology or big data or Hadoop technologies. This is built with a brand-new query engine designed to work on the cloud.

Snowflake is also referred to as a self-managed service because:

- No hardware is required to set up or maintain the running of Snowflake.

- No software is required to install or configure to access Snowflake.

- No maintenance or licensing is required to run Snowflake as it manages everything.

Snowflake's self-managed data platform can be set up on any public cloud, such as AWS, Google Cloud Platform, and Microsoft Azure. Snowflake utilizes the cloud resources to deploy the compute, storage, and cloud services required to run it. Snowflake offers account setup on one or more regions on each cloud. You can host one account on one cloud as an organization account and set up other accounts on the other two cloud platforms as Snowflake accounts. This follows an organizational account hierarchy, which you will learn more about in the subsequent section of this chapter.

Snowflake offers multiple editions, and you can choose any one of the editions based on your business or organization's needs. There are four editions available, and each successive edition consists of features of the previous edition and a set of additional features. The following are the editions available, and each of them has specific offerings and limited features:

- **Standard edition:** The standard edition is the introductory edition, and you have access to all standard features of Snowflake.

- **Enterprise edition:** The enterprise edition has all the features from the standard edition and additional features that require organization or enterprise-wide implementation.

- **Business critical edition:** The business-critical edition is the successive edition with all features from the enterprise, along with additionally enhanced security and data protection to store, process, and manage highly sensitive information.

- **Virtual Private Snowflake (VPS):** The last edition, VPS, is the highest edition, in which organizations have strict policies and need to implement sensitive data processing. For example, financial institutions.

Snowflake is committed to providing a seamless experience to the users. Snowflake product teams work relentlessly to optimize existing services and add new features. These features are released in various phases: Private Preview, Public Preview, and General Availability. These releases share new features, fixes, and enhancements to the existing services weekly. There are two types of releases: Full release and Patch release.

Snowflake also shares the releases that have behavioral changes to the platform monthly. You can visit **https://docs.snowflake.com/en/release-notes/new-features** to get details of new features released this week.

Snowflake's unified architecture enables users to integrate various applications into the data platform. You can refer to *Figure 1.1,* which represents the three layers of Snowflake architecture.

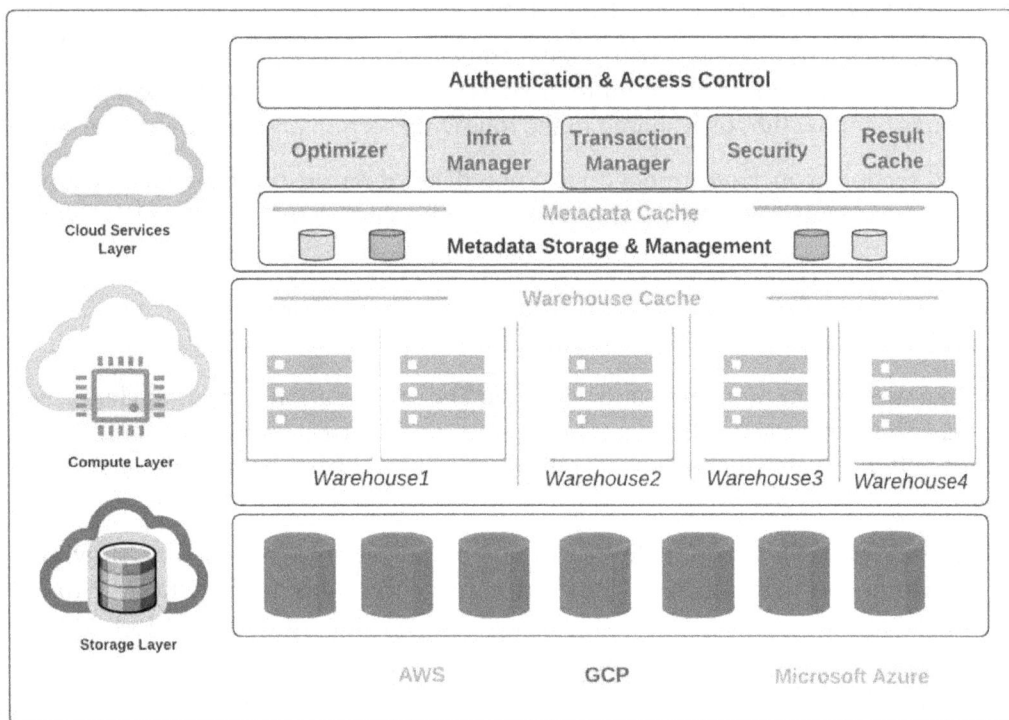

Figure 1.1: Three layered architectures

Snowflake architecture consists of three layers: the cloud services layer, the compute or virtual warehouse layer, and the storage layer. Let us take a look at them in detail:

- **Cloud services layer:** This is the very first layer of architecture that takes care of metadata management, authentication, and authorization, parsing and generating query plans, maintaining the result cache to serve the same query results from the cache, etc. This is also referred to as the *Brain* of the platform, as it controls and manages the key activities.

- **Warehouse layer:** This is the second layer and is referred to as the **compute layer**. This layer allows users to create various warehouses depending on their application and business needs. There are different types of warehouses available to be set up, such as standard and Snowpark-optimized. This layer also maintains a local cache referred to as the warehouse cache that holds the data processed for subsequent queries.

- **Storage layer:** This is the third and last layer of the architecture that caters to the storage requirements to store the data. This layer offers storage to store the data and the backup copy of the data as part of data protection.

These layers are designed to serve all your application needs with efficient implementation. You will learn more about Snowflake's architecture and the offerings of each layer in *Chapter 2, Unraveling the Three-Tier Architecture*.

Snowflake offers a trial account with $400 credits for your personal training and learning purposes. You can set up the account to learn as you learn with upcoming chapters in the book. You can follow the steps shared in the following section and set up the trial account.

With this section, you have understood Snowflake: data on the cloud and have been introduced to the unified architecture of Snowflake. In the following section, you will learn to set up the organization account and manage Snowflake accounts.

Account and organization setup

Snowflake supports organization and accounts. The organization is the first-class object in Snowflake that connects multiple accounts set up for business entities. Organizations are used for better account management, billing, data replication, data sharing, and admin tasks.

You can have multiple accounts linked to one organization, which can be provided by different cloud providers as well. You can manage accounts using ORGADMIN role. You can manage the admin role and grant privileges to the admin role to take care of organizations or accounts.

It is recommended that you enable **multi-factor authentication (MFA)** to secure admin logins. You can enable MFA while creating users or by using the **ALTER USER** command. You can complete the MFA setup from UI.

Refer to *Figure 1.2*, which represents a use case where an organization has three accounts associated, and each of the accounts is set in three different clouds and regions.

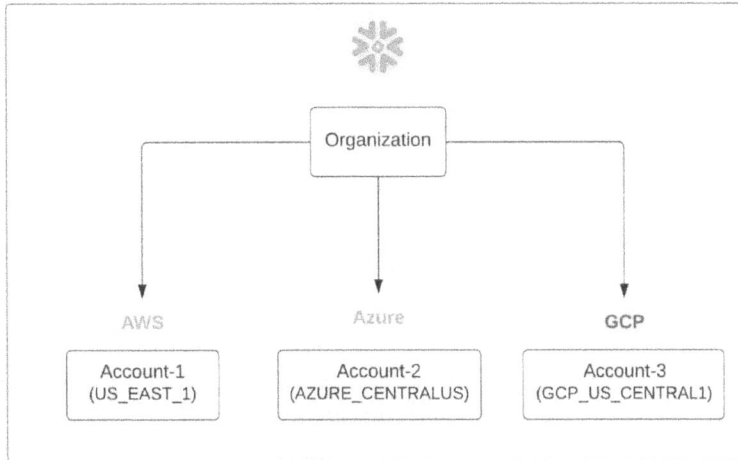

***Figure 1.2:** Snowflake Org setup*

Organization can be set up when you want to create multiple accounts and manage them for different domains or workloads. If your existing Snowflake platform has only one account, you may not need ORGADMIN and Org setup. Whenever you need to set up another account on the same or a different cloud, you can create an account and manage both accounts as part of the organization. You can enable the ORGADMIN role and allow the admin to create accounts. You will learn about maintaining accounts in an organization in the subsequent sections of this chapter.

Using ORGADMIN

You cannot create an organization directly while setting up the Snowflake account. You can create an account first based on the choice of edition and cloud provider. You can also enable the ORGADMIN role and grant users access using the **GRANT** command.

You can enable the ORGADMIN using the following SQL commands:

- Enabling ORGADMIN for an account:
  - **USE ROLE orgadmin;**
  - **ALTER ACCOUNT account1 SET IS_ORG_ADMIN = TRUE;**
- Disabling the ORGADMIN for an account:
  - **USE ROLE orgadmin;**
  - **ALTER ACCOUNT account1 SET IS_ORG_ADMIN = FALSE;**

You can enable the ORGADMIN role to a maximum of eight Snowflake accounts, and this cannot be enabled for a READER account.

Note: You cannot remove the ORGADMIN from the current account if you are enabling it for the first time. If you want to remove it from the current account, then you need to enable the ORGADMIN in another account and then remove the ORGADMIN from the current account. ORGADMIN must be associated with an account within an organization. If you have only one account within the organization then you cannot delete ORGADMIN.

Setting up accounts

Once you enable the ORGADMIN, you can view the accounts created and active in the ORG. You can use the **SHOW ORGANIZATION ACCOUNTS** command to list the accounts in the organization. You can create the accounts using the ORGADMIN role and using UI options as well as SQL commands.

Example 1: Set up an account with a new region and cloud provider.

In this scenario, consider that you want to set up the account in the AWS US WEST 2 region within the organization:

```
Use role ORGADMIN;
Create account sales_account
  admin_name = admin
  admin_password = 'Demp@2024'
  first_name = Pooja
  last_name = Kelgaonkar
  email = 'pk_email@org.com'
  edition = enterprise
  region = aws_us_west_2;
```

Example 2: Set up an account in an existing region.

Consider that you already have an account in the AWS region of AWS US EAST 1 and want to set up a new account using the ORGADMIN role in the same region:

```
Use role ORGADMIN;
create account hr_account
  admin_name = admin
  admin_password = 'Demo2024'
  email = 'pk_gmail@org.com'
  edition = enterprise;
```

Deleting accounts

You can drop an account created using the ORGADMIN role. Only **ORGADMIN** can drop the accounts. However, **ORGADMIN** cannot drop the accounts logged into. You can also drop an account with a grace period to retrieve the account, as shown:

```
USE ROLE ORGADMIN;
DROP ACCOUNT hr_account GRACE_PERIOD_IN_DAYS = 14;
DROP ACCOUNT hr_account; --without grace period
```

Snowflake offers a feature that allows you to retrieve dropped objects using **UNDROP**. Only **ORGADMIN** can restore the account. You can use the **UNDROP** command to restore the account:

```
USE ROLE ORGADMIN;
UNDROP ACCOUNT hr_account;
```

UNDROP is an SQL command used to recover objects dropped accidentally. You will learn more about this command in the *Data protection and governance* of *Chapter 5, Implementing Data Governance*.

Organization usage

Snowflake offers **USAGE** views to query the utilization of resources. Snowflake shares read-only **USAGE** schemas such as **ORGANIZATION_USAGE** and **ACCOUNT_USAGE**. You can use **ORGANIZATION_USAGE** to get the usage details at the organization level. **USAGE** schema consists of a bunch of views that share usage details of accounts, storage, compute, serverless services used in accounts, rate sheet daily, and usage in currency on a daily basis. Some of the key views are listed as follows:

- **ACCOUNTS**: This is a view in the **USAGE** schema that shares information about **ACCOUNTS** for a given organization.

- **METERING_DAILY_HISTORY**: This view consists of details of the daily credit usage as well as a cloud services rebate for an organization within the last 365 days (one year).

- **RATE_SHEET_DAILY**: This view consists of the effective rates that are required for calculating usage in the organization. This gives details of the currency rates and conversion of Snowflake credits.

- **USAGE_IN_CURRENCY_DAILY**: This view shares information on daily usage in credits as well as usage in currency.

You can use these USAGE views to monitor the usage and send alerts. You can also use Snowsight to build dashboards and share them with teams. You can use Snowflake's native features to monitor and generate alerts. You will learn these features in upcoming sections of this book.

In this section, you have learned to set up the organization and multiple accounts. You can also manage the accounts using SQL commands as well as GUI features and options. In the following section, you will learn to set up a trial account that will be essential to perform the labs and exercises from this book.

Set up a trial account

Snowflake offers trial accounts to help learners create their temporary accounts and perform **proof of concepts** (**POCs**), complete quickstarts, and learn with hands-on experiences.

You can set up the trial account using your mail ID, and this is valid for 30 days with $400 credits for learners. You can get your trial account for the labs and use cases demonstrated in this book.

Note: **Requirements for sign-up: You will need these details before you sign up for the trial account: your email ID, region, Snowflake Edition (you can opt for Standard, Enterprise, or Business Critical; it is recommended to get the Enterprise edition to complete labs in this book), the cloud provider, i.e., GCP, AWS, or Microsoft Azure (you can choose your choice of cloud, however, it is recommended to get the AWS setup as some of the preview features are available for AWS accounts).**

You can use the following steps to set up your trial account:

1. You can visit **https://signup.snowflake.com/** and set up a trial account. You can follow the forms shared here and complete the setup. You can get your trial account verified and get started with the trial version. Refer to the following figure:

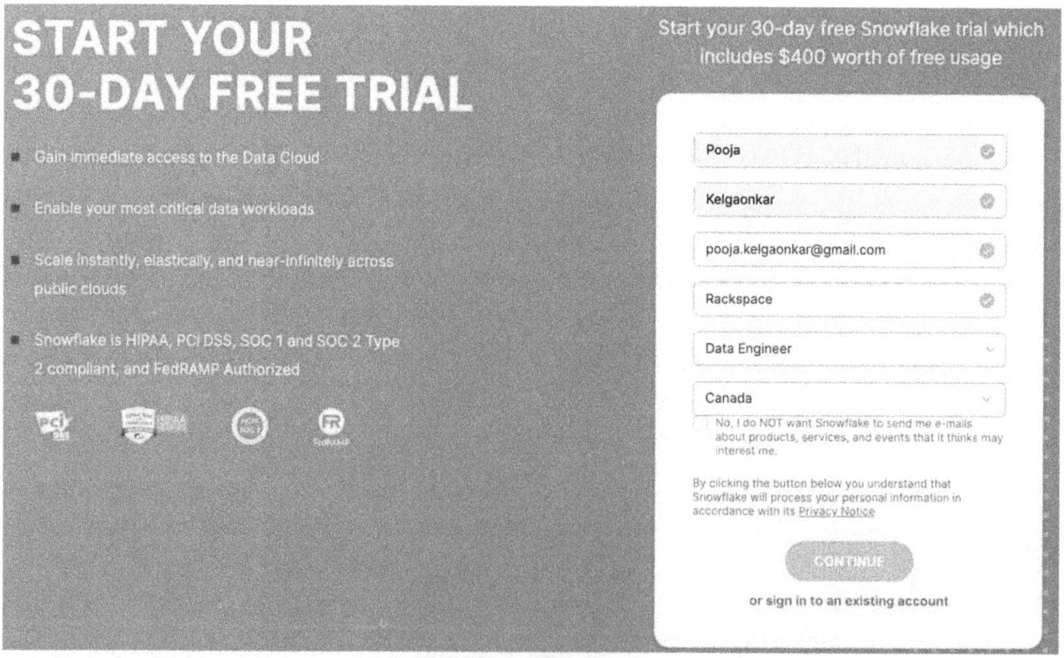

Figure 1.3: Trial account setup

2. Provide your details as shown in the form:

    a. First Name

      b. Last Name

      c. Email address

      d. Company name

      e. Role

      f. Country

3. Click on **CONTINUE** to get the next form to select your choice of cloud and region, as shown in the following figure:

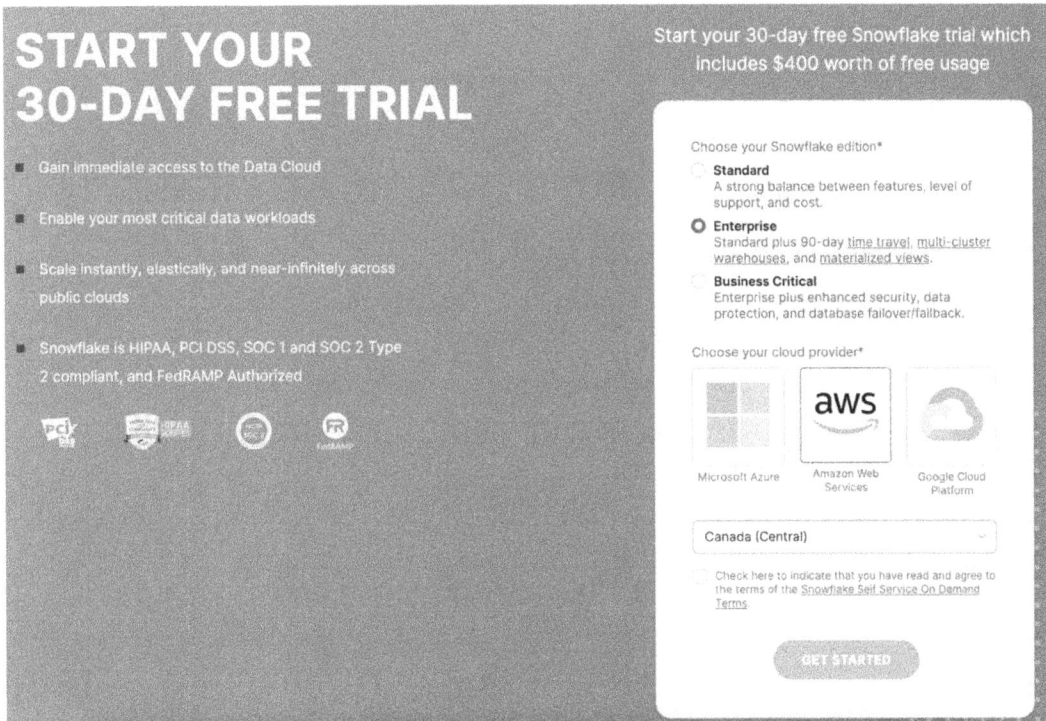

Figure 1.4: Trial account setup, page 2

4. Once you click **GET STARTED**, you get an email with a welcome message routed to the Snowflake account.

Note: Please do not forget to capture your account identifier.

You can log on to the trial account created using the the Snowflake app link: **https://app.snowflake.com/**. You can provide the account identifier to log on to the account. Snowsight is the default Web UI for all the new accounts being signed up. It is an intuitive GUI with various features to support developers, admins, and engineers to continue with their development life cycle. You will learn more about this in subsequent sections of this book.

CLI setup

Snowflake offers SnowSQL as a CLI, and you can download it from the web UI. You can follow the given steps to download and configure the SnowSQL interface:

1. Go to **https://developers.snowflake.com/snowsql/**

2. Select the version as per the operating system's requirements.

3. Download and install the CLI.

4. You can find the directory at `~/.snowsql/config`, which can be used to store config files.

5. You can also use the CURL command from cloud endpoints to download the interface.

6. You can use the `$ snowsql` prompt to connect to Snowflake and perform SQL or programmatic development.

7. You can use `$ snowsql -v` and get the version of the SnowSQL.

8. You can use `~/.snowsql/config` to store your login details, i.e., username, password, Snowflake account identifier, etc.

9. You can use the following parameters in the config file:

Parameter	Description
`-a / --accountname`	Account identifier
`-u / --username`	Username
`-P`	Password (prompts interactively)
`-d / --dbname`	Database name
`-s / --schemaname`	Schema name
`-r / --rolename`	Role in setting the context
`-w / --warehouse`	Warehouse to be used
`-f`	File name, it is the sql file that can be executed from the command line
`-c / --connection`	Connection parameters to connect to Snowflake

Table 1.1: SnowSQL parameters

You can use the **snowsql** command to connect to Snowflake as CLI. Refer to the following examples to connect and use SnowSQL:

- Connect to Snowflake account to run interactive queries using SnowSQL. You can use the following **snowsql** command with parameters to connect and run queries:

```
snowsql -a accountname -u poojak2024 -P -d POC_DEV_DB -r DATA_ENG
```

- Connect to Snowflake and run a query as CLI. You can use the snowsql query parameter to run a query as a command prompt and get the following result:

```
snowsql -c pk_connection -d poc_dev_db -s poc -q 'select * from
sales limit 10'
```

In this example, the **-q** parameter is used to specify the query to be run interactively using a command prompt.

- Connect and execute an SQL file from the command prompt. You can use **snowsql** command with an export file to export data to an output file and specify the output file properties using snowsql options:

```
snowsql -a accountname -u poojak2024 -f /tmp/sql_export.sql -o
output_file=/tmp/sales_report.csv -o quiet=true -o friendly=false -o
header=true -o output_format=csv
```

In this example, the -o parameter used:

- o **Header = true:** Adds a header to the output file.

- o **Output file:** Provides a file name to save the result of the query, export file.

- o **Quiet:** It is provided to turn off the standard output.

- o **Friendly:** It is used to turn off the standard and existing messages.

- o **Output_format:** This is the file format used to specify the output file.

SnowSQL commands options syntax may vary a bit with operating systems, namely, Windows, MacOS, and Linux. You can also refer to **https://docs.snowflake.com/en/user-guide/snowsql-config** to complete config setup.

Once you log on to your trial account, you can use the system-defined roles to implement the various use cases in the book. In a real scenario and production implementation, it is recommended that custom roles be set up as per your application requirements and platform integrations. You will learn more about access control and role management in the following section.

Access control setup

Snowflake's access control approach consists of features from access frameworks: **Discretionary Access Control (DAC)** and **Role-Based Access Control (RBAC)**. Access control frameworks, DAC and RBAC models, have different features to support access management. They are:

- **DAC:** In this framework, each database object has an owner, and each owner grants access to other users.

- **RBAC:** In this framework, access is granted to the roles. Various roles are created to manage access and grant these roles to the users.

Access control implementation in Snowflake follows features that let owners manage objects and create roles with required access privileges. You need to understand some of the key concepts to get started with the Snowflake access control setup. They are as follows:

- **Object:** An object is a securable entity. You can grant access to the entity.

- **Role:** Role is an entity used to grant access to objects. These roles are assigned to the users.

- **Privilege:** This is the level of access that can be granted to the roles or users.

User: This is an identity used to identify users in Snowflake. This can be associated with a person or program.

Refer to *Figure 1.5*, which represents these two types of access control frameworks, DAC and RBAC:

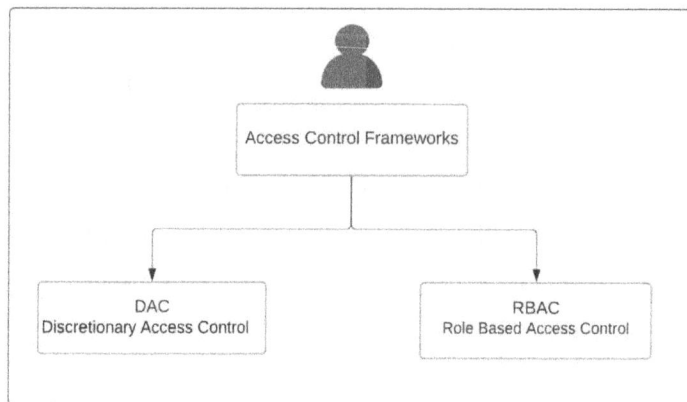

Figure 1.5: Access control frameworks

A role can be granted to another role, and this leads to the role hierarchy. Access control follows the hierarchy to grant access to the roles, users, and objects. Snowflake offers system roles and allows users to create custom roles. System defined roles are given to manage users, roles, systems, accounts, and security as admins. Let us take a look at them:

- **ORGADMIN:** This is the ADMIN at ORG level, and this role can manage accounts at ORG. User with this role can create or manage accounts within an organization and view their usage.

- **ACCOUNTADMIN:** This is the ADMIN at the ACCOUNT level, and this role can manage ACCOUNT. This is the top-most role for an account, and this is a super user role. This is granted to a very limited number of users who can manage accounts. It is recommended to enable MFA for ACCOUNTADMIN.

- **SECURITYADMIN:** This is a security admin that manages the care of objects, users, and roles, and grants the required privileges to the users.

- **SYSADMIN:** This is the role used to create and manage Snowflake resources like warehouses and databases.

- **USERADMIN:** This is the role designed for user and role management. This can be granted to a user who is allowed to manage users and roles.

- **PUBLIC:** This is the pseudo role granted to the users.

    These are the six system defined roles that users can use to access objects. Refer to *Figure 1.6*, which represents system defined roles:

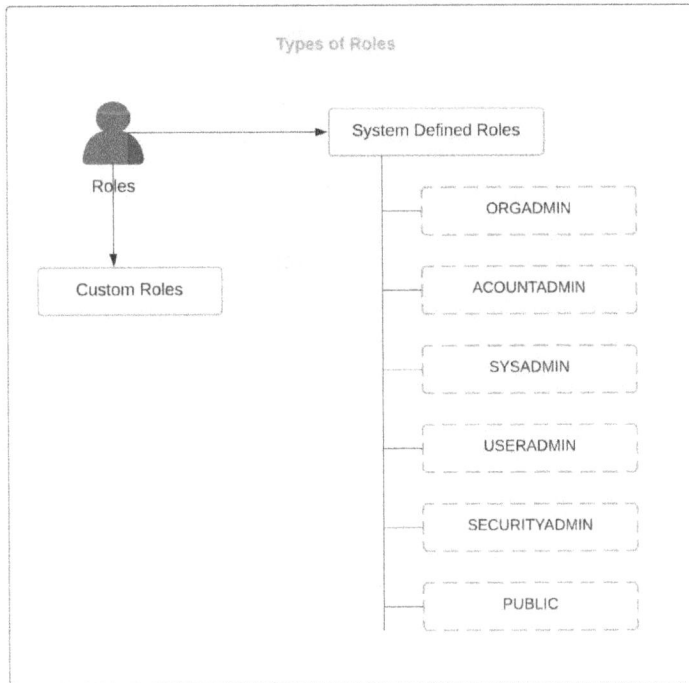

Figure 1.6: System defined roles

You can create custom roles as per your application requirements and assign the system defined roles to the custom role. Active role is the role that sets the authorization for a given session. You can use the system defined role or custom role as an active role for a session. This sets the role and permissions required to perform operations in the given session. You can set the active role using the **USE** command, as follows:

```
/* set active role */
USE ROLE SYSADMIN;
```

Consider a scenario where you are an account admin and onboarding teams. As an admin, you would like to maintain roles that can be assigned to the users as per their requirements. You can create roles as per application needs: data engineer to build pipelines, ML engineers to implement AI/ML use cases, and data analysts who need view permission to some of the databases to build reports. You create these roles and grant permissions to manage resources and objects. You can run these SQL commands to create roles and assign roles:

- **Create role for data engineers: DATA_ENG** is the role setup for data engineers. These users can be used to build engineering pipelines. Use the following **CREATE ROLE** statement to set the data engineering role:

```
/* create role for data engineers */
USE ACCOUNTADMIN;        --set active role
CREATE ROLE data_eng
COMMENT = 'This role is for engineering team';  --creates role for
data engineers
GRANT ROLE SYSADMIN to ROLE data_eng;
/*grant usage on objects for specific objects*/
```

- **Create role for ML engineers: ML_ENGINEER** is the role setup for ML engineers and these users have access to create and manage resources required to develop ML pipelines. Refer to following **CREATE** statement:

```
/* create role for ML engineers */
CREATE ROLE ml_engineer;  --creates role for data engineers
GRANT ROLE SYSADMIN to ROLE ML_ENG /*grant usage on Snowflake objects
in place of SYSADMIN*/
COMMENT = 'This role is for ML team';
GRANT OPERATE ON WAREHOUSE dev_ml_wh TO ROLE ml_engineer;
```

- **Create role for data analysts: DATA_ANALYSTS** is the role setup for data analytics user to run analytical workloads. These can be BI engineers or business users that run queries to analyze data. Refer to following **CREATE** statement:

```
/* create role for Data analysts */
CREATE ROLE data_analysts
COMMENT = 'This role is for data analysts team';  --creates role for
data engineers
GRANT SELECT ON ALL TABLES IN SCHEMA database.schema to ROLE data_
analysts;
GRANT OPERATE ON WAREHOUSE compute_wh TO ROLE data_analysts;
```

- You can assign custom roles created for users. Multiple roles can be assigned to the user, and the user gets the access inherited from the roles. In the given use case, custom roles created can be assigned to a user using **GRANT**, as shown:

```
/*assign roles to the user*/
GRANT ROLE data_analysts TO USER jsmith;
GRANT ROLE ml_engineer TO USER jsmith;
```

Refer to *Figure 1.7*, which represents privileges inherited from one role to another. The user who is assigned multiple roles gets various permissions to the account. You can implement accesses, grant privileges, and manage users and roles in the access control setup. You can also implement a role hierarchy with a set of custom roles and privileges assigned.

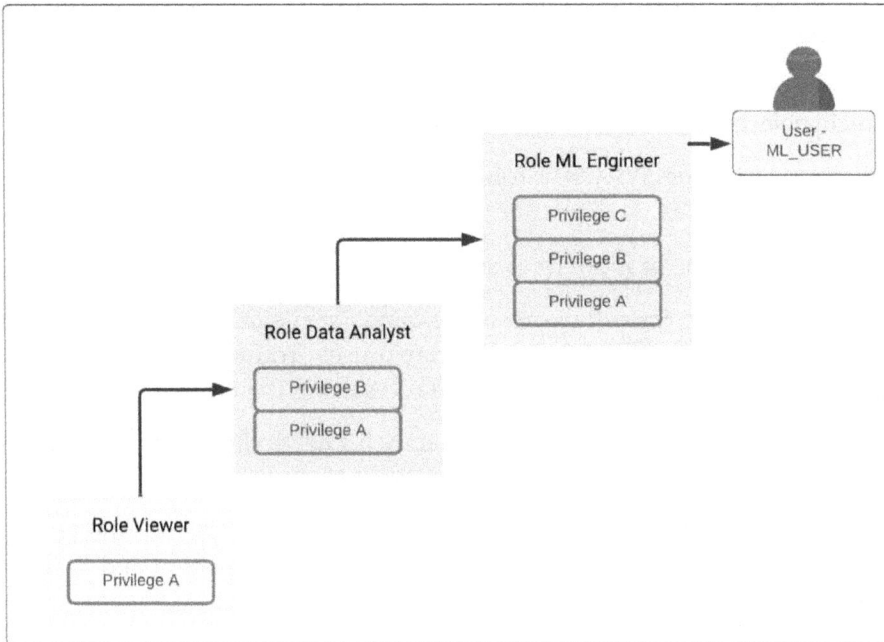

***Figure 1.7:** Role and access management*

Here, Role Viewer can be considered as a basic role that has view-only permissions to specific databases and schemas. Role Data Analyst is a viewer along with write permissions to a specific database and schema to implement analytics. Data analyst inherits the view role from role viewer. Similarly, ML engineer have further roles added to create and manage resources required to implement ML use cases using Snowflake Cortex. ML engineer inherits permissions of the viewer and analyst. ML engineer is granted to a user who essentially inherits the permissions of two other roles.

We have learned system defined roles, custom role creation, role assignment, and hierarchy setup for role implementation. You will learn in the following section, with a real-time use case, how to implement access control RBAC.

Access control with RBAC

You can implement access control with various roles and privileges on Snowflake securable objects. You need to consider the system defined functions, and their privileges to define the custom roles. Snowflake recommends the following considerations while designing access management:

- **ACCOUNTADMIN** is a super user and avoids assigning this as a default role to any user.

- You can set more than one **ADMIN** as **ACCOUNTADMIN** to administer the account.

- Enable **MFA** for the users. To enable **MFA**, ensure users are verified with their email addresses.

- Avoid creating objects using **ACCOUNTADMIN** until it is necessary to have **ADMIN** create objects like storage integrations.

- Recommend using **SYSADMIN** role to create securable objects and grant privileges to the custom roles.

- You can grant one or more roles and privileges to the custom role.

- You can manage Snowflake resources and privileges to use and operate these resources. For example, Snowflake warehouses. You can create a warehouse and grant **USAGE** or **OPERATE** to the custom roles using them.

- You can create read-only roles for users who need view only permissions to the account.

- You can use **GRANT** to assign permissions to the role as per the requirements. Follow the minimal access required to perform the operation and grant only that permission to the role.

Snowflake allows **GRANT** to allow permissions to all objects like warehouses, databases, schemas, procedures, functions, integrations, tasks etc.

You can implement access control using SQL commands as well as using Snowflake Web UI. The following steps are used to create roles using Web UI:

1. Log in to Snowsight. (**https://app.snowflake.com/**).
2. Login with your account identifier, username, and password.
3. Select the role **ACCOUNTADMIN** (as shown in *Figure 1.8, Step 1*).
4. Go to **Admin** (as shown in *Figure 1.8, Step 2*).
5. Select **Users & Roles** (as shown in *Figure 1.8, Step 3*).

You get a list of existing users and roles in the account. You can view the users in the users tab and roles in the roles tab present in the Snowflake account.

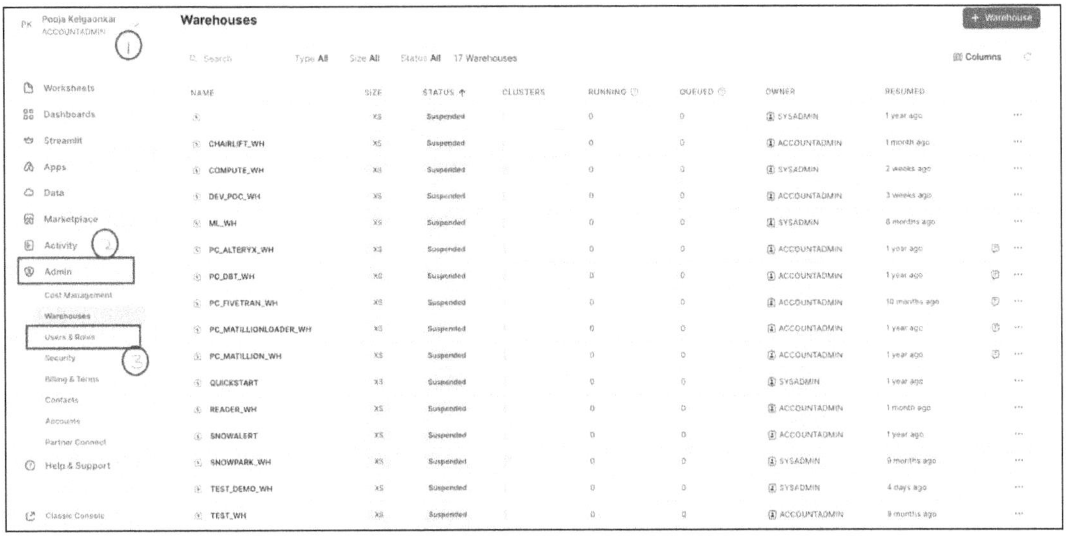

Figure 1.8: *Snowsight user management*

You get a view of existing roles in a graphical representation and a tabular view. Refer to *Figure 1.9*, which shares a graphical view of roles present in the account:

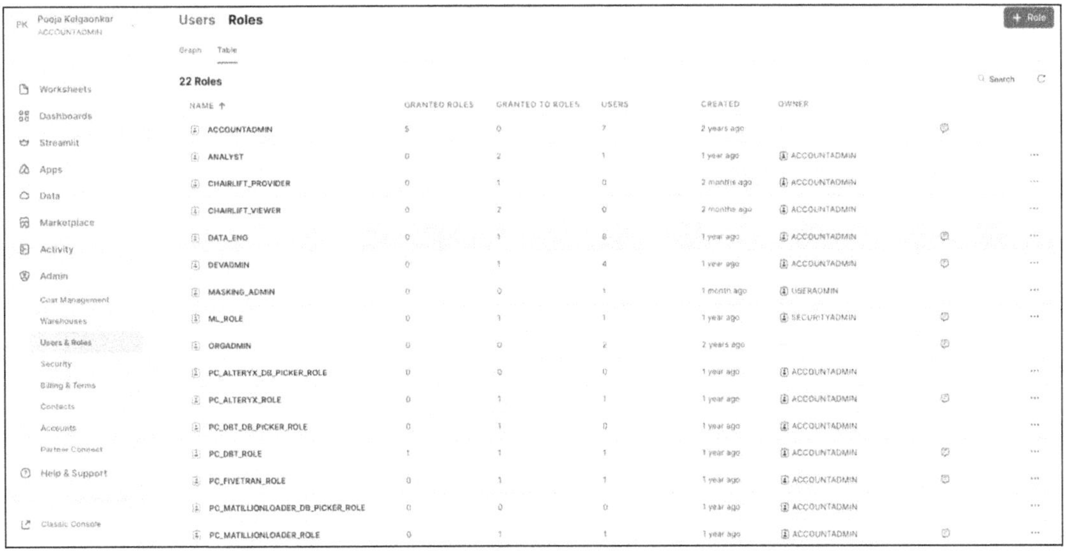

Figure 1.9: *Roles view in account*

Add users using **Create User** using Web UI (Refer to *Figure 1.10*). Follow the given steps:

1. Go to **Users & Roles**.

2. Click on the **+Users** in the top right corner.

3. Provide the following details to create a user:

a. **User Name**: Name of the user being onboarded.

b. **Email**: Email address of the user.

c. **Password**: Temporary password for the user.

d. **Comment**: User onboarding comment.

4. **Click on the check box**: Enable force user to change password on the first time. This is essential to allow password reset.

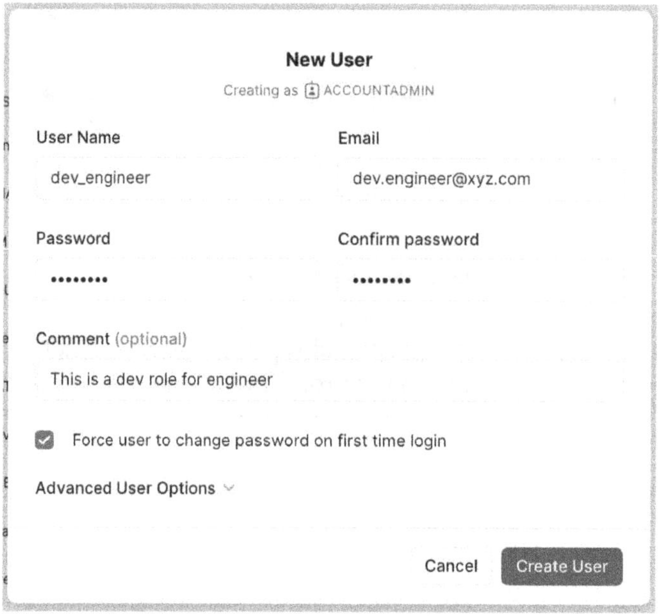

Figure 1.10: New user creation form

Roles can be created or added with **Create Role** using Web UI (Refer to *Figure 1.11*). Follow the given steps:

1. Go to **Users & Roles**.

2. Click on the **+Roles** in the top right corner.

3. Provide the following details to create a role:

a. **Name**: The name of the role being created.

b. **Grant to the role**: The existing role that can be granted to the user. This is optional, you can grant permissions once the role is created as well.

c. **Comment**: Provide comment on role creation.

Figure 1.11: *New role creation form*

Owners are the users who create and own an object within Snowflake. You can grant access to the users as well as roles. Refer to *Figure 1.12*, which represents an owner who creates two objects: Database and Warehouse. Now, the owner can assign privileges on these objects to the roles and users as needed. The database object permissions are granted to the users via custom roles created.

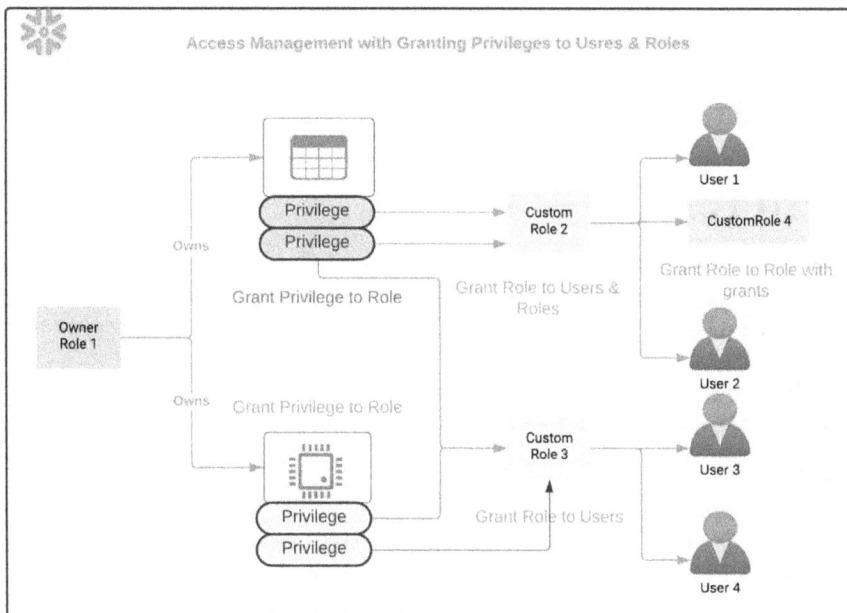

Figure 1.12: *Role management*

You can use the following set of SQL statements to create and manage object permissions.:

```
/*set context */
USE SYSADMIN;
CREATE DATABASE POC_DEV_DB;
CREATE SCHEMA POC;
CREATE or replace WAREHOUSE dev_poc_wh with warehouse_size='XSmall';
CREATE ROLE ml_engineer;
/*grant roles and users */
GRANT USAGE on WAREHOUSE dev_poc_wh to role ml_engineer;
GRANT SELECT on ALL TABLES IN SCHEMA POC to role ml_engineer;
```

You have learned to create and manage roles and users. You can manage resources using SQL commands as well as UI based options.

Conclusion

In this chapter, you have learned what Snowflake, data on cloud is and its unified, three-layer architecture. Snowflake's unified architecture with separate computing and storage makes it stand out in the market. Many customers are adopting Snowflake due to its parallel scalability to serve compute and storage requirements independently. Snowflake organizations, account setup, and user management with RBAC allow admins to manage resources the same way as cloud user management.

In the next chapter, you will learn more about Snowflake architecture, the three layers, and the services of each layer. You will also learn about Snowflake caching and how caching helps in resulting queries faster. You will learn Snowflake data storage and understand micro-partitions and clustering, which are essential to learning Snowflake data designs.

Points to remember

Snowflake platform brings various key features and data platform capabilities. We will learn more as we drive through subsequent chapters of this book. This chapter shares the following key takeaways:

- Snowflake is designed from scratch for cloud. It is a unified architecture that isolates computing and storage from each other. You can scale compute and storage irrespective of the other. This feature overcomes the biggest challenge of traditional data platforms, i.e., scalability and capex.

- Snowflake account is a self-managed data platform. You can set up the account on your own to manage your organization, accounts, and resources. You do not need any additional hardware, software, or licenses to set up the platform. This is the simplest platform to manage and configure, reducing the admin efforts.

- Snowflake architecture is a three-layered architecture: Cloud services layer, Warehouse layer, and storage layer. Each layer has its own set of responsibilities to cater to Snowflake's features, such as scalability, efficiency, maintainability, and operational excellence. Snowflake maintains cache at various layers to support performance efficiency.

- You can get started with Snowflake with a trial account. Snowflake offers a trial account with $400 credits, and this is sufficient to get hands-on experience in designing and deploying data use cases with native features. Your trial account is valid for 30 days. Snowflake also offers student accounts that are valid for 60 days.

- Snowflake allows users to create organizations and accounts within an organization. You can create Organizations and Accounts within your data platform using SQL commands. You can create accounts on different cloud platforms and regions. ORGADMIN can manage accounts within the organization and ACCOUNTADMIN can manage account resources like users, roles, warehouses, databases, objects, etc.

- Snowflake offers access management with features of RBAC and DAC. You can manage access at the object level using roles and granting privileges to the roles. You can create custom roles using system defined roles. Additional permissions can be added using GRANT statements on the resources. The owner of the object has all the rights to maintain the object.

- Snowflake also offers a command line interface: SnowSQL. This is used to connect with Snowflake over the command line interface. You can use commands to connect to Snowflake for an interactive interface and execute SQL commands. You can also access Snowflake objects over CLI and create objects programmatically.

- Snowflake lets users manage organization, accounts, and resources using SQL commands and web UI. You can manage object privileges and access using SQL commands. Snowflake's extended SQLs help users to create, manage, and deploy objects using SQL.

Join our Discord space

Join our Discord workspace for latest updates, offers, tech happenings around the world, new releases, and sessions with the authors:

https://discord.bpbonline.com

CHAPTER 2
Unraveling the Three-Tier Architecture

Introduction

Snowflake's unique three-layered architecture delivers performance, scale, elasticity, and concurrency in organizations. The three-layered architecture consists of storage, compute, and cloud services layers that are integrated to serve data needs. This also supports the scalability with independent scaling of each layer, which helps workloads scale independently, making it an ideal platform for data solutions. You will learn about the responsibilities of each layer present in Snowflake architecture. This chapter also covers Snowflake caching, exploring how Snowflake leverages cache to achieve performance excellence, and how these caches are being maintained.

Structure

This chapter consists of the following topics:

- Three-layered architecture
- Cloud services layer
- Compute layer
- Storage layer
- Snowflake caching

Objectives

By the end of this chapter, you will be able to understand Snowflake's three-layered architecture and how this data platform differentiates from traditional or enterprise platforms. You will also be able to understand features and services offered by each layer of the architecture and how these layers contribute in executing any type of workload on the platform.

Three-layered architecture

Snowflake's unified architecture differentiates it from other data platforms available in the market. The architecture allows users to scale the compute and storage irrespective of each other. Scalability is the most common challenge of traditional data platforms. Increasing compute adds storage as well. In the case of Snowflake, you can scale compute without adding any storage, as storage and compute are independent of each other.

You can refer to *Figure 2.1*, which represents the three layers of Snowflake architecture.

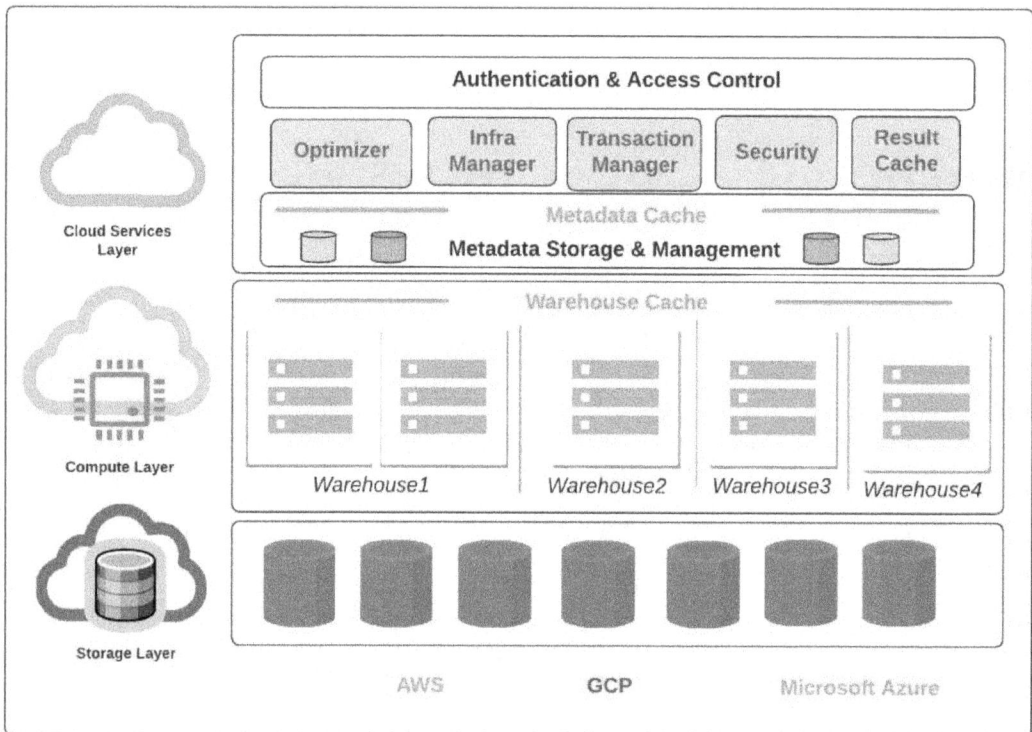

Figure 2.1: Three-layered architectures

Snowflake architecture consists of three layers: cloud services layer, compute or virtual warehouse layer, and storage layer. Refer to the following layers of the architecture:

- **Cloud services layer:** This is the top layer of architecture and is usually referred to as the *brain of the platform*. This layer takes care of metadata management, authentication, and authorization, parsing and generating query plans, maintaining the result cache to serve the same query results from the cache, etc. This layer takes care of security and allows users to configure the policies to restrict unwanted access to the platform. You will learn more about the components of this service in a subsequent section.

- **Warehouse layer:** This is the middle layer of Snowflake architecture, also known as the **compute layer**. Users can create various warehouses depending on their application and business needs. Users can set up multiple warehouses in one platform and allow users to use them as per their needs. Snowflake also offers a variety of warehouses in t-shirt sizes. T-shirt sizes are the size references from extra small (XS) to six times extra-large (6XL), depending on the compute nodes associated with each size. Warehouse sizes are represented in the form of t-shirt sizes, hence referred to as t-shirt sizes (XS to 6XL). Along with the sizes of warehouses, Snowflake also offers several types of warehouses: Standard and Snowpark-optimized. This layer also maintains a cache referred to as the warehouse cache that holds the data processed for subsequent queries. This is also referred to as the processing engine of Snowflake. You will learn more about creating and using warehouses in the following section of this chapter.

- **Storage layer:** This is the bottom layer of the architecture that caters to the storage requirements to store the data. This is the centralized storage that can be concurrently accessed by various warehouses in the platform. Users can use the same storage to store their data and query in parallel. Snowflake has a unique way to store the data and partition them to ensure faster retrieval. Snowflake stores data in the form of micro partitions. These partitions are optimized, compressed, and stored in columnar format. These can also be referred to as immutable partitions. Snowflake also creates clustering on top of the micro partitions depending on the relativity by defining the dept index of the partitions. Data stored is protected by AES encryption by default. This layer offers storage to store the data and a backup copy of it as part of data protection. You will learn more about this layer in the subsequent section of this chapter.

Snowflake's architecture allows users to implement distinct types of workloads on top of Snowflake. You can implement various data designs and patterns to cater to your business requirements. Snowflake offers various objects and extended support to ANSI SQL that enables users to implement the use cases in SQL way. Implementing the use cases with simple SQL-like features allows users to onboard quickly and get started with the implementation. You will learn about the unique features of architecture in the upcoming sections.

Cloud services layer

As you know, this is the **brain** of the platform. This layer takes care of various activities and performs the roles and operations, as necessary. This section will help you learn the various functionalities of the cloud services layer. This layer also manages the metadata of the platform, which is used to derive the query optimization plan, maintains the cache details, and contributes to the query parsing. Based on the nature of services offered by the cloud services layer, this layer also contributes to the Snowflake cost and usage. The overall platform cost has cloud services cost as one of the components. You can refer to *Figure 2.2* to understand the different functionalities of the layer:

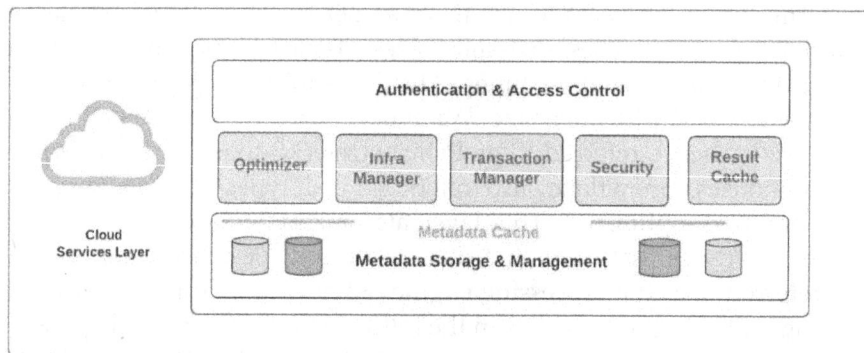

Figure 2.2: Cloud services layer

Cloud services layer takes care of the following services and operations:

- Authentication and authorization
- Performance and query optimization
- Metadata management
- Result cache management
- Security management
- Infrastructure management

Snowflake uses the metadata maintained at this layer to improve the performance of queries. The services of the layer are billed, and this is one of the components of Snowflake billing or usage, along with other components like storage, compute, serverless services, etc. You will also learn about identifying the cloud services cost and finding queries that are using the metadata information from this layer.

Authentication and authorization

Authentication is the key to logging on to any platform. There are many ways users can be authenticated for the data systems. Authorization is the way you authorize users to use your platform once they are authenticated successfully. Authentication method is used to authenticate the user logon and allow users to access to the platform using logon details, whereas authorization is the method used to validate the user permissions set up to access services as well as features of the platform. You can control the authorization using various access control techniques. In the case of Snowflake, the cloud service layer offers services that allow you to authenticate and authorize users. Let us look at them:

- **Authentication:** You can also integrate the authentication with your existing **Active Directory (AD)** and route the logon to **Single Sign On (SSO)**. Snowflake allows users to use Okta and Microsoft AD to configure the federated login. Snowflake also allows users to configure **Security Assertion Markup Language (SAML)** for users using Google GSuite, Microsoft AD, OneLogin, and PingOne. You can learn more about configuring and using SSO here: **https://docs.snowflake.com/en/user-guide/admin-security-fed-auth-overview**.

- **Authorization:** You have learned about access control in *Chapter 1, Navigating Snowflake Account Setup and Configuration,* and you can use the same to authorize users to perform operations on the platform. Snowflake supports **Role-Based Access Control (RBAC)**, and you can use SQL commands to create and manage users. You can also use Snowsight: Snowflake's web UI to manage users.

Performance and query optimization

This is the optimizer service of the layer that helps in preparing a plan for query execution. As the name suggests, this takes care of various query aspects like parsing query for syntax errors, generating optimized query plans based on the metadata information stored, as well as result cache maintained at the layer. The metadata maintained and the result cache persisted play a significant role in devising the query plan. This is the first step before queries are submitted to the compute layer for processing.

Metadata management

This layer takes care of the platform's metadata information. This layer stores the information and helps in deciding the fastest query path. The metadata information stored caters to the SQL queries, and some of the queries are answered directly from the metadata, like `SELECT COUNT(*)`. Snowflake also maintains the metadata of various **Data Definition Language (DDL)** and **Data Manipulation Language (DML)** operations on top of any object. DDL queries allow users to create, manage, alter, and delete objects, whereas DML is the set of queries users can use to perform data operations like load, update, delete, merge, etc. The layer takes care of all DDL operations as these are metadata-specific operations, and they do not need any compute to run these commands. Snowflake supports ANSI SQL standards. Hence, all DDL commands used to create Snowflake objects are run by this layer, and metadata information about them is maintained as part of metadata management.

Result cache management

Snowflake maintains distinct types of cache to cater to faster query executions. Users can run queries on Snowflake, and the result of the query is stored in the result cache. If the user runs the same query again, then the result is shared directly from the result cache. This cache is global and maintained for all users. Two different users running the same query can also result in sharing results from the cache. However, users may not have access to the cache directly. Users can see whether the answer resulted from the cache or not. Typically, the result cache is maintained for 24 hours and automatically purged. Whenever users submit a query, the optimizer checks for the available cache, and this is the first cache checked to validate the query against the cache. In case of queries being resulted from the result cache, the compute is not used, hence the usage is also limited to the cloud services layer.

Security management

The security services of the layer take care of data security. This is separate from access control. You can define the network policies and rules to allow or block users to connect to the Snowflake platform. You can configure them using SQL or using Snowsight. We will learn more about security features and services in the subsequent chapters of the book.

The cloud services layer is a highly available service that runs on multiple availability zones of the cloud region. The result cache is maintained at each available zone where cloud services are available.

> **Note:** This layer also supports scaling of cloud services, where it can scale independently. This is an automated process and does not need any direct manipulation by end users.

Usage of cloud services layer

As you know, the usage of the services layer is also part of overall Snowflake usage (billing). Ten percent of the overall usage is offered as a FREE bucket for cloud service layer's billing. If your service layer usage is below the ten percent threshold, then there will not be any additional usage for the service layer. If the consumption is more than 10%, then you will be charged additionally for the additional use of the service layer.

The following scenarios will contribute to the usage of cloud services layer:

- Large, complex queries with multiple joins.
- Simple queries with session variables or using session information.
- Row level operations in place of batch loads.
- Any third-party tools with JDBC or ODBC connectors to read or write data to Snowflake.
- Any metadata queries against INFORMATION_SCHEMA.

You can view the usage by using **ACCOUNT_USAGE** schema views. The most common view used to view the query details is **QUERY_HISTORY**. You can run the following SQL to fetch details and analyze the pattern where cloud services are being used:

```
select * from account_usage.query_history;
```

The preceding command can be executed on Snowsight (Snowflake Web UI) as well as using SnowSQL (Snowflake CLI). This query output is a tabular result that shares information about all types of queries being executed on the platform.

We can refer to the column **CREDITS_USED_CLOUD_SERVICES** that represents the cloud services usage. You can also use the following SQL:

```
select * from account_usage.query_history where CREDITS_USED_CLOUD_SERVICES
> 0;
```

You can also get the usage view using warehouse metering history view of **USAGE** schema. Refer to the following SQL:

```
select sum(credits_used) as total_credits, sum(credits_used_compute) as
compute_credits, sum(credits_used_cloud_services) as cloud_services_credits
from
account_usage.warehouse_metering_history where datediff(day,cast(start_time
as date),current_date)= 60;
```

Here, the date range can be of the month or quarter, or bi-weekly, depending on your use case.

You can monitor the usage and maintain the threshold below 10% to avoid any additional cost to the overall usage. You can also work on the query patterns and workloads to optimize the use of the layer.

Compute layer

Snowflake virtual warehouse is the compute power required to execute SQL queries as well as workloads on the platform. Snowflake offers two types of warehouses: Standard and Snowpark optimized. You can configure the warehouse with a type of warehouse, size, and scaling policy. Warehouses can be set up as stand-alone or single-cluster and multi-cluster warehouses. Stand-alone warehouse can be set to suspend and resume automatically. The clustered warehouse can add additional nodes as part of auto-scaling. We can resize the warehouse as and when needed while you have operations running on the warehouse. Choices of the warehouses are based on the type of workloads and concurrency. We will learn more about using stand-alone clusters vs clustered warehouses in the following sections of the chapter. Refer to *Figure 2.3*, which represents the Snowflake compute layer and warehouses setup to execute multiple workloads:

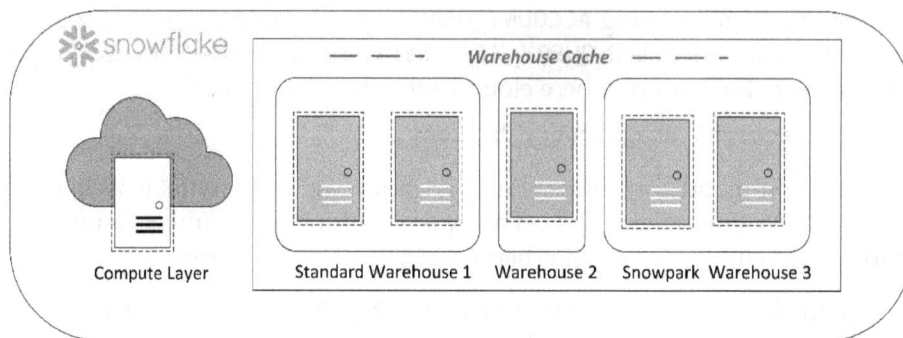

Figure 2.3: Compute or warehouse layer

Snowflake recommends setting up the warehouses as per the workload requirements, user, and application onboarding. You can refer to *Chapter 1, Navigating Snowflake Account Setup and Configuration* for role setup and hierarchy. You can consider the following use case scenario to set up the account, users, and roles. The same can be used for warehouse allocations:

- You have a development platform setup on AWS us-east-1 region. Now, you are setting up roles to onboard application teams. These roles are:

  o **Data engineering team:** This is the engineering team developing data pipelines. The development team needs access to read, write, and process data. The team will be building pipelines to read, process, transform, and aggregate data. These operations need compute power to complete execution. You can set up a warehouse and grant it as the default warehouse to the data engineering role. As you know, the development team might need varying capacities to test the workloads. Hence, you can create a multi-cluster warehouse of a small size with a minimum of 1 and a maximum of 2/3 clusters with auto-scale mode.

  o **Data analysts:** This team runs queries to generate reports and dashboards. Some of the report queries can be medium complex, or some queries might be highly complex and need higher compute power. You can set up a single standard warehouse with a medium size to develop and test dashboards.

  o **Ad hoc users:** This team uses the platform to run some auditing queries and ad-hoc SQL to generate customized reports using SQL queries. You can set up a small-sized standard warehouse and assign it to the role.

You can assign warehouses to the roles as default warehouses and grant permissions to use warehouses to the role. You can use the following commands:

- `Use role accountadmin;`
- `Create role dev_adhoc_user;`
- `Create role read_only_user;`

- Use role sysadmin;
- Create warehouse dev_adhoc_wh with warehouse_size='Small' INITIALLY_ SUSPENDED=TRUE;
- GRANT OPERATE ON WAREHOUSE dev_adhoc_wh TO ROLE dev_adhoc_user;
- GRANT USAGE ON WAREHOUSE dev_adhoc_wh to role dev_adhoc_user;

OPERATE is granted the role of controlling the operations of the warehouse. Users with this grant allow users to suspend or resume the warehouse. **USAGE** is granted to allow users to use the warehouse.

You can create warehouses using SQL commands as well as Web UI features. To create a warehouse, you need to specify the size, scaling policy, cluster size: minimum and maximum nodes, auto suspend and auto resume, etc.

Single cluster warehouses

These are defined to be used as a standalone cluster that cannot be scaled up and down. We can create them with available warehouse sizes. These warehouses can be resized and suspended automatically. These are typically used to run batch loads or complex queries. Any workloads that do not need concurrency can be run in this warehouse. Snowflake offers two types of computes to support the different workloads. Standard compute is used to handle standard workloads like tasks, streams, functions, SQL-based workloads, SQL scripting, etc. Snowpark optimized compute is recommended to be used for workloads that execute Snowpark workloads that may have large memory required, along with **machine learning** (ML) workloads. The following are the properties of a single cluster warehouse:

- **Type:** Specify the type: Standard or Snowpark-optimized.

- **Size:** You can specify the size of the warehouses. Pick up the appropriate size from the offered T-shirt sizes (XS to 6XL).

- **Resize:** You can resize the warehouses anytime, even when the loads are being run.

- **Auto-suspend:** Automatic suspension of the clusters when they are not in use. Specify the minutes of inactivity to suspend the warehouse.

- **Auto-resume:** Automatic resuming of the clusters when the query is submitted to be executed on the warehouse. If the submitted query does not need a warehouse, then the warehouse is not resumed. Queries resulting from any available cache or metadata information do not need a warehouse to serve them.

Multi-cluster warehouses

These are defined to be used as multiple instances in a cluster. You can create the cluster with the available warehouse sizes. These are used to run concurrent loads, queries, and concurrent requests. This also has the same properties as a single warehouse, along with a few additional parameters as follows:

- **Minimum clusters:** Minimum number of nodes in the cluster. The default is 1.

- **Maximum cluster:** Maximum nodes to be spun in the cluster.

- **Scaling policy:** Define policy as Standard or Economy to set the automatic scaling of the warehouse nodes in the multi-clustered warehouse.

Warehouse scaling

Snowflake supports auto scaling, and users can define policies to scale up and down. There are two types of scaling possible for warehouses:

- **Scaling up:**
  - Snowflake's scaling up refers to the resizing of warehouses.
  - Resize the warehouse from a smaller size to a larger size. This is referred to as scaling up.

Scaling up refers to the resizing of a warehouse. Scaling can be applied to single-cluster warehouses where a single instance is being run and used. This cannot be applied to multi-cluster warehouses.

- **Scaling in and out:**
  - Snowflake supports scaling in and out of nodes in a multi-clustered warehouse with auto-scaling.

Users can define policies to add and remove warehouses from the cluster depending on the workload and resources required to complete processing. This is referred to as scaling in and out.

- **Scaling modes:**
  - There are two modes for defining scaling policies with multi-cluster implementation:
    - **Maximized**: This is the mode where the minimum and maximum number of nodes or clusters are the same. This will provide a steady performance for the users.
    - **Auto-scaled**: This is the mode where minimum and maximum clusters are different. Maximum clusters can be defined up to 10 clusters. You can use this mode when you do not have steady concurrent users, and you want to scale up and down based on the end-user or the concurrent user hits.

Note: **Snowflake recommends starting with auto-scale mode and with a small number of clusters. You can change the maximum cluster count based on the warehouse loads until you determine the upper and lower number of clusters in a multi-cluster warehouse. Snowflake also recommends experimenting with different types of queries along with different warehouse sizes to determine the best way to manage warehouses effectively and efficiently.**

Setting up warehouses

You can create warehouses using the Snowflake console as well as SQL queries. Refer to the following reference use cases to set up warehouses, standard, Snowpark-optimized, single, and multi-clustered warehouses:

```
/* creating standard warehouse */
CREATE OR REPLACE WAREHOUSE ADHOC_WH WITH WAREHOUSE_SIZE='Small';
/* creating clustered warehouse */
CREATE OR REPLACE WAREHOUSE DEV_POC_WH WITH
 WAREHOUSE_SIZE='Small'
  MAX_CLUSTER_COUNT = 02
  MIN_CLUSTER_COUNT = 01
  SCALING_POLICY = STANDARD
  AUTO_RESUME = TRUE
  INITIALLY_SUSPENDED = TRUE
 COMMENT = 'This is a test multi-cluster warehouse'

/* creating snowpark-optimized warehouse */
CREATE OR REPLACE WAREHOUSE DEV_ML_WH
WAREHOUSE_TYPE = 'SNOWPARK-OPTIMIZED'
WAREHOUSE_SIZE='Medium';
```

Billing and usage of compute

Snowflake warehouse billing is calculated based on the size of the warehouse, the number of warehouses, and the total time clusters were up and running. Snowflake bills every second and calculates the credits consumed. Warehouse bills for 1 minute initially, followed by per second billing. Snowflake warehouse billing is calculated based on the size, and in case of re-size, the billing is calculated based on the warehouse size earlier and later for the time it is running.

You can use **ACOUNT_USAGE** views to gather details on the warehouse consumption. You can consider the following use cases as reference use cases to get started with warehouse usage computation:

- **Query consumption**: Queries that need warehouses and the consumption is captured per query in **QUERY_HISTORY**.

- Identifying the query that takes more credits.

- Identifying top queries that contribute to the overall usage: Refer to the following query that runs on **QUERY_HISTORY** view to list queries that use cloud services credits:

```
select * from account_usage.query_history where CREDITS_USED_CLOUD_
SERVICES  > 0 limit 10;
```

- Warehouse usage is also captured in two dedicated views of **ACCOUNT_USAGE**: **WAREHOUSE_METERING_HISTORY** and **WAREHOUSE_LOAD_HISTORY**. You can also get hourly credit usage details from **METERING_DAILY_HISTORY** & **METERING_HISTORY** views.

- Warehouse consumption per day.

Warehouse usage for a month, quarter, or selected time. Refer to the following sample queries that can be run on **USAGE** views to capture warehouse usage metrics:

```
/*warehouse metering history query */
select sum(credits_used) as total_credits, sum(credits_used_compute)
as compute_credits, sum(credits_used_cloud_services) as cloud_
services_credits  from account_usage.warehouse_metering_history
where datediff(day,cast(start_time as date),current_date) = 60;

/*view sample records from metering history*/
select * from account_usage.warehouse_metering_history limit 10;

/*quarterly usage view */
select sum(credits_used) as total_credits
from account_usage.METERING_HISTORY
where NAME = 'COMPUTE_WH'
and datediff(day,cast(start_time as date),current_date) = 90;
```

You can capture the usage details and set up alerting using Snowflake resource monitors to avoid any additional costs. You can also use **USAGE** views and set up monitoring dashboards using Snowsight. You will learn about these two features in the subsequent chapters of this book.

Storage layer

The storage layer is the centralized storage where data is stored, including structured and semi-structured data. Refer to *Figure 2.4*, which represents the compressed storage layer:

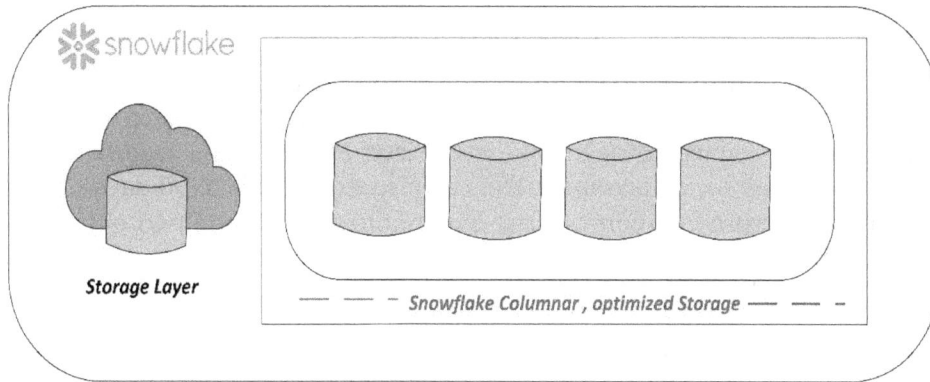

Figure 2.4: *Storage layer*

Data is stored in an internally optimized, compressed, columnar format. Snowflake uses underlying cloud storage to store the data where it is hosted: AWS, GCP and Azure. Users cannot access data from the Snowflake data layer directly. This data is accessible only via SQL queries.

Data storage format

Snowflake stores data in the form of snowflake objects, and this follows a hierarchy. The hierarchy also follows the object hierarchy: Snowflake account | Databases | Schemas | Tables and other objects. Table data is stored in the form of micro partitions, and this helps not only to store but also to improve the performance of queries and accessing data from the storage layer. Table data stored as micro partitions are stored in optimized, immutable, compressed columnar format encrypted using AES-256 encryption.

The data stored is encrypted and compressed. Snowflake can store data up to petabytes with no impact on the warehouse layer. Snowflake storage layer supports two unique features: Zero copy cloning and time travel. We will learn about these features along with data protection in *Chapter 5, Implementing Data Governance*.

Micro-partitions

Snowflake uses micro-partitions to store the data. The data gets divided into micro-partitions automatically as and when data is loaded or stored. Each micro-partition can be of size between 50MB and 500MB. One table can have multiple micro-partitions, each partition holds a set of individual rows stored in columnar format. Micro-partitions allow granular pruning of the data, even for huge tables. Like the metadata information stored for a table or object, the micro-partition stats are also gathered and stored as part of table metadata information. Each partition has a range of values and a set of distinct values. The metadata also consists of a set of additional properties required to run queries efficiently. The metadata captured helps in pruning the data as part of query execution.

Time-travel

Time-travel is the **Continuous Data Protection** (**CDP**) feature that allows users to access historical data at any point. The historical data can be data that has changed, deleted, or dropped objects. You can retrieve data and objects as part of this feature. The default time-travel is one day for all accounts. You can also extend this to 90 days (about three months) for the enterprise edition. Storage required to store data as part of time-travel is also considered as a component to calculate storage cost.

You can run this SQL query to access data present point in time:

```
SELECT * FROM RETAIL_DB.POC.SALES AT(OFFSET => -60*5); --to access data at
5 mins back
```

You can also query the state of the data before a specific operation or query has been run. You need a query ID to run the following SQL. Query ID can be found in the query profile as well as the query history view. Snowflake assigns a unique ID to each query, and this can be used to track the query executions, performance, etc.:

```
SELECT * FROM RETAIL_DB.POC.SALES BEFORE(STATEMENT => '1e5d0ca7-050e-21e8-
b959-a1f5b32c7562');
```

Failsafe

Failsafe is another CDP feature that ensures the availability and maintenance of the data. This feature is used for **disaster recovery** (**DR**) of historical data. Unlike time-travel, failsafe data retrieval can be done only up to seven days and only by the Snowflake support team. Users cannot access failsafe data using queries. This feature is standard to all accounts, and no additional licensing is required to enable this feature. This needs additional storage, and this cost gets added as part of failsafe storage and overall storage usage and billing.

Data cloning

You can run a data clone command to clone the data to create a snapshot of the data. Users can create snapshots and set up the environment quickly for development or testing. Data cloning works at a metadata level, and actual cloning does not take place. Each cloned object points to the same micro-partitions and underlying data as the original table until data is changed, modified, or deleted. For any recent changes, a new storage is created and maintained for clones. Additional storage contributes to the storage cost whenever data is modified in clones.

Storage usage and billing

Storage cost is computed monthly. The cost is calculated based on a flat rate per terabyte. The cost depends on the type of storage (capacity or on demand) and the region. Storage billing is calculated based on the following usage parameters:

- Files stored for bulk data loading/unloading (stored compressed or uncompressed).

- Database tables with historical data for time travel.

- Storage associated with fail-safe for database tables.

- Database clones.

You can use **ACCOUNT_USAGE** views to view the storage usage. You can use **STORAGE_USAGE** view. The following are some of the reference use cases to get the storage details:

- **Database storage by date**: You can use this query to identify the storage growth over the period and databases or objects contributing to the growth:

```
SELECT TO_DATE(USAGE_DATE) AS USAGE_DATE, DATABASE_NAME,
SUM(AVERAGE_DATABASE_BYTES+AVERAGE_FAILSAFE_BYTES)/(1024*1024) AS
STORAGE_MB FROM SNOWFLAKE.ACCOUNT_USAGE.DATABASE_STORAGE_USAGE_
HISTORY
GROUP BY TO_DATE(USAGE_DATE), DATABASE_NAME ORDER BY TO_DATE(USAGE_
DATE) DESC;
```

- Overall storage for a month with categorization of total space, space occupied by failsafe, and space occupied by stages:

```
SELECT SUM(STORAGE_BYTES)/(1024*1024) AS TOTAL_STORAGE_MB, SUM(STAGE_
BYTES)/(1024*1024)      AS      STAGE_STORAGE_MB,      SUM(FAILSAFE_BYTES)/
(1024*1024) AS FAILSAFE_STORAGE_MB
FROM SNOWFLAKE.ACCOUNT_USAGE.STORAGE_USAGE
WHERE USAGE_DATE BETWEEN '2024-01-01' AND '2024-01-31';
```

- You can change the SQL to get the storage in GB or TB as well as get it for a quarter using the date column.

- Also note that there are a few more **STORAGE** views in **ACCOUNT_USAGE** that can be used to generate the usage metrics. You can view **TABLE_STORAGE_METRICS** to get table storage details.

- You can use **STAGE_STORAGE_USAGE_HISTORY** to get a historical view of storage occupied by the stage. Based on the overall stage utilization, you can plan to add archival policies to archive the files from the stage.

You have learned the three layers of Snowflake architecture, their features, and computing the usage of each layer. You can also set up automated monitoring and reporting to avoid unnecessary bills. You will learn more about reporting, alerting, and automated monitoring with the data architecture patterns in subsequent chapters of the book. The following section helps you understand Snowflake caching and why the cache is critical to improving the performance of Snowflake query workloads as well as the platform.

Snowflake caching

Snowflake maintains various caches to cater to the query workloads. The queries submitted look out for the available cache first, followed by the execution of the query. These caches are maintained and helpful in designing the query execution plan. Refer to *Figure 2.5*, which represents the three types of cache: result cache, metadata cache, and warehouse cache:

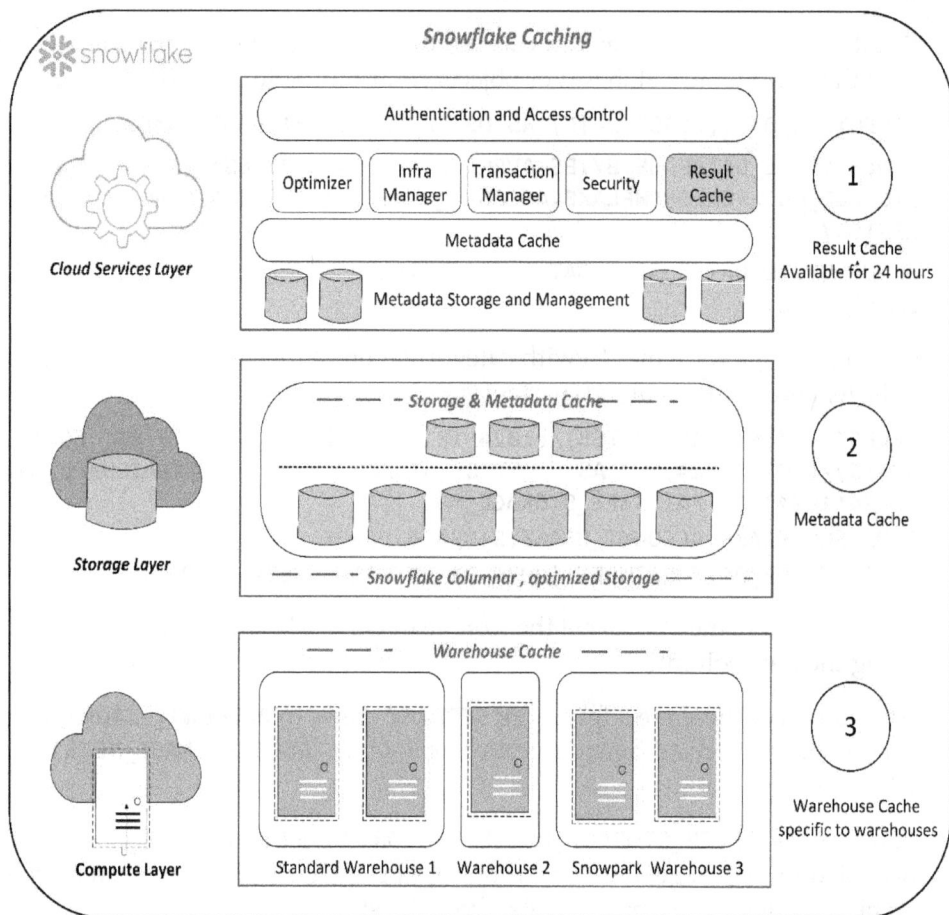

Figure 2.5: Snowflake's available cache

Each cache maintained has its own benefits, and Snowflake architecture layer resources maintain the cache at the layer. The result and metadata cache are maintained at the cloud services layer, and the warehouse cache is maintained at the warehouse layer. Whenever a user submits a query, the parser validates the query, and the optimizer looks out for the available cache in the store to cater to the query submitted. Refer to *Figure 2.6*, which represents the query execution flow with cache and no cache. You will learn more about each cache in the subsequent section.

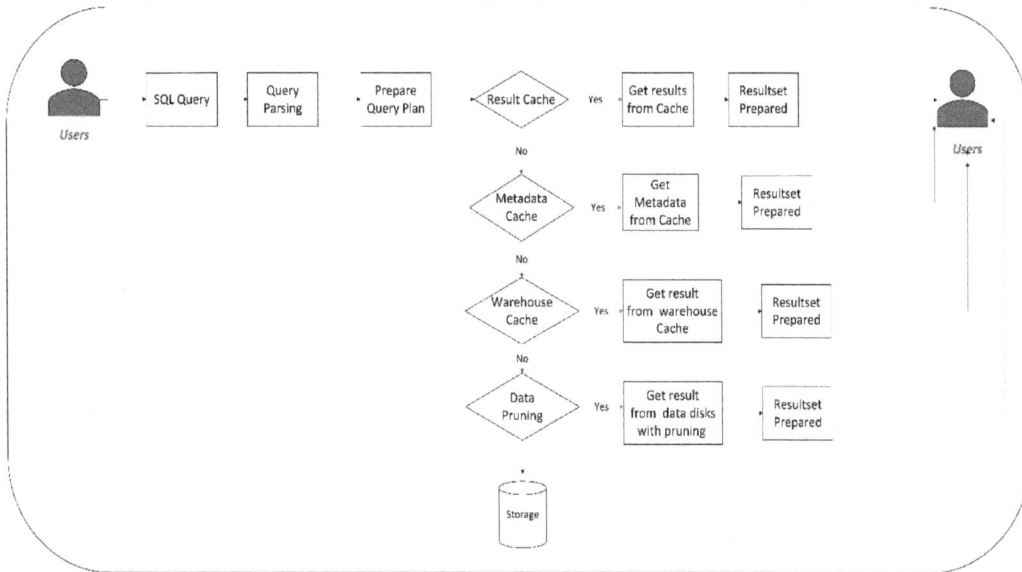

Figure 2.6: Query plan with cache

Whenever a user submits a query, the query is parsed and sent to the optimizer. The optimizer looks for a cache available to prepare the optimized query plan. If the result cache is available, it will be used to generate the query result. If this is not available, the optimizer will check for the metadata cache to generate results. Next, it will look for the warehouse cache if the result or metadata cache is not available to generate the result. At the end, it will run the query on the warehouse to fetch results from the storage layer if none of the cache is available to produce the result of the query being executed. We will learn more about each of the caches and their persistence in the following section.

Result cache

This is the first level of cache or the first checkpoint to validate if the query can be catered using the result cache. This is the fastest way to generate the result and access data from Snowflake. Snowflake builds the cache from the various queries run on the platform and persists the results for 24 hours. This cache is maintained for a limited time and purged every 24 hours. This cache is managed by the cloud services layer and is available across all warehouses, users, and roles.

Query results are cached and accessible to any user on the platform. Consider user A runs a query in the morning, and user B runs the same query in the evening, then the second query results from the cache available and created by user A in the morning. If another user, C, runs the same query the next day in the afternoon, then the cache will not be available, and considering the execution is the first execution of the query on a given day and time, it results and stores as a cache for subsequent users, if any. Typically, these caches are maintained internally and cannot be accessed directly by users. However, this can be used across users while generating an optimized query plan. This is the only cache that can be controlled by the user by running SQL queries for specific sessions.

Metadata cache

This is another cache that is maintained and managed by the cloud services layer. Users do not have any control over the metadata cache. Snowflake generates, captures, and manages details of the objects, micro-partitions, and clustering. The metadata information consists of the metadata for tables that can be stored in the form of row count, table total size, file references, and table versions.

Consider user A submits a query that can be fulfilled by metadata cache, like getting count, then this query execution may not need any warehouse in active state. Snowflake optimizer generates a query plan based on the available caches and checks if the warehouse is needed to execute a query and generate a plan.

Typically, Snowflake metadata stores object information as metadata like table definitions, and micro partitions with these details for each micro-partition of the Snowflake object:

- Range of values stored in micro-partitions with MIN and MAX values
- Count of NULL values
- Count of distinct values

Metadata cache also consists of details like the total number of partitions and depth of overlapping partitions to store clustering details. Queries with MIN, MAX, and counts result from this cache.

Warehouse cache

This is the third type of cache maintained at the warehouse layer. This cache is usually built, maintained, and managed at the warehouse level. Each warehouse is nothing but a compute with CPU and pre-defined storage (local SSDs) according to the size of the warehouse. Queries that are executed on the warehouse help in building the cache at this layer.

This cache is specific and local to the warehouse. Unlike the result cache, this cache is maintained and accessed locally, this cannot be accessed across warehouses. Consider user A submits the query, and there is no other cache available. Hence, this is submitted to be executed in the warehouse. The query checks the data available in the cache first and validates if the query can be fulfilled by the cache available. The query results from the cache if it satisfies the requirement, or it gets submitted to the data layer and gathers data to be maintained at a cache. In this case, whatever data is extracted from storage is maintained as a cache for the time the warehouse is up and running to cater to the queries.

The cloud services layer manages the freshness of the data. All warehouse cache is maintained at the warehouse layer and recorded as metadata. The optimizer checks data freshness and all available caches before producing a query plan. A certain rule is followed to persist and refresh the cache. The cache is persisted until the warehouse is running and active. The cache is discarded and freed whenever the warehouse is suspended.

Like the result cache, you can control the warehouse cache by managing the uptime. In some cases, it has been observed that the usage of keeping the warehouse running and submitting queries to the storage layer to pull results is the same or more. In this scenario, you can analyze the workloads, queries, query plans, and usage to calculate the warehouse usage. You can keep the warehouse running and maintain the cache if you know your workloads and the time they will be executed. These workloads will benefit from the cache.

You can use `ACCOUNT_USAGE` schema view `QUERY_HISTORY` to analyze the queries submitted and cache leveraged. There is a set of columns that help to understand whether the query is executed from the cache or not. You have learned about the three caches maintained at the cloud services and warehouse layer.

Conclusion

We have learned the basics of Snowflake: snowflake architecture, the three layers, and usage of each layer with the first two chapters. We have also learned about Snowflake Cache and its usage to optimize SQL workloads.

Next, we will learn more about the architecture framework, pillars, data platform designs, and use cases in the subsequent chapters. The next chapter gets you on board the data architecture world and guides you to learn the fundamentals of architecting data platforms.

Points to remember

In this chapter, you have explored the three layers of Snowflake architecture. The following are the key takeaways from this chapter:

- Snowflake architecture is referenced as a three-layered architecture with its three layers: cloud services layer, warehouse layer, and storage layer.

- Each layer has its own components, resources, and services that help to cater to any type of workload and requests in the platform.

- The cloud services layer is the top layer that caters to some of the essential features like authentication and authorization, security implementation, parsing the queries, and the optimizer to prepare the query plans, and metadata management to store the metadata information of Snowflake resources.

- The cloud services also hold the first type of cache: result Cache. This cache is maintained and available only for 24 hours. This cache is available across the platform, users, and objects. The optimizer checks the availability of the result cache first while preparing for the query plan.

- The next layer is the warehouse layer, and this is the processing engine that executes the workloads. You can create warehouses and manage them with GRANT. Warehouses can be created and altered at any point in time. You can create it in available t-shirt sizes and two types: standard and Snowpark-optimized.

- The warehouse layer maintains the warehouse cache: the local cache of each warehouse. This is the second type of cache that the optimizer looks for while preparing a query plan. This is available only until the warehouse is up and running. This is also local to the warehouse and cannot be accessed across other warehouses running in the system.

- The third layer, i.e., the storage layer, is the centralized storage of the data. The data stored is compressed and encrypted. The data retrieval is often referred to as data pruning and micro-partitions accessed. Snowflake offers clustering on top of micro partitions to cluster the data. You can enable automatic clustering.

- Snowflake also offers failsafe and time-travel to protect from data loss and recover historical data in case of accidental loss or DR.

- Data cloning is another interesting feature of Snowflake that allows users to setup parallel environments without copying the data.

- You can use ACCOUNT_USAGE schema and its views to monitor, manage, and report the consumption of these layers, overall platform usage, and bills.

- You can use QUERY, WAREHOUSE, and STORAGE views to gather specific information on the usage of these layers.

- Cloud services consumption is critical. You get 10% of the overall compute credits as a discounted window. When your service layer consumption is more than 10%, you will be billed for additional usage.

Join our Discord space

Join our Discord workspace for latest updates, offers, tech happenings around the world, new releases, and sessions with the authors:

https://discord.bpbonline.com

CHAPTER 3
The Pillars of Architectural Excellence

Introduction

Nonfunctional requirements (**NFRs**) are equally important as the functional requirements. Whenever you work on designing any system: distributed system, web-app system, or data system, you need to follow certain design pillars. These core NFRs are also referred to as architecture framework pillars. You can slit the pillars based on their features to extend support to maintain, operate, manage, enhance, and develop the system. These core pillars of distributed systems design are also applicable to the data platform designs. This chapter helps to understand the core principles of security, reliability, cost-effectiveness, performance, and scalability, along with their importance in architecture design implementation. This is the foundation of any data platform architecture and design.

You will learn about the design pillars and understand the requirements to implement them. This chapter also covers the corresponding features of Snowflake that allow you to design a data platform with all core pillars.

Structure

This chapter consists of the following topics:

- Unveiling the architectural pillars
- Applying pillars to the platform design
- Benefits of design principles

Objectives

By the end of this chapter, you will be able to understand the architecture pillars and the importance of considering them while working on any architecture design. These can also be referred to as system design pillars. These are also referred to as non-functional requirements and play an essential role while working on architecture design.

Unveiling the architectural pillars

Typically, an architecture is designed in consideration of two types of requirements: Functional and non-functional. Functional requirements are the business requirements that are converted to technical requirements and implemented using technical skills. An architecture is weighed as a well-designed architecture when it caters to both requirements. Often, functional requirements take precedence over non-functional, hence resulting in an architecture that has heavy or considerate efforts required to maintain the ecosystem infrastructure as well as maintenance efforts (data pipeline, break fixes, support, etc.). NFRs are the typical requirements that take care of system performance, efficiency, maintenance, operations, optimizations, availability, **disaster recovery** (**DR**), etc. We will learn more about the functional implementation of data platform architecture in subsequent chapters of this book. This section is mainly designed to cover system design principles. Architecture pillars are the core principles of system design and referred to as **non-functional requirements** (**NFRs**). Refer to *Figure 3.1*, which shares some pillars of the system design. You can refer to them as follows:

- Availability
- Reliability
- Scalability
- Maintainability
- Fault tolerance
- Efficiency, i.e., cost and performance

Each pillar of the design is equally important as it states the state of the system and provides you with metrics or KPIs to evaluate the design. Refer to the following figures:

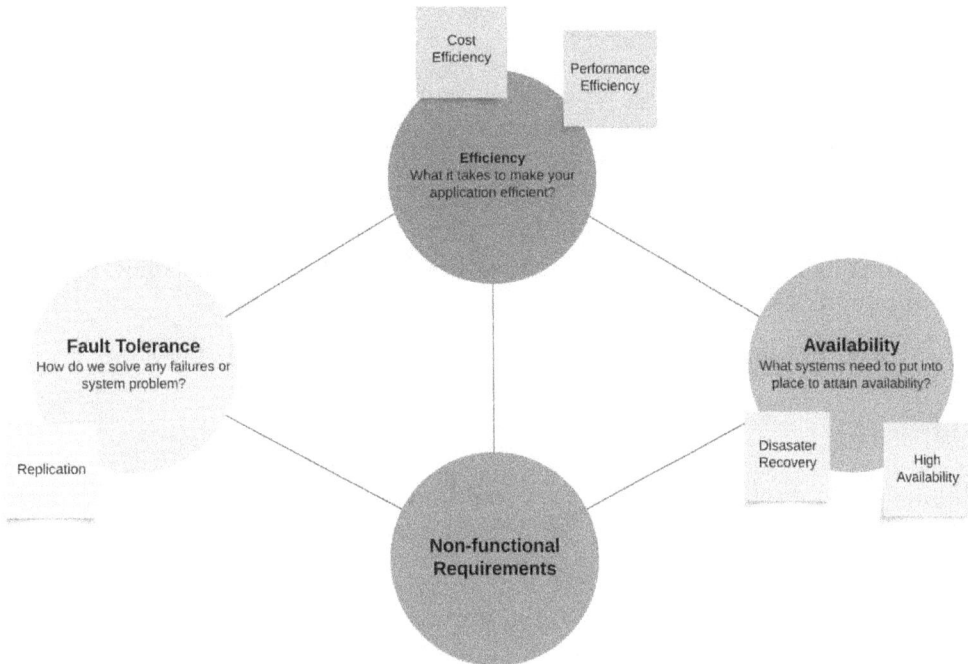

Figure 3.1: *System design pillars, part I*

The following figure illustrates some more pillars of system design:

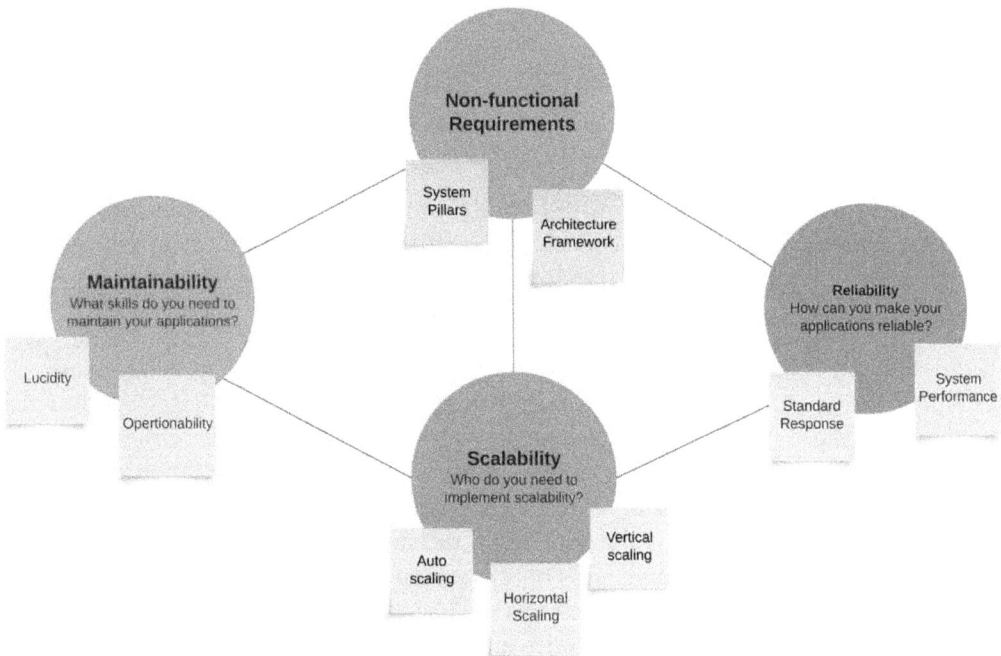

Figure 3.2: *System design pillars, part II*

Availability

Availability is the percentage of time the system is available to the users under given normal conditions. It is the time when the system is up and running for the clients or end users. Your design should consider the availability time of the system, not only under normal conditions but also in case of any downtime. You might have heard this term with most of the cloud services, where the cloud provider states that the service is available 99.99% of the time. Availability is usually measured in the form of percentage and number of 9s. You can measure the availability using the following equation:

Availability (A)= (Total time – down time) / Total time * 100

Reliability

Reliability is the measure that shares the details of the probability of a service performing its expected functions for a given time. R is the reliability measured to evaluate the service performance under varying conditions.

As you know, R is the probability of the performance. Hence, it is usually calculated by using the number of times the failure happens and the number of times taken to repair the failure. This is usually considered the **mean time between failures** (**MTBF**) and the **mean time between repairs** (**MTBR**). You can refer to the following formula to derive the R metric:

MTBF = Total elapsed time – Total downtime / Total number of failures

MTTR = Total maintenance time / Total number of repairs

For the best system design, lower MTTR and higher MTBF values are recommended. More robust services make your system more reliable.

The first two pillars, availability and reliability, are the two critical measures to derive the **service level objectives** (**SLO**). These are related to each other, availability tells the downtime. However, the impact of the downtime is measured in reliability. We can design the system to minimize the impact due to downtime.

Consider a web app-based application that has web-based application used by end users and data platform supporting the web app. In case of any issues with database downtime, the front end should not be impacted. The availability of a web app in case of any issues with the front end or back end defines availability, whereas the availability of the same features without any downtime or minimal downtime defines the reliability index. This app can be designed to repoint the rendering queries to a backup database in case of unavailability of the primary database. This system can be designed with high availability and reliability. Typically, these two measures are used to gauge the health of the service. It is recommended to have a high availability and a high reliability index.

Disaster recovery

This technique is part of the pillar that ensures the system is available in normal as well as failure conditions. Typically, the DR is set up to redirect the workloads or requests to the replicated or backed-up system or data to serve the user requests. With cloud adoption and implementation, managing DR is simpler than earlier on-premise configurations, procurement, and managing the hardware and software for the system. Most of the cloud services are **highly available (HA)**. Cloud services availability and HA index are dependent on the type of service and availability, e.g., storage services are available at 99.99%, while computing might have a different index of availability. We can use cloud availability features to set the applications as highly available.

Scalability

Scalability, as the name says, is the ability to scale to serve the growing need of the system without impacting the performance. There are two types of scaling, horizontal and vertical scaling.

Vertical scaling

This is also referred to as scaling up by providing additional capabilities or power to the existing system. In this case, you add more CPU or RAM to provide additional power to the existing node. You get additional hardware and software in this case. The cost to get vertical scaling is usually high, as you may need to get exotic resources to scale up. Refer to *Figure 3.2*, which represents vertical scaling versus horizontal scaling:

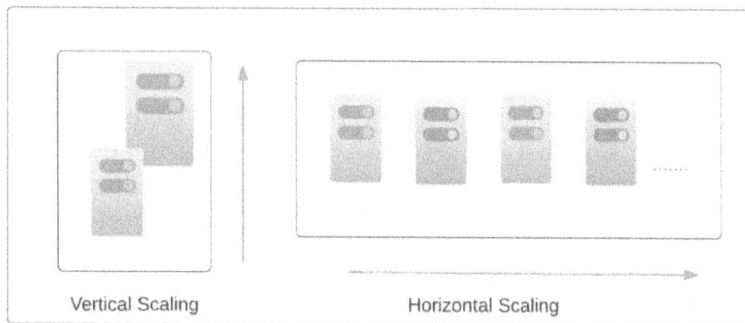

Figure 3.3: Scaling options

Horizontal scaling

This is also referred to as scaling out by adding more nodes to the existing system. In this case, you add one or more nodes or commodity machines as nodes to offer the horizontal scale to split the workload between these nodes. With cloud implementations, it is easy to get horizontal scaling as resources can be allocated for a given time or the selected timeframe of workload. Any extra added nodes are deallocated as and when the workloads are reduced. Managing the scaling in and scaling out of the nodes is referred to as auto-scaling.

Consider a scenario where daily batch loads are running and loading data from source files to the tables as a landing zone. In the case of regular runs, the size of the cluster suffices. However, towards the month's end, the size may be restricted due to the increased volume of the incoming data files. The time taken to load increased volume with the existing cluster size may delay the daily batch towards the month end and have an impact on the time of data availability. This impacts the **service level agreements** (**SLA**) of data. In this case, the scaling can be considered to address the increased demand towards the month end and meet SLAs.

This is the third pillar that helps to analyze the workloads and system performance. You can define the SLA and ensure your system or platform meets the requirements. You can implement either of the scaling options depending on the workload and application requirements.

Maintainability

This is the next critical pillar that guides you to consider the efforts and tasks required to maintain the system or platform once you build it. This caters to the maintenance of the platform, supporting the ongoing activities to maintain the health, identifying bugs or issues, fixing them, ensuring platform performance, etc. Usually, maintainability is divided into three underlying aspects:

- **Operability:** This is the ease of operations to ensure the system is running as expected under normal conditions, as well as achieve the normal state in case of failure or faulty conditions.

- **Lucidity:** This aspect considers the simplicity of the code. The maintenance time depends on the simplicity of the code. It is recommended to have simpler and easy-to-understand code for everyone. This helps in reducing the maintenance window as well as reducing the time to onboard the support team to maintain the system.

- **Modifiability:** As the name suggests, this aspect considers the system's design to accommodate any new changes, features, or extensions to support the upcoming features or business use cases. This is a crucial aspect while designing the system and considering some of the near-future enhancements and business value adds.

Typically, maintainability is measured in the form of probability. It is the probability of the system restoring within a given downtime. This is the measure of the system regain and how smoothly a system is up and running. This is calculated the same as the reliability **metric, mean time to repair (MTTR):**

MTTR = Total maintenance time / total number of repairs

This is the average time required to fix the issue and restore the system or application. It is recommended to have a low MTTR value. You can also relate to reliability. MTTR in maintainability is the time required to repair, whereas in reliability, it is the time taken to repair the failure. Maintainability and reliability together help you to derive availability, downtime, and uptime insights.

Fault tolerance

This is the second-last pillar of the design and refers to the system's availability to the end users in case of any component failures. In this case, the component failures can be hardware or software failures. There are two techniques to cater to the application needs and make your system a tolerant system.

Replication

Replication-based fault tolerance is the most widely used technique. In this technique, the services, as well as the data, are replicated. You can switch to the replicated services or data in case of failure of primary services. In this case, the replicas are maintained, and the data or changes are reflected in the replicas as and when the changes are made to the primary system. In the case of data platforms, the storage is replicated and maintained with automated sync-ups.

Checkpointing

This is another technique used to check the system's state or health. Checkpointing can be used in various application designs to ensure the service is available before you hit the service. This can also be used to check for the nodes or the servers to ensure they are available to use. This maintains the state in the storage. You can implement checkpointing for web-app databases, microservices, or service mesh architecture to ensure the services are available for the users before they use it or hit it. This is an ongoing check and can be automated to check the state and maintain the status at state storage. Most of the data platforms have built-in checkpointing implemented to store the state of the system and restore in case of failure or revert required.

Efficiency

This is the last pillar of the system design. Efficiency consists of two aspects: performance efficiency and cost efficiency. The earlier pillars ensure that the system or data platform designed is available, reliable, scalable, maintainable, and fault-tolerant. You have the initial five pillars considered in your system design. Now, you would want to consider the performance and cost of the system as part of the design as well. This is usually considered a part of the maintenance or operations. However, efficiency is an essential pillar of design to help you design the services and choose the right set of options and features to design the system or platform loads.

Performance efficiency

This is the aspect of efficiency where you ensure the performance of the system is optimal, and you have the right scalability techniques implemented to meet your performance requirements. You can design the compute choices based on the type of workloads and requests to be served versus the time required to serve the requests. You can consider the scalability and optimization techniques to maintain the performance of the system. Snowflake offers serverless services that can scale automatically to meet performance efficiency. We can consider using serverless services like dynamic tables, materialized views, snowpipes, etc., that meet efficiency without any additional configurations to specify the scaling method. We can also design automatic scaling to handle performance efficiency based on the metadata information and timely review of overall query performance.

Cost efficiency

This is the aspect of efficiency that ensures you have the system running with cost efficiency. You cannot have a system with increasing cost while maintaining it as a performance-efficient system. You can also consider this while designing the system, adding the cost of the system, and performing a forecast based on the growing volume of user requests for the system soon. You can implement automated monitoring that monitors the application, platform, and system usage and billing and generates reports and alerts based on the billing threshold setup. You can maintain the cost of the system and monitor it to avoid any additional costs. Snowflake offers various options to monitor, log, and generate alerts, as well as set up budgets for cost efficiency. We can setup Snowflake budgets and track consumptions. We will learn more about using various options to optimize cost and performance in subsequent chapters of this book.

Applying pillars to the platform design

You can apply all the pillars explained in the previous section while designing the Snowflake data platform. You can consider some of the following features to map the design pillars while architecting the Snowflake data platform:

- **Availability:** Snowflake is built on the cloud from scratch. The platform leverages all the cloud benefits. Hence, Snowflake offers all its services: compute, storage, serverless services, as well as the cloud service layer as highly available services.

- **Reliability:** Snowflake offers data protection and replication by default to maintain a data copy in case of any failures. You can also enable the replication if you want to maintain your data replication on your own. You will learn more about this feature in the next chapter.

- **Scalability:** Snowflake offers both types of scaling. i.e., horizontal and vertical scaling. You can resize your warehouse as and when needed to handle complex queries. You can also define the clustered warehouse with minimum and maximum nodes with a scaling policy to manage the increasing need to run the workloads concurrently. You have learned about warehouse setup in the previous chapter.

- **Maintainability:** You can use Snowflake native features to develop the code, applications, and workloads with easy-to-understand code. You can also use automated alerting, error handling, and reporting for proactive and reactive monitoring. You will learn more about these features in upcoming chapters.

- **Fault tolerant:** Snowflake offers services for replication, DR, and managing workloads. You can use Snowflake native features to restore the tables or data dropped accidentally using simple SQL commands. You can also retrieve the data stored and maintained by Snowflake with failsafe mode. You will learn more about these features in the data governance chapter of this book.

- **Efficiency:** Snowflake is rich in services that cater to performance and cost monitoring. You can use Snowflake's USAGE views to monitor the performance of workloads, queries, and the cost of the platform. You can set alerts and monitor them using native features like tasks, Snowsight dashboards, and notification integrations.

We will learn about all these native features of Snowflake in subsequent chapters of this book. We will also learn to apply these features along with the system design patterns and designs. We will also learn to use these pillars and mapped native features to design the data platforms to implement data warehouse, data lake, and data mesh architectures patterns.

Benefits of design principles

Often while designing data applications, not all principles are considered. Considering all principles and selecting appropriate features brings multiple benefits. Refer to some of the following benefits:

- Enhanced scalability
- Higher reliability
- Improved performance
- Better maintainability

These benefits can be achieved by implementing the application design principles explained in an earlier section. Let us understand these benefits one by one.

Enhanced scalability

Snowflake architecture separates compute and storage. Data platform designed to handle workloads with Snowflake native features can be scaled independent of each other. This allows users to handle growing needs of data access. Applications integrated with Snowflake can be scaled horizontally as well as vertically. Data and application workloads can be designed to scale with scalability design principle.

Higher reliability

Applications designed with availability and reliability design principles are used to build robust workloads. These workloads are designed to be less error prone and have high stability with robust error handling. Data and applications that are available for more than 99% and used to design workloads that cater to 24x7 applications. Applications designed with fault tolerance and fall back to restore data in case of unavailability of primary data store or center. Applications that are highly available and reliable with automated processes, design is the key of architecture design.

Improved performance

Data workloads that can be scaled based on the application needs provide performance efficiency. Applications designed with principles offer performance and cost efficiency. Designing performance-efficient solutions offer users the ability to implement workloads that offer improved performance along with data growth and application usage. Users can obtain and maintain the steady performance of applications, workloads, and data platform with scalability.

Better maintainability

This is one of the key benefits achieved with the help of the maintainability design principle. Automated error handling, bug fixing, and maintenance of existing pipelines or workloads allow users to simplify reporting and maintaining data workloads. Often, maintainability is overlooked and adds complexity to workloads as part of post-maintenance. Implementing maintainability allows users to maintain workloads better.

These are some benefits of designing applications and workloads with design principles. These principles can be applied to both data platforms and application designs.

Conclusion

In this chapter, we explored the architectural pillars of any system design. There are many underlying benefits to following the design principles as laid out in the previous section.

This chapter is the foundation of the data architecture section. Every chapter of this book is designed to help you understand the core principles and features and map them to design architecture patterns with real-time use cases. As part of the design journey, you will start understanding security features in the next chapter.

Points to remember

Here are some of the key takeaways from this chapter:

- NFRs are equally important as functional requirements while designing the systems. There are six pillars of the system design: availability, reliability, scalability, maintainability, fault tolerance, and efficiency.

- All pillars apply to any system design, web apps, data platforms, microservice-based applications, etc. You can design a system that is performance and cost-efficient.

- You can apply all system principles while designing Snowflake data platform's data architecture patterns like a data warehouse, data lake, data mesh, etc.

- You can map Snowflake native features, platform services, and serverless offerings to meet the system design requirements.

Join our Discord space

Join our Discord workspace for latest updates, offers, tech happenings around the world, new releases, and sessions with the authors:

https://discord.bpbonline.com

CHAPTER 4
Understanding Snowflake's Security Features

Introduction

Security is a key to designing any type of system. Security is part of the foundational setup required to be set up before you get started with any development activities. The security design and implementation become crucial when you start working on designing a data platform that persists, processes, transforms, and stores the **data**. There are different aspects of security in data platform designs.

You will learn about the security aspects and understand the need to implement them. This chapter also covers the security features of Snowflake that allow you to start considering native features while designing security for the data platform.

Structure

This chapter consists of the following topics:

- Data guardrails
- Time travel
- Failsafe
- Data replication

Objectives

By the end of this chapter, you will be able to understand the essentials of Snowflake security features. This chapter introduces you to Snowflake security features and how these can be used to implement data guardrails.

Data guardrails

You have learned the foundation and core pillars of platform design in *Chapter 3, The Pillars of Architectural Excellence*. You can start applying the pillars learned while designing a platform. When you start with platform design, the first pillar you consider is security. Usually, you end up asking some of the following questions to the data teams:

- Who are all the users of the platform?

- How will they be accessing the platform?

- How often will users use the platform?

- How will the users or applications interact with the platform?

- What are the integrations required to bring in the data, process, and share data as part of the consumer model?

- Who are the users allowed to access the platform?

- What is the network requirement that allows users to access the platform?

You might ask some more questions based on the details shared by the data teams. One thing you need to design is the guardrails around your data and datasets. You need to restrict any unauthenticated, unauthorized access to the platform. You would also want to define the boundaries through which users can access or the platform can share the data. Snowflake has a variety of features that allow users to define security policies. Refer to *Figure 4.1*, which shows the security aspects:

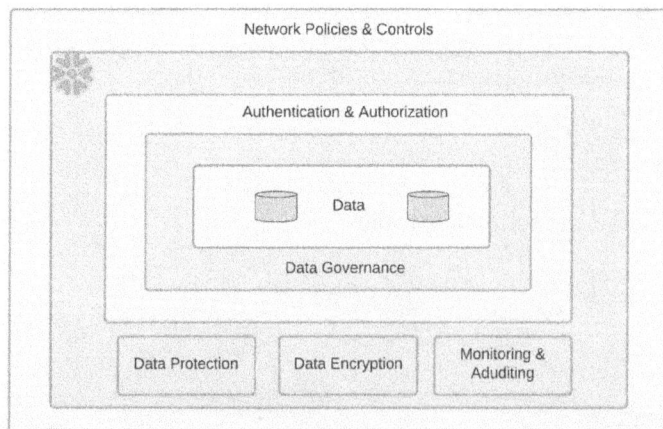

Figure 4.1: Security layers Snowflake

These are the security aspects considered, listed as follows:

- Network controls
- Authentication
- Authorization
- Data encryption
- Data protection
- Data governance
- Data compliance

Each aspect of the design is equally important as it caters to the state of security, protection, and compliance. You can also consider these as KPIs to evaluate the security design.

Network controls

This is the topmost layer or the first layer of security setup. You can define the policies in terms of network rules on ingress or egress traffic to control incoming as well as outgoing connections or traffic. You can relate to the network rules and firewall rules that can be set for cloud or any system connectivity. Snowflake allows you to create network rules in the form of simple SQL statements to allow or block a range of IP addresses or specific addresses. You can also use Snowsight features to create the rules. You can use either the allow list or the block list to restrict connectivity to the Snowflake account. When you specify the allow list, you do not have to specify any additional list to blocked IP ranges, as it allows users from the given IP range to connect to the Snowflake account successfully. Any additional connections that fall beyond the specified range of allowed users will fail to connect to the platform.

You can create a network rule to allow or block IP ranges and attach them to the network policies. You can have multiple network rules set up for an account. Refer to the following code snippet for the same:

```
/* allow only specific traffic from given IP ranges */
CREATE NETWORK RULE allowed_traffic_rule
  MODE = INGRESS
  TYPE = IPV4
  VALUE_LIST = ('192.2.1.0/24');

/* block any traffic from public ips*/
CREATE NETWORK RULE blocked_traffic_rule
  MODE = INGRESS
  TYPE = IPV4
  VALUE_LIST = ('0.0.0.0/0');
```

```
/* Create policy with network rules*/
CREATE NETWORK POLICY account_nw_policy
  ALLOWED_NETWORK_RULE_LIST = ('allowed_traffic_rule')
  BLOCKED_NETWORK_RULE_LIST=('blocked_traffic_rule');
```

Here, you are allowing only specific IP ranges. Typically, you add the IP range of a **virtual private network** (**VPN**) and block the public IP range (connection over public internet). You can also create the same rules using Snowsight. Refer to *Figure 4.2* to create network rules using Snowsight. The steps to do so are as follows:

1. **Create a network rule**: Ingress or Egress and login to Snowsight, **https://app.snowflake.com/**.

   a. Select role; **ACCOUNTADMIN** or **SECURITYADMIN**

   b. Go to | **Admin** | **Security**

   c. Network rules tab

   d. Select +**Network** Rule button from the top right corner

   e. Fill in the details of the rule and traffic mode ingress or egress or internal stage

   f. Provide the list of IP ranges to allow or block

   g. **Create Network Rule**

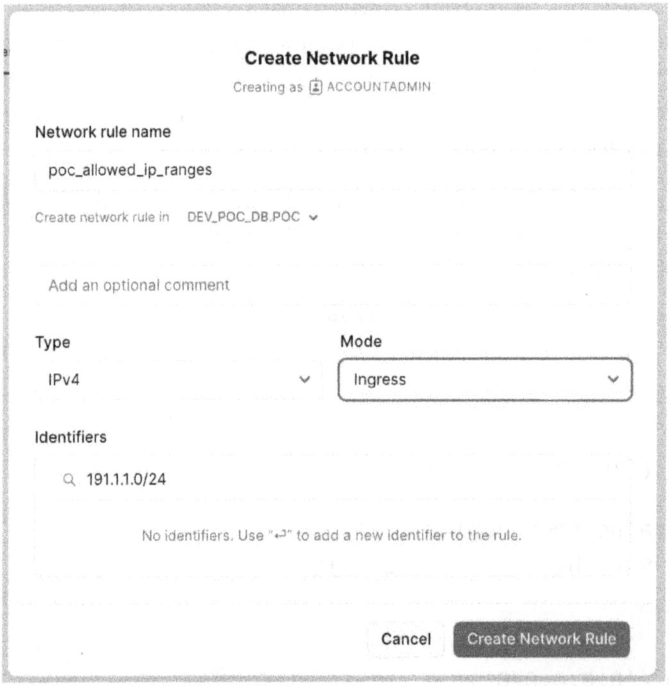

Figure 4.2: Network rule setup

This saves the network rule as an object in the database and schema provided.

2. **Create a network policy**: To create a network policy, refer to *Figure 4.3* to create network rules using Snowsight.

    a. Logon to Snowsight at **https://app.snowflake.com/**

    b. Select role, **ACCOUNTADMIN** or **SECURITYADMIN**

    c. Go to **Admin | Security**

    d. Go to the **Network Policies** tab

    e. Select the **+Network Policy** button from the top right corner

    f. Fill in the details of the policy and select the allow rules and blocked rules from the list

    g. Create a new rule if needed using create rule option

    h. Create a policy to set the policy for the account

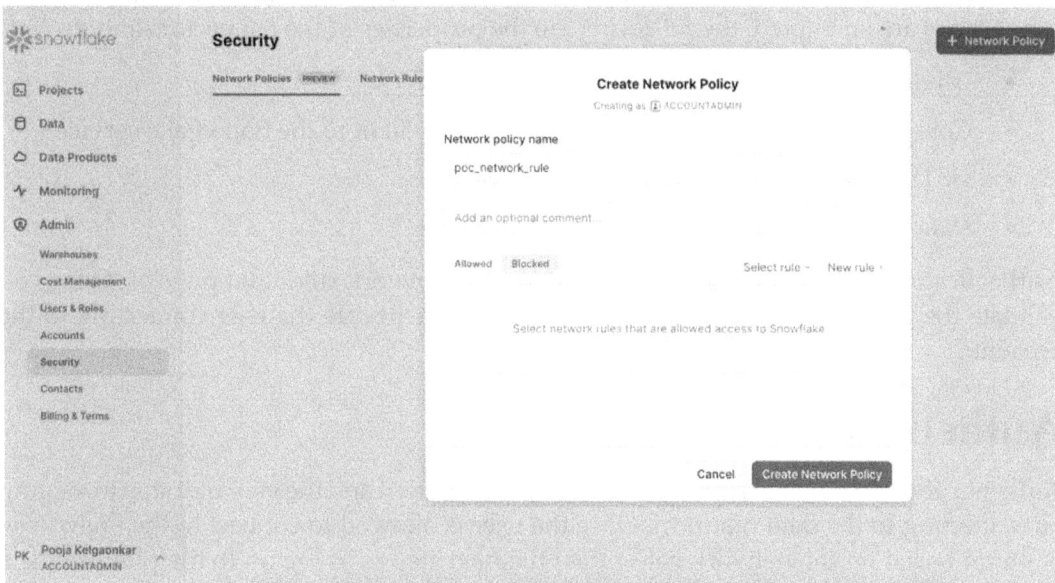

Figure 4.3: Network policy setup

The next important step is to activate the policies. You can follow the steps listed in this section to create rules and policies. Now, you need to activate the policies setup using **Activate** button on the Snowsight policy view or you can run the following SQL:

```
USE ROLE ACCOUNTADMIN;
ALTER ACCOUNT SET NETWORK_POLICY = account_nw_policy;
```

You can also set up the policies for specific users, for example, you need to onboard a team or user to work on development activities then you can set up the policy to add the rule to specific users to allow them to connect to the Snowflake account. You can also use the SQL commands to create, alter, describe, drop, and show network rules set up in an account:

```
USE ROLE USERADMIN;
ALTER USER smith SET NETWORK_POLICY = account_user_policy;
```

You can also connect to Snowflake through a programmatic interface. You can set up the rules to connect over the application interface, for the programming interface Snowflake encrypts the connections end-to-end. The following are some of the drivers and connectors to Snowflake:

Kafka	JDBC or ODBC	.NET
Cor C++	R or Python	Spark
Node.js	Hive	Golang

Table 4.1: Snowflake programming drivers

Here, every connector or driver connects to the Snowflake account in the same way. All connections are encrypted, the following are the properties of the connectors and drivers:

- All data flows over HTTPS
- Connections are encrypted using TLS1.2 from client to the Snowflake service
- HSTS enforced all client communications
- Data is encrypted at rest

Authentication is the next step once you set up the network rules and policies. Once you validate the connection traffic, then you need to authenticate the user connecting to the account.

Authentication

Authentication is the next layer in security implementation and the very first step to logging or connecting to the data platform. Once the user is allowed to connect to the Snowflake platform based on the network rules, then the next step is to log on to the platform as a Snowflake user. Snowflake authenticates the user and allows them to access the platform. The access is based on the authorization. You can set the user's access policies to access any objects within the platform. Refer to *Figure 4.4*, which represents the logon workflow with network rules and policies:

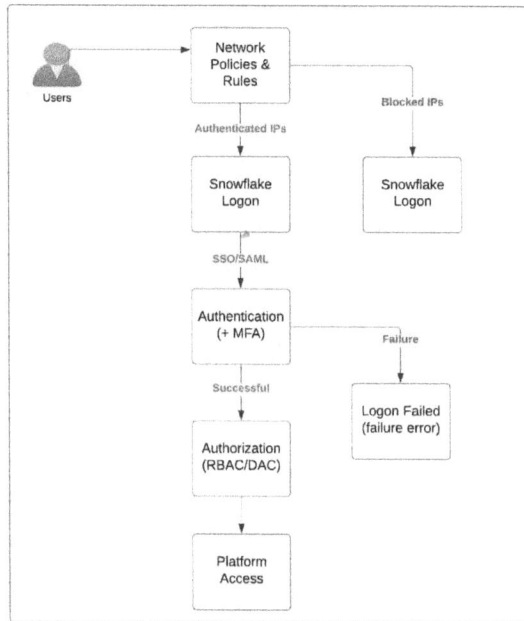

Figure 4.4: Logon workflow

You can authenticate users using various techniques in integration with **Active Directory (AD)**, **Single Sign On (SSO)**, etc. You can set up the authentication with any provider that offers SCIM authentication methods. You can use any of the following methods to set up the authentication:

- Federated authentication and SSO
- Key-pair authentication
- **Multi-factor authentication (MFA)**
- **OAuth**: Snowflake OAuth and External OAuth

We will learn more about authentication techniques with upcoming sections of this chapter.

Federated authentication and SSO

To set up a federated authentication, you need a service provider and one **identity provider (IDP)**. In this case, Snowflake is the service provider, and you can integrate with IDPs like Okta, and Microsoft ADFS. You can also integrate it with IDPs that offer SAML 2.0 compliant, like Gsuite, Ping, OneLogin, and Microsoft AD.

Key pair authentication

Snowflake supports key pair authentication for enhanced authentication which is also an alternative to the existing authentication such as username and password. You can set up the key pair authentication using public and private key-pair generated using OpenSSL. You can refer to the Snowflake documentation page to set the key pair authentication: **https://docs.snowflake.com/en/user-guide/key-pair-auth**.

Multi-factor authentication

Snowflake supports MFA as an additional security to authenticate users. It is recommended to enable MFA for all admins of the Snowflake account. MFA can be enabled using SQL command to manage users as well as individuals can set up the MFA from the Snowflake account. You can follow the steps to set MFA from Snowflake documentation **https://docs.snowflake.com/en/user-guide/security-mfa**.

OAuth

Snowflake enables users to set the OAuth for clients using integration. Snowflake integration is an object that provides an interface between Snowflake and third-party services. There are two protocols supported for authentication and authorization using Snowflake OAuth as well as External OAuth. You can refer to the configuration steps from Snowflake documentation **https://docs.snowflake.com/en/user-guide/oauth-snowflake-overview**

Authorization

Snowflake enables users to set up the authorization using an access control framework. Once the user is authenticated using one of the authentication methods, the user can access the Snowflake objects based on the roles and access control setup. There are two types of authorization, **Discretionary Access Control (DAC)** and **Role Based Access Control (RBAC)**. Access management can be managed for all Snowflake objects like databases, schema, stages, file formats, warehouses, functions, stored procedures, etc.

Role Based Access Control

RBAC is one of the access frameworks to manage access. Snowflake offers system-defined roles to grant permissions to the users. Snowflake also offers user-defined or custom roles to manage accesses. You can create and manage roles using SQL as well as Snowsight features. Snowflake offers six system-defined roles, ACCOUNTADMIN, SYSADMIN, USERADMIN, SECURITYADMIN, PUBLIC, and ORGADMIN. The following are the usage of the system-defined roles:

- **ORGADMIN**: This is the system-defined role that manages the organization and accounts in that organization.
- **ACCOUNTADMIN**: This role is a super user role for a Snowflake account.
- **SYSADMIN**: This role allows users to create and manage Snowflake objects.

- **USERADMIN**: This role allows users to manage users.

- **SECURITYADMIN**: This role allows users to implement and manage security for an account.

- **PUBLIC**: This is the default role assigned to every user.

You can grant access to the system-defined roles using the **GRANT** command as follows:

```
GRANT ROLE SYSADMIN to USER devuser;
```

You can create a custom role using the **CREATE ROLE** command. You can grant system-defined roles to the custom role created. You can also add object-specific permissions to the custom role:

```
USE ROLE ACCOUNTADMIN;
CREATE ROLE DATA_ANALYST;
GRANT ROLE SYSADMIN TO ROLE DATA_ANALYST;
GRANT OPERATE ON WAREHOUSE DEV_POC_WH TO ROLE DATA_ANALYST;
```

You can also grant multiple roles to a user and roles can be assigned in a way to create a role hierarchy.

Discretionary Access Control

This access control framework allows users to manage access at object level. You can grant access to read, operate, write, and manage Snowflake objects. You can grant access using the **GRANT SQL** command.

Data governance

This is the second last pillar of the design and refers to the system's availability to the end users in case of any component failures. In this case, the component failures can be hardware or software failures. There are two techniques to cater to the application needs and make your system a tolerant system:

- **Replication**: This is the most widely used technique, replication-based fault tolerance. In this technique, the services as well as the data replicated. You can switch to the replicated services or data in case of failure of primary services. In this case, the replicas are maintained, and the data or changes are reflected in the replicas as and when the changes are made to the primary system. In the case of data platforms, the storage is replicated and maintained with automated sync-ups.

- **Checkpointing**: This is another technique used to check the system's state or health. This can be used with various application designs to ensure the service is available for use before you hit the service. This can also be used to check for the nodes or the servers to ensure they are available to use. This maintains the state in the storage, you can implement this for web-app databases or microservices, or service mesh architecture to ensure the services are available for the users before they use it or hit it. This is an ongoing check and can be automated to check the state and maintain the status at state storage.

Data protection

Data protection is an essential pillar of data security. This allows users to protect their data. Snowflake protects the data and offers features that help users recover or retrieve the data if needed. You can protect the data at the table fields as well using dynamic data masking. This helps you to avoid any unauthorized access to the data and data privacy. You will learn more about data protection and masking in the upcoming *Chapter 5, Implementing Data Governance*. It includes:

- **Time travel:** Time travel is one of the data protection features that allows users to set the historical days they can look back. This is an enterprise and above feature. You can have time travel up to 90 days. You do not have to enable or disable time travel, as the time travel will be enabled by default as standard practice for one day. You can extend the time travel for 90 days using the SQL command. This is used to recover the data that is accidentally dropped, you can use the SQL command to recover the data using time, query ID, and action. You will learn more about managing data backups using time travel in the following section of this chapter.

- **Failsafe**: Failsafe is a data protection method that caters to data recovery in case of any **disaster recovery (DR)**. This feature is available with enterprise and above editions of the platform. You cannot enable or disable failsafe on Snowflake objects. This is not a user managed and configuration driven feature. This is standard and default offered by Snowflake for DR. The standard objects are maintained for seven days failsafe. In case of any DR incident, you will need Snowflake support to recover your data. You will learn more about failsafes in the later sections of this chapter.

Data encryption

Snowflake stores the data in internal, compressed, and columnar formats. Snowflake encrypts data stored at rest as well as in transit. The data is encrypted automatically. You can also use your encryption keys and manage them using SQL commands. Data encryption is enabled by default for all accounts and all types of storage, like databases, stages, etc.

These are the layers of security implementation for a Snowflake account. With layered security, you can store, process, and access your data securely. You can also secure data from loss and use features like time travel and failsafe to recover the data. You will learn more about these features in the following sections.

Time travel

Time travel enables users to protect historical data and access the data at any point in time. The data stored can be transformed or changed with any type of DML statement. You can restore and access the data, as well as objects, using this feature. Time travel allows users to use the following features:

- Restore any deleted or dropped objects (dropped accidentally or intentionally), and restore objects like databases, schemas, and tables.
- Restore data based on the key points or events in the past using query ID or action taken.
- Retrieving the data over a specific period in case of any incorrect updates or processing.

Time travel can extend the backup up to 90 days. The backup storage is based on the type of objects and edition of Snowflake. You can restore the data using SQL commands like **SELECT** or **CLONE** at any point in time within the time travel bucket. Temporary and transient tables do not have the time travel for more than one day as these tables are used to store temporary datasets or data.

SQL commands

SQL commands are used to retrieve data or objects. You can use the following commands:

- **SQL with AT | BEFORE**: This is used to identify the time or period to restore the data. This is the parameter that accepts the following values:
- **Timestamp**: Timestamp before or at to retrieve the data
- **Offset**: Time difference in seconds from the current timestamp
- **Statement**: Query ID statement to identify the operation that has changed the data or deleted the objects
- **SQL with UNDROP**: This is more like a DDL command that retrieves the objects
- **UNDROP DATABASE**: Retrieve the database and all objects within the database
- **UNDROP SCHEMA**: Retrieve schema and all objects within
- **UNDROP TABLE**: Retrieve any tables dropped

Time-travel enables users to retrieve data as well as objects dropped.

Managing time travel

Time travel is set automatically and as a default. You cannot enable or disable the feature, however, you can manage the period to maintain the historical data using SQL commands. You can set the time travel duration at the account level or the object level.

Usage cost

As you know, this feature stores the data as a backup and hence has storage costs associated with it. The storage cost is calculated every 24 hours from the time data has been changed. The storage cost is based on the type of table and retention period. The overall storage cost is calculated based on the percentage of the table modified. If an object is dropped, then the full copy or data is maintained.

Examples

Data retention feature is used to set to retain the data. You can use the data retention while creating the table and **ALTER** table to set it. The following are the examples used to set the data retention for the tables:

```
/* setup a table data retention to 90 days */
CREATE TABLE poc_db.poc.store_info(store_nm String,Store_no NUMBER, Store_
loc String, Store_start_date DATE, Store_close_dt DATE) DATA_RETENTION_
TIME_IN_DAYS=90;
/* Modifying the data retention for existing table */
ALTER TABLE  poc_db.poc.store_info SET DATA_RETENTION_TIME_IN_DAYS=30;
```

Time travel allows users to access historical data using the AT clause. The following are the examples to query the historical data using the AT clause with different parameters like **TIMESTAMP**, **OFFSET**, and **STATEMENT**:

```
/* accessing historical data using time travel with AT clause */
SELECT * FROM poc_db.poc.store_info AT(TIMESTAMP => 'Mon, 26 Feb 2024
05:30:00 -0700'::timestamp_tz);
/* accessing historical data using a query offset or query that is run 10
minutes back */
SELECT * FROM poc_db.poc.store_info  AT(OFFSET => -60*10); --OFFSET is
always in the form of seconds
/* Restore or access data before a query is executed - using query id */
SELECT * FROM poc_db.poc.store_info BEFORE(STATEMENT => '2e7d0ca5-006e-
33e6-b354-a8f4b29c2618');
```

You can clone the table using the AT timestamp to choose the snapshot time to take the snapshot to clone the data:

```
/* Clone a table using AT clause and a timestamp*/
CREATE TABLE poc_db.poc.store_info_backup CLONE poc_db.poc.store_info
  AT(TIMESTAMP => 'Mon, 26 Feb 2024 05:30:00 -0700'::timestamp_tz);
```

You can recover the database objects by recovering the database objects using **UNDROP**. The following are some of the examples to recover the dropped objects like database, schema, and table:

```
/* restore dropped database objects */
undrop database poc_db;
undrop schema poc;
undrop table store_info;
```

Time travel is an essential feature in retrieving the data or objects that have been modified as part of engineering processes. You can restore them by yourself using SQL commands. Failsafe is another feature that helps to restore data however this can be done only with the help of the Snowflake support team.

Failsafe

The failsafe feature is completely different from time travel. The data protected as part of time travel is moved to the failsafe to store it for an additional seven days. The data stored and maintained is used as part of DR in case of system failure or any other event. This feature is available for enterprise edition and above. Snowflake maintains the data copy or backup to restore whenever needed. You cannot modify the retention time or objects to be protected. By default, and at maximum, data is protected for seven days.

> **Note: Please note that this is not an alternative to the time-travel, this is additional to the existing data protection methodology to store data backup.**

Failsafe is not meant to be an extended method to access data beyond time-travel. This is used only by Snowflake to recover data lost due to operational or natural calamities. Snowflake support is needed to retrieve the data, data cannot be restored using SQL commands.

Usage and cost

Like time travel, Snowflake maintains the data copy for seven days and has storage costs associated with it. Along with time-travel storage cost, failsafe storage cost is also considered while computing storage cost for an account. You can view this storage as part of usage using UI, Snowsight, as well as a query on metadata view. You can use the metadata view and SQL to query the usage. You can also view the usage by following steps to access on Snowsight:

- Logon to Snowsight
- Change the role used to view cost
- Go to **Admin**
- Select **Cost management | Consumption**
- Select **All usage types and Storage**

This list down storage costs associated with failsafe. Failsafe has storage costs associated, as this needs additional storage to maintain failsafe version for identified tables and data.

Temporary and transient tables do not have any failsafe cost as this does not need to maintain table beyond the session. Permanent tables are stored for seven days as failsafe period.

Like any other feature, USAGE views can be used to get storage details of table using **TABLE_STORAGE_METRICS**. Only **ACCOUNTADMIN** role can be used to query this view. This view has columns **ACTIVE_BYTES**, **TIME_TRAVEL_BYTES**, and **FAILSAFE_BYTES** that can be used to generate storage metrics.

STORAGE_USAGE view from **ACCOUNT_USAGE** can also be used to gather details of failsafe bytes. However, these views give a consolidated view of usage on daily basis. If you want to capture details of failsafe based on table, **TABLE_STORAGE_METRICS** can be used.

Data replication

Database replication is supported between Snowflake accounts that are in the same organization. Replication also supports cross-region and cross-cloud platform replication. Data replication can be enabled for all types of tables, including transient and temporary tables. Replication can be set up between primary and secondary databases. Once you enable the database, that becomes the primary database, and all objects from the database can be replicated. Secondary databases can be set up in the same or cross-accounts within the same organizations. Data is replicated periodically in secondary databases. You can set up the replica using the SQL command.

The replication supports only database objects, and the replication does not replicate permissions granted to the database objects. Snowflake recommends account replication to replicate the database data. Replication features have some of the following limitations:

- Replication cannot be enabled on primary databases that contain external tables, event tables, and hybrid tables
- Any databases created from data shares cannot be replicated
- You cannot create a secondary database from a replica with TAGs

You can create a replication group to set up replications of multiple databases or objects. You can set up the replication schedule, and Snowflake recommends setting up automatic refresh. You can use the **REPLICATION SCHEDULE** parameter. When you set up replication, the data gets refreshed automatically. However, you need to set up the schedule to run the replication with frequency. You can use the following SQL command to set the replication and schedule:

```
CREATE REPLICATION GROUP replicate_poc_db
    OBJECT_TYPES = DATABASES
    ALLOWED_DATABASES = DEV_POC_DB, DEMO_DB
    ALLOWED_ACCOUNTS = org.account2, org.account3
    REPLICATION_SCHEDULE = '30 MINUTE'; /* this is used to automate the
refresh */
```

```
/*Manually refresh from target account */

ALTER REPLICATION GROUP replicate_poc_db REFRESH;
```

There are a set of replication features that are supported only for business-critical editions. The following is the list of features supported:

- Integration replication
- Network policy replication
- Parameter replication
- Resource monitor replication
- Roles and grants replication
- User replication
- Warehouse replication

You can use the data replication feature to replicate the data required in case of DR or failure. You can use this as a DR feature to back up your data.

Conclusion

You have learned about Snowflake security features used to secure data platforms. You can set up the network policies and rules to set up a secure connection to the platform. You can also use Snowflake's data protection and recovery features to protect the data and recover Snowflake objects. Snowflake time-travel can be used to protect data as well as objects using SQL commands. Snowflake also offers failsafe an extended data protection to protect data from loss beyond time-travel.

In the next chapter, you will learn extended security features to implement data governance with Snowflake. Snowflake features from *Chapter 4, Understanding Snowflake's Security Features,* and *Chapter 5, Implementing Data Governance,* are used to design the data governance framework and implementation.

Points to remember

In this chapter, we have explored Snowflake features for security and data protection implementation:

- Snowflake offers various layers that cater to security implementation.
- Network policies are set up to allow users to connect via a secured network connection. You can define the controls that allow users to connect by using IP ranges.

- You can also restrict IP to block access to the account. The Allow IP ranges work as a complement to restrict controls. It is recommended to use ALLOW network controls to define the IP ranges.

- Once you set the network policies, you can set up authentication and authorization for users. There are various authentication techniques supported to authenticate users.

- You can use RBAC or DAC access policies to authorize users to access any database object within the account. You can use system-defined roles and grant them to users.

- You can also create custom roles, grant them required system roles or object permissions to use, operate, manage, etc. It is recommended to set up the custom rules as per application requirements and teams to be integrated with Snowflake account.

- You can use data protection techniques like time travel to recover data and dropped objects. You can use the UNDROP DDL command to recover dropped objects. You can also recover a database or schema with its objects.

- You can retrieve the data before any changes or historical data or data snapshot for a given point in time using SELECT or CLONE command with the AT or BEFORE clause, offset clause, or using query id. You need to consider the storage utilization and storage cost while enabling the time travel for a longer duration, as it adds to the additional storage cost to maintain the modified records or data.

- You cannot retrieve data on your own in case of failsafe. You need to get help from Snowflake support to recover your data.

- You can also use replication to replicate the data in case of DR. You can create a replication group, set replication frequency, and enable replication using the SQL command.

Join our Discord space

Join our Discord workspace for latest updates, offers, tech happenings around the world, new releases, and sessions with the authors:

https://discord.bpbonline.com

CHAPTER 5
Implementing Data Governance

Introduction

Data is at the center of every technology implementation. AI and Gen AI are the buzzwords these days, and you need a strong data platform and data readiness to adopt any AI strategy. You might have observed that the data topics are hot and being discussed once again to ensure data meets the quality and standards, and maintains data boundaries to implement AI use cases. For any data and AI strategy, data governance is the most critical pillar. This chapter covers data governance and implementation using Snowflake native features. This chapter focuses on implementing data security, row-level and column-level data security.

You will learn dynamic masking, role-based policies, object tagging, and object-tagged policies. This chapter also covers the implementation of data governance features of Snowflake that allow you to start considering them while implementing or reviewing for data readiness.

Structure

This chapter consists of the following topics:

- Data governance demystified
- Implementing dynamic masking

- Using role-based policies
- Object tagging

Objectives

By the end of this chapter, you will be able to understand the need of data governance and implementing data governance with Snowflake native choices. You will learn to handle sensitive data in the platform using various masking choices. You can use trial account setup to perform various exercises of this chapter.

Data governance demystified

Data governance is one of the critical pillars of data platform architecture. Data governance consists of various aspects of data security. Data protection is one of the aspects that allows users to implement strategies to protect data.

Data protection enables users to secure data from unauthorized access that may cause potential data loss. Any unauthorized access to data is often referred to as a data breach. Data breaches cause data loss, and data loss can happen due to assets, data transmission, or any loss over a network. You can implement data protection policies to prevent data loss due to breaches. Data availability is one of the critical aspects of data management that ensures data is available as part of business continuity. Data management is data lifecycle management that allows users to maintain its phases.

Snowflake offers features to support all the aspects of data governance and its components, like data protection, data security, data management, **data quality** (**DQ**), and data management. Let us explore the key aspects and features.

Data protection and data security

Snowflake offers a variety of features to protect data. There are key aspects of data governance framework components that cater to data protection and data security, which we will discuss in this section.

Data protection

As part of data protection, you can protect the data using column-level and row-level access policies. You can restrict the users from viewing sensitive information like **Personally Identifiable Information** (**PII**) or any confidential information stored as part of table fields. Row-level security can be implemented using views to filter out rows that contain sensitive information. Column level security can be implemented using masking or tokenization, where you can mask the data field value. You can protect the fields based on the metadata information. You will need to protect the fields like email, address, phone number, **Social Security Number (SSN)**, **Tax Identification Number (TIN)**, or **Unique Identifier (UID)**, etc., and restrict users from reading them using masking.

Data access control

Authentication and authorization implementation to allow only authorized users to access the data within the platform based on the grants. You have learned features supported to implement authentication and authorization in the previous chapter.

Data encryption

Snowflake stores data in an encrypted form. The data is automatically encrypted using AES-256. All data stored in the internal stage as part of loading and unloading is encrypted. Data is encrypted at rest as well as in transit to ensure data security.

Data recovery

Data recovery offers support to recover the data that is being modified or deleted. As you have learned, Snowflake supports using Time-travel and Failsafe. Time-travel maintains the historical copy of the changes, and you can restore it using SQL commands. Failsafe stores the data for up to seven days and can be recovered with the help of the Snowflake support team. Refer to *Figure 5.1*, which represents the data governance framework with its various components:

Data Governance Framework

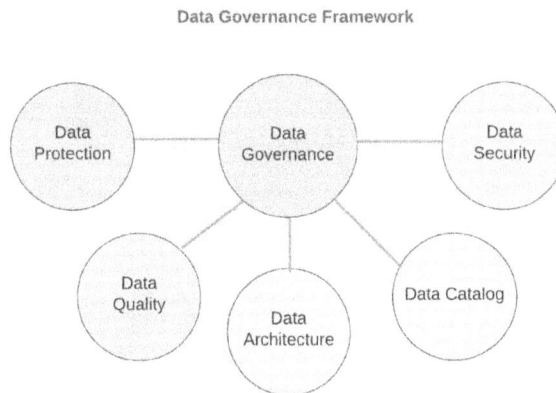

Figure 5.1: Data governance framework

Data replication

As you know, data is usually replicated to create an additional copy in case of data unavailability due to any disaster or system failures. Snowflake supports cross-regional as well as cross-cloud replication to protect the data. You can set up the replication by following simple steps to enable it for the given objects.

Data masking

This is one of the data security features where you mask the entire data or tokenize the data to be exposed to all users. You can enable a set of users to see the original form of the data and for the rest, the data is displayed in masked format. Snowflake supports dynamic masking. You can implement the masking using a simple set of SQL commands. You can also create the policies as a centralized repository and tag them to the corresponding fields in the databases to mask the PII data. Some of the common sensitive fields include name, address, phone number, SIN, SSN, TIN, any UID that can be used to identify a person. All the fields can be categorized as PII.

Data quality

DQ is one of the important aspects of data validation. This indicator indicates the quality of the data. This is a crucial factor as data drives the values and business insights. Incorrect data or poor-quality data leads to poor decisions, hence impacting the business overall. You can implement DQ checks to validate the data being processed and mark them with quality indicators if it meets standards or not. Data stewards define DQ standards, practices, and rules to validate the data.

The following are some of the common practices followed across the industry to implement DQ:

- Identify the **data stewards** who can define the standards, layout practices, and the DQ rules required to validate the data as per the business requirements and domain requirements.

- **Data architects** work on understanding the defined business rules and convert them to technical implementation using existing tools and technologies or using third-party tools for centralized implementation.

- **Data engineers** work on developing DQ engines or pipelines that validate data and rank them against the defined rules. The following table shares the responsibilities of each aforementioned role:

Role	Responsibilities
Data stewards	• Define the DQ rules with the help of business analysts and business users. • Identify the database objects to apply DQ rules and share with architects. • Convert the defined rules to the technical approach of implementation.
Data architects	• Convert the business rules to technical implementation using existing tools and technologies or using third-party tools for centralized implementation. • Design the DQ framework to implement DQ. • Work with the engineering team to implement DQ rules.
Data engineers	• Set up automated reports and alerts to share the DQ checks. • Get the data rectified and corrected to maintain the data records.

Table 5.1: Data roles and responsibilities

Data catalog

Data cataloging is one aspect where you can define the metadata of the data and manage it. You can use cataloging to manage the metadata information used by business users and analysts. This helps to tag the business terminologies with the technical fields. This is also useful in building data lineage that will help to analyze and debug any issues in the data as well as pipelines.

Data architecture

Data architecture is the way of data platform design and implementation. You have learned about the data architecture pillars in *Chapter 3, The Pillars of Architectural Excellence*. The architecture pillars allow users to design platforms with scalability, reliability, resiliency, and high availability. Data architecture is one of the aspects of governance design.

You have learned to implement security features like time travel, failsafe, and replication in the previous chapter. You will learn more about implementing data protection using dynamic masking and implementing masking policies using roles and tags within the platform.

Implementing dynamic masking

Data masking is a feature that masks data to prevent it from unauthorized access or usage. Dynamic masking in Snowflake allows users to define the policies once and apply them to multiple fields, tables, or objects to protect the data. Masking can be applied to the columns or table fields and hence used to implement column-level security. Masking is used to implement column-level security in the form of masking policies. Masking policies are used to mask the data selectively. These policies are schema-level objects and can be created once. You can implement dynamic masking only on tables and views. These policies are applied at run time whenever the columns masked are accessed.

Snowflake offers great support and extends the feature implementation using SQL commands. You can use a set of commands to create, view, and apply the masking policies. As part of the data governance umbrella, you can create these policies at a centralized place and apply them to the fields. Snowflake offers DDL commands to create, drop, alter, show, and describe masking policies.

Snowflake offers two types of masking policy setup, i.e., normal as well as conditional. You can create a policy that specifies the field and type of masking with normal masking. You can also define policy as a condition based on the role that is accessing the data with conditional masking. You will learn more about these in the following section.

Creating masking policy

You can use the **CREATE** or **REPLACE** command to create a new policy in a specified schema or to replace a policy in the schema. As you know, you need a masking policy field to define the policy. You can also attach a condition to the policy in case of conditional implementation.

Normal masking policy

In normal policy, you can protect the sensitive information stored in fields used to identify a person (PII data). Consider that you have a customer table that has fields like email, name, and TIN, and you want to define the policy to protect these columns. Refer to the following code snippet to create a policy using the SQL command:

```
/* set the context */
Create database POC_DB; --if not exist
create schema POC; --if not exist
use database POC_DB;
use schema POC;

/* Policy to mask the email */
CREATE OR REPLACE MASKING POLICY email_mask AS (val string) returns string
->
  CASE
    WHEN current_role() IN (‹ACCOUNTADMIN›) THEN VAL
    ELSE ‹*********›
  END;

/* Policy to mask Tax identification number */
CREATE OR REPLACE MASKING POLICY TIN_mask AS (val string) returns string ->
  CASE
    WHEN current_role() IN (‹ACCOUNTADMIN›) THEN VAL
    ELSE NULL
  END;

/* mask the name */
CREATE OR REPLACE MASKING POLICY name_mask AS (val string) returns string
->
  CASE
    WHEN current_role() IN (‹ACCOUNTADMIN›) THEN VAL
    ELSE sha2(VAL)
  END;
```

As you refer to the aforementioned three policies, there are three distinct types of values returned as output of the masking policies:

- The email masking policy masks the value to a hard coded value of string with *. Hence, this returns a value of a string with ******* every time the field is accessed.

- The TIN masking policy masks the value to NULL and hence returns the NULL as and when the column or field is accessed.

- The name masking policy masks the value to a hashed value using a hash function, hence returning the hash value of the field being accessed.

Conditional masking policy

In the case of conditional masking, you can set a condition to check the current role accessing the field or the visibility column value being masked.

You can implement these policies where you need to allow specific users to see the original value of the field and restrict a few users from accessing the field values. You can check the role display the original value and set the masked value for restricted users. You can refer to the following example of conditional masking and implement using SQL commands shared:

```
/*create policy for email based on the visibility and role */

create masking policy email_visibility as
(cust_email varchar, visibility string) returns varchar ->
  case
    when current_role() = ‹ACCOUNTADMIN› then cust_email
    when visibility = ‹Public› then cust_email
    else ‹***MASKED***›
  end;

/* create policy based on the role */
create masking policy email_visibility_policy as
(Val string) returns string ->
  case
    when current_role() = ‹ACCOUNTADMIN› then Val
    when current_role() = ‹DATA_ANALYST› then regexp_
replace(val,'.+\@','*****@')
    else ‹*******›
  end;
```

The masking policy implementation workflow can be shown as a flow diagram as follows:

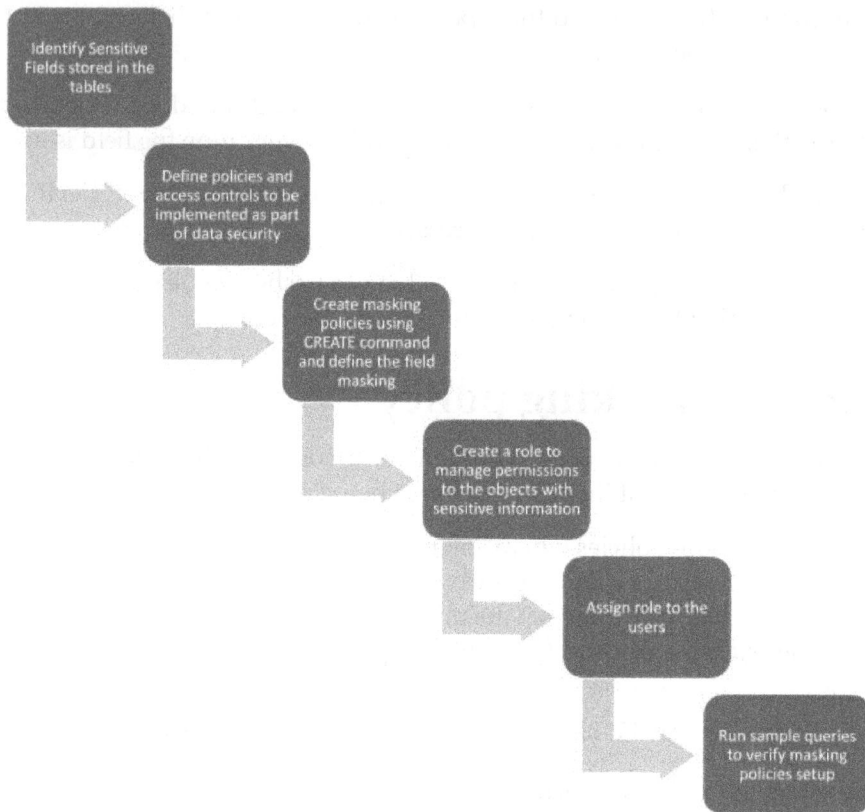

Figure 5.2: Policy implementation workflow

Refer to the preceding two policies set for the email field:

- The first policy masks the email column based on the role and field visibility. You can use the visibility field to set the users to view original or masked fields.

- The second policy masks the email column based on the roles given when two different users access the fields and how they will view the field value. REGEX function tokenizes the email in place of masking it to a fixed value of strings.

Using role-based policies

As you know, you can define masking policies and apply them to database objects. These policies are applied when users start accessing the tables to protect the data being exposed. You need a security officer or a data steward to define the masking policies as per the data classifications.

You can use the following steps to define the roles and manage policies:

1. Create a custom role for the security officer.

2. Grant masking policy privileges to the custom role created for the security officer role.

3. Grant the security officer custom role to a user.

4. Create masking policies.

5. Apply masking policies to the database and objects.

6. Execute queries on the tables to validate the policy applied.

You can use SQL commands to implement steps defined as part of policy implementation. We will detail the steps as follows:

1. **Create custom role**: You can manage users using **USERADMIN** role as well as **ACCOUNTADMIN**. You can use the **CREATE** command to set the role:

```
Use role USERADMIN;
/*--create security role--*/
Create role account_security_admin;
/*--Grant permissions to the custom role --*/
GRANT CREATE MASKING POLICY on SCHEMA poc_db.poc to ROLE account_
security_admin;
GRANT APPLY MASKING POLICY on ACCOUNT to ROLE account_security_
admin;
```

Once you create a custom role, you can assign it to a user. You can create a role as per your business requirements or application requirements.

2. **Grant custom role to a user**: **GRANT** is used to allow privileges to a user. You can use the **GRANT ROLE** command to grant privileges to the user:

```
/* Grant role created in step 1 to a user*/
GRANT ROLE account_security_admin TO USER poojak;
```

You can grant roles to multiple users that are data stewards as well as manage accounts using **ACCOUNTADMIN**.

3. **Create masking policy**: Use the custom role to create masking policies. These policies can be created once as a centralized policy:

```
/* set context */
USE database poc_db;
USE schema poc;

/*--use new custom role--*/
use role account_security_admin;

/*--use role and create policy--*/
CREATE OR REPLACE MASKING POLICY sensitive_masking AS (val string)
returns string ->
  CASE
```

```
      WHEN current_role() IN (<ACCOUNTADMIN>) THEN VAL
      ELSE NULL
    END;

/*--create email masking policy-- */
CREATE OR REPLACE MASKING POLICY email_masking AS (val string)
returns string ->
    CASE
      WHEN current_role() IN (<ACCOUNTADMIN>) THEN VAL
      ELSE <***@**.com'
    END;

/*--grant policy to table owner role--*/
GRANT APPLY ON MASKING POLICY sensitive_masking to ROLE data_owners;

GRANT APPLY ON MASKING POLICY email_masking to ROLE data_owners;
```

Now, you can apply the policy created to a table or view.

4. **Apply masking policy to the database objects**: Policies can be applied to the table or view while creating tables or views. You can also apply the policies using the **ALTER** command:

```
/* create table */
Create table poc_db.poc.cust_info
(
Cust_id int,
Cust_name string,
Cust_email string,
Cust_addr string,
Cust_status string
);

/* apply masking policy to an existing table column */
ALTER TABLE IF EXISTS poc_db.poc.cust_info MODIFY COLUMN cust_addr
SET MASKING POLICY sensitive_masking;

/* create view */
Create view poc_db.poc.v_cust_info as select * from poc_db.poc.cust_info;

/* apply the masking policy to a view column */
ALTER VIEW v_cust_info MODIFY COLUMN cust_email SET MASKING POLICY
email_masking;
```

5. **Query data and validate masking policies**: Once you apply the policies, users querying the tables or views can see masked data. You need to validate the data masked by using distinct roles. As set in the policies, only **ACCOUNTADMIN** can view the original values. You can use **ACCOUNTADMIN** to run the query on the table to get the original values. You can also use another role to run the same query and get masked data. You can validate the data by comparing the result between two queries:

```
/* using the ACCOUNTADMIN role */
USE ROLE ACCOUNTADMIN;
USE database poc_db;
USE schema db;

/* run sql query to view customer address and email */
SELECT * from poc_db.poc.cust_info;

/* use another role */
USE ROLE DATA_ANALYST;
SELECT * from poc_db.poc.cust_info;

/*capture results of both queries and verify the columns masked */
```

As you have observed, the policies are conditional and created as per rules. You can follow the steps and set up masking rules as per your business requirements. The following section covers object tagging and using tags to setup the policies.

Object tagging

You can create the policies along with tagging to create the tag-based masking policies. You can create masking policies using the **CREATE POLICY** command. TAGs are also one of the Snowflake objects. You can use the **ALTER** command to align the policies using TAGs. Tags are also attached to the tables and fields. Once you attach these tags, policies are applied automatically. The columns are protected with masking policies.

Once you define a tag-based policy then you do not need to assign the masking policies to the table columns. This gets assigned automatically wherever you create tables and columns with object tags defined. This is a simplified approach to implementing policies.

There are numerous benefits of tag-based policies:

- **Easy to implement**: Maintaining policies and assigning them to tags is simple. You can implement them without impacting any pipeline workflows.

- **Scalability**: You can set up the policies as a one-time activity and assign them to the Snowflake objects with TAGs. One tag can have multiple policies. These columns are protected automatically as soon as policies are applied.

- **Flexibility**: You can assign policies using **CREATE** or **ALTER** statements. You can assign the policies while defining the tables as well as add them using **ALTER** command.

- **Future objects**: Policies are applied to the existing databases and schema objects. These get enforced on any new objects being added to the databases. Any objects added get the masking policies applied automatically.

Masking policies can be applied to Snowflake objects with role-based and tag-based implementation. Implementing tag-based policies has a set of limitations:

- Tag-based policies are specific to a data type. You can create data type-specific tags and cannot assign them to any other data types.

- Snowflake has system tags, and these policies cannot be assigned to system tags.

- You cannot drop a policy or a tag if it is combined.

- There is a limitation to creating materialized views if masking policies are assigned to a table.

- Columns that are already masked cannot be used in defining the masking policy or as part of a condition in the masking policy signature.

- You cannot assign policy to a virtual or derived column.

Object tags can also be defined as a centralized implementation by defining and maintaining tags for an account centrally. You can define the tags and implement tag-based policies to mask sensitive information. You will learn to implement tag-based policies in the following section.

Implementing tag-based policies

Like role-based policies, tag-based policies also follow a set of steps for implementation. Refer to the following steps:

1. Create a tag using the **CREATE TAG** command.
2. Create a masking policy using **CREATE MASKING POLICY**.
3. Set the masking policy to a tag using the **ALTER** command.
4. Set the tag to Snowflake objects using the **ALTER** command.

You can refer to the following implementation steps and sample use case:

```
Create tag
Create tag using CREATE TAGcommand:
CREATE TAG sensitive_data COMMENT = 'data classification tag';
```

To assign a policy to the tag, create a masking policy.

Create policy

You can create policies using **CREATE POLICY** statement:

```
/* Policy to protect email address */
CREATE OR REPLACE MASKING POLICY email_
masking AS (val string) RETURNS string ->
CASE
WHEN CURRENT_ROLE() IN ('ACCOUNTADMIN') THEN val
ELSE '******@***.com'
```

```
END;

/* policy for identification columns */
CREATE OR REPLACE MASKING POLICY identity_
masking AS (val string) RETURNS string ->
CASE
WHEN CURRENT_ROLE() IN ('ACCOUNTADMIN') THEN val
ELSE '********'
END;
```

You can create policies to protect sensitive information. These policies are used for column-level security.

Set policies to tags and objects

You can use **SET** command to assign policies to the tags and Snowflake objects:

```
/* assign policies to the tags */

ALTER TAG sensitive_data SET MASKING POLICY email_masking;
ALTER TAG sensitive_data SET MASKING POLICY identity_masking;

/* assign policies to the objects */
ALTER TABLE poc_db.poc.customer_info SET TAG sensitive_data = 'tag-based
policies';
ALTER TABLE poc_db.poc.transaction_details SET TAG sensitive_data = 'tag-
based policies';
```

You can validate the data masked by querying the tables.

Identifying tag-based policies

You can use **USAGE** views to identify the TAGs. You can use **INFORMATION_SCHEMA** to discover the policies and tags references using the **POLICY_REFERENCES** function. You can use the **USAGE** view: **POLICY_REFERENCES** that can help to determine whether a masking policy and a tag reference each other by looking at the following columns:

- TAG_DATABASE
- TAG_SCHEMA
- TAG_NAME
- POLICY_STATUS

You can also have tag-based policies defined on Snowflake objects and create a data share. These policies are automatically enforced on the consumer account. Your data remains protected even if the consumer creates a new database from share. Data is never exposed to the consumers if policies are applied to tables in the data share.

Conclusion

In this chapter, you have taken a deep dive into Snowflake's data governance features: data protection, row-level, and column-level security.

The next important aspect of the data platform architecture design is optimization. Snowflake offers various features that lead to performance and cost optimization. You will learn about the Snowflake performance and optimization techniques in the next chapter.

Points to remember

Here are some of the key takeaways from this chapter:

- Snowflake offers features for data protection: row-level and column-level security. You can use masking policies to mask the data as part of column-level security.

- You can use dynamic masking to mask the data on the fly. The data stored in the storage is not masked. The data is masked on the read while accessing the columns.

- You can use a centralized approach to define and maintain the data access policies as part of masking policies. Data stewards are the owners who define the data policies and maintain them.

- You can also create, manage, alter, and maintain the data masking policies using SQL commands. Defining policies is a one-time activity, and you can use the defined policies to map them to the objects.

- You can use the mapping while creating the objects or the ALTER command to assign the policy. You can use role-based as well as tag-based policies.

- You can use role-based policies to create and manage custom roles using CREATE, ALTER, and GRANT SQL commands. You can create custom roles and assign them to users. Users with custom roles can create masking policies and maintain them.

- You can also create TAGs and assign the sensitivity level to assign tags to them. You can use data classifications to set the TAGs for sensitive, confidential, internal, and public access levels.

- You can set the TAGs and assign them to Snowflake objects using the ALTER command, or you can assign them while creating objects. You can manage the TAGs to maintain the data classifications and data access controls.

- TAGs can also be associated with data shares. The secure data shares carry the TAGs and data protection policies to the consumers.

- Role-based and tag-based implementation allows users to protect the data as part of data protection. Data protection is one of the pillars of data governance implementation.

CHAPTER 6
Evaluating and Optimizing Snowflake's Performance

Introduction

Optimization is the critical pillar that focuses on the maintenance, performance, and cost-effectiveness of the data platform. This chapter focuses on understanding Snowflake's performance elements and evaluation process. You will learn to use Snowflake metadata views to compute the usage and performance of the account, which also helps you learn performance optimization techniques.

You will learn to measure Snowflake performance using USAGE views and optimize the performance of Snowflake layers. This chapter also covers the implementation of serverless services like query acceleration, **materialized views** (**MV**), and using dynamic tables to optimize the transformations.

Structure

This chapter consists of the following topics:

- Measuring Snowflake's performance
- Performance computation
- Evaluating data models
- Performance optimization techniques

- Query acceleration service
- Materialized views
- Dynamic tables

Objectives

By the end of this chapter, you will be able to understand Snowflake data platform optimization techniques. You will also learn to use optimization options to improve the performance of data workloads. You can use the trial account setup to perform various exercises in this chapter.

Measuring Snowflake's performance

As you know, Snowflake architecture is a three-layered architecture. The unified architecture allows users to scale warehouse and storage independently. Snowflake platform's performance can be measured with the performance of three layers: cloud service layer, warehouse layer, and storage layer. Along with these layers, Snowflake also maintains three types of cache. Hence, the performance is also dependent on these caches: metadata cache, warehouse cache, and storage cache. Overall, the Snowflake platform's performance is not only dependent on the layers and cache but also on platform design, component design, and usage play a vital role in deciding the platform performance. The following are some of the critical components of platform performance computation:

- Warehouse performance
- Storage performance
- Cloud services layer utilization
- Query usage
- Query performance

Snowflake offers USAGE metadata that can be leveraged to monitor and compute the usage as well as billing of the platform. You will learn about USAGE views and use them to generate performance metrics. In the following section, you will learn each of the performance components to help you define metrics and derive them using USAGE views.

Warehouse performance

Warehouses are the compute used to perform operations or query executions. The warehouse performance is dependent on the warehouse size, workloads, and concurrency. The performance is calculated by measuring the query performance and warehouse queueing. This is also referred to as warehouse usage. Warehouse usage is the credits consumed by warehouses. As you know, you will be billed for performance usage, and if you are not using the warehouse, you will not be billed for it. You can consider the following metrics for warehouse performance analysis and computation:

- Warehouse consumption or credit usage (total)
- Warehouse usage by warehouse
- Queries per warehouses
- Query execution trend (based on time)
- Queries in queue (wait state)

You can use USAGE views to compute the preceding metrics. You will learn more about performance metrics computation in the upcoming section.

Storage performance

The storage layer contributes to the data stored and storage bytes required to implement data protection features like time travel, failsafe, etc. Snowflake stores the data in the form of micro-partitions, and pruning is done while retrieving the data from the storage layer. The performance of the storage layer is dependent on the overall storage, data retrieval, and query spillage. Data storage is calculated as the daily average in bytes. You can define some of the metrics for storage usage as follows:

- Total storage usage for an account
- Storage usage by databases
- You can use USAGE views to compute storage metrics. You will learn more about storage metrics computation in the upcoming section.

Cloud service layer performance

As you know, this is the topmost layer of the Snowflake and maintains metadata. This metadata information is used by the query parser to generate an optimized query execution plan. The service's usage is billed based on the overall compute usage. Service layer consumption is not billed if it is below 10% of the overall credits consumed. If the cloud services usage exceeds the 10% threshold, then this is billed for the account. You can define and use the following metrics:

- Cloud service layer consumption (total)
- Top logon failures

You can use USAGE views to service layer usage and metrics. You will learn more about the computation of these metrics in an upcoming section.

Query performance

Query performance is the time required to run a query, i.e., the execution time. The overall execution time of the query consists of the following metrics:

- **Wait time**: The time a query was in flight or queue
- **Compilation time**: Query compilation time
- **Execution time**: Query execution time

You can use the query profile to review the query plan generated by the parser and analyze the performance. A query profile is nothing but an execution plan with stepwise execution, time taken for each stage, disk spilling, etc. Query profile shares overall time. However, another important aspect of query execution is query design. Snowflake uses pruning to scan the data stored and access it through queries.

Query usage

Snowflake enables users to access queries and analyze them using `query_id`. `Query_id` the unique identifier used to identify and analyze queries. You can also access the Query profile using `query_id`.

Snowflake's metadata schema `ACCOUNT_USAGE` consists of a set of views used to compute the various performance metrics, analyze the platform performance, and optimize it. Query usage plays a crucial role as this is a major component of performance optimization as well as usage computation. You can use `QUERY_HISTORY` to analyze queries.

You can refer to some of the following metrics for query usage computation:

- Active queries in an account
- Failed queries by users
- Top failed queries
- Long running queries in an account
- Long running queries per warehouse
- Total jobs running per warehouse
- Queries by database
- Queued queries by warehouses
- Costly queries by warehouses
- Costly queries in an account

You can use `USAGE` views to derive usage and metrics. You will learn more about query performance metrics computation in the next section.

Performance computation

As you have learned in the previous sections, various performance metrics can be calculated using Snowflake's metadata views. Snowflake offers Snowflake as a shared resource with **USAGE** schemas. The following are the **USAGE** metadata schemas available for all accounts:

- **ACCOUNT_USAGE**
- **ORAGANIZATION_USAGE**
- **INFORMATION_SCHEMA**
- **DATA_SHARING_USAGE**
- **READER_ACCOUNT_USAGE**

As you see, these **USAGE** schema offers metadata details of account, organization, data sharing, reader account usage etc. **INFORMATION_SCHEMA** consists of a set of views that captures metrics and metadata information before it is available in **USAGE** schema views. The retention is different between **INFORMATION_SCHEMA** and **ACCOUNT_USAGE**.

You can refer to the metrics and reference queries discussed in this section.

Total storage usage for an account per month

Run a query on **STORAGE_USAGE** view to count the total storage in TB:

```
select date_trunc(month, usage_date) as storage_usage_month,
avg(storage_bytes + stage_bytes + failsafe_bytes) / power(1024, 4) as
billable_storage_tb
from snowflake.account_usage.storage_usage
group by 1
order by 1;
```

Total queries by warehouses

Using **QUERY_HISTORY** view to derive the total number of queries being run on a warehouse to date:

```
select
WAREHOUSE_NAME,
count(*) as total_number_of_queries
from
snowflake.account_usage.query_history
where start_time >= date_trunc(month, current_date)
group by warehouse_name;
```

Total number of jobs running in an account

Using **QUERY_HISTORY** view to derive the total number of jobs being run actively in an account to date:

```
select
count(*) as total_number_of_jobs
from
snowflake.account_usage.query_history
where start_time >= date_trunc(month, current_date);
```

Total credit consumption by warehouse

QUERY_HISTORY to derive metrics that calculate the overall credits consumed to date:

```
select
warehouse_name,
sum(credits_used) as total_credits_used
from snowflake.account_usage.warehouse_metering_history
where start_time >= date_trunc(month, current_date)
group by 1, order by 2 desc;
```

Overall credits consumed by warehouse

Use **WAREHOUSE_METERING_HISTORY** to calculate overall credit consumption:

```
select
warehouse_name,
sum(credits_used) as total_credits_used
from
SNOWFLAKE.ACCOUNT_USAGE.WAREHOUSE_METERING_HISTORY
group by warehouse_name;
```

You can use **USAGE** view to derive various performance metrics that must be monitored for your platform usage and application requirements.

You can also refer to **https://docs.snowflake.com/en/sql-reference/account-usage** for more details and reference queries to monitor and measure account usage. These are standard queries used for performance, usage, and billing monitoring. You can also customize them to generate custom metrics as per your application's need. In the next section, you will learn optimization techniques to improve performance.

Evaluating data models

You can design data models along with data architecture design. Data models enable users to define the system to integrate existing and new systems. There are several types of data models: conceptual data model, logical data model, and physical data model. You can use any type of data model to define the system models using entities and relations, and pick the relevant model technique like Snowflake, Data Vault, and Star Schema. Snowflake supports all techniques of data model implementations.

Data architecture and data modeling align to play the critical role in system design, integrations, and implementation. While you work on analyzing the performance of a data platform and optimizing techniques, evaluating data models defined also plays a key role. You can use the following techniques to evaluate your existing data models:

- **Clustering keys:** You can define the table cluster while creating table and include as part of your data model definitions. You can define clusters based on your entity relationships, integrations, and usage to derive the system functionalities. You can also use the automatic clustering feature to improve the performance of the queries. You can learn more about identifying and redefining the clustering keys from Snowflake documentation: **https://docs.snowflake.com/en/user-guide/tables-clustering-keys**. You can use the following system functions to monitor the clustering metadata of a table:

    ○ `SYSTEM$CLUSTERING_DEPTH`
    ○ `SYSTEM$CLUSTERING_INFORMATION`

- **Choosing the appropriate object:** You can leverage the distinct types of tables supported in Snowflake, i.e., permanent, temporary, transient, and external tables while defining the data model. You can use temporary as well as transient tables for intermediate processing and storing intermediate results. You can also use external tables to bring in the source data without loading the data to the Snowflake storage.

- **Using extended Snowflake objects:** You can use hybrid tables, dynamic tables, and MV to define data models. Based on the application integrations and processing needs, you can leverage these tables to achieve better performance and optimized usage. You can define them as part of the model instead of using them as one of the optimization techniques to improve the performance later.

- **Using constraints:** Snowflake supports constraints, and you can define them while creating objects (for example, tables). You can consider adding constraints while defining your data models as well. Snowflake supports inline as well as out-of-line constraints. You can define unique, primary, and foreign key constraints along with create. You can evaluate if the defined constraints are essential as per your system and application needs.

You can leverage the Snowflake extensions and support to the various data models and modeling techniques to evaluate your data model. You can also validate the queries using these Snowflake objects to identify if these objects need to be modified to meet the performance needs. You can use performance optimization techniques to identify the potential queries, objects, services, or components that need to be optimized for better performance and usage. You will learn more about these techniques in the next section.

Performance optimization techniques

You have learned the performance components and metrics used to measure the platform's performance. Several optimization techniques can be applied to improve or optimize performance. The following are the optimization techniques that can be used:

- Warehouse optimization
- Storage optimization
- Improved cache utilization
- Query optimization

You will learn more about each of the techniques in this section. You will learn Snowflake recommendations, techniques, and additional optimization services that can be used to optimize the performance of Snowflake components.

Warehouse optimization

You can use **WAREHOUSE** view to measure performance. You can analyze the performance, configurations, concurrent workloads, and compute credits using these views. Snowflake recommends using the strategies discussed in this section to optimize the warehouse to improve the query performance.

Reduce queue time

You can find queued queries from the **USAGE** view and the warehouse view of Snowsight. You can reduce the queue time by changing the warehouse size or reducing the concurrent loads in the warehouse. You can identify the *queued* queries and find the ratio of queries being executed and queued to optimize the performance. You can use this as one of the critical aspects to consider warehouse sizing. You will learn about warehouse sizing in the next section. You can run the following query to identify queue time:

```
SELECT
warehouse_name,
SUM(avg_queued_load) AS average_queued_time
FROM
snowflake.account_usage.warehouse_load_history
where avg_queued_load > 0
GROUP BY 1
ORDER BY 1 desc;
```

Resolving or avoiding memory spillage

If the warehouse runs out of memory while executing a query, then the performance of the query gets impacted as it spills the memory to the local disk. In some queries, if it needs further memory, then it spills to the cloud storage as well. If this is the case with queries or workloads, then this results in the worst performance of the queries. You can also refer to the Snowflake documentation: **https://docs.snowflake.com/en/user-guide/performance-query-warehouse-memory** for memory spillage. You can run the following SQL query to identify impacted queries and optimize them or change warehouse size:

```
SELECT
query_id,
substr(query_text,1,50) as partial_query,
bytes_spilled_to_local_storage as query_spilled_bytes,
bytes_spilled_to_remote_storage as query_storage_bytes,
user_name,
warehouse_name
FROM
snowflake.account_usage.query_history
WHERE (bytes_spilled_to_local_storage > 0
OR  bytes_spilled_to_remote_storage > 0 )
ORDER BY
bytes_spilled_to_remote_storage, bytes_spilled_to_local_storage DESC
LIMIT 10; --sample limit to the rows
```

Changing warehouse size

Queued and query spilling due to memory issues cause query performance and warehouse performance issues. You can use the metrics derived in the preceding sections to analyze the warehouse performance. Identify the warehouse performance with respect to workloads and queries. You can resize the warehouse at any point in time without affecting existing workloads. Resizing is considered the best choice when you have workloads running on the same warehouse and getting into the wait queue for a long time, waiting for resources to execute the workloads.

Restricting the concurrent workloads or queries

As you know, warehouses can be standalone as well as set up in clusters. You can run concurrent workloads on clustered warehouses as well as standalone warehouses. Snowflake offers a parameter that can be set on warehouses to allow concurrent queries or jobs to be run. The concurrent queries executed in the warehouse consume more or all resources, adding the rest of the queries to a queue. The queued queries wait until the resources are available. You can use **MAX_CONCURRENCY_LEVEL** parameter to set the concurrent execution. Refer to the following **ALTER** query to set the parameter to 5:

```
ALTER WAREHOUSE DW_POC_WH SET MAX_CONCURRENCY_LEVEL = 5;
```

Improved cache utilization

You can also optimize the warehouse cache to improve the performance of the warehouse or queries. As you know, warehouses maintain their cache and the queries are served from the cache if the cache is valid and applied to the query. You can plan to use the cache by maintaining it. If you have auto suspend enabled on your warehouse, then the cache becomes invalid and gets deleted. You can analyze the workloads, queries and identify the queries that can be served by using cache. In this scenario, you can compare the warehouse's minimal cost versus the query pruning cost in case the cache is invalidated. You can use the following query to analyze the cache used in queries:

```
SELECT
warehouse_name
,SUM(bytes_scanned) AS Total_bytes_scanned
,SUM(bytes_scanned*percentage_scanned_from_cache) / SUM(bytes_scanned) AS
bytes_scanned_from_cache
,SUM(bytes_scanned*percentage_scanned_from_cache) AS bytes_from_cache
,COUNT(*) AS count
FROM
snowflake.account_usage.query_history
WHERE
bytes_scanned > 0
GROUP BY 1
ORDER BY 3 DESC;
```

You can optimize the workloads by maintaining various cache available. Warehouse cache can be maintained if the warehouse is up and running, and you can compare the warehouse uptime versus cache utilization. You can maintain the cache if the cost is equivalent to or less than the storage scan or query execution cost on the warehouse in case of non-availability of cache.

Storage optimization

Storage cost is computed based on the average data stored. However, to optimize the storage cost, you need to analyze the following storage components:

- Physical data stored
- Data storage used for time-travel
- Data pruning

As you know, Snowflake stores data in micro-partitions and uses pruning to scan the data to be shared as query responses.

Analyze physical data stored

You can evaluate the data and bucket them in terms of hot, warm, and cold data. The cold data can be stored on the cloud storage and queried using external tables, as it is not queried often. You can save storage cost for cold datasets or data that can be archived or rolled to storage buckets on a monthly basis.

Data storage used for time-travel

Time-travel maintains the historical snapshot of the data and needs additional storage to maintain them. Storage associated with time-travel is also considered while calculating the usage of the storage layer. You can restrict the usage by enabling the time-travel only for critical tables where you really need to maintain the history for specific days. Analyze and review the existing time-travel policy setup for databases or tables in the account. You can set up longer windows for the critical tables and shorter windows for intermediate tables.

Data pruning

Pruning is a mechanism used to scan the data and generate results as response to the queries. Snowflake stores data in compressed, columnar format called micro-partitions. Snowflake also creates clustering on top of the micro partitions to reduce the scan and result pruning time. You can use automatic clustering to specify the custom key to be used for larger tables.

Enabling automatic clustering

Snowflake creates and manages cluster keys to cluster data based on micro partitions and dimensions. Snowflake creates clusters automatically; however, you can also define the clustering key. The cluster key is used to organize the data within micro partitions. The clustering key can be used to improve the performance of a query that contains filters, joins, or aggregates using the columns defined in the cluster key. You can enable automatic clustering to update the micro partitions as and when new data is added to the table.

Typically, automatic clustering is used to benefit queries that access the same set of columns from a given table. You need to analyze and pick the queries depending on the frequency and latency requirements to choose the clustering keys. These keys can be used to improve the performance of queries, especially where filters, joins, or aggregates on the same set of columns are used.

Query optimization

Query optimization can be done by following the standard SQL optimization practices as well. You can consider the following steps to identify queries to be optimized:

1. Identify long running queries
2. Identify queued queries
3. Analyze the identified long running queries and list down **query_ids**
4. Use **query_profile** to analyze the plan using **query_ids**
5. Identify the reason of the long execution of SQL optimization:
   a. Memory spillage
   b. SQL optimization
   c. Joining or filtering enhancements using clustering keys

Based on your analysis of identified queries using the aforementioned steps, you can plan to use the following options to optimize queries:

- Materialized views
- Search optimization
- Query acceleration service
- Automatic clustering keys
- Snowflake offers these serverless services to optimize the queries that cater to specific operations

Search optimization

This is a serverless optimization service of Snowflake that improves the performance of queries that are used to filter or look up the data. Snowflake recommends this to be used if it is required to have a low latency lookup.

Snowflake offers a set of SQL commands to enable this service for a table or specific columns in a table. The prerequisite to set up a column is to have selective values, substring searches, geo searches, and equality searches against those columns. You can use this feature for structured as well as semi-structured data.

Search optimization and MV are enterprise and above features. These services have limited scope as they can be used for single or given tables and for queries where the subset of table data is accessed.

You can also plan to apply multiple strategies to improve the query performance. Typically, it is recommended to get started with automatic clustering or search optimization, as this helps to improve the performance of similar queries on the table. You can refer to the following table, which lists the considerations for choosing these optimization techniques:

Optimization technique	Pre-requisites and considerations
Automatic clustering	Benefits if queries consist of WHERE clause to filter records for given columns. Any operations on the selected column. If queries have filters that are either inequality or equality filters. Limited to be defined on single column.
Materialized Views	Expensive queries consist of frequent calculations, e.g., aggregates, analysis of semi-structured data. Can be used for subqueries or specific query execution. Can be used to improve the performance of external tables.
Search Optimization	Focused on operations used for matching using LIKE or ILIKE. Can be used for VARIANT or GEO data types. Improves the performance of lookup queries.
Query Acceleration Service	Used for ad-hoc analysis. On any workloads that have unpredicted data patterns or queries that have large data scans.

Table 6.1: Optimization techniques

In the following section, we will introduce you to query acceleration service, MV, and dynamic tables. You can use these services to improve the performance of workloads and queries.

Query acceleration service

This is a serverless service offered as an enterprise edition feature. This offers acceleration service by accelerating parts of the workloads. This service can be enabled for a warehouse to improve the performance of the warehouse. This improves performance by reducing the impact of the queries that need more resources than usual queries.

The service offloads the work to extended shared compute resources offered by the service. You can use this service for the following workloads:

- Ad-hoc analysis
- Workload with unpredicted data volume
- Queries that scan larger datasets

The service adds resources to the existing execution, enabling queries to run in parallel to reduce scanning and filtering time. This service is used to improve the performance of the warehouse. You can use system functions to identify the eligible workloads and warehouses. You can use the function **SYSTEM$ESTIMATE_QUERY_ACCELERATION** to identify eligible warehouses. You can also use **QUERY_ACCELERATION_ELIGIBLE** view to identify warehouses that might benefit from this service.

Identifying workloads and warehouses

As you know, this service cannot be used for all types of workloads. If you have queries with the following operations, then these are not eligible for this service:

- Queries that do not have any filters and aggregates.
- Query that has smaller filters and is not selective enough.
- Queries that access the table and not enough partitions.
- Queries with **LIMIT** clause.

You can run **SELECT** query on the view to list down queries that can benefit from this service.

Identifying queries

You can run **SELECT** to fetch the **query_ids** from the view and use **query_id** to identify the queries. You can review and analyze the queries identified in this view before enabling the service for warehouses. You can run various queries on the view to capture the query details. You can refer to the following sample query:

```
SELECT
query_id,
eligible_query_acceleration_time
FROM
SNOWFLAKE.ACCOUNT_USAGE.QUERY_ACCELERATION_ELIGIBLE
where warehouse_name='DEMO_POC_WH'
ORDER BY eligible_query_acceleration_time DESC;
```

You can also identify the warehouses if they are eligible for this service. You can refer to **https://docs.snowflake.com/en/user-guide/query-acceleration-service** and get more details about using the query acceleration service to find eligible queries or warehouses.

Identifying warehouses

Run the **SELECT** on the view to get the warehouse names from the view. You can also get the eligible time by using the following SQL:

```
SELECT
warehouse_name,
SUM(eligible_query_acceleration_time) AS total_eligible_time
FROM
SNOWFLAKE.ACCOUNT_USAGE.QUERY_ACCELERATION_ELIGIBLE
GROUP BY warehouse_name
ORDER BY total_eligible_time DESC;
```

Once you identify the warehouse or queries running on the warehouse to be benefited, then you need to enable the service. You can enable the service while creating the warehouse or use **ALTER** statement to enable it for existing warehouses.

Enabling acceleration service

Use the following SQL to enable query acceleration while creating the warehouse:

```
Create warehouse DEMO_POC_WH with
ENABLE_QUERY_ACCELERATION = TRUE;
```

Use the **ALTER** command to enable and set the acceleration scale factor:

```
ALTER WAREHOUSE DEMO_POC_WH
SET ENABLE_QUERY_ACCELERATION = true
QUERY_ACCELERATION_MAX_SCALE_FACTOR = 0;
```

The scale factor allows users to set the upper bound on the number of resources the warehouse can lease to query acceleration service.

Query acceleration usage

Like other usage factors, query acceleration usage is also calculated using **USAGE** view. You can use **QUERY_HISTORY** view to compute the usage of the service. You can use the following columns from query history that are used to identify service usage:

- **QUERY_ACCELERATION_BYTES_SCANNED**
- **QUERY_ACCELERATION_PARTITIONS_SCANNED**
- **QUERY_ACCELERATION_UPPER_LIMIT_SCALE_FACTOR**

Use the following **SELECT** query on **QUERY_HISTORY** view to find the workload that is consuming most of the bytes:

```
SELECT
query_id,
query_acceleration_bytes_scanned as bytes_scanned,
query_acceleration_upper_limit_scale_factor as scale_factor,
query_acceleration_partitions_scanned as partition_scanned
FROM
SNOWFLAKE.ACCOUNT_USAGE.QUERY_HISTORY
WHERE
query_acceleration_partitions_scanned > 0
ORDER BY query_acceleration_bytes_scanned DESC;
```

You can gather metrics to analyze the usage of the service. The service can be billed based on the usage, and you can compute the billing using usage view.

Billing query acceleration service

This is the serverless service of Snowflake. The billing is computed based on the usage per second. You can get the billing details from querying the view as shown:

```
SELECT
warehouse_name,
SUM(credits_used) AS total_credits_used
FROM
SNOWFLAKE.ACCOUNT_USAGE.QUERY_ACCELERATION_HISTORY
WHERE start_time >= DATE_TRUNC(month, CURRENT_DATE)
GROUP BY 1
ORDER BY 2 DESC;
```

You can use this service along with search optimization to optimize the performance of queries and workloads. You can also view the usage on the Snowsight billing dashboard. Refer to **https://docs.snowflake.com/en/user-guide/query-acceleration-service#query-acceleration-service-cost** to get more details on the cost of the acceleration service. You will learn about MV and dynamic tables to optimize the SQL operations and automate the DML operations.

Materialized views

MV are nothing but pre-calculated data that is stored in the form of a table on top of the **SELECT** statement. You get better performance for the queries running on MV as they access the pre-calculated data. Typically, these views are used to simplify the processing of queries where complex processing, aggregations, or operations are performed. As of now, you can implement these views on a single table and not on more than one table. You can create this view to optimize the performance of queries, as this stores the pre-computed results of the **SELECT** query and has data ready for usage. We will learn to implement MV and use cases supported in this section.

Use cases of materialized views

As you know, MVs are used to preserve the intermediate results as a table. The following are some of the use cases where MVs can be used to store results and improve performance:

- Store results of queries that hold a small number of rows or columns in comparison with the base table used to create MV.

- Use view if the query requires significant processing, including:

   o Semi-structured data analysis

   o Longer or huge aggregates that take longer than usual

- View that refers to the external table and is used to improve the performance of queries on top of external tables.

- Create view on top of the base table that does not change often.

Maintaining materialized views

Snowflakes maintain these views automatically. Snowflake runs service in the background to reflect the changes from base table to the MV. This is an automatic and more efficient process in comparison with manual updates.

Creating materialized views

You can create views that refer to the **SELECT** statements. You cannot create MV for any DML statements like **INSERT**, **UPDATE**, or **DELETE**:

```
CREATE MATERIALIZED VIEW demo_mv
COMMENT='Demo view'
AS
SELECT
Set of columns,
Transformed columns,
Aggregated columns
FROM
Base_table;
```

You can manage views using DDL statements like **ALTER**, **SHOW**, **DESCRIBE**, **DROP**, and **TRUNCATE**. You can use MVs on top of **SELECT** statements of single base table. However, you can use dynamic tables on top of multiple tables with complex operations. Dynamic tables allow you to create tables that refer to a complex SQL statement by joining tables. You will learn more about dynamic tables in the following section.

Dynamic tables

Dynamic tables are the type of tables available in preview to all accounts. These are typically used to simplify the data engineering processes in Snowflake. This implementation caters to cost-effective, reliable, and automated data transformations.

In any data implementations, users write data pipelines that work on enrichment, transformations, and preparing data for the next data layer. In this case, dynamic tables replace the data engineering pipeline that reads from a set of tables, transforms data, and loads it to the target table. With dynamic table implementations, target tables are refreshed automatically based on the transformation logic used to load the table. This also materializes the results and manages the automated refresh.

As you know, dynamic tables are used to materialize the result. Hence, you cannot run any DML queries, such as insert, update, and delete rows, in a dynamic table.

Use cases

You can use dynamic tables to refresh the target tables automatically. The following are use cases to be considered for dynamic tables:

- Users do not want to write code to track dependencies and manage data refresh.
- Avoid complexities of streams and tasks.
- Users need to maintain the result of the query on multiple tables.
- When users need to use multiple tables to build the result set or the target table.

You can define the table refresh, lag, or latency to refresh the data in the target tables. You can use **CREATE** statement, as shown:

```
CREATE OR REPLACE DYNAMIC TABLE demo_dynamic_table
TARGET_LAG = '30 minutes'
WAREHOUSE = demo_poc_wh
REFRESH_MODE = auto
INITIALIZE = on_create
AS
SELECT
Column names
FROM table A;
```

You can use either of the serverless services to optimize the performance of the queries. You can also use warehouse optimization services to optimize the performance of the warehouses.

Conclusion

In this chapter, you explored Snowflake's performance optimization features: query performance, warehouse performance, storage performance, and serverless services. Optimization is one of the critical aspects of platform operations and maintenance. You can use optimization services and techniques to improve the performance of the platform. Snowflake offers a set of serverless services as features that lead to performance optimization. Once you understand the usage and optimization of the services, then you can compute the cost and implement cost monitoring.

You will learn about Snowflake's cost monitoring and optimization techniques in the next chapter.

Points to remember

Some key takeaways from this chapter are as follows:

- Snowflake offers serverless features to optimize the performance of the platform.

- You can use warehouse optimization techniques to analyze and optimize the overall performance. You can also use USAGE views to generate the performance metrics and monitor them.

- You can use storage optimization techniques to reduce storage costs and utilize storage effectively.

- You can use cloud services layer optimization techniques to identify the usage of cache and optimize the service layer usage.

- You can use query optimization techniques to identify long running, queued queries and optimize them.

- You can use serverless services, such as search optimization, query acceleration service, MV, and dynamic tables for performance improvements.

- You can manage the billing and view usage of overall serverless services using USAGE views as well as Snowsight features.

- You can use MV to store the result of single table operations to optimize performance.

- You can use search optimization to optimize the search operations using LIKE or ILIKE, or bucket filters to search the records in a table.

- You can use query acceleration service to offload some of the workloads or queries to the parallel resources of the service. You can use this service with warehouses to offload resources and improve the performance of the warehouses.

- You can use dynamic tables to store the result of operations on more than one table.

Join our Discord space

Join our Discord workspace for latest updates, offers, tech happenings around the world, new releases, and sessions with the authors:

https://discord.bpbonline.com

CHAPTER 7

Unlocking Snowflake's Cost and Performance

Introduction

Performance and cost efficiency is one of the architectural pillars of data platform design. This chapter focuses on understanding Snowflake's cost components. This focuses on calculating the cost using Snowflake metadata views, pricing, and serverless services usage. This also covers the derivation of various usage metrics and shares details of implementing these identified usage metrics. This chapter also helps to learn various cost optimization techniques and monitoring costs.

You will learn to use resource monitors to monitor the warehouse usage, monitoring overall performance of the platform using Snowsight tasks, alerts, and metrics. This chapter also covers the implementation of dashboards, alerts, and checkpoints to watch the platform's usage.

Structure

This chapter consists of the following topics:

- Understanding Snowflake cost
- Understanding serverless services
- Monitoring Snowflake usage metrics

- Monitoring using Snowsight dashboards
- Cost optimization techniques

Objectives

By the end of this chapter, you will be able to understand the Snowflake cost components and optimize the overall spending of the platform. You will also learn about the various metrics and options to setup the monitoring process to get timely alerts. Trial account setup can be used to perform various exercises throughout this book.

Understanding Snowflake cost

Snowflake's unified architecture is made up of three primary layers: the cloud services layer, the warehouse or compute layer, and the storage layer. In the previous chapter, you also learned about Snowflake performance components and optimizing the performance of each layer. The overall cost of the Snowflake platform is computed based on the cost model, as shown in *Figure 7.1*. Snowflake cost model not only caters to the three layers of architecture but also includes the serverless services and data transfer services used as part of optimization or platform design. You need to consider the cost model to derive the overall cost of the platform.

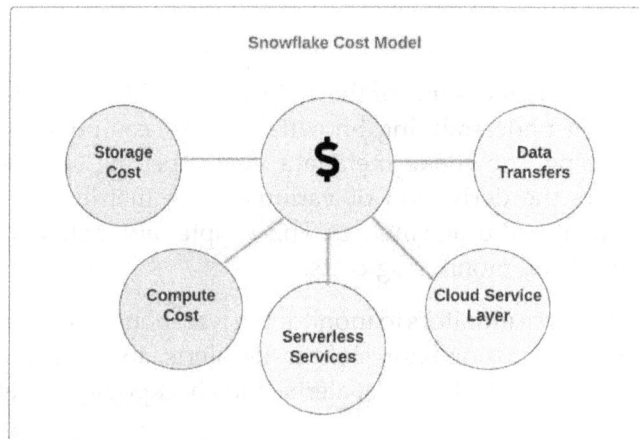

Figure 7.1: Snowflake cost model

Each component in the Snowflake cost model consists of various usage components to calculate the overall usage. You can refer to *Figure 7.2*, which represents the various components of each service that caters to the platform cost:

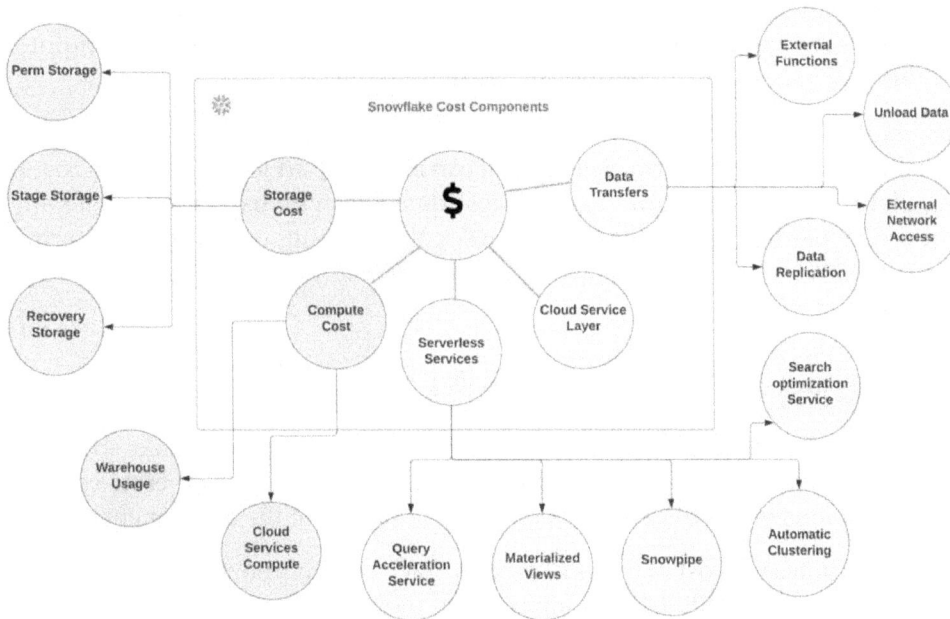

Figure 7.2: Snowflake cost components

As you can see, each layer or service has a set of services or operations that contribute to the platform component cost. Let us take a look at the following:

- Storage cost is computed as an average of daily storage utilized for permanent storage, stage storage, and storage used for data protection features like time-travel or failsafe.

- Compute cost is compute usage as part of the warehouse layer and cloud services layer. The compute cost is dependent on the size of the warehouse and uptime.

- Serverless services are the next major contributor to the platform cost, as most of the optimization techniques and Snowpipe are used to load real-time data. Apart from the components mentioned in the figure, there are also a set of other components to the cost, including hybrid tables, external tables, copy files, logging, tracing, etc.

- Data transfer cost is the cost incurred for data replication, data unloads, external functions, or external network access. Data can also be transferred or copied over to different regions or availability zones for **High Availability (HA)** or **Disaster Recovery (DR)**. This yields additional cost as part of data transfer, this also applies to any data unloads or accessing data from external systems.

- Cloud services cost is the cost incurred to maintain the metadata, cache, and SQL statements used to set the context: role, database, schema, warehouse, or any DDL or metadata queries. Cloud services cost is considered as consumption with respect to the compute usage. If the cloud services cost is less than 10% of the overall compute cost, then it is free and not attributed to any additional cost of the cloud services layer. If the cost bucket exceeds 10% of the overall compute, then this is billed as per the edition and costing model.

You can use this cost model and cost components while designing the platform to calculate the probable cost of the platform. This model can also be used to maintain the cost for the existing platform. The costing model and cost details can be used to calculate any new application onboarding to the platform or track the ongoing cost of the platform. Also, you can use **USAGE** views to calculate the cost of the platform, which is what we will be exploring next.

Computing cost using USAGE views

As you know, there are various **USAGE** schemas that are shared as Snowflake share. You can use the metadata views present in the **USAGE** schema to query and generate cost metrics. You can use various views to gather the credit information of the component usage.

Snowflake computes the cost in terms of **credits**. Each cost component of Snowflake usage is maintained in the **USAGE** schema along with the performance metrics. You can use **CREDIT** columns from these metadata views to calculate the platform's usage.

As you know, you can have multiple Snowflake accounts as part of your organization, and you can compute the cost at the account as well as the organizational level. There is a separate **ORGANIZATION_USAGE** schema to cater to organizational usage components. You can also use the conversion metadata view to get the conversion rate of the credits to the dollar values.

You can use the following set of **ACCOUNT_USAGE** views to calculate the various cost components:

- `warehouse_metering_history`
- `query_history`
- `storage_usage`
- `EVENT_USAGE_HISTORY`
- `QUERY_ACCELERATION_HISTORY`
- `PIPE_USAGE_HISTORY`
- `REPLICATION_USAGE_HISTORY`
- `SEARCH_OPTIMIZATION_HISTORY`
- `SERVERLESS_TASK_HISTORY`
- `SNOWPARK_CONTAINER_SERVICES_HISTORY`

The following are the **ORGANIZATION_USAGE** views used to calculate the account costs:

- `METERING_DAILY_HISTORY`
- `RATE_SHEET_DAILY`
- `WAREHOUSE_METERING_HISTORY`

- **`STORAGE_DAILY_HISTORY`**
- **`USAGE_IN_CURRENCY_DAILY`**

You can use the views listed previously and use SQL statements to generate the set of usage metrics to review the platform usage. You can also use these views and metrics to monitor the overall usage. You will learn more about monitoring and using these usage metrics in the following section.

Understanding serverless services

As you understand, the serverless services are the managed services of Snowflake. The resource allocation, sizing, and usage are managed by Snowflake. You can use these serverless services and compute the cost using Snowflake serverless services views. Costing of serverless services consists of the following services:

- Materialized views
- Search optimization service
- Query acceleration service
- Snowpipe
- Automatic clustering
- Hybrid tables
- Snowflake managed services to track data changes in the platform

You can use the corresponding **USAGE_VIEWS** to calculate the usage of the services. You can also view the usage by using Snowsight navigation menu. *Figure 7.3* shows serverless usage:

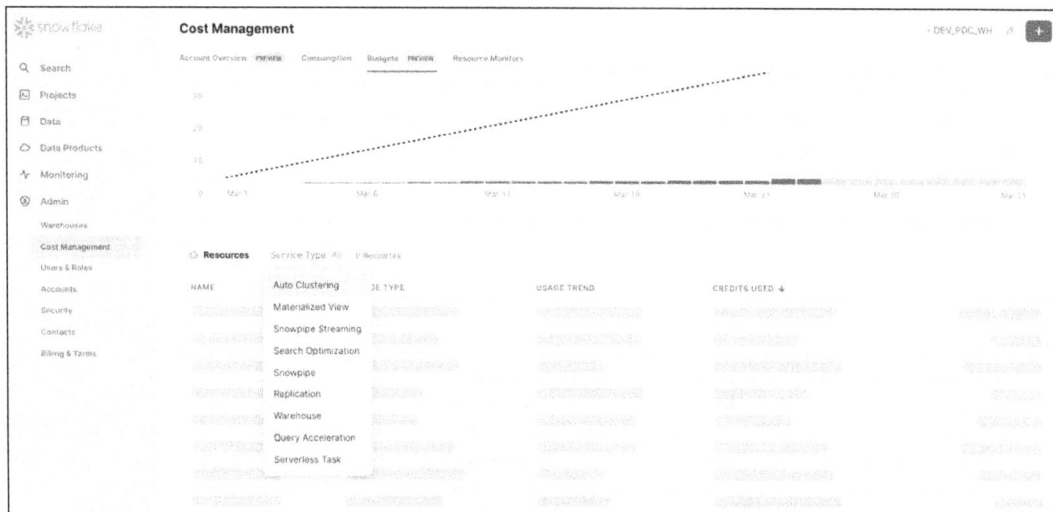

Figure 7.3: Snowsight cost management view

To list the view of Snowflake account cost and usage, go to Snowsight (**https://app.snowflake.com/**) | Logon with your details | Choose role to **ACCOUNTADMIN** or custom role setup to view usage permissions | Open **Admin** from the navigation menu | **Cost Management** | **Budgets**.

A drop down menu lists all the serverless services and warehouses. The page shows usage details of the services used in the account. Budgets and resource monitors are used to monitor the overall usage. You will learn about monitoring usage in the following section.

Monitoring Snowflake usage metrics

Monitoring and maintaining the usage within the defined threshold is the most critical part of cost management. You need to ensure that you are defining the right thresholds and setting up alerts and notifications to manage the overall consumption of the platform. The following are the important aspects of the monitoring:

- Monitor and generate alerts if it reaches the threshold.
- Monitor and act on the usage.
- Define a limit and monitor the usage on a monthly basis.
- Reporting or dashboarding for the usage metrics.

You can use Snowflake native components to implement the usage monitoring. You can implement them using the following features or services:

- Resource Monitors
- Budgets
- Snowsight Dashboards

These are easy to configure and use features that are essential for usage tracking and monitoring. These services are provided to implement the preventive measures and may have costs associated. For example, Snowsight dashboard cost is based on the queries' cost used to render the charts within the dashboards. Budgets and resource monitors are used to setup the thresholds and help monitor usage. The following section helps you understand and implement these monitoring features.

Resource monitors

Resource monitors are used to monitor warehouse usage. You can set up a resource monitor to monitor the warehouse usage and take some actions based on the threshold, and if it reaches the threshold. This is helpful to avoid any additional usage costs to the account. Warehouses are charged for the time they are up and running. You can set the action to suspend the warehouse, send notifications, etc.

As you know by now, resource monitors need input parameters to set the threshold, warehouse actions: notify or suspend, and frequency of the monitoring. The following are the parameters or properties of the resource monitors used to configure them:

- **Schedule:** This is used to set the frequency or interval to start monitoring. By default, this is applied immediately and starts monitoring. You can set the frequency to daily, weekly, monthly, or yearly. You can also set the start and end dates if you want to configure the resource monitor to run for a specific duration.

- **Quota:** This is the threshold set to Snowflake credits that are used to review the warehouse usage. You can set the credit quota for user managed warehouses as well as cloud services warehouses.

- **Type:** This is used to specify the resources to be monitored. You can set it up as an account resource monitor or warehouse monitor. Warehouse monitor monitors the specific warehouse and its credit consumption. The account type of resource monitor monitors all the warehouses present in the account. You can specify one or more warehouses to warehouse monitor and track the credit consumption of multiple warehouses with the same threshold or quota.

- **Actions:** As you know, this is used to specify what action is to be taken when a monitor reaches the quota limit or the percentage threshold. You can specify three types of actions here:

  o **Notify:** Sends a notification without taking any action to the warehouse.

  o **Notify & Suspend:** Send notification and suspend the warehouse once all the statements or workloads are completed. This waits for the execution completion of the queries being executed.

  o **Notify & Suspend Immediately:** This sends a notification and suspends the warehouse on an immediate basis, even if there are any statements being executed.

- Snowflake recommends using resource monitors to keep track of the warehouse usage and avoid any additional usage. Admins can set up multiple monitors to monitor the usage of warehouses using **CREATE** statements or by setting them using Snowsight console features.

- Resource monitors can be created using **CREATE DDL** and managed using other DDL statements like **ALTER**, **SHOW**, **DROP**, etc. These are created and maintained by ACCOUNTADMINs only. However, **ACCOUNTADMIN** can grant a role to manage them to a custom role by granting **MONITOR** and **MODIFY** grants.

- These notifications are sent to the users with verified email addresses. You need to ensure that the recipient of the notification verifies their account using Web UI, Snowsight.

The following are some of the examples or references to set the resource monitors:

- Setup the monitor with a credit limit of 80% and send a notification if it reaches 80%:

```
USE ROLE ACCOUNTADMIN;
/*use previously created warehouse poc_demo_wh to set the resource
monitor */
CREATE OR REPLACE RESOURCE MONITOR demo_wh_monitor WITH CREDIT_
QUOTA=1200
TRIGGERS ON 80 PERCENT DO NOTIFY;

/* attach the resource monitor created above*/

ALTER WAREHOUSE poc_demo_wh SET RESOURCE_MONITOR = demo_wh_monitor;
```

- Setup monitor with a credit limit of 80% and notify to suspend and suspends if it reaches 90%.

```
USE ROLE ACCOUNTADMIN;
/*create a new warehouse */
CREATE OR REPLACE WAREHOUSE dev_compute_wh WITH WAREHOUSE_
SIZE='SMALL';
CREATE OR REPLACE RESOURCE MONITOR dev_wh_monitor WITH CREDIT_
QUOTA=800
TRIGGERS ON 80 PERCENT DO NOTIFY
        ON 100 PERCENT DO SUSPEND;
/* attach the resource monitor created above*/

ALTER WAREHOUSE dev_compute_wh SET RESOURCE_MONITOR = demo_wh_monitor;
```

- Setup monitor with a credit limit of 85% and suspend. In case of 95%, suspend immediately:

```
USE ROLE ACCOUNTADMIN;
/*create a new warehouse */
CREATE OR REPLACE WAREHOUSE dev_eng_wh WITH WAREHOUSE_SIZE='MEDIUM';
CREATE OR REPLACE RESOURCE MONITOR de_dev_monitor WITH CREDIT_
QUOTA=1000
TRIGGERS ON 85 PERCENT DO NOTIFY
        ON 95 PERCENT DO SUSPEND;
/* attach the resource monitor created above*/

ALTER WAREHOUSE dev_eng_wh SET RESOURCE_MONITOR = de_dev_monitor;
```

- Resource monitors are useful to setup monitoring at account usage or warehouse usage. Snowflake also offers budgets to set up limits on the usage, which we will explore next.

Maintain usage with budgets

Snowflake's budget is now an available (**Generally Available (GA)**) feature that lets users define the limit at account and custom group of objects. Resource monitors are associated with the warehouse spend and usage, whereas budgets are used to monitor the spending limits and send notifications when it is projected to reach the limit. Users with verified mail will get email notifications. Users who are entitled to get email notifications receive notifications. There are types of budgets that can be set to track usage, account, and custom budgets. This section covers details of the budget's set-up and implementation.

Account budgets

The account budget is used to monitor the spending of all supported objects in the account. You can set the budget using the following set of steps and SQLs:

1. Activate the budgets.

2. Assign limits to the budgets:

```
/* Step 1: Activate Budgets */
CALL snowflake.local.account_root_budget!ACTIVATE();
/* Step 2: Assign limits to budget */
CALL snowflake.local.account_root_budget!SET_SPENDING_LIMIT(2500);
```

3. Create notification integration for Snowflake users or admins to receive the budget notification using the following SQL command:

```
/* Create notification integration */
CREATE NOTIFICATION INTEGRATION budgets_notify_integration
TYPE=EMAIL
ENABLED=TRUE
   ALLOWED_RECIPIENTS=('poojakelgaonkar@xyz.com','accountadmin@example.com');
```

4. Grant permissions on the notification integration to the account:

```
GRANT USAGE ON INTEGRATION budgets_notifiy_integration
TO APPLICATION snowflake;
```

5. Assign the email notification to the Snowflake budgets:

```
CALL snowflake.local.account_root_budget!SET_EMAIL_NOTIFICATIONS(
'poojakelgaonkar@xyz.com','accountadmin@example.com');
```

Now you have learned to set up the budgets, and these can be set up on Snowflake objects like tables, materialized views, schemas, databases, warehouses, pipes, and tasks. This also supports serverless features to be added as part of spend limits. Only **ACCOUNTADMIN** can activate the budgets. Typically, custom roles are set up for budget creation, and grant roles are to create budgets. Snowsight features can also be used to set up the budgets with the console menu.

Custom budgets

You can set up the custom budgets using SQL commands and follow a similar set of steps as account budgets. In the case of custom, you create customized budgets and assign resources to add to the budget monitoring:

```
/* create database and schema for budgets */
create database snowflake_budgets;
create schema budgets;

use database snowflake_budgets;
use schema budgets;

/* Create custom budget */
CREATE SNOWFLAKE.CORE.BUDGET dev_budget();
/* assign spend limit */
CALL dev_budget!SET_SPENDING_LIMIT(50);
/* assign notification integration */
CALL dev_budget!SET_EMAIL_NOTIFICATIONS('budgets_notify_integration',
'poojakelgaonkar@xyz.com');
/* assign resources to custom budgets */
CALL snowflake_budgets.budgets.dev_budget!ADD_RESOURCE(
    SYSTEM$REFERENCE('WAREHOUSE', 'DEV_POC_WH', 'SESSION', 'applybudget'));
```

You can use Snowsight features to create budgets. Refer to *Figure 7.4* and provide the following details:

1. Login to Snowsight.
2. Select role | **ACCOUNTADMIN**
3. Go to **Admin** | **Cost Management**
4. Select the **Budgets** tab
5. Click on + on the top right corner to add budget.

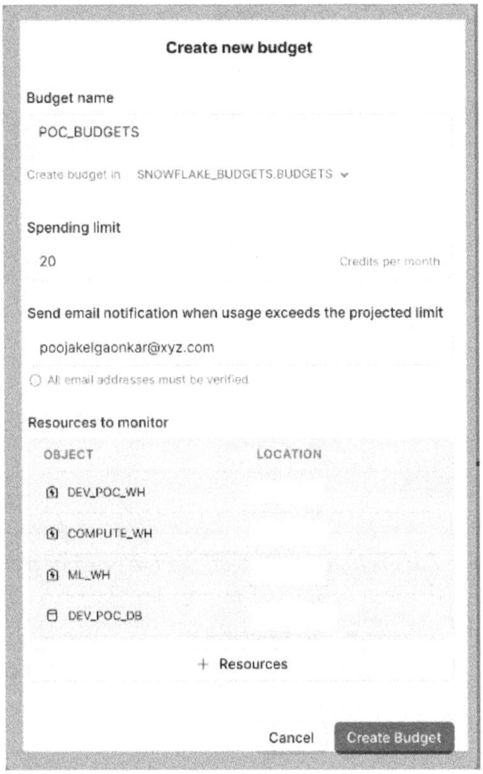

Create new budget

Budget name

POC_BUDGETS

Create budget in   SNOWFLAKE_BUDGETS.BUDGETS ⌄

Spending limit

20   Credits per month

Send email notification when usage exceeds the projected limit

poojakelgaonkar@xyz.com

○ All email addresses must be verified

Resources to monitor

OBJECT	LOCATION
ⓢ DEV_POC_WH	
ⓢ COMPUTE_WH	
ⓢ ML_WH	
🗄 DEV_POC_DB	

\+ Resources

Cancel   Create Budget

Figure 7.4: Budget creation using Snowsight

Now, you have learned to implement usage monitoring with resource monitors and budgets. Next step is to setup dashboards for visual monitoring and tracking for performance and cost usage. You will learn to set up monitoring dashboards in the following section.

Monitoring using Snowsight dashboards

You can use Snowflake dashboards to create monitoring dashboards using Snowflake metadata views and defining metrics to monitor usage and billing. You can create Snowflake metrics using metadata views to monitor the usage of warehouses, storage, cloud services layer, long-running queries, etc.

Refer to *Figure 7.5* and follow the given steps to create monitoring dashboards:

1. Login to Snowsight
2. Select role **ACCOUNTADMIN**
3. Go to **Projects | Dashboards**
4. Click on +**Dashboard** in the top right corner.
5. Provide appropriate dashboard name | **Create Dashboard**.

6. Select **New Tile** | from SQL worksheet.

7. Select context | database, schema, warehouse

8. Run SQL to generate metrics

Figure 7.5: Snowsight SQL worksheet to generate metrics

9. Click on the **Charts** tab from the result set.

10. Select chart type, metrics, and measure. Refer to *Figure 7.6*, which shows the chart options and displays a sample chart:

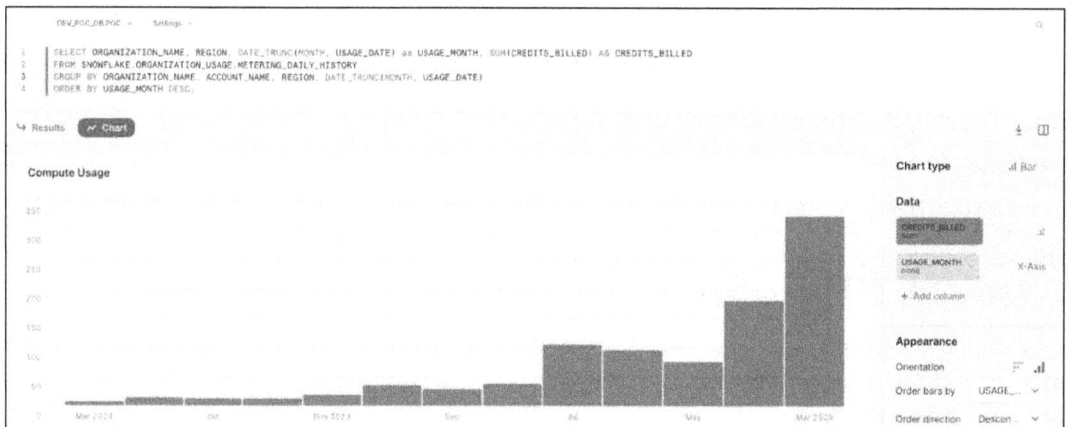

Figure 7.6: Chart configuration on Snowsight dashboard

11. Use SQL queries on top of metadata views. You can generate the following metrics for usage, billing, and operational dashboards:

    a. **Operational**: Long running queries, top 10 failed queries, top 10 queued queries.

    b. **Usage**: Compute usage, cloud services usage, storage usage, overall monthly usage for an account, and overall usage for an organization.

c. **Billing**: Account credit consumption, overall cost per month, account cost, and bill in $ for an organization.

Refer to *Figure 7.7* for the sample dashboard. You can set up a similar dashboard with chart types of your choice.

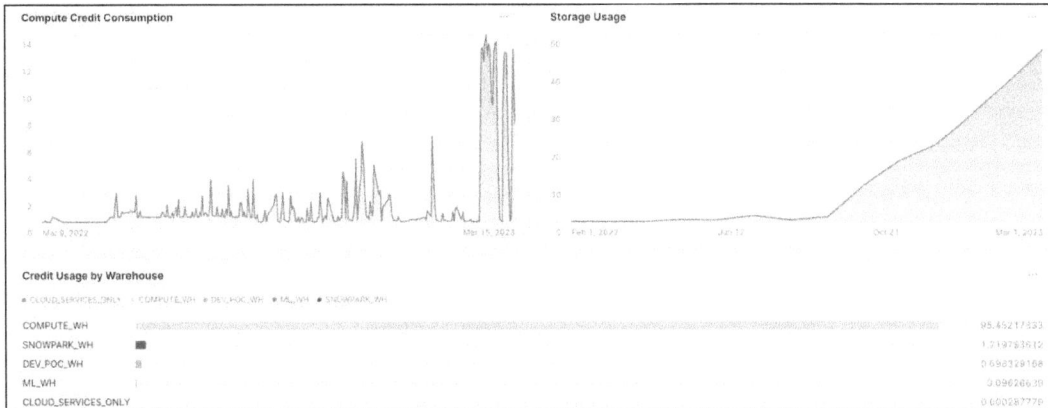

Figure 7.7: Sample usage dashboard

You can use these dashboards to monitor and share with your operational teams. Budgets, Resource Monitors, and Snowsight dashboards are used to monitor the account performance. Once you implement cost and performance monitoring, the next important aspect is cost optimization. The following section covers details of optimization and techniques.

Cost optimization techniques

Snowflake costing has various components to compute the overall usage of the platform. You need to optimize the use of components like Compute, Storage, Cloud Services, serverless services, etc., to optimize the usage of the platform.

Compute optimization

Compute is warehouse usage used to perform SQL, DML, and data load operations. You can follow the given strategies to optimize the cost:

- **Warehouse setup:** Avoid granting access to multiple users to manage warehouses. Set up separate warehouses for each team based on their types of workloads. Snowflake recommends a centralized approach to creating and managing warehouses in an account.

- **Right sizing the warehouse:** Snowflake recommends trying different workloads with the warehouse sizes before picking up a size for the warehouse. It is recommended to use a smaller size and increase the size of the warehouse to test for the workload if you are not sure of the warehouse sizes. Warehouse cost is associated with the size and uptime of the warehouses.

- **Adding query time limits:** Compute cost is associated with the queries executed in the warehouses, and if you have multiple queries being executed or queued, then warehouse usage goes up. Snowflake recommends using **STATEMENT_ TIMEOUT_IN_SECONDS** parameter to set the limit to avoid additional costs. You can avoid such queued queries using the **STATEMENT_QUEUED_TIMEOUT_IN_SECONDS** parameter. These parameters can be set at account, at user, at session, or at a specific warehouse.

- **Setup auto suspend and auto resume:** Every warehouse has auto-suspend enabled by default. The warehouse costs only when it is up and running. It does not incur costs when suspended. Auto resumes warehouses when workloads are submitted on them. Auto suspending avoids any additional cost when the warehouse is idle.

- **Enforce spend limits:** You can enforce the limits using resource monitors and budgets. These allow users to monitor the spend and put a threshold on spend.

Storage optimization

Storage cost is computed as a daily average of data stored in compressed data format. The storage cost is computed on the flat rate of storage. You can optimize storage costs by using the storage strategy to store hot data:

- **Store only required data:** You can use transient or temporary tables for intermediate processing. You can also use internal or external stages to reduce the storage cost of the data. You can use the stage in the same region where data copy is FREE. As a best practice, you can always store the data necessary or the data used frequently, usually termed HOT data, in the storage layer.

- **Configure time-travel only for critical tables:** Snowflake offers failsafe and time-travel to protect the data and prevent data loss. You can configure the time-travel of the tables to required days as it consumes storage cost. Snowflake recommends setting up time-travel only for the required and critical tables for specific days.

Cloud services optimization

Cloud services cost is computed separately for any metadata queries or context queries being run. If your cloud services cost is within 10% of the compute usage, then you still have room to use the SQL commands that leverage the cloud services bucket. Cloud services cost for any usage more than 10% of compute cost. You can use some of the following recommendations to reduce the overall cloud services cost:

- Reduce the context queries that use **USE** queries to set database, schema, role, warehouses, etc. You can configure the context while using queries or setting up the default role, warehouse for the users, and roles.

- Queries that run count(*) or count(1) on tables or using table information from schema views.

- Analyze the queries to check if they can be run from the cache stored at various layers.

You can use these optimization strategies to evaluate and reduce the usage cost of the account. Snowflake recommends implementing monitoring and setting up appropriate alerts for the admin or users.

Conclusion

In this chapter, you explored Snowflake's cost and learned the cost components. Snowflake cost optimization and monitoring features enable users to maintain the cost as well as usage of the platform.

Snowflake cost and understanding the cost components play vital roles in developing pipelines and using the platform. You can develop the pipelines and calculate the usage of the compute, cloud services to monitor query performance. You can use these cost optimization techniques to monitor, optimize, and report usage of your application. This is essential to understand the overall platform usage.

In the next chapter, you will learn to share data with teams or applications using data sharing. You will also learn to use data cloning to set up the data environments.

Points to remember

This chapter shares the following key takeaways:

- Snowflake cost is computed based on the Snowflake components, features usage: cloud services, compute layer, storage, serverless services, etc.

- Snowflake cost is computed in terms of **credits**. Credits are the units used to calculate platform usage.

- Snowflake warehouse cost is computed based on the size of the warehouse and the time it is up and running.

- Snowflake storage cost is computed based on the daily average of the storage, storage associated with permanent storage, stages, time-travel, failsafe, data recovery, and temporary storage.

- Snowflake cloud services cost is associated with the usage of the layer to query metadata information, cache, context setting, etc.

- You can use warehouse optimization techniques to optimize the overall performance. You can use warehouse optimization techniques to optimize warehouse usage.

- You can use storage optimization techniques to reduce storage costs and utilize storage effectively.

- You can use cloud services layer optimization techniques to identify the usage of cache and optimize the service layer usage.

- You can use query optimization techniques to reduce compute usage for long running, and queued queries.

- You can use monitoring features like resource monitors to monitor the usage of warehouses at the account level or custom warehouses.

- You can use budgets to set the spending limit on the account to monitor overall account spend. You can also set up custom budgets to monitor the spending of custom resources or objects in an account.

- You can use Snowsight dashboards to get a consolidated view of overall account usage and metrics. You can set up the dashboards and share them with your teams.

Join our Discord space

Join our Discord workspace for latest updates, offers, tech happenings around the world, new releases, and sessions with the authors:

https://discord.bpbonline.com

CHAPTER 8
Implementing Data Integrations

Introduction

Data integration is an integral part of data platform design. Source and target systems need to be integrated with the data platform as part of data integration. Applications that consume data from the platform are called consumer applications. Snowflake offers data sharing and cloning features to share data with consumer applications and users. Data sharing allows us to share data with Snowflake and non-Snowflake users.

This chapter focuses on consumer integration and helps to understand Snowflake's unique feature, namely, data sharing. This also covers data cloning, maintaining multiple environments with optimal space. The chapter covers the need to have data consumers and consumer models. This also helps to learn the benefits of data sharing and cloning.

Structure

This chapter consists of the following topics:

- Understanding consumer data integrations
- Data sharing
- Data cloning
- Data exchange
- Snowflake data marketplace

Objectives

By the end of this chapter, you will be able to understand the need for various data integrations and how Snowflake caters to need of data integrations. You will also learn about Snowflake features like data cloning, sharing, exchange, and sharing data with consumers. You can use the trial account setup to perform various exercises throughout this book.

Understanding consumer data integrations

In a typical data platform design, there are sets of consumer applications, users, and data analytics requirements to serve BI, AI/ML applications. Refer to *Figure 8.1*, which shares a view of platform consumer integrations that consume and read data from the platform.

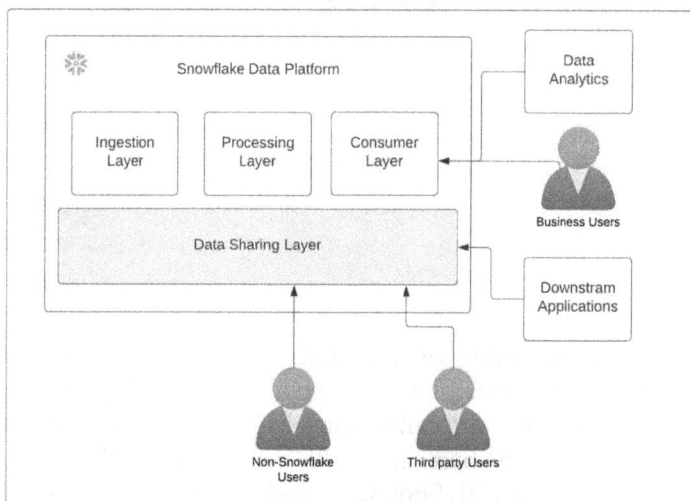

Figure 8.1: Data consumer integrations

As seen in *Figure 8.1*, the following are the typical consumers and integrations set up with the data platform, these are standard users, and there can be more consumers and customized integrations based on the application requirements:

- **Data analytics:** This is a type of consumer integration where applications and users run analytics, BI reporting, and dashboarding requirements. You can also have the AI/ML applications integrated to consume data from the platform.

- **Business users:** These are the type of business users that consume data from the platform to validate business use cases as well as business requirements.

- **Downstream applications:** These are the type of applications that consume data from the Snowflake platform as a data source. Snowflake acts as a source of data for these applications, providing the data in the form of tables and data file feeds.

- **Third-party users:** These are the type of users who consume data from the platform as external users. You can share the data required as reference data with these users.

- **Non-Snowflake users:** These are the type of users that are a subset of third-party users that are not onboarded to the Snowflake data platform. Snowflake allows data sharing with non-Snowflake users via reader accounts.

Typically, the users who can be onboarded to the Snowflake platform are granted access to the consumer layers, databases, and objects. You can create a consumer database and grant required access to the consumer users. In some cases, consumer data applications expect data in the form of feeds or files. Hence, data pipelines are required to generate these data feeds as per application requirements. This adds an overhead to manage the pipelines as well as data consistency.

The following options can be used to share data using Snowflake data sharing capabilities:

- **Listings:** Share data privately as well as publicly with users on Snowflake marketplace.

- **Direct share:** Share data with one or more Snowflake accounts in the same region.

- **Data exchange:** Share data as private listings with specific accounts or individual users.

You will learn about data sharing options in the subsequent sections of this chapter.

Data sharing

Snowflake offers secure data sharing. However, not all objects that are created and deployed can be shared as part of secure data sharing. You create and share the following objects:

- Databases and objects: schema, tables
- Secure views and secure materialized views
- Dynamic tables, iceberg tables, external tables
- Secure **user-defined functions** (**UDFs**)

Data shares can be created and shared by providers. Consumers can use shared data as imported data. Data sharing follows the provider-consumer model. You can refer to *Figure 8.2* for secure data sharing. Providers are the Snowflake users who create secure data shares, and consumers are the users who consume data. Provider data sharing is enabled by default for most of the Snowflake accounts, though not for all accounts. You can reach out to Snowflake support in case provider sharing is not enabled for your account.

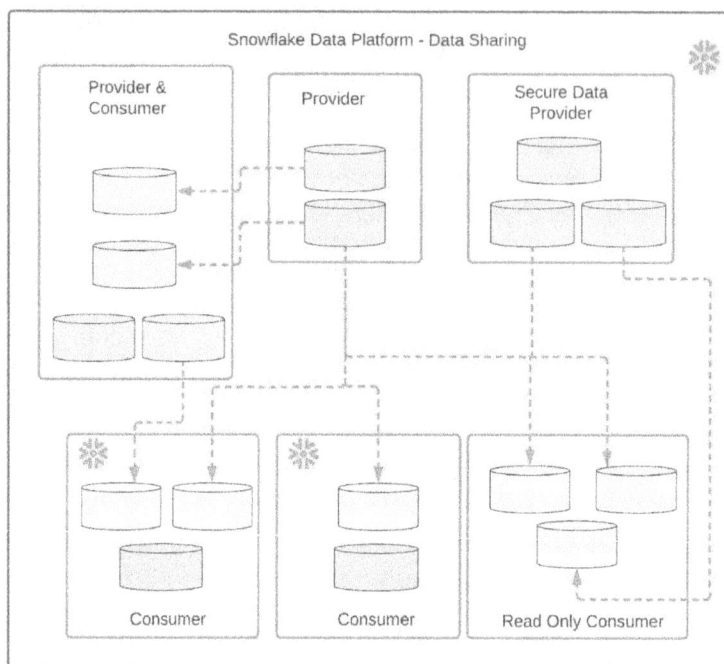

Figure 8.2: Snowflake secure data sharing

Data providers can share the data as a direct share as well as with a database role. You can grant required privileges to the database objects and secure data shares. Snowflake allows users to create shares and share them with Snowflake and non-Snowflake users. As a provider, you can create secure data share using the **CREATE** command as well as use Snowsight UI features.

Snowflake recommends using secure views and other secure objects to be included in a database or schema to create a data share. These secure objects enable users to protect the metadata, column, and object level details from the provider accounts. Secure views can be used to share the data between multiple databases, Snowflake also allows users to create secure views in the same or different databases. Secure views are recommended to be created if you need to add them as part of data shares, as well as have access granted to end users who may not have access to the metadata details. Secure views are less performance efficient than regular views. Based on the use case and requirements to implement efficient views is key to choose between regular views vs secure views. Snowflake data shares can be created and shared with any user. This section will help you understand the process and steps required to create the data shares.

Sharing data with Snowflake users

Snowflake treats *Share* as an object. This is like any other database object, and we can create share using DDL commands. This share can be shared with individual users or as a database role. A share consists of multiple objects from one or more databases that can be shared as one share with users. You can use the following options to create the share as a provider:

- Using database role
- Creating direct share

We will explore both options in detail.

Using database role

Database roles are the same as traditional roles created at the account level. Roles and permissions can be granted on the database role within the same database.

Follow the given steps to create a share using the database role:

1. Create database role.
2. Grant privileges to the database objects to the role created in *Step 1*.
3. Create a data share.
4. Grant USAGE privileges on the database to the share.
5. Add the required objects to be shared as part of secure data share.
6. Share the secure share created with consumers.

You can refer to the following SQL commands to implement the preceding steps:

```
/* create database */
CREATE DATABASE DATA_SHARE;
CREATE SCHEMA POC;
USE DATABASE DATA_SHARE;
USE SCHEMA POC;

/* create roles */
CREATE DATABASE ROLE share_role1;
CREATE DATABASE ROLE share_role2;

/* create objects */
CREATE TABLE DEMO_TABLE(ID INTEGER,NAME STRING);
CREATE SECURE VIEW DEMO_VIEW AS SELECT * FROM DEMO_TABLE;
```

Once you have objects ready to be shared and the database role used to create the share, the next step is to grant permissions to the schema, table, and view to both roles created in the preceding step. The following are the SQL commands used to grant permissions on the object's setup:

```
/*grant privileges to the role1*/
GRANT USAGE ON SCHEMA DATA_SHARE.POC TO DATABASE ROLE DATA_SHARE.share_role1;
```

```
GRANT SELECT ON VIEW DATA_SHARE.POC.DEMO_VIEW TO DATABASE ROLE DATA_SHARE.
share_role1;

/*grant privileges to the role2*/
GRANT USAGE ON SCHEMA DATA_SHARE.POC TO DATABASE ROLE DATA_SHARE.share_
role2;
GRANT SELECT ON VIEW DATA_SHARE.POC.DEMO_VIEW TO DATABASE ROLE DATA_SHARE.
share_role2;
```

Now, you have objects and roles set up. All required permissions are granted to the database roles. Next is to create the database share using the **CREATE** command. SQL commands can be used to create the data share and share it with the consumer accounts. Create and share data share by using the following SQL commands:

```
/*create share*/
CREATE SHARE DEMO_SHARE;

/*GRANT PERMISSIONS*/
GRANT USAGE ON DATABASE DATA_SHARE TO SHARE DEMO_SHARE;
GRANT DATABASE ROLE DATA_SHARE.share_role1 TO SHARE DEMO_SHARE;
GRANT DATABASE ROLE DATA_SHARE.share_role2 TO SHARE DEMO_SHARE;

/*SHARE WITH PROVIDERS */
ALTER SHARE DEMO_SHARE ADD ACCOUNTS = org1.consumer1,org1.consumer2;
```

You can use the preceding reference SQL to create secure data share using database role Option 1.

Creating direct share

Unlike database role set up for sharing, you can also grant sharing with direct users with secure data sharing. You can follow these steps to create secure data share:

1. Create a secure share.
2. Add objects and permissions to the share.
3. Add consumer accounts to the share.

You can use the following SQL commands to create secure data share:

```
/* Create share */
USE ROLE ACCOUNTADMIN;
CREATE SHARE POC_SHARE;

/* Grant permissions */
GRANT USAGE ON DATABASE DATA_SHARE TO SHARE POC_SHARE;
GRANT USAGE ON SCHEMA DATA_SHARE.POC TO SHARE POC_SHARE;
GRANT SELECT ON TABLE DEMO_TABLE TO SHARE POC_SHARE;
```

```
/* Share with consumers as direct share */
ALTER SHARE POC_SHARE ADD ACCOUNTS=abc12345,pq67890; --share with Snowflake
accounts
```

You can use the preceding reference SQL shared to create secure data share using direct shares Option 2. Data sharing with a database role is preferred while creating shares and managing them at the account level. Sharing data as direct sharing with individual users using access permissions to create and manage shares is not a feasible choice.

Data sharing can be shared with any Snowflake as well as non-Snowflake users. However, you need to follow different sets of steps to share the share created. This section helps you create data shares that are shared with Snowflake users. The following section will help you set up a reader account, manage the reader account, and share the data with the reader account.

Sharing data with non-Snowflake users

You can share the data with non-Snowflake users using reader accounts. Reader accounts are the consumers managed by providers. Providers can create shares and grant usage to the consumer reader accounts. Provider accounts allow consumers to use the compute required to access the data as well as run queries. Reader accounts are owned and managed by providers. These accounts have restricted permissions to execute queries to access the data shared as secure data share. Reader accounts cannot create new tables or entities within Snowflake account as a consumer. Provider accounts can manage credits, warehouses, and the cost of the reader accounts using resource monitors and usage queries.

You can create and manage reader accounts using DDL statements like **CREATE**, **ALTER**, **SHOW**, and **DROP** SQL commands. Snowsight can also be used to create reader accounts via web interface over SQL queries. You can run these queries on Snowsight as well as using SnowSQL. Refer to the following SQL commands to create a user:

```
/* Create user using SYSADMIN or ACCOUNTADMIN */
CREATE MANAGED ACCOUNT consumer_reader
ADMIN_NAME = reader_account , ADMIN_PASSWORD = 'Demo123' , TYPE = READER;

/* view existing reader accounts */
SHOW MANAGED ACCOUNTS;
```

You can create a reader account using the Snowsight feature by following these steps:

1. Logon to Snowsight: **https://app.snowflake.com/**
2. Navigate to the menu | **Data products**.
3. Private sharing | **Reader accounts**.
4. Use **+New** to create a reader account. Provider username, password, and account name.

This creates the reader account link to access the data as a consumer. Share the location link with the consumer, reader account logon details to access the data.

To share data shares with Reader accounts, follow the given steps:

1. Logon to Snowsight: **https://app.snowflake.com/**

2. Navigate to the menu | **Data products**.

3. Private sharing | **Shared by Your Account**.

4. Open the share listed in this section and select **Add Consumers** from the top right corner.

5. Search for the reader account locator to find the reader account.

6. Select +**Add** to add a consumer.

7. Go to | **Reader accounts** and open reader accounts, locate the share shared with the reader account.

8. Refer to the following figure, which represents the preceding steps shared:

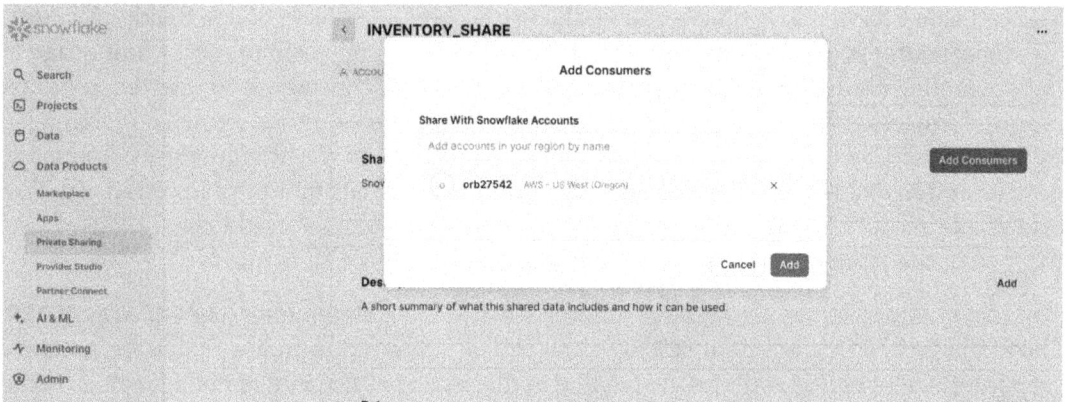

Figure 8.3: Sharing data with reader accounts

Snowsight Web UI is an intuitive interface that can be used to perform admin tasks. Follow the steps shared to create a reader account and share the data with them. From a consumer perspective, follow these steps to access the data shared:

1. Logon to Snowsight at **https://app.snowflake.com/**

2. Use the account locator or location link to connect to the consumer account.

3. Logon with the reader account user ID and password.

4. Go to the navigation menu | **Data Products** | **Private sharing** | **Shared with You**.

Reader accounts can query the data shared. Readers can **SELECT** query to access the consumer data. You can also use data sharing options, such as listings, data exchange, and direct data share, to share the data with consumers. Also, the data cloning feature can be used to clone the data to set up multiple environments without moving or copying the data. You will learn more about implementing data cloning in the following section.

Data cloning

There are several processes to be maintained to maintain the data platform and data availability. Data backup, restore, archival, and copy are some of the examples of standard processes to be followed in any data platform. Data archival and copy are the processes that allow users to create a copy of the data as well as archive the historical data to another database or storage. Data backup is a process where users can create backups of the data to ensure that data is available to restore in case of any disaster recovery. Snowflake offers **Zero Copy Cloning** feature to create snapshots of Snowflake data objects like databases, schemas, and tables. Cloning can be used to create backups and copy data for development or testing. We will learn about the features of clones next.

Features of data clones

Data cloning allows users to create copies of the data required to set up the backup and an environment. Snowflake data clones are also treated as objects with the following distinguishing features:

- Data clones do not copy the data or create additional storage of the objects.

- Snowflake clones create snapshots of the data and point to the same storage, hence sharing the underlying storage.

- These can be used to create backups without adding any extra cost to the account. These are also used to set up the data environments for development and testing.

- Users can create new objects from the cloned data objects.

- Users can also run processes on top of the cloned object to load or modify data into clones.

- Clones can attribute to the additional storage required for any new or modified data in the clones.

We will be exploring data cloning and the process of creating the clones in the following subsections.

Understanding clones

Data cloning is implemented and maintained at the metadata layer. Snowflake creates a unique ID associated with every table in an account. Along with a table ID, Snowflake also maintains **CLONE_GROUP_ID**. The **CLONE_GROUP_ID** is maintained for the table clones. However, this ID is the same as the table ID in case there are no clones created for a table. You can view these IDs in the **TABLE_STORAGE_METRICS** view. You can create clones for databases, schemas, and permanent tables. Refer to *Figure 8.4*, which represents the data cloning and storage maintenance for existing and new data loads to the clones:

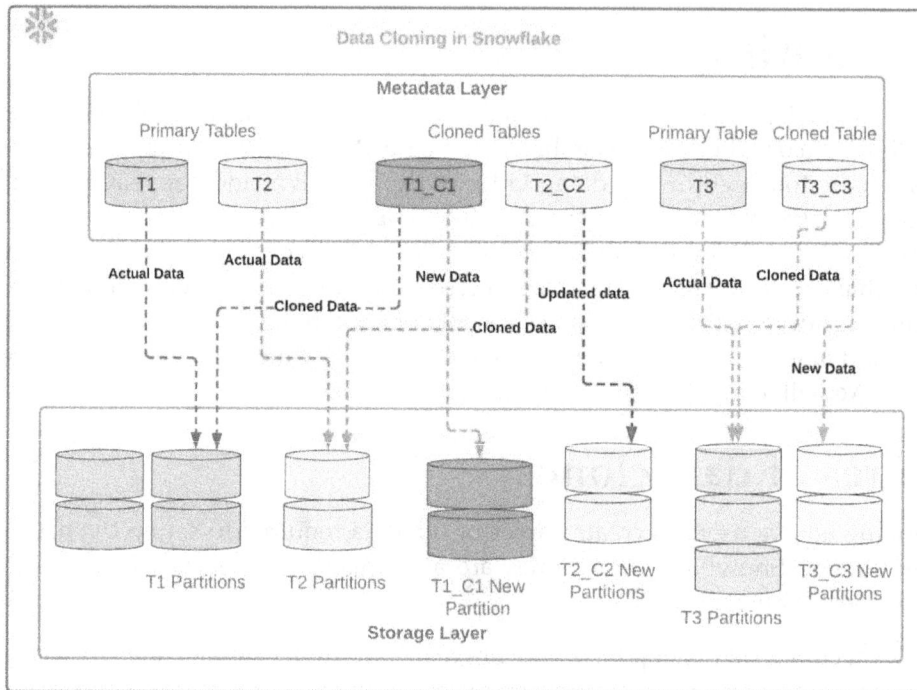

Figure 8.4: Snowflake data cloning

In the given scenario with *Figure 8.4*, there are three primary tables: T1, T2, and T3, and their corresponding clones are represented as T1_C1, T2_C2, and T3_C3. The clones share the underlying storage and create new partitions as soon as new data is inserted into cloned tables. Any changes made to the cloned data create and store the data in new micro-partitions. The storage and clone copies are maintained at the metadata layer.

You can also use tables with time-travel to create snapshots of the data. As you have learned in *Chapter 5, Implementing Data Governance*, time-travel allows users to retrieve the data that is changed or deleted accidentally at any point in time. You can also retrieve the data using time-travel to create a clone of the data using time-travel SQL. **CREATE DDL** statement can be used to create clones. The cloned databases and schemas also clone the grants inherited as part of child objects. Clones do not inherit the privileges granted to the source or the database. You can also clone Snowflake objects like sequences, stages, clustering keys, pipes, streams, tasks, event tables, etc.

Implementing data clones

Data clones can be created and managed by users with specific privileges. You can create clones if you have the following permissions on the Snowflake objects:

- Database **OWNERSHIP** privileges as well as **CREATE DATABASE ROLE** on the target database.

- For Schema objects, privileges depend on the managed or unmanaged schema.

- **SELECT** privileges on the tables.

- **OWNERSHIP** privileges on Alerts, Tasks, Pipes, and Streams.

- **USAGE** privileges on the rest of the Snowflake objects.

These permissions can be granted to a role and assigned to a user who needs to create CLONEs. Usually, it is recommended to have ADMIN working on setting up CLONEs. **GRANT** command can be used to grant all required permissions to a role.

You can use **CLONE DDL** statements to create the clones and set up the backup or environments for the development lifecycle. You can consider the scenario of setting up multiple environments, DEV, QA, UAT, and PROD, for the development lifecycle. You can create the CLONE of PROD objects in a non-prod environment. Refer to the following SQL commands used to set the clones:

```
/* Create a UAT environment with clone from PROD database*/
CREATE DATABASE RETAIL_DB_CLONE CLONE RETAIL_DB;

/* Create DEV clone from PROD database for data based on the AT clause and
taking snapshot */
CREATE TABLE SALES_DB_CLONE CLONE SALES_DB
  AT (TIMESTAMP => TO_TIMESTAMP_TZ('04/09/2024 11:10:34', 'mm/dd/yyyy
hh24:mi:ss'));
```

Once you create the clone, all cloneable database objects are cloned to the database clone. You can use the following query to view the storage and clone details, if any:

```
/* QUERY TABLE_STORAGE_METRICS USAGE VIEW*/
SELECT * FROM SNOWFLAKE.ACCOUNT_USAGE.TABLE_STORAGE_METRICS;
```

You can use CLONEs to setup the backup as well as set up the testing environment for Snowflake testing. Snowflake recommends using data cloning as standard practice to maintain the development environments. As an architect, you can leverage the recommended practice and set a process to refresh the data required for development or **User Acceptance Testing (UAT)** before deploying it to **Production (PROD)**. Like data cloning, Snowflake offers a set of features to enable users to manage their data without any additional overhead of processes and pipelines. You have learned that data sharing allows users to share the data without copying or moving it out of the platform. Similarly, data exchange is another feature that allows users to share data. We will now learn about data exchange.

Data exchange

Data exchange is a data hub that offers secure collaboration of data with selected users or groups. This allows you to publish data as a provider, and consumers can discover it by participating in data exchange.

Refer to *Figure 8.5,* which shares an overview of the data-sharing flow as part of data exchange. This also shows the relationship between data providers and consumers:

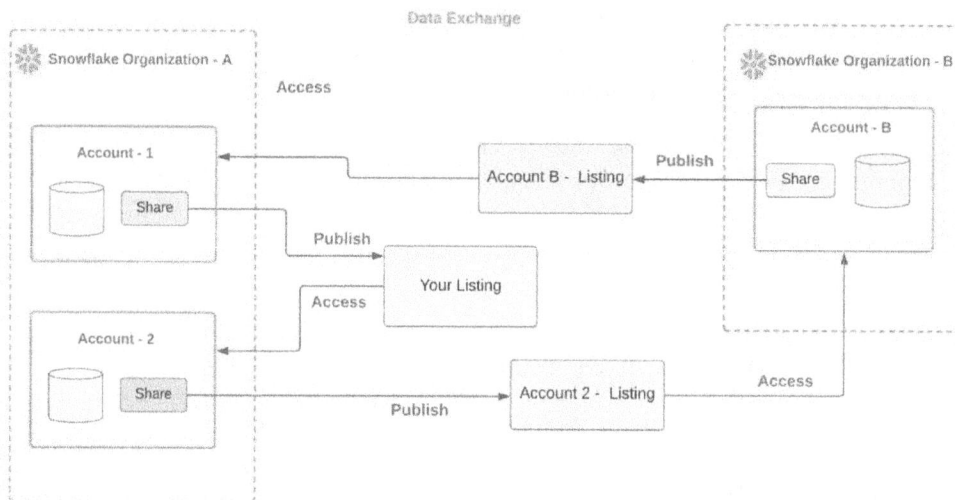

Figure 8.5: Data exchange between Snowflake accounts

A provider can create a share and list it as a list to be consumed by other consumers. The color code in the figure follows the path of provider to consumer. Data providers can publish the shares, and consumers can raise access requests to them. We will explore the role of data providers and consumers next.

Data providers

Data providers are the users who provide data to the users or groups of specific users. You can create data provider profiles if you have **ACCOUNTADMIN** permissions. **ACCOUNTADMINs** can create data listings, review listings, and provider profiles. You can use Snowsight to create a provider profile using the feature as shown:

1. Logon to Snowflake account at **https://app.snowflake.com/**
2. Change the role to **ACCOUNTADMIN**.
3. Navigate to **Data products** | **Provider Studio**.
4. Select **Add Profile** with **+Profile**.
5. Provide the required details to create a profile.

You can also refer to **https://docs.snowflake.com/en/user-guide/data-exchange-becoming-a-provider** for data provider profile management.

Data consumers

Data consumers are the users who consume data. Consumers can subscribe to the data and consume data from the marketplace as well as private sharing (specific to accounts only). All users can see the data listings in the data exchange. However, not all users can access the data from the exchange. Users with `ACCOUNTADMIN` as well as `IMPORT SHARE` privilege can import or request the data.

You can view the listings on the Snowsight using the given steps:

1. Logon to Snowsight from **https://app.snowflake.com/**
2. Change the role to `ACCOUNTADMIN`.
3. Navigate to **Data Products** | **Private sharing**.
4. Open the tab named **Shared with You** to view the listings shared with you.

You can also view the reader accounts from Snowsight by following the steps mentioned previously. Reader accounts are the non-Snowflake users who can consume or access the data as consumers.

You can use data exchange to share the data with internal users and vendors, as well as publish it to be used as public data share on the Snowflake data marketplace. You will learn more about the data marketplace in the following section.

Snowflake data marketplace

Snowflake marketplace connects you to over 540 providers, offering more than 2,400 live, ready-to-use data services, and Snowflake native apps (as of January 31, 2024).

Snowflake shares the data securely in the form of listings, which follow the same provider-consumer model. Listings add the following additional capabilities on top of the secure data sharing:

- Listing as a public share on Snowflake marketplace.
- Charge consumers to access the data shared in listings.
- Monitor the usage and interest in the listings to share the data.
- Provide metadata about the listings as data share.

These listings can be shared in private as well as public mode. **Private listing** is the data shared with restricted users, selected individuals, and groups. Private listing allows users to share the data with other Snowflake users. **Public listings** allow users to share the information publicly with other Snowflake users simultaneously. In the case of private sharing, you need to maintain the individual users and data shares, whereas for public data shares, you can manage the shares for multiple users at the same time.

You can refer to *Figure 8.6*, which shares the view of the Snowflake data marketplace from Snowsight, the Web UI, and its offerings:

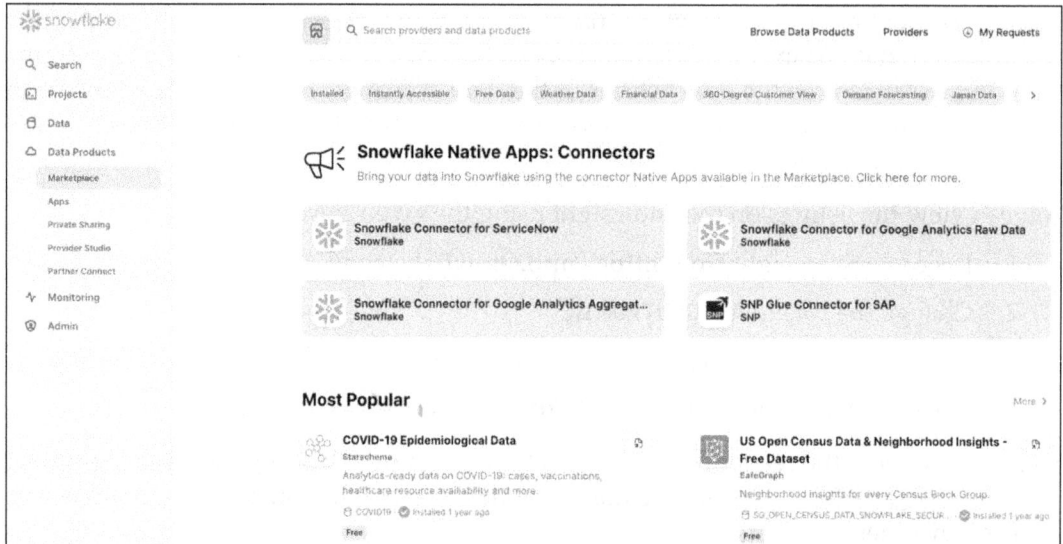

Figure 8.6: Snowflake data marketplace

As you can see in the preceding figure, Snowflake marketplace shares more than just data. This is the landing page of the marketplace where you can see the native app connectors and get them added or downloaded as ready-to-use connectors. You can also get your native apps listed here in the marketplace as a provider. The following subsection lists various features of the marketplace.

Data marketplace features

Marketplace not only offers data but also native apps. You can search for the data products by providers, free data, and domains. The following are some of the distinguishing features of data marketplace:

- **Beyond the data:** Marketplace not only offers a variety of data but also offers data services, native apps from the providers. Consumers can search and request the data, services, or apps required as per their business needs.

- **Integrating third-party data providers:** Marketplace is the platform or a place where multiple providers share data or apps. This reduces the overall cost and maintenance process required to process data, share, and maintain freshness, data redundancy, and data quality. With this feature, a provider does not need to maintain any additional process for the shares. Snowflake features and security features can be leveraged to share data securely. A provider can also share the data apps or native apps, same as secure data share.

- **Search and buy data and apps faster:** Self-serve portal and direct access to the data and apps made available on the Snowflake marketplace.

As you can see in *Figure 8.7*, the data products are listed as part of marketplace offerings:

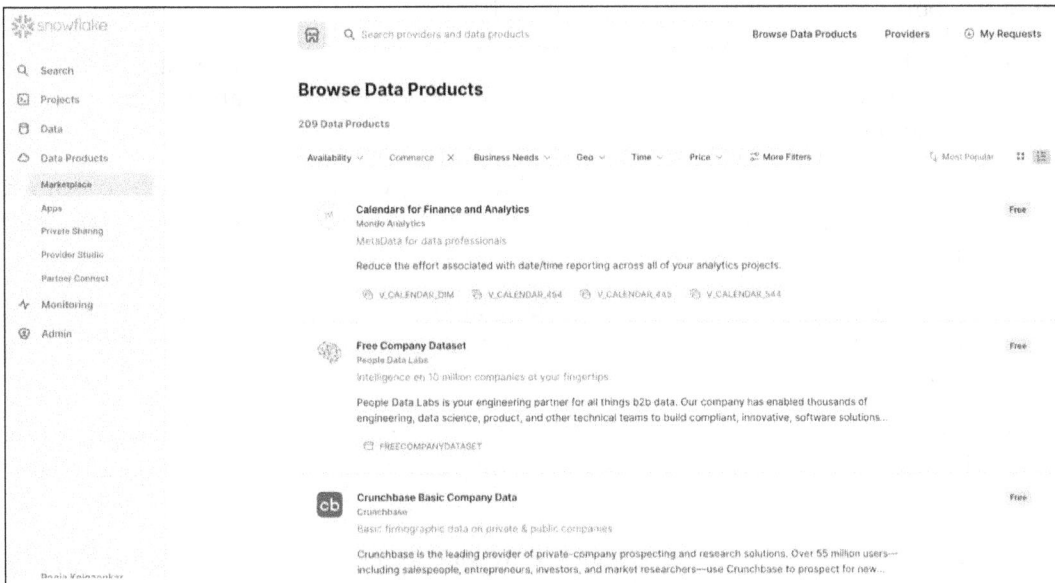

Figure 8.7: Snowflake data marketplace data providers

These products can be filtered and searched based on the domain, price, time, location, or business needs. You can also search for the provider's name if looking for a specific provider or data shared by a provider. A request can be made to these data products as a consumer and share your details to get the data available in your account.

Conclusion

In this chapter, you have taken a deep dive into data sharing and cloning of Snowflake features. You have learned to use data sharing and cloning features to implement data collaborations as part of platform design and architecture. You have learned about all the data platform design architecture pillars till this chapter. Now, you are ready to start working on the data designs, engineering design patterns, and building data platform designs like data warehouse, data lakehouse, etc. There are various patterns of data platform designs. Every platform design must follow the architecture pillars defined as part of **Non-Functional Requirements (NFRs)**. The platform's design depends on the data requirements as their functional requirements. However, there are a few standard patterns and best practices to be followed while designing the data platforms.

You will learn about the standard frameworks, architecture patterns, and recommendations in the next chapter. The following chapter sets the foundation to the data designs and solutions.

Points to remember

Here are some of the key takeaways from this chapter:

- In a typical data platform, data consumption is critical in enabling consumers to consume it. Data analytics, BI, and AI/ML capabilities are the most critical consumer integrations for the data platform.

- Snowflake's data sharing feature enables users to share the data with consumers without needing to manage any additional data pipelines to maintain data freshness or data consistency.

- Data sharing also offers data to be shared in listings, direct share, and data marketplace. Some of the providers can also earn by sharing the data in the marketplace.

- You can share the data between one or more Snowflake accounts as part of the Data Exchange feature. You can share the data within an organization as well as with a different organization.

- Data can also be shared with non-Snowflake users as reader accounts. However, reader accounts need additional maintenance of the resources, compute, and overall spend ($) utilization.

- In any real-time scenario, data needs to be copied into multiple development and testing environments for development and testing phases. This needs an additional process to copy the data from PROD to lower environments for development, testing, or to run UAT. Snowflake offers a data cloning feature that allows users to clone the data to create backups or data snapshots. These are effective as no additional pipeline or process is required to copy the data. This is also an easy maintenance and low-cost solution, as data copy does not utilize additional storage until modified.

CHAPTER 9
Designing Data Solutions

Introduction

Design is the critical aspect of data platform architecture as well as engineering implementation. Design plays a crucial role in implementing optimized workloads and well-defined, optimized performance and cost-efficient data platforms. You have learned the data architecture pillars and their need to build a data platform. From this chapter onwards, you are going to learn to apply these pillars and principles to design the data platforms.

This chapter sets the foundation of data solution designing based on the data architecture pillars. This covers the most important integrations in any data application, like logging, monitoring, error handling, altering, auditing, etc. You will learn these standard practices that are followed in data application design.

This chapter focuses on guiding and sharing the best practices to implement the features essential as part of operational, maintainability, and performance efficiency. These are standard frameworks you can use to design and implement any data platform.

Structure

This chapter consists of the following topics:

- Understanding standard practices
- Using event tables
- Altering and notification integrations
- Implementing alerting with AWS SNS
- Implementing data metric functions

Objectives

By the end of this chapter, you will be able to implement standard data frameworks using Snowflake native features and services. You will also learn to integrate various options to design error handling, notification, and data quality checks with this chapter. You can use the trial account setup to perform various exercises throughout this book.

Understanding standard practices

There are defined standards and best practices implemented in any typical application, data, or engineering process. You can refer to the **non-functional requirements (NFRs)** to implement the best practices shared in this section. Most of the time, the NFRs are treated at a lower priority than business requirements to implement applications. However, these requirements are critical and essential to implement an optimized, efficient data platform. The following are some of the standard practices that are followed to implement enterprise data platform:

- Error handling
- Alert and notifications
- Audit batch control

These are implemented as part of reusable components with automated frameworks. You can use Snowflake native features to implement these automated, modular units to integrate with data engineering pipelines.

Error handling

Error handling is the module where you can handle errors and implement error handling with engineering pipelines. You can use error codes and make decisions, process jobs, or invoke specific functions and procedures based on the errors and error codes.

You can use the following approaches to implement the module based on Snowflake features and pipeline design:

- **Exception handling:** You can use exception handlers to capture and raise exceptions while processing the data with scripting.

- **Event table:** You can use the event table to capture the log messages and events from **stored procedures (SPs)**, **User Defined Functions (UDFs)**, and **User Defined Table Functions (UDTFs)**.

You can use error code capture and scripting integration to develop errors, except handling modules. You can use a programming language as per your preference and application design to build an automated framework. This can be generated as an automated framework as Python modules and integrated with pipelines.

You can refer to the following SQL commands to set up the exceptions:

```
DECLARE
  sp_exception EXCEPTION (-20002, 'Raised SP_EXCEPTION.');
BEGIN
  LET counter := 0;
  LET should_raise_exception := true;
  IF (should_raise_exception) THEN
    RAISE sp_exception;
  END IF;
  counter := counter + 1;
  RETURN counter;
END;
```

You can use **DECLARE** to define the exception and **RAISE** to raise the exception, as shown in the preceding code. You can also refer to the **https://docs.snowflake.com/en/developer-guide/snowflake-scripting/exceptions** documentation page to learn and use exceptions along with Snowflake scripting.

You will learn to use event tables to capture exceptions and raise exceptions in the following section.

Alerts and notifications

This is the next critical aspect of standard practices implementation. You can implement alerting and notifications to notify the users in case of failure or success scenarios of data pipelines. Snowflake features like notification integrations, cross-cloud integrations, and system functions allow users to generate notifications.

Snowflake features allow you to integrate with cloud messaging services. You can use one of the following Snowflake integrations to implement alerting or notification:

- Email notification integration
- Notification Integration with cloud messaging services like **Amazon Simple Notification Service (AWS SNS)**, GCP Pub/Sub, and Azure Event grid.

Notification integration can be setup to be used with Snowflake tasks to send error notifications. Snowflake objects like notification integrations and tasks can be set up to automate alerting and notifications. These integrations with engineering pipelines and tasks can be used to implement error-handling frameworks. These integrations can also be implemented to standardize and automate the monitoring as part of operational tasks.

Resource monitors are great for warehouse monitoring and generating alerts. These monitors can be set to notify as well as act. You have already learned about resource monitors as part of warehouse optimization as part of cost optimization in *Chapter 7, Unlocking Snowflake's Cost and Performance.*

Audit batch control

Audit batch control is also referred to as the ABC of the data engineering pipeline implementation. This is a custom framework developed and used in most of the data engineering implementations. As the name suggests, this is used to maintain the pipeline metadata and execution metadata information to be used as audit information. This is explained as one of the common frameworks here. We can implement it by leveraging the Snowflake features, SQL, and support to the extended SQL functions.

Typically, the ABC framework is used to implement pipeline monitoring and reusability. You can use the following tables as a control table and to store execution metadata information:

- **Audit control table:** The control table to store the metadata information and static information of pipeline. Static information caters to the information of pipeline, like name, userid, type of job, etc.

- **Audit log table:** Log table to store the pipeline execution logs. This is not only used to maintain the pipeline execution, but also used to restart pipelines or implement restart ability.

Refer to the sample table DDL and audit columns used to maintain the control information. You can start implementing the auditing using the following sample code to set up the audit table:

```
/* Audit Batch Control table*/
CREATE DATABASE AUDIT_DB;
CREATE SCHEMA AUDIT;

/* SET CONTEXT*/
USE DATABASE AUDIT_DB;
USE SCHEMA AUDIT;

/* CREATE CONTROL TABLE */
CREATE TABLE AUDIT_BTCH_CTL
(
```

```
SRC_SYS_CD STRING,
SRC_SYS_NM STRING,
JOB_ID INT,
JOB_NAME STRING,
JOB_TYPE STRING,
STATUS STRING
);
```

You can also refer to the following data model to implement audit control and batch log:

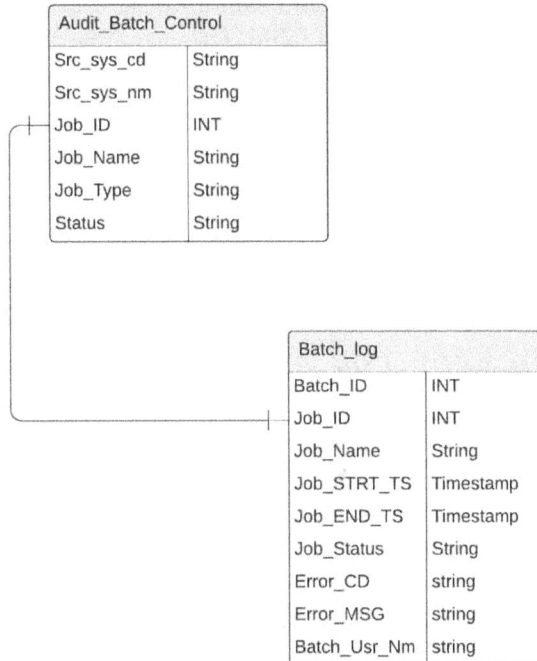

Audit_Batch_Control	
Src_sys_cd	String
Src_sys_nm	String
Job_ID	INT
Job_Name	String
Job_Type	String
Status	String

Batch_log	
Batch_ID	INT
Job_ID	INT
Job_Name	String
Job_STRT_TS	Timestamp
Job_END_TS	Timestamp
Job_Status	String
Error_CD	string
Error_MSG	string
Batch_Usr_Nm	string

Figure 9.1: Batch control table

Once a control table is created, you can use a control table and create a batch log table to log the execution details, as shown:

```
/* set the context */
USE DATABASE AUDIT_DB;
USE SCHEMA AUDIT;

/* CREATE BATCH LOG TABLE */
CREATE BATCH_LOG_TBL
(
        BATCH_ID INT,
        JOB_ID INT,
```

```
    JOB_NAME STRING,
    JOB_STRT_TS TIMESTAMP,
    JOB_END_TS TIMESTAMP,
    JOB_STATUS STRING,
    ERROR_CD STRING,
    ERROR_MSG STRING,
    BATCH_USR_ID STRING
);
```

This is one of the sample logging tables you can define as per your requirements. This is defined as a physical table and used as a table. These are the control and log tables used to maintain control entries and log details. You can use a modular approach to create a function or stored procedure to automate the log entry as well as modification.

Here, **BATCH_ID** is the unique identifier used to identify a particular load, hence batch processing the incoming data files. This specifies the occurrence of pipeline execution as per the schedule. You can use a table to create execution monitoring, alerting to monitor or log the data for the given day or batch loads. You will learn to implement the frameworks defined in this section with a real time use case in the upcoming section.

Note: **This is added as a part of the generic frameworks used to implement non functional requirements (NFRs). This is not a service or feature offered by Snowflake, but this can be implemented as a custom framework using Snowflake features and objects.**

Using event tables

Snowflake enables users to capture the activities of the functions and stored procedure handler code with the help of log messages and event traces. Snowflake captures log messages and event traces as and when code is being executed. This is stored as part of the log data and can be queried to analyze. Snowflake offers event tables to capture the logs and events. You can create an event table and start capturing the log messages as well as events.

You can follow the given steps to set and use the event tables to analyze the failures:

1. Create an event table.
2. Initiate log messages and events with the help of handlers. Snowflake captures the logs and events data in the event table.
3. Query event table data to analyze the failures.

Snowflake allows users to use SQL commands to implement the preceding steps. In the following section, we will be exploring the SQL commands and code blocks that can be used to initiate logging and tracing.

Creating event table

You need to create an event table and associate it with an account to start capturing the logs and events for that account. The event table is created with predefined columns and follows system standards to capture the details. The event table is also treated as an object of Snowflake. However, this table has distinguishing properties as follows:

- This table structure is predefined with a set of columns to capture the log messages and event details.

- Event table can be associated with an account to capture all the log details for an account in this table.

- There can be only one event table associated with one account. Hence, there can be only one active event table that gets associated with an account.

- You can control the severity level and verbosity of events captured in an event table.

- All the log messages, event details, and handler code exceptions are captured in the event table. You can customize and set the exceptions and handler code for SPs and functions (UDFs and UDFTs). Any exceptions raised by these objects are automatically stored in the event table.

You can create a table using **CREATE DDL**. You can set up a separate database to capture log details, create a **log_db** as a database, and set the event table in it. Refer to the following code snippet to set up the table:

```
/* create event table*/
Create database log_db;
Use database log_db;
Create schema logs;
Use schema logs;
CREATE EVENT TABLE log_events;
```

You can create a table with the **CREATE** statement, and you do not need to specify the DDL, as it is created with a predefined format. There are three steps to set up an event table for an account:

1. Once you have an event table created, you need to assign it to the account to capture all log events. Refer to the following SQL command:

```
/* associate event table with an account */
ALTER ACCOUNT SET EVENT_TABLE = log_db.logs.log_events;
```

2. Once the event table is associated with an account, you can set the error level, severity, and log level to capture the logs and events in the log table. You can use SQL commands to set the log level or error level for SPs, UDFs, and UDFTs. You

can set the log level at object, schema, or database level to capture the events for objects. Refer to the following sample SQL command to set the log level:

```
/* set the log level for database and UDF (user defined functions) */
USE ROLE ACCOUNTADMIN;
ALTER DATABASE RETAIL_DB_POC SET LOG_LEVEL = ERROR;
ALTER FUNCTION demo_function(int) SET LOG_LEVEL = WARN;
```

3. You can also set the role to manage the events and log data metrics. This role can be granted to the engineering role to allow them to specify the log events or level at the object level or session level. Typically, these can also set the log level for a given session to capture the events. These log levels can be set at the session level to **DEBUG**, **WARNING**, and **INFO**, shown as follows:

```
/* create role and grant permissions*/
CREATE ROLE LOG_ADMIN;
GRANT MODIFY LOG LEVEL ON ACCOUNT TO ROLE LOG_ADMIN;
/*grant log_admin to the engineering role*/
GRANT ROLE LOG_ADMIN to ROLE DATA_ENG;
/* use DATA ENG role to develop the code and test*/
USE ROLE DATA_ENG;
ALTER SESSION SET LOG_LEVEL = DEBUG;
```

Now, you have an event table set and associated with an account. You also have a role set and granted to engineers to capture the log events or ignore them in case of **DEBUG** mode. Now, you can use the programming handlers to emit the exceptions.

Raising exceptions

As you know, you can use the programming languages supported by Snowflake to create SPs, UDFs, and UDFTs. You can use the equivalent code standards to define the log levels in each of the objects while defining and setting the exceptions and error codes. You can use Java, JavaScript, Python, Scala, and Snowflake scripting to define the objects as well as log handling. You can refer to the following sample code as a reference for Snowflake scripting:

```
/* Sample to set the log level to error, warning, debug, trace, and fatal
error */
SYSTEM$LOG_ERROR('Error message');
SYSTEM$LOG_WARN('Warning message');
SYSTEM$LOG_DEBUG('Debug message');
SYSTEM$LOG_TRACE('Trace message');
SYSTEM$LOG_FATAL('Fatal message');

/* use below function to pass the corresponding message and log level */
```

```
SYSTEM$LOG('error', 'Error message');
SYSTEM$LOG('warning', 'Warning message');
```

You can use the corresponding language syntax to set the same using other languages supported in Snowflake. Like log levels, events tracing can also be set. Refer to the following Snowflake scripting example that shows event additions:

```
/* Adding two events */
SYSTEM$ADD_EVENT('SProcEmptyEvent');

/* adds event with an attribute specified in key-value pair*/
SYSTEM$ADD_EVENT('SProcEventWithAttributes', {'key1': 'value1', 'key2':
'value2'});
```

You can refer to the following sample stored procedure definition using Snowflake scripting:

```
CREATE OR REPLACE PROCEDURE demo_pi_proc()
  RETURNS DOUBLE
  LANGUAGE SQL
  AS $$
  BEGIN
    -- Add an event without attributes
    SYSTEM$ADD_EVENT('pi_testing');

    -- Add an event with attributes
    LET attr := {'score': 89, 'pass': TRUE};
    SYSTEM$ADD_EVENT('pi_testing', attr);

    -- Set attributes for the span
    SYSTEM$SET_SPAN_ATTRIBUTES({'key1': 'value1', 'key2': TRUE});

    RETURN 3.14;
  END;
  $$;
```

You can use the **CALL** statement to call the stored procedure and test. Now, you also have a set of objects defined that are written on the events table in case of log events or trace events. Next, you will learn to use an event table and query it to analyze the log data.

Using events table

Event tables can be queried using a **SELECT** statement. You can query to get the log messages as well as event details. The attributes can be specified for the events in the form of key value pairs. These attributes provide additional information on the logs and events that might be essential for debugging. Refer to the following sample command to get the log messages:

```
/* set the event table name */
SET event_table_name='log_db.logs.log_events';

/* use SELECT to query the log data*/
SELECT
  TIMESTAMP as time,
  RESOURCE_ATTRIBUTES['snow.executable.name'] as log_executable,
  RECORD['severity_text'] as log_severity,
  VALUE as log_message
FROM
  IDENTIFIER($event_table_name)
WHERE
RESOURCE_ATTRIBUTES['snow.executable.name'] LIKE '%demo_pi_proc%'
AND RECORD_TYPE = 'LOG';
```

Here, the **record_type** is log. You can also use the scope name to represent Snowflake scripting. You can also use the **python_logger** or **scala** exception handler based on the programming language used. You can also use the table to query the events data. You can also refer to the Snowflake documentation to learn more about specific programming support and using them to generate log messages and events: **https://docs.snowflake.com/en/developer-guide/logging-tracing/logging-tracing-overview**.

Once you start capturing the log messages and event data, you also need to start reporting and generating alerts and notifications. You will learn more about implementing notification integrations and using them to generate alerts.

Altering and notification integrations

Snowflake is rich in integration features. You can use Snowflake cloud integrations as well as cross-cloud integrations to implement extended functionalities. You can use notification integration to set up the notifications. You can use it to leverage the Snowflake native MAIL integration with the **SENDMAIL** system function, as well as use the same to integrate with cross-cloud to send messages and notifications using cloud-native messaging services.

Notification integration

Snowflake offers integration as an object that offers an interface between Snowflake and third-party messaging services. You can also use email integrations as part of notification integration to send email notifications. You can create integration using **CREATE** statement.

EMAIL notification

You can use users with registered and verified email IDs. You can use the following SQL command to create notification email integration:

```
create notification integration app_email_int
    type=email
    enabled=true
    allowed_recipients=(firstname.lastname@xyz.com')
;
```

You can use the notification created in the preceding example to send email notifications using the Snowflake function **SYSYEM$SEND_EMAIL()**. Refer to the following SQL command to send email alerts:

```
CALL SYSTEM$SEND_EMAIL(
    'app_email_int',
    'first_name.last_name@example.com, firstname.lastname@example.com',
    'Email Alert: Pipeline completed Successfully.',
    'Data load job has successfully finished.\nStart Time: 08:00:00\nEnd
Time: 11:35:15\nTotal Records Processed: 214567'
);
```

You need to have users verified before you add their email IDs here as part of mail integration and mail recipients. You can follow the given steps to verify the email address:

1. Sign in to Snowsight: **https://app.snowflake.com/**.

2. Select your username, and then select **Profile**.

3. Configure your email address.

4. Check the email address and confirm. If you do not have an email address, then enter the email address in the **Email** field and save.

5. If you are not able to enter the email address, then contact the **ACCOUNTADMIN** to help you get the email address added.

6. You get an email to verify. If you do not receive an email, then click on **Resend verification email**.

7. Open your email, and then select the link in the email to validate your email address.

Email verification is required to add users to email integration and get notifications for resource monitors. Like email notification integration, you can also integrate with cross cloud messaging services.

Notification integration with cloud messaging services

Snowflake allows users to integrate with cross cloud messaging services and create notification integration to send notifications. Snowflake integrates with cloud messaging services:

Cloud provider	Cloud messaging services
AWS	Notification integration with AWS SNS
GCP	Notification integration with GCP Pub/sub
Microsoft Azure	Notification integration with Azure Event grid

Table 9.1: Snowflake messaging integrations

You can also use the cloud storage services in integration with messaging services to automate the data loads for real time as well as batch loads. You can refer to the following references to integrate and implement integrations with cloud services:

- GCP Pub/Sub integration: **https://docs.snowflake.com/en/user-guide/tasks-errors-gpc**

- Azure Event grid integration: **https://docs.snowflake.com/en/user-guide/tasks-errors-azure**

You can also set it to generate alerts based on any events by using Snowflake TASKS. TASKS can be used to configure the error alert and set up a schedule to send alerts in case of errors. TASKS can also send notifications by using **ERROR_NOTIFICATION** parameter of the **TASK**. Refer to the following **CREATE TASK** statement to set the notification integration:

```
/* create task to send notification and log alerts using SP */
CREATE TASK log_monitor
  SCHEDULE = '15 MINUTE'
  ERROR_INTEGRATION = log_notification_int
  AS
 call snowflake_alerts_sp();

/* alter the task to set the notification if already exists*/
ALTER TASK log_monitor
SET ERROR_INTEGRATION = log_notification_int;
```

Here, you can use the cross-cloud integrations with cloud messaging services as **ERROR_INTEGRATION**. **log_notification_int** is the integration object and setup to integrate cloud notification services.

You can integrate and use the cloud messaging service based on your application and data platform design. You can refer to the subsequent section to learn more about implementing alerting using AWS SNS.

Implementing alerting with AWS SNS

As you know, you can integrate with AWS SNS and use SNS topics to generate Snowflake alerts. You can then subscribe to the SNS topics and get notifications on the choice of your platform, like Slack, Teams, email, etc. You can also use Snowflake SNS to integrate with Snowflake Snowpipe to automate the data loads as and when load files are available on S3.

For this section, you will learn to use AWS SNS and create a notification integration to send alerts to SNS topic.

Implementation steps

To create an integration between Snowflake and AWS SNS, you need to have an active AWS account to implement this use case. If you do not have an AWS account setup, then you can get one setup as a trial account: **https://signin.aws.amazon.com/**. Follow the steps outlined as follows:

1. **Create SNS topic:** You can go to your AWS account, select SNS, and create a topic. Once you create a topic, record the **Amazon Resource Name (ARN)** of that topic. It is recommended to set up the SNS topic in the same region as the Snowflake region to avoid egress charges and to send notifications. Follow the given steps:

   a. Go to AWS Account | SNS.

   b. Select create topic and give a topic name.

   c. Record the ARN once the topic is created.

   Record the SNS ARN created in this step on a notepad. You will need to record a few other ARN and details before you create the Snowflake integration. Note these details and keep them handy.

2. **Create IAM policy:** This step will add or modify the policy to allow taking actions on the topic created in *Step 1*. Follow the given steps:

   a. Go to **IAM** | **Account Settings**.

   b. Go to Security Token Services Region | found account | view the status, and activate if it is inactive.

   c. Choose **Policies** from the left-side navigation pane.

   d. Choose **Create Policy** and go to the JSON tab.

   e. Add the following code snippet and change the SNS topic ARN with the ARN captured in *Step 1*.

   f. Click on **Review Policy** and create policy, as shown:

```
{
    "Version": "2012-10-17",
    "Statement": [
      {
        "Effect": "Allow",
        "Action": [
```

```
            "sns:Publish"
        ],
        "Resource": "<sns_topic_arn>"
    }
  ]
}
```

Record the policy name, as you must attach it to a role to be created in the following step.

3. **Create IAM role:** You can create an IAM role and capture the role ARN for Snowflake integration. Follow the given steps to create a role and capture ARN:

    a. Go to **IAM | Roles**.

    b. Click on **Create Role**.

    c. Select another AWS account as trustee type.

    d. Add your own AWS account ID in the ACCOUNT ID for now.

    e. Select **Require external ID** and enter dummy **0000** for now.

    f. Click on **Next** and select the policy created in *Step 2*.

    g. Click on **Create role**.

    h. Record the role ARN once the role is created from the role page

       Once you create the role, record the ARN as a separate role ARN for your record, along with the SNS topic ARN captured in the first step.

4. **Create notification integration:** Go to Snowflake console and create an integration with the details captured in the initial steps. Follow the given steps to create an integration: Copy the following SQL command:

```
/* create integration*/
CREATE NOTIFICATION INTEGRATION log_notification_int
  ENABLED = true
  TYPE = QUEUE
  NOTIFICATION_PROVIDER = AWS_SNS
  DIRECTION = OUTBOUND
  AWS_SNS_TOPIC_ARN = 'arn:aws:sns:us-east-2:111122223333:sns_topic'
  AWS_SNS_ROLE_ARN = 'arn:aws:iam::111122223333:role/error_sns_role';
```

    a. Replace the **AWS_SNS_TOPIC_ARN** and **AWS_SNS_ROLE_ARN** in the aforementioned command with the ARN captured in the preceding steps.

    b. Run updated SQL command to create the integration.

Once you create the integration, you need to grant access to the AWS SNS topic created.

5. **Grant Snowflake access to the SNS topic:** You need to allow the user to send notifications to the AWS SNS topic. You can retrieve the AWS User ARN and External ID from Snowflake. Follow the given steps:

    a. Run **DESC** SQL command as follows:

```
DESC NOTIFICATION INTEGRATION log_notification_int;
```

    b. Capture the **SF_AWS_IAM_USER_ARN** and **SF_AWS_EXTERNAL_ID** required to be updated on AWS to allow integration to send traffic to the SNS topic.

    c. Capture the details on the same notepad where you captured the initial AWS details and ARN.

6. **Update the AWS Trust relationship:** You need to go to the AWS and IAM role to update the trust policy. Follow the given steps to update the policy:

    a. Go to AWS Account | **IAM**

    b. Go to **Roles** | select the role created in *Step 3*.

    c. Click on **Trust Relationship** | click **Edit trust relationship**.

    d. Modify the policy document to reflect the External ID, AWS USER ID captured in *Step 5*.

    e. Use the given code snippet to update the policy.

    f. Click on update trust policy to update the policy.

```json
{
  "Version": "2012-10-17",
  "Statement": [
    {
      "Sid": "",
      "Effect": "Allow",
      "Principal": {
        "AWS": "<sf_aws_iam_user_arn>"
      },
      "Action": "sts:AssumeRole",
      "Condition": {
        "StringEquals": {
          "sts:ExternalId": "<sf_aws_external_id>"
        }
      }
    }
  ]
}
```

Here, as you can notice, you need to update the **sf_aws_iam_user_arn** and **sf_aws_external_id** with the details captured in *Step 5*.

7. **Using notification integration:** You have completed the setup of the notification integration, allowing the user to send notifications to the AWS SNS topic. Now, you can use this integration to test and use it along with TASKS to send alerts and notifications. Refer to the previous section to set up the TASK.

You can follow the preceding steps or use the Snowflake documentation reference page for AWS SNS Integration: **https://docs.snowflake.com/en/user-guide/tasks-errors-aws**.

You can integrate with other cloud messaging services as well. Refer to the following reference links to integrate with GCP and Azure messaging services:

- GCP Pub/Sub integration: **https://docs.snowflake.com/en/user-guide/tasks-errors-gpc**

- Azure Event grid integration: **https://docs.snowflake.com/en/user-guide/tasks-errors-azure**

Implementing data metric functions

Snowflake brings in distinct features to implement data platform design patterns. Snowflake's native **data metric functions (DMF)** are used to implement data quality checks. We will learn more about using Snowflake native functions as well as defining custom user functions. DMFs can be used for the following table and object types:

- Dynamic tables

- External tables

- Event tables

- Standard tables, including temporary and transient tables

- Iceberg tables

- Views, including materialized views

These metric functions are used to validate the state and integrity of the data. Some of the typical data quality checks cater to data consistency, validity, and freshness.

Using Snowflake native functions

Snowflake offers bunch of system functions to be used natively to monitor and report data issues. Snowflake system functions can be categorized into accuracy, freshness, uniqueness, statistics, and volume. These functions can be run on top of a column. Refer to *Table 9.2*, which shares details of system DMFs:

Category	Function	Details
Accuracy	BLANK_COUNT	Used to get blank values of a column
	BLANK_PERCENT	Used to return the percentage of blank values for a specified column from the table
	NULL_COUNT	Used to get the number of NULL counts for a given column
	NULL_PERCENT	Used to return the percentage of NULL values for a specified column from the table
Statistics	AVG	Used to return the average value of a column
	MAX	Used to return the maximum value of a column
	MIN	Used to return the Minimum value of a column
	STDDEV	Used to get standard deviation of a column
Freshness	FRESHNESS	Used to check the freshness of the data present in the table based on the timestamp column.
Uniqueness	DUPLICATE_COUNT	Used to get the duplicate values present in a column, including NULL
	UNIQUE_COUNT	Used to determine the unique values of a column
Volume	ROW_COUNT	Gives the total row count from the table

Table 9.2: Snowflake system DMF

These system functions are used natively with appropriate **GRANT** permissions. Refer to the following sample examples to use these functions:

- **Validate null records present using NULL_COUNT:** This query checks the number of null records present in a column of a table. **Cust_id** is a unique column used to identify the record for a customer:

```
SELECT SNOWFLAKE.CORE.NULL_COUNT(
  SELECT
    Cust_id
  FROM retail.public.cust_info
);
```

- **Validate uniqueness of a column using UNIQUE_COUNT:** This query checks the uniqueness of column:

```
SELECT SNOWFLAKE.CORE.UNIQUE_COUNT(
  SELECT
    Emp_id
  FROM hr.tables.empl_info
);
```

System functions are useful to validate the quality of the data, but these may not suffice all the needs of data quality checks. Typically, data quality checks are implemented based on the business rules and logic to validate the data present in the system. We will learn to create custom functions and use them to validate the data in the following section.

Implementing custom DMFs

DMFs can be created as custom functions using the **CREATE** statement. There are other DDL commands supported while working on custom functions like **CREATE**, **ALTER**, **DESCRIBE**, **DROP**, and **SHOW**. DMF can be assigned to a table or column using the **ALTER** command for a table or view. Once functions are created, **USAGE** needs to be granted on the functions to the users. Refer to the following use case example:

- Creating a custom function to verify the input column contains valid values based on the input columns:

```
CREATE OR REPLACE DATA METRIC FUNCTION dq_checks.public.count_valid_
values(
   Input_t TABLE(
      inp_c1 NUMBER,
      inp_c2 NUMBER,
      inp_c3 NUMBER
   )
)
RETURNS NUMBER
AS
$$
   SELECT
      COUNT(*)
   FROM sales
   WHERE
      inp_c1>0
      AND inp_c2>0
      AND inp_c3>0
$$;
```

Once the function is created, grant permissions to the users or roles.

- Grant permissions to the role data_engineers:

```
GRANT USAGE ON FUNCTION
   dq_checks.public.count_valid_values(TABLE(NUMBER, NUMBER, NUMBER))
   TO dev_data_eng;
```

Now, the data engineer role in the dev environment is granted usage permissions on the functions. Next is to assign the function to the table or column.

- Set the DMF to a table and set the frequency of execution:

```
ALTER TABLE retail.public.sales SET
  DATA_METRIC_SCHEDULE = '5 MINUTE';

ALTER TABLE retail.public.sales
  ADD DATA METRIC FUNCTION dq_checks.public.count_valid_values
  ON (c1, c2, c3);
```

These functions can also be set to run on a schedule, like cron job or trigger on changes. These are viewed using **SHOW PARAMETERS** on a table. DMFs are set on tables to implement custom functionality to run data quality checks. These functions return scalar values and are monitored using **USAGE** view data quality monitoring.

Conclusion

In this chapter, you explored and learned about the standard frameworks and architecture patterns implemented across data platforms. You have learned to implement them using Snowflake native features and cross cloud integrations.

Once you have the standard practices implemented, you can also setup the standard processes to implement some of the most common data use cases like data ingestions, data validations, data quality, data reconciliation, change data capture, and data sharing. You will learn about all these standard processes throughout the following chapters of this book. You will learn to implement change data capture, bulk data loads, and real-time loads with Snowpipe in the next chapter.

Points to remember

The following are some of the key takeaways from this chapter:

- Data platform architecture pillars are critical to design and implement the data platforms. Some architecture pillars cater to deriving value from the data and driving the business. However, some pillars are essential to implement the NFRs for any platform and application design.

- This chapter shared some of the standard frameworks and automated modules that can be implemented to integrate with any data engineering and data platform features to capture the operational details.

- Operational excellence as well as maintainability are the pillars of the platform design that cater to the ease of the platform maintenance as well as operational capabilities that allow users to automate the processes and generate timely reports, alerts, and notifications to share with operations.

- These frameworks can also be used to integrate and implement other pillars like performance efficiency and cost efficiency. You can set the thresholds, resource monitors, query performance monitors, and use the alert to generate alerts to share the performance and cost metrics with you.

- You can design and implement alerts and notifications with Snowflake native notification integration and using SYSYEM EMAIL function to send alerts to verified users.

- You can also use notification integration to integrate with cloud messaging services to send notifications and alerts. Cloud messaging service can be used to subscribe with any other tools, third-party tools, or integrate with ticketing tools to raise a ticket.

- You can integrate with AWS SNS and send alerts to SNS TOPIC. You can use this and subscribe to SNS topics to send notifications to tools like Teams, Slack, or any third-party tool.

- You can use **audit batch control** (**ABC**) to set up the auditing process for your data pipelines. This can be used to set up the daily monitoring process, reports, and alerts. ABC adds to the maintainability pillar and improves the platform capability to not only maintain but also restart, with features to restart any failed pipelines automatically without worrying about any data issues.

- Error handling is the key to implementing engineering pipelines and data applications. You can use Snowflake native features to generate errors, log messages, and trace events. You can use event tables to capture the log messages and trace data for the events. This can be set up to capture an entire account. Event table can be created and set to be used as an active event table for an account.

- You can use event tables to capture the exceptions, errors, and log data for Snowflake objects like SPs, UDFs, and UDFTs. You can use Snowflake programming languages supported, like Java, JavaScript, Scala, Python, and Snowflake scripting, to generate errors, set log levels, and generate event trace data.

- The event table captures the data automatically, and you can query the data by using a SELECT statement. You can use predefined metadata and columns of the event table to filter out the data for various logs and events based on the logger. The logger is the program through which the event data is captured.

- You can use the Snowflake TASKS to set the automated notifications. You can integrate the event tables, alerting, and Tasks to automate the monitoring. You can also create an SP to send alerts if there are any errors captured or based on the log level captured in the event table.

CHAPTER 10
Designing Data Engineering Pipelines

Introduction

Data engineering (**DE**) is part of the data platform design that takes care of data integrations, data transformations, data quality, data aggregations, and data readiness for consumption. This chapter focuses on designing and implementing engineering pipelines with Snowflake. This chapter helps to understand various data pipelines as per the data loads and frequency. This will also help you understand the streaming and batch use cases to design the data pipelines to ingest data to the Snowflake tables.

This chapter sets the foundation of DE and designing data pipelines. This covers the most important aspects of engineering, batch data loads, real-time loads, change data capture, data transformations, using programming connectors and drivers, etc. You will learn to implement DE pipelines using Snowflake native features.

This chapter focuses on guiding and sharing the best practices to implement the engineering pipelines, considering the architecture principles, performance, cost efficiency, maintainability, reusability, etc.

Structure

This chapter consists of the following topics

- COPY for batch loads
- Understanding Snowpipe

- Using Snowpipe
- Automating loads with Snowpipe
- Snowflake recommendations
- Snowflake streams
- SQL transformations with UDF and UDFT
- Creating and using stored procedure

Objectives

By the end of this chapter, you will be able to understand the various engineering choices and designs with Snowflake services and features. This chapter will help you to distinguish between design choices and help you to design DE pipelines that take care of real time as well as batch data processing. You can use the trial account setup to perform various exercises shared in the chapter.

COPY for batch loads

Learn to load batch data loads using Snowflake native utilities and features of **COPY** Snowflake offers **COPY INTO** to load data from named stages, internal and external stages. You can also load data from external locations. You can use **COPY** to load data in the form of batch loads. Snowflake **COPY INTO** offers various features to manage errors and transform data on the fly. Snowflake **COPY INTO** parameters can be specified into the following categories to support the bulk load to Snowflake tables:

Feature category	Features	Parameters
File Features	File Format, Files, File Pattern, File compression, File header properties, File delimiter properties, File features for field properties, NULL and ESCAPE character handling	`FILES, PATTERN, FILE_ FORMAT, COMPRESSION, FILE_ FORMAT, RECORD_DELIMITER, FIELD_DELIMITER, SKIP_ HEADER, ESCAPE, NULL_IF`
Error Handling Features	Error handling, skip loading, skip file, fail load, continue to load	`ON_ERROR` parameters `CONTINUE, SKIP_FILE, ABORT_ STATEMENT, SKIP_FILE_<num>, SKIP_FILE_<num%>`
Metadata or File Handling Features	Forcefully load files in case of duplicate files, remove files from stage post loading, return files failed to load, Boolean parameters	`PURGE, FORCE, RETURN_ FAILED_ONLY`
Data Transformation Features	Select required columns, re-arrange columns, and transform columns using substring	`SELECT COLUMNS FROM` stage

Table 10.1: COPY INTO features

Snowflake maintains the log and metadata of files loaded using **COPY**. The metadata is maintained to avoid loading the same files causing data duplicates. **COPY** looks for the metadata by default and skips the file if it is already loaded. You can use the **COPY** option, **FORCE** to load the file forcefully. Refer to *Figure 10.1*, which shares one of the use cases to load data from cloud storage buckets to the Snowflake landing layer using the **COPY INTO** command:

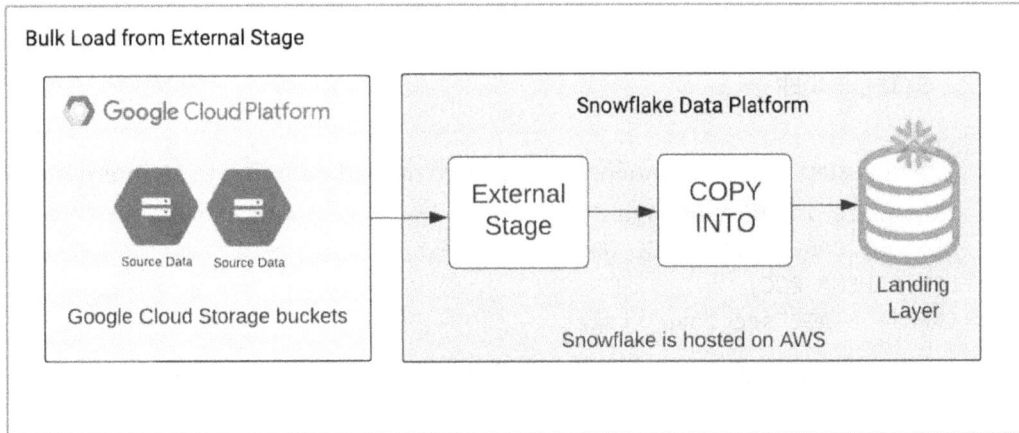

Figure 10.1: Batch load using COPY INTO

As you can observe from the preceding image, the Google Cloud Storage buckets are integrated as an external stage to read the data files. Based on the type of data and format of the file, **COPY** options are used to implement the load use cases. Refer to some of the load use cases and scenarios discussed in the following sub-section.

Load use case 1

Use **COPY** to load delimited files from the internal stage. Batch load with data feed features as specified in *Table 10.2*:

1. File Property Check	2. Indicator
3. Delimited File	4. Yes
5. Field Delimiter	6. Pipe (|) delimited
7. Header Record Present	8. Yes
9. Error Handling	10. Fail load in case of any error
11. Duplicate load check	12. Avoid duplicate loads

Table 10.2: File feed properties

To implement the use case defined above with file properties specified in *Table 10.2*, start following these steps to load data into the Snowflake table using **COPY INTO**:

1. Define the file format as a Snowflake object with file specifications and properties. Follow the code snippet to create a file format:

```
/* create file format */
USE DATABASE RETAIL_POC_DB;
USE SCHEMA POC;
CREATE OR REPLACE FILE FORMAT src_file_format
  TYPE = CSV
  FIELD_DELIMITER = '|'
  SKIP_HEADER = 1
  ;
```

2. The next step is to create an internal stage to upload data files to an internal stage:

```
/* create internal stage */
USE DATABASE RETAIL_POC_DB;
USE SCHEMA POC;
CREATE STAGE src_load_stage;
```

3. Now, upload data files to the internal stage. The **PUT** command can be used to upload files from the local to the internal stage:

```
/* upload files to internal stage*/
PUT file:///download/data/retail_load.csv @src_load_stage;
```

Here, you can specify the file path as per your local system file path.

4. Once data feeds are uploaded to an internal stage, use the **COPY INTO** command to load the files to the Snowflake table:

```
COPY INTO retail_load
FROM @src_load_stage
FILE_FORMAT = (FORMAT_NAME = src_file_format)
  ;
```

In the preceding example, the **retail_load** table is loaded to load files from the **src_load_stage** internal stage. **COPY** does a metadata check for files being loaded by default and skips the file. Here, the **FORCE** is not specified as the default of **FORCE** is **FALSE**. Files are not loaded forcefully if they are found in the metadata. Also, the failure action is not specified as the default action is **ABORT STATEMENT**. We can use relevant copy options as per our requirements. Refer to the following sample example to specify the copy options as per our use case and requirements to handle data loads:

```
COPY INTO retail_load
FROM @src_load_stage
FILE_FORMAT = (FORMAT_NAME = src_file_format)
FORCE = TRUE
ON_ERROR = SKIP_FILE
;
```

Load use case 2

The next use case is to load JSON files from the external stage to the Snowflake table. One of the critical load properties is to skip the file load if the load reaches 10 error records. *Table 10.3* shares the file properties to be considered while setting up the data load:

File Property Check	Indicator
File Format	JSON
Error Handling	Skip load of the file if error records are more than 10
Location	Files are on external stage

Table 10.3: File feed properties

You can continue to use **COPY** to load JSON format files. Like the structured delimited files load use case defined in the preceding section, Snowflake objects need to be created to support data loading. Follow these steps to implement the semi-structure loading use case with JSON data:

1. **Create an account for the external stage**: To set up an external stage outside the Snowflake trial account. You can set up another trial account on **Google Cloud Platform** (**GCP**). You can integrate the GCP cloud storage with a Snowflake account.

2. Create a Google Cloud integration to create an external stage. Follow this code snippet to create an integration:

```
CREATE STORAGE INTEGRATION gcp_int
  TYPE = EXTERNAL_STAGE
  STORAGE_PROVIDER = 'GCS'
  ENABLED = TRUE
  STORAGE_ALLOWED_LOCATIONS = ('gs://source_dir/source_path1/',
  'gs://source_dir/source_path2/');
```

3. Create an external stage using the GCP integration created in the previous step:

```
CREATE STAGE gcp_ext_stage
  URL='gs://retail/source_files/'
  STORAGE_INTEGRATION = gcp_int;
```

4. Define the file format for JSON files. Use the create file format to define the source file format:

```
CREATE OR REPLACE FILE FORMAT json_file_format
  TYPE = JSON;
```

5. Next is to use the external stage and file formats created in the preceding steps to load the files using **COPY INTO** as batch load:

```
COPY INTO transactions_load
  FROM 'gs://retail/source_files/transactions.json'
  STORAGE_INTEGRATION = gcp_int
  FILE_FORMAT = (FORMAT_NAME = json_file_format)
  ON_ERROR = SKIP_FILE_10
;
```

COPY INTO options can also be specified as needed to load data files from named stages. **COPY** can load any type of bulk load for all supported file formats, like structured delimited files, semi-structured files, and open-source format files like Parquet, Avro, and ORC. Next, we will learn how to use Snowpipe to load data in real-time as well as near real-time.

Real-time loads with Snowpipe

Real-time loads are other types of loads where data is received in smaller chunks and at higher frequencies. Snowflake managed feature, namely Snowpipe, can be used to load the data in near real-time. You can use small data files with greater frequency to load using Snowpipe.

Understanding Snowpipe

Snowpipe allows users to load the data as soon as it is available in the source location or stage. This is used to load data in micro-batches, smaller volumes with higher frequencies, unlike bulk loads, which are used to load data in high volume and small frequencies. Snowpipe is a Snowflake object defined as a wrapper on top of the **COPY** command to load data files. Pipe contains **COPY** command and invokes based on the Snowpipe feature to invoke the data loads as well as automate the data loads using cloud messaging services.

You can load data from all three clouds, AWS, GCP, and Microsoft Azure. All **COPY** features are supported, and all supported file formats can be loaded using pipe. In comparison with bulk load using **COPY**, the pipe maintains the load history for 14 days. Snowpipe metadata is used to avoid data duplication and load the same files again. Snowpipe loads data into smaller chunks and multiple transactions based on the size of the data, volume, and table rows. Snowpipe is Snowflake's managed object is also referred to as serverless service, where compute resources are managed by Snowflake. Snowpipe billing is like Snowflake and computes billing model, i.e., pay as you use. This is the warehouse cost associated with Snowpipe to load the data in real-time. Refer to *Figure 10.2*, which represents micro batching load using Kafka | Storage buckets | Snowpipe | Snowflake table:

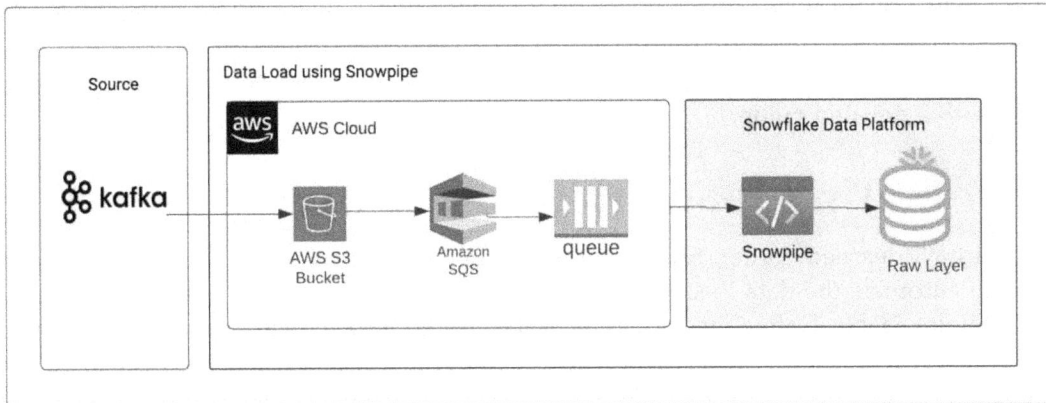

Figure 10.2: Data load with Snowpipe

As you observe in *Figure 10.2*, Amazon SQS and queue are used to push the files to the queue as soon as they are available on the storage bucket. Snowpipe picks it up from the queue and loads it to the table.

Snowflake recommends a data file size of 100-250MB compressed to be loaded as part of Snowpipe and bulk load. Snowflake manages the data load queue for each pipe object, data files are loaded as they are staged in the load. Though the files are loaded in the order received, there is no guarantee of data load in a given sequence. Snowpipe can be created by using the **CREATE PIPE** statement. You can use DDL commands to create and manage Snowpipe objects.

Using Snowpipe

You can use the **CREATE** statement to create the pipe to load data files from the named stage. Refer to the following steps to load data in micro-batches:

1. If you have data files received on the named stage. Use the **CREATE** pipe to load the data from the stage as and when it arrives:

   ```
   create pipe retail pipe as copy into retail_table from @retail_
   stage;
   ```

2. COPY options and properties can also be used to transform the data and load it to the table using Snowpipe, shown as follows:

   ```
   create pipe transaction_pipe as copy into transaction(C1, C2) from
   (select $5, $4 from @retail_stage);
   ```

3. Use the **ALTER** command to change the pipe properties as well as the pipe execution status if needed:

   ```
   alter pipe retail_pipe SET PIPE_EXECUTION_PAUSED = true;
   ```

Cloud-native messaging services can be used to load the data automatically to the Snowflake table by triggering the Snowpipe. The following section covers the steps used to automate the data load using messaging services. You will learn to automate Snowpipe loads with a detailed guide.

Automating loads with Snowpipe

As you have learned earlier, Snowpipe loads data in micro batches. Snowflake allows users to automate the data load to trigger the Snowpipe to load data in micro batches to the Snowflake table. Define the Snowpipe that contains **COPY** to read data from an external stage and leverage cloud messaging services to automate the ingestion of files from cloud storage. Refer to *Figure 10.3* using AWS S3 as an external stage, integrating storage with Snowflake. You can use AWS **Simple Queue Service (SQS)** notifications for the AWS S3 bucket.

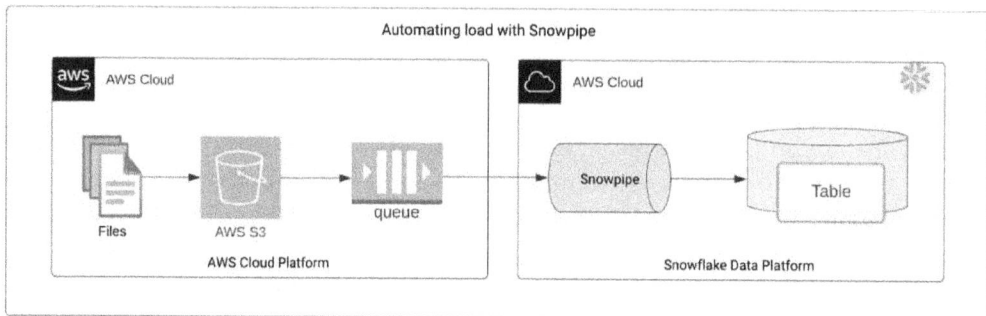

Figure 10.3: Automating Snowpipe

As you know, to integrate the AWS S3 bucket with Snowflake access securely, we need to define the storage integration and allow access to read data from the AWS storage bucket. Follow the storage integration steps to create a storage integration to read data from AWS S3. In the following section, we will have a recap to create storage integration.

Create storage integration

Create an AWS S3 storage bucket to upload data files for testing. If you do not have an active AWS account, then you will need a trial account to be set up to create storage objects in AWS S3. The steps are as follows:

1. Create a bucket on AWS S3.

2. Create an IAM policy to allow access to the S3 bucket, use the following policy reference and add the S3 path and prefix to the policy:

```
{
    "Version": "2012-10-17",
    "Statement": [
```

```
{
     "Effect": "Allow",
     "Action": [
       "s3:GetObject",
       "s3:GetObjectVersion"
     ],
     "Resource": "arn:aws:s3:::<bucket>/<prefix>/*"
},
{
     "Effect": "Allow",
     "Action": [
         "s3:ListBucket",
         "s3:GetBucketLocation"
     ],
     "Resource": "arn:aws:s3:::<bucket>",
     "Condition": {
         "StringLike": {
             "s3:prefix": [
                 "<prefix>/*"
             ]
         }
     }
}
  ]
}
```

3. Create an IAM role with your AWS account ID and external ID as 000 temporary ID to be updated. Attach the policy to the AWS IAM role created in the preceding step. Save the role. Copy the role ARN once the role is created.

4. Create storage integration on Snowflake using the **CREATE STORAGE INTEGRATION**. The reference code is as follows:

```
CREATE STORAGE INTEGRATION aws_external_int
  TYPE = EXTERNAL_STAGE
  STORAGE_PROVIDER = 'S3'
  ENABLED = TRUE
  STORAGE_AWS_ROLE_ARN = '<aws_iam_role>'
  STORAGE_ALLOWED_LOCATIONS = ('s3://<bucket>/<path>/',
's3://<bucket>/<path>/')
  [ STORAGE_BLOCKED_LOCATIONS = ('s3://<bucket>/<path>/',
's3://<bucket>/<path>/') ]
```

Here, update the AWS role ARN with the ARN copied in the aforementioned step.

5. Describe the integration created in *Step 4* and copy the Snowflake user and external ID details. Run the **DESCRIBE** command:

```
DESC INTEGRATION aws_external_int;
```

6. Copy these two field values from the storage description:

STORAGE_AWS_IAM_USER_ARN and STORAGE_AWS_EXTERNAL_ID

7. Grant IAM permissions to access the bucket created in *Step 1*. You can add a trust relationship to the role created:

```
{
    "Version": "2012-10-17",
    "Statement": [
      {
        "Sid": "",
        "Effect": "Allow",
        "Principal": {
          "AWS": "<snowflake_user_arn>"
        },
        "Action": "sts:AssumeRole",
        "Condition": {
          "StringEquals": {
            "sts:ExternalId": "<snowflake_external_id>"
          }
        }
      }
    ]
}
```

Here, you can paste the Snowflake user ARN and Snowflake external ID copied in the earlier step. Once this is updated, save the policy.

Now, we have the AWS bucket, bucket integration, and external stage setup to access the data stored on AWS S3. Next is to choose the automation option to automate the Snowpipe loads. Snowflake supports diverse options to integrate the trigger. We will learn to choose the option and implement the SQS integration to automate the loads in subsequent sections.

Choose automation integration option

There are two feasible options to automate the data load using AWS services. You can use one of the following options:

- **New S3 event notification:** Create an event notification to send a notification to Snowpipe via SQS queue as and when files are available.

- **Existing event notification:** Configure AWS **Simple Notification Service (SNS)** to share notifications for a given path with multiple endpoints.

- **Amazon Event bridge to automate Snowpipe:** You can use Amazon Event bridge for S3 buckets and set rules to send notifications to SNS topics.

You can use one of the above options to automate the data load using Snowpipe. You can choose AWS messaging or notification service to notify the pipe that files are ready to be loaded.

Setup pipe and configure notifications using SQS

To set up automation to load files from the external stage, we need to create an external stage by using storage integration created in the previous section, *Create Storage integration*. The next step is to create a pipe object with auto ingest. Refer to the following SQL commands:

```
/* create external stage*/
USE DATABASE RETAIL_POC_DB;
USE SCHEMA POC;
CREATE STAGE pipe_stage
  URL = 's3://retail/load/pipe_files'
  STORAGE_INTEGRATION = aws_external_int;

/* create snowflake pipe */
Create retail_poc_db.poc.retail_pipe auto_ingest=true as
  copy into retail_poc_db.poc.transactions
  from @retail_poc_db.poc.pipe_stage
  file_format = (FORMAT_NAME = src_file_format);
```

Once a Snowpipe is defined, you can use the **SHOW** command to list the pipe and copy the ARN. Follow these steps to configure the pipe and notification service on AWS:

1. Run the **SHOW PIPE** command and copy ARN to keep it handy.

2. Go to the AWS console.

3. Configure the event notification. You can refer to AWS documentation: **https://docs.aws.amazon.com/AmazonS3/latest/userguide/enable-event-notifications.html** to configure and provide the following details:

    a. **Name:** Provide the name of the event.

    b. **Events:** Select all applicable from the options list.

4. Send to select SQS queue from the list.

5. Add SQS ARN copied in the earlier step and save.

If you have old files in the S3 bucket and want to load them as part of the historical load, then you can use the **COPY** command to load them. You can also use **ALTER PIPE**. **REFRESH** command to refresh the pipe and load data from the previous seven days. If there are older files than seven days, you can use **COPY** to load files from the external stage to the table.

You can also delete the staged files from the external stage. The load files can be skipped in case picked to be loaded using Snowpipe. You can use the **REMOVE** command to remove the files, and Snowflake recommends removing the staged files periodically.

You can follow the steps listed previously to automate the data loads. Similarly, you can follow the steps to configure the notification services, SNS, or event bridge to automate the data loads using Snowpipe.

You can refer to Snowflake documentation at **https://docs.snowflake.com/en/user-guide/ data-load-snowpipe-auto-s3** to configure SNS or Event bridge to automate data loads.

With the recent updates and release, Snowflake's Snowpipe also supports streaming loads, and this is referred to as Snowpipe streaming. You can use Snowpipe to load data in micro batches and Snowpipe streaming to load data in real-time.

Snowpipe streaming

Implement automated near-real-time data loads using Snowpipe and AWS SQS. Snowpipe is recommended for micro batches, and small data files with greater frequency. Snowpipe streaming can be integrated with Kafka for streaming loads. Refer to *Figure 10.4*, which represents the Kafka to Snowflake using Snowpipe streaming. This figure also shows the difference between Snowpipe streaming and Snowpipe:

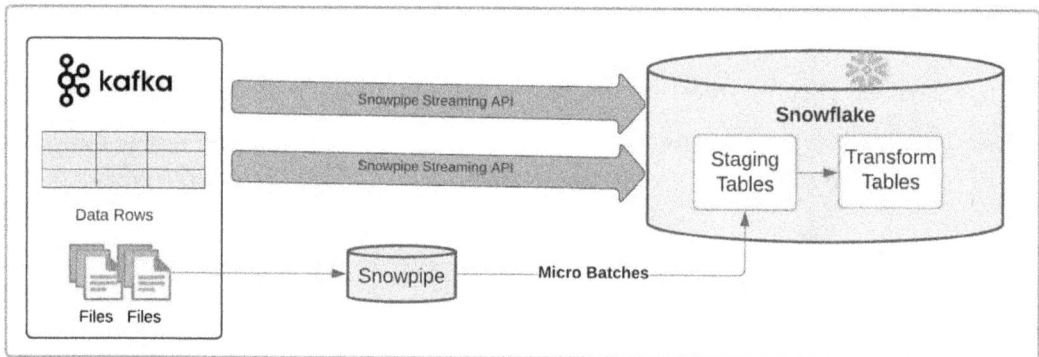

Figure 10.4: Snowpipe Streaming vs Snowpipe

As you observe here, Snowpipe reads data in the form of files from the storage location and loads it to the table in micro batches, whereas Snowpipe streaming reads it directly from Kafka topics and loads it to the Snowflake table. Refer to **https://docs.snowflake. com/en/user-guide/data-load-snowpipe-streaming-kafka** to learn more about Kafka streaming to Snowflake. We can use Snowpipe as well as Snowpipe streaming to get the data in smaller volumes and higher frequency to Snowflake. There are a few best practices and recommendations shared by Snowflake to achieve cost and performance efficiency.

You will learn more about some of the best practices to implement Snowpipe as optimized workloads in an upcoming section.

Snowflake recommendations

Snowflake recommends best practices for implementing Snowpipe streaming API. The following are some of them:

- **Cost optimization**: Snowflake recommends using fewer Snowpipe streaming clients to write more data per second. The API aggregates the data across multiple target tables in an account. A single Snowpipe streaming client opens multiple channels to send data. The channels do not affect the client's cost; hence, it is recommended to use multiple channels per client for better performance and cost optimization. If you use the same table for batch load as well as streaming load, then the computer cost associated with the load is also reduced.

- **Performance optimization**: It is recommended to maintain the size of each row at 16MB. If there are multiple rows to be loaded, then insert rows are more performant. You can also pass values for **TIME**, **DATE**, and **TIMESTAMP** columns as one of the supported types in the Java package.

You can use the Snowflake Kafka connector with Snowpipe streaming to load data in real-time. You can refer to **https://docs.snowflake.com/en/user-guide/data-load-snowpipe-streaming-kafka** for Kafka configuration. You can also refer to the Snowflakes QuickStart to get started with streaming integration **https://quickstarts.snowflake.com/guide/data_engineering_streaming_integration/index.html#0**.

Once data is loaded into the Snowflake staging layer, the next task is to transform the data. The data needs to be transformed, enriched, processed, and moved from one layer to another as part of data processing. The following sub-sections cover data export using the **COPY INTO** command.

Data unloading using COPY INTO

Data unloading is one aspect of data consumption and consumer integration. Snowflake allows users to share the data in multiple ways. You have already learned about data sharing, data marketplace, and listings as part of data sharing in *Chapter 8, Implementing Data Integrations*. In some of the scenarios, data feeds need to be generated and shared with the downstream applications, external consumers, or users. In the case of feed generation, a data feed (file) is generated and pushed to another storage or server or to a **network-attached storage** (**NAS**). Snowflake offers **COPY INTO**, which can also be used to unload the data in the form of batch exports, the same as data loading as part of batch loads.

As you know, to load data into a table, **COPY INTO** can read from any named stages and load. In case of data unloading, **COPY INTO** can read from a table and export data to any named stage or location. File formats, named stages, external stages, as well as storage integrations, can be used to set the export job. Snowflake Tasks can also be used to automate the export or schedule it on the required frequency. This can be used in any scenario where data needs to be rolled monthly from the database to storage as part of a monthly roll or run an archival process to export data from the Snowflake table and push it to storage buckets. The historical data or archived data can be made available in the form of external tables in the Snowflake platform in case you need to run any queries or access data.

COPY INTO follows similar features, parameters, and copy options as it offers to the data loads. Refer to the sample SQL commands used to export data to the named external stages:

```
/* set the context*/
USE DATABASE RETAIL_POC_DB;
USE SCHEMA POC;

/* use the external stage created in the load step */

COPY INTO 'gcs://retail/exports/'
FROM sales
STORAGE_INTEGRATION = gcs_int;
```

There are a few considerations while exporting the data to the cloud storage buckets. The following are some of the critical considerations:

- Snowflake exports data into multiple part files by default and allows users to use the **SINGLE** copy option to set to **TRUE** to export data into a single file.

  ```
  copy into @retailstage/sales_monthly.csv.gz from sales
  file_format = (type=csv compression='gzip')
  single=true
  max_file_size=4900000000; --this is maximum size supported 5GB
  ```

- Snowflake allows users to export data into JSON format, **OBJECT_CONSTRUCT** can be used to convert the data into JSON format to be exported. In this case, the row is converted into a single **VARIANT** column.

- Snowflake also supports exporting data in the form of open file formats like Parquet. You can define the file format to set the format on export.

- You can also customize the fields being exported to be enclosed with quotes. In some of the cases where you want to export data in the form of CSV, however, the data feed also contains the feed with a comma in it, then in this case, you can use the enclosed option to enclose each column field into quotes. **FIELD_OPTIONALLY_ENCLOSED_BY** can be used to set the parameter to export the enclosed fields.

Data unloading might be required when you are integrating the platform with some of the existing platforms, multi-cloud, or hybrid applications. The data feed can be generated to cloud storage and from there pushed to the required server. Data exports are still being used with Snowflake, though it offers a variety of data sharing features. The next critical part of engineering is to capture the changes and apply changes to the target data systems. This is often referred to as change data capture, and you will learn more about it in the following section.

Change data capture with streams and tasks

Change data capture is a process in which changes are identified and applied to the data. There are diverse types supported to be implemented as part of change data capture. **Slowly Changing Dimensions (SCD)** is a process to implement change data capture. Typically, SCD Type II is implemented where historical data is maintained as log history of changes, and new data is refreshed. You can implement SCD Type II using SQL commands. However, Snowflake offers extended features to implement CDC using streams and tasks.

Snowflake streams

Stream is a snowflake object used to capture the changes in the form of metadata information and metadata action. This object stores the offset of the source object without storing the actual data or columns. You can query streams like any table object using the **SELECT** command. Streams maintain additional columns catering to metadata information and metadata action. Refer to the following columns that define the metadata changes:

- **METADATA$ACTION**: This captures the action taken in the form of DML, **INSERT**, **DELETE**, and **UPDATE**

- **METADATA$ISUPDATE:** This is an indicator that indicates whether the operation taken was part of the **UPDATE** statement or not. This is a Boolean column, -TRUE or FALSE.

- **METADATA$ROW_ID**: This is a unique and immutable ID for the row and is used to track changes.

You can create a stream using the **CREATE** command. Refer to the following command:

```
/* create stream */
USE DATABASE RETAIL_POC_DB;
USE SCHEMA POC;
CREATE STREAM transaction_stream ON TABLE transactions;
```

There are distinct types of streams available based on the metadata recorded.

Stream types

Snowflake offers three types of streams, listed as follows:

- **Standard:** This is the type of stream that can be used for tables, directory tables, and views. The **standard** stream tracks all DML changes on the source object. This type of stream cannot be used to track changes for geospatial data type.

- **Append-only**: This type of stream can be used for standard tables, directory tables, and views. This type of stream tacks only inserts operations on the source. As the name says, it captures only inserts, while the rest of the DML operations, like update, delete, or truncate, are not captured.

- **Insert-only**: This type of stream is supported only for external tables. As the name suggests, this captures only the rows inserted. No DML transactions are captured.

You can create streams on views as well. The streams can be created on standard views as well as secure views. Streams cannot be used for materialized views. Streams can be created for views. However, there are a few limitations on the view:

- All tables used in the view are native tables.

- The view contains specific operations or limited operations like filters, inner or cross joins, **UNION ALL**, etc.

- Views with selected columns and multiple where conditions.

- Streams are not supported for views that use clauses, like **GROUP BY**, **QUALIFY**, **LIMIT**, **DISTINCT**, subqueries in the FROM clause, and correlated queries.

- The underlying tables in view should have changed tracking to enable streams.

Stream cost

As you know, Snowflake's cost is associated with the computing or storage required. Stream cost is associated with the warehouse time required for processing. You can view the billing or usage of streams using metadata views. You can also view the usage on Snowsight.

Streams can be implemented and used using SQL commands. You can refer to the following use case and SQL commands to implement streams and capture changes using streams:

```
/* create stream and query stream to read data from stream */
CREATE DATABASE DEMO;
USE DATABASE DEMO;
CREATE SCHEMA POC;
USE SCHEMA POC;

/* create a sample table to demo stream capability */
CREATE OR REPLACE TABLE library_membership (
  member_id number(8) NOT NULL,
  mem_name varchar(255) default NULL,
  mem_fees number(3) NULL,
  mem_type varchar(20)
);

/* create stream to track changes in the table*/
CREATE OR REPLACE STREAM members_changes ON TABLE library_membership;
```

Now, you have set up the demo database, schema, table, and stream that looks out for any changes to the source table as defined. Next is to load some sample records to the table created above to track changes using stream. The following code snippet shares the load statements to load data:

```
/* load sample records to the table */
INSERT INTO library_membership  VALUES
(1010,'Smith',0, 'Short Term'),
(1011,'Andrew',0, 'Annual'),
(1012,'Angela',0, 'Life Long'),
(1013,'Rose',0, 'Temporary Pass');
```

You can enhance these statements to add more details or modify them. With the preceding load statements, sample records are loaded to the table, hence an activity is captured in streams. View stream data using **SELECT** on streams as follows:

```
/* you can view the stream to check the metadata records and action captured*/
SELECT * from members_changes;

/* get changes to the membership table */
INSERT INTO library_membership  VALUES
(1014,'Shivam',0, 'Annual'),
(1015,'Maggie',0, 'Annual');

/* you can view the stream to check the metadata records and action captured*/
SELECT * from members_changes;
```

Streams are used to capture any changes made to the source table. In this case, the loads and inserts are captured into streams. The next part of the use case is to get another table to apply the changes captured in streams. Follow these steps:

```
/* Every year the charges are renewed for the membership */
CREATE TABLE MEMBERSHIP_CHARGES( mem_id int, member_type string,
membership_fees int);

/* create stream on the table */
CREATE OR REPLACE STREAM members_stream ON TABLE MEMBERSHIP_CHARGES;

/* Add new records to the fees table*/

INSERT INTO MEMBERSHIP_CHARGES(1012,'Life Long',199);
INSERT INTO MEMBERSHIP_CHARGES(1011,'Anual',99);
INSERT INTO MEMBERSHIP_CHARGES(1014,'Anual',99);
INSERT INTO MEMBERSHIP_CHARGES(1015,'Anual',99);
INSERT INTO MEMBERSHIP_CHARGES(1010,'Short Term',49);
INSERT INTO MEMBERSHIP_CHARGES(1013,'Temporary Pass',19);
```

As you observe here, new sample records are loaded to the **MEMBERSHIP_CHARGES** table, and this needs to be applied to the **MEMBERSHIP** table. Refer to the following code snippet to apply the changes to the table:

```
/* apply the changed fees to the membership */

MERGE INTO library_membership  a
USING
MEMBERSHIP_CHARGES b
ON a.member_id = b.mem_id
WHEN MATCHED THEN UPDATE SET a.mem_fees = b.membership_fees;

/* view the stream to check the metadata records and action captured*/
SELECT * from members_changes;
```

Refer to the above SQL statements to implement streams. You can also refer to Snowflake quick starts to use streams and access them in a programmatic way: **https:// quickstarts.snowflake.com/guide/getting_started_with_streams_and_tasks/index. html?index=..%2F..index#0**.

Once the streams are defined, set the change data capture to apply changes to the target table. You can also use Snowflake tasks to schedule the changes to be applied. This code can also be wrapped in a program or **stored procedure** (**SP**) and invoked using tasks. Refer to the following sample code to set up the task that applies data to the table based on the changes captured in streams:

```
create or replace task change_capture_tsk
schedule = '20 minute'
when
system$stream_has_data('members_stream')
as
merge into library_membership a
  using (select var:mem_id id, var:mem_type type, var:membership_fees fees
from members_stream) s on a.member_id = s.id
when matched then update set a.mem_fees = s.fees;
```

You can set the task to call the change capture and apply changes to the table. Transformations is the next phase where you can apply changes as part of transformations using UDF and UDFT. You will learn more about it in the next section.

SQL transformations with UDF and UDFT

UDF is a user-defined function that can be used to develop custom functionality and used as a reusable feature. UDF can be used as part of an SQL statement to extend the functionality. **CREATE FUNCTION** is used to create the user-defined function, and Snowflake supports multiple languages to develop the UDF. Snowflake supports two types of functions: scalar and tabular. The scalar function returns one row as output to each input row and is referred to as UDF. Tabular functions generate results in a tabular form for each input row, which is referred to as UDFT.

Snowflake UDFs and UDFTs can be built using Java, JavaScript, Python, Scala, and SQL. Developers can use their choice of language to develop the custom functionality. Like any other PL/SQL functions, you can develop functions with handlers to handle exceptions.

Exception handlers

There are two types of handlers, in-line handler and staged handler. In-line handlers are coded in line with the UDF code. In the case of in-line handlers, you do not need to manage the handler code separately.

In the case of staged handlers, the handler code is compiled and staged in a different location. When you have a standard piece of code to be integrated with functions for exception handling, you can plan to compile the code and store it as part of staged handlers. This helps to reduce the code size as well as implement a standard block of code. You can use staged handlers for UDFs as well as SPs. The stage handlers have a dependency on the file. If the file name is modified for the staged code, then the corresponding functions or procedures need to be modified to point to the correct location and file.

Create functions

You can use the **CREATE FUNCTION** DDL to define a function. You can use programming languages like Java, JavaScript, Scala, Python, and SQL to develop the function. The function can have input parameters as well as output as a single value or multiple values. Refer to the following section for the function types and corresponding reference code to define the function using SQL.

Scalar function

The scalar function returns a single output as function output. Refer to the following SQL used to define the UDF:

```
CREATE FUNCTION rectangle_area(length FLOAT, breadth FLOAT)
  RETURNS FLOAT
  AS
  $$
    length * breadth
  $$
  ;
```

You can use this function to calculate the area of the rectangle. Similarly, you can create functions to implement reusable functions. **GRANT** can be assigned to the functions and allow permissions to the users to execute the function.

Tabular function

The tabular function returns results in tabular format. Refer to the following UDF definition to create a UDF that returns the tabular result:

```
CREATE OR REPLACE FUNCTION get_promotions(region varchar )
  RETURNS TABLE (promo_code varchar, promo_details varchar, promo_validity
varchar)
  AS 'select promo_code, promo_details , promo_validity
      from promotions a
      where a.region = region
      and promo_status='active'';
```

This function is created to return the tabular result for a given input. This function accepts customer ID as input and shares the promotional details for the customer. These tabular functions can be used as a table to query using **SELECT** queries. Refer to the following sample query to run on a tabular function:

```
select *
    from table(get_promotions('US')) promos
    order by promo_validity asc;
```

Refer to the result, as shown here:

```
+--------------+----------------+--------------+-----------|
|PROMO_CODE|  PROMO_DETAILS                 |PROMO_VALIDITY. |
|—+-----|—-----—+—-----------—|—----------—|
|30USMCY|30% off on Macy's for $150 spend |Till 30/04/2024|
|50USHNM|50% off on HNM shopping over $200|Till 30/06/2024|
+--------------+----------------+----------|----------|-----
```

You can use the function as part of the SQL statement to invoke the function. In the case of a scalar function, you can use it to transform the function as a **SELECT** statement. You can use the tabular function in the **FROM** clause to query the data. These tabular functions can also be used to manage access to databases, data, and tables.

Function references

As you know, functions can be defined using Java, JavaScript, Scala, and Python as well. You can refer to the following reference links to define the functions:

- **JavaScript: https://docs.snowflake.com/en/developer-guide/udf/javascript/udf-javascript-introduction**

- **Java: https://docs.snowflake.com/en/developer-guide/udf/java/udf-java-introduction**

- **Scala: https://docs.snowflake.com/en/developer-guide/udf/scala/udf-scala-introduction**

- **Python**: **https://docs.snowflake.com/en/developer-guide/udf/python/udf-python-introduction**

Snowflake also shares quick starts to start learning and implementing Snowflake features. Refer to **https://quickstarts.snowflake.com/guide/getting_started_with_user_defined_sql_functions/?index=..%2F..index#0** to get started with user-defined SQL functions.

Like UDFs, SPs can also be used to define the transformations and build modular code. Snowflake supports various languages to define SPs and extends support with Snowflake scripting to develop SPs as a procedural language. We will learn more about implementing SPs in the following section.

Snowflake stored procedures

A SP is a block of statements that contains logic to process the data, transformations, and generate the target output. SPs can be used to generate and execute dynamic SQL and execute code with required privileges. SPs can also be used to automate multiple statements that need to run frequently. SPs can also be used to replace the long and complex SQLs to make the code modular code.

Sample examples

SPs can be used to modularize the code in the following scenarios:

- Generating dynamic SQLs to implement a functionality like data quality
- Automate the error-handling modules
- Modularize the code required to implement DML functionalities
- Generalizing the DML operations to clean up the data, taking backups, or monthly rolls
- Generating code or SQL to generate the modular code for data operations

Supported languages

Snowflake allows users to create SPs with their choice of programming language to develop the SP. Snowflake supports programming languages like Java, JavaScript, Python, Scala, and SQL as Snowflake scripting. As a developer, you can use one of these languages to develop the SP. You can refer to **https://docs.snowflake.com/en/developer-guide/stored-procedure/stored-procedures-usage** to create SPs with standards, best practices, and naming conventions.

Creating and using stored procedure

CREATE STORED PROCEDURE is used to create the SP and CALL to invoke the SP. A SP can be invoked with CALL and generate the result. SPs can also be set to be invoked with

Snowflake tasks, which can be scheduled with dependencies to execute the SP. You can use the handler modules with SPs as well to handle exceptions and manage error handling. A SP can also be used to generate the tabular output:

```
/*set the context*/
USE DATABASE DEMO_POC;
USE SCHEMA POC;
/* create stored procedure */
CREATE OR REPLACE PROCEDURE locate_promo_cd(cust_id integer)
RETURNS TABLE (promo_cd varchar, promo_date date)
LANGUAGE SQL
AS
DECLARE
  res RESULTSET DEFAULT (SELECT promo_cd, promo_date FROM promotions WHERE
customer_id = :cust_id);
BEGIN
  RETURN TABLE(res);
END;
```

The preceding procedure provides the promo code for customers eligible for promotions.

Next is to invoke the SP using the **CALL** command as shown here:

```
 /* call to execute the SP */
CALL locate_promo_cd(010011);
```

This call statement returns the output as defined in the form of two columns: **promo_code** and **promo_date**. SP can be invoked as part of any **Extract, Load, Transform** (**ELT**) job, as well as can be added in Snowflake task to be invoked as per cron schedule. Generally, we can create SP to implement data transformations as SQL code. This is the simplest form of approach to leverage platform capabilities and implement ELT workloads with push down optimization. SP can also be used to automate processes as well as setup re-usable components to implement generalized processes. For example, monthly rolls archive or aggregates processes that run every month and follow the same rules across databases or tables.

Logging and tracing

Snowflake offers **EVENT** tables to capture the log messages and trace the events. The event table is one of the table types supported in Snowflake. This table is used with Snowflake SPs and functions. You have learned to use the event tables as part of the standard practice of error handling and exception handling in *Chapter 9, Designing Data Solutions*.

It is recommended to use functions and SPs to implement modularity. These are treated as Snowflake objects and used to automate the transformations and functionalities. Snowflake also offers features like Snowpark that allow developers to develop data pipelines with dataframes. You will learn to implement Snowpark in the following section.

Snowpark dataframes and pipelines

Snowpark is a library that offers query and processing data at scale in Snowflake. Snowflake allows developers to develop pipelines using Java, Python, and Scala. This is used to build applications that run within the Snowflake platform and process data without moving from the platform. Snowpark code runs at a scale as part of a serverless and elastic Snowflake engine. Snowpark enables users to develop data pipelines using dataframes. This is like Spark functionality. However, this has numerous benefits over Spark. The following are some of the benefits of Spark:

- Snowpark enables users to interact with data using libraries and patterns without compromising the performance of the functionality. Snowpark development uses local tools to develop code, such as IntelliJ, Jupyter, VS Code, etc. It supports Pushdown optimization to push the workloads to the Snowflake platform. All the heavy lifting and transformations are pushed to the Snowflake platform.

- Snowpark does not need any separate clusters or environments to run the data pipelines. All transformations and computations required to perform transformations are performed within the data platform. The computer resources are managed by Snowflake. Snowpark allows users to develop the functionality using SQL and create UDFs as inline functions. Refer to *Figure 10.5*, which represents the Snowpark execution within the data platform:

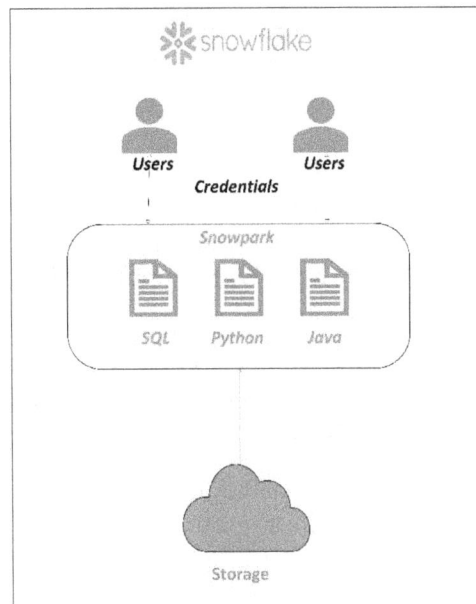

Figure 10.5: Snowpark

Here, as represented in *Figure 10.5*, Snowpark pipelines can be developed using Python, Scala, and Java. Snowpark allows users to build data pipelines in several ways. Refer to *Figure 10.6*, which shows Snowpark development ways using Client API and libraries:

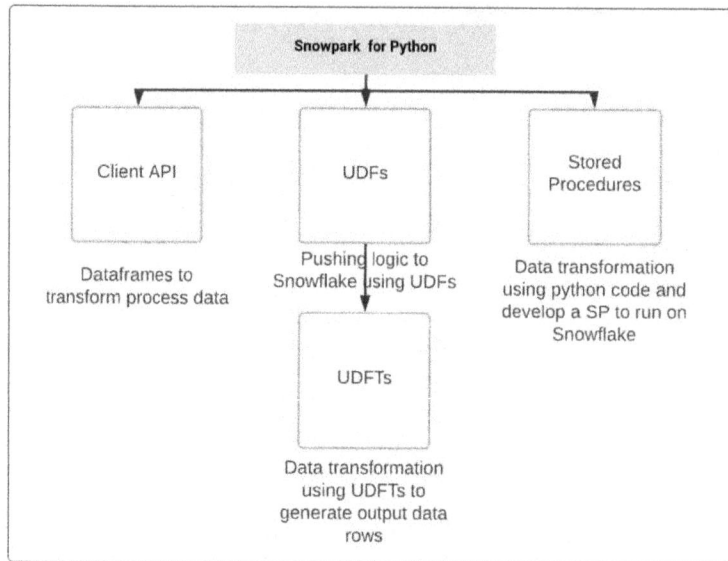

Figure 10.6: Snowpark ways to develop pipeline

As represented in *Figure 10.6*, the following are the options and objects that can be developed using Snowpark:

- Snowpark data pipelines using Client APIs and libraries
- Snowpark UDF and UDFTs
- Snowpark SPs

Snowpark objects can be created and used in the same way as any other Snowflake objects. The data pipelines, using client APIs, can be invoked as data pipelines within the Snowflake platform. Snowflake offers Snowpark-optimized warehouses to support Snowpark workloads. You can create a Snowpark-optimized warehouse and allow users to use it to build and test data pipelines.

Refer to Snowflake QuickStart to start developing a data pipeline using Snowpark **https://quickstarts.snowflake.com/guide/data_engineering_pipelines_with_snowpark_ python/index.html?index=..%2F..index#0**.

Snowflake also allows users to use the existing data pipelines and connect to Snowflake with a set of connectors and drivers. In migration or modernization use cases, you do not need to convert all pipelines, as you can use programming connectors. The following section will cover the drivers and connectors available.

Programming connectors and drivers

Snowflake offers a variety of drivers to develop applications that perform operations on the Snowflake platform. You can develop applications in any of these languages supported and drivers extended by Snowflake. The following are the drivers and connectors supported:

- Go Snowflake driver

- JDBC and ODBC driver

- .NET driver

- Node.js driver

- PHP PDO driver

- Snowflake connector for Python

These drivers offer an interface to develop applications using a programming language to connect to Snowflake to perform all required operations. Snowflake allows users to download these drivers and configure them. Refer to the following links to download these drivers:

- **ODBC Driver download: https://docs.snowflake.com/en/developer-guide/odbc/odbc-download**

- **Install Node.js Driver: https://docs.snowflake.com/en/developer-guide/node-js/nodejs-driver-install**

- **Download JDBC Driver: https://docs.snowflake.com/en/developer-guide/jdbc/jdbc-download**

- **Complete install and setup for Go driver: https://github.com/snowflakedb/gosnowflake**

- **Install Python connector: https://docs.snowflake.com/en/developer-guide/python-connector/python-connector-install**

Python connectors can be used to develop applications using Python. You can perform all standard operations using this connector, like Snowflake object creation, DML queries, and querying data. pandas dataframes are also supported with a Python connector, which you can use to analyze as well as manipulate the data. You can also use the Snowflake Python connector API to perform operations on the platform.

Once you have pipelines developed and tested in the DEV environment, the next step is to migrate the data pipelines from the DEV to the PROD environment. Snowflake allows users to implement continuous integration and deployment as CI/CD. You will learn about the integration features in the following section.

Data pipeline management with CI/CD

Continuous integration (**CI**) and **continuous deployment** (**CD**) are the needs of engineering design and implementation. In earlier implementations, a developer needs to follow a complete development cycle from development ∣ unit testing ∣ QA ∣ Integration testing ∣ **User Acceptance Testing** (**UAT**) ∣ Sign off ∣ PROD. It was difficult to capture the errors and rectify all issues before deploying it to production. The cycle was long, and it was challenging to detect errors early. With CI, the developed code is integrated with the shared repository and automatically deployed. This helps in identifying the errors in the early phase of the development cycle and rectifies most of the issues before it goes live. CD caters to releasing the features to the production automatically as soon as they are tested, validated, and passed.

As you know, CI and deployment are integrated with most of the versioning tools. Typically, developers use one of these tools: GitHub, Gitlab, Bitbucket, etc. There are a variety of tools available in the market that are integrated with actions to initiate or trigger the deployment cycle. In this section, GitHub is used for versioning and acts as a code repository. GitHub actions are the triggers that can be used to set the deployment cycle.

You can also use open-source change management to integrate and deploy the changes to the Snowflake platform. For any database changes, Snowflake allows users to use SchemaChange. SchemaChange is the tool built by the Snowflake community, and it is not part of the Snowflake product offerings or integrations. However, you can use it to integrate and identify the changes to run CI/CD.

A typical CI/CD architecture looks as follows:

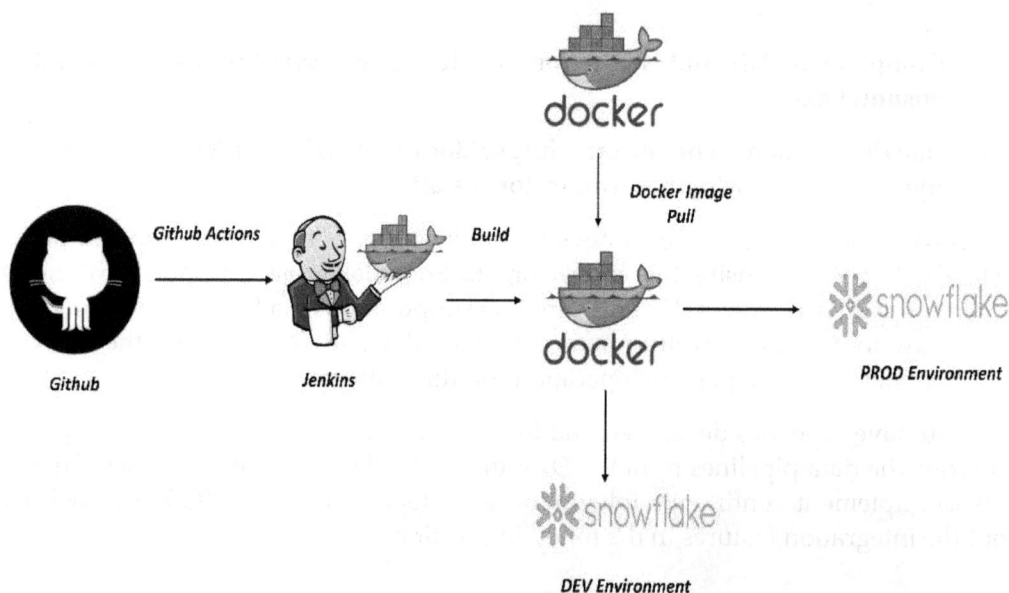

Figure 10.7: Snowflake CI/CD reference architecture

Snowflake Quick Starts has references to set up the CI/CD pipeline with open-source change management tools.

Snowflake also supports implementing the changes with Terraform. You can create the Terraform to deploy the Snowflake objects and resources, such as IaaC, and automate the deployment. Set up the configuration to connect to Snowflake and action workflows on Terraform actions. Terraform offers the easiest way to define the objects and deploy. Refer to the Snowflake quick starts to get started with GitHub and terraform for CI/CD: **https://quickstarts.snowflake.com/guide/devops_dcm_terraform_github/index. html?index=..%2F..index#0.**

Refer to **https://quickstarts.snowflake.com/guide/devops_dcm_schemachange_github/ index.html?index=..%2F..index#0** to perform a hands-on with SchemaChange and GitHub.

Also, complete this lab **https://quickstarts.snowflake.com/guide/devops_dcm_ schemachange_jenkins/index.html?index=..%2F..index#0** to get hands-on with SchemaChange and Jenkins.

CI/CD is the final part of the engineering efforts where you automate the integration and deployment process for all the pipelines, code, and objects being developed. CI/CD is the foundation block of DevOps implementation for any platform architecture and design. This is essential and critical to set up the change management cycle for any platform implementation.

Conclusion

This chapter sets the foundation for DE aspects and approaches to implement various use cases with Snowflake. DE patterns like ingestion, export, change data capture, and data transformations implemented across data platforms can be implemented with Snowflake native features. You have learned to implement them with different approaches and integrations.

As part of engineering designs and pipelines, this chapter helped you to learn Snowflake native features and resources to be used to implement various engineering aspects of data platform setup. Data integrations, ingestions, data transformations, processing, change data capture, and CI/CD cover the broader umbrella of engineering.

The next essential aspect is to understand the two aspects and approaches of DE implementations, **Extract, Transform, Load** (**ETL**), and ELT. The next chapter not only explains ETL and ELT approaches but also takes a deep dive into the pros and cons of each approach.

Points to remember

The following are some of the key takeaways from this chapter:

- Snowflake COPY INTO is used to load data in batches and micro batches. COPY supports various file formats, features, and offers COPY Options that can be leveraged to automate, configure, or manage load jobs.

- Snowflake's Snowpipe can be used to load data that is available in near real time in the form of micro batches. Snowpipe loads can be automated using cloud native messaging services.

- Snowpipe also offers streaming, and this can be configured with Kafka connectors to read data from Kafka topics and push the data in the form of streams to the table.

- COPY can be used to unload data into file feeds as well. Data feeds can be generated and shared with users over an external stage with users.

- Streams and Tasks can be used to automate the data transformations as part of **Change Data Capture (CDC)**.

- Snowflake data objects, UDFs and UDFTs, can be used to apply changes or transformation on the table using SQL commands.

- SPs are used to perform complex data transformation and generalize code generation.

- Snowflake's Snowpark is the recommended programming approach to implement any programmatic pipeline approach. This is the most widely used feature to implement any AI/ML pipelines.

- CI/CD can be implemented to apply changes to the Snowflake data model, data pipelines, or platform in integration with code repositories like GitHub, GitLab, or many others. Jenkins can be used to implement **Continuous Integration (CI)**. Docker container is used to implement the changes to the platform. There are a few open sources available in integration to implement the changes, like Sqitch or SchemaChange, etc.

CHAPTER 11
Designing ETL and ELT With Snowflake

Introduction

This chapter focuses on guiding and sharing the best practices to implement the features as part of the ETL or ELT approach. This is the foundation of upcoming data workload pattern designing.

By the end of this chapter, you will be able to understand the need for a Snowflake data platform over traditional or enterprise platforms. You will also be able to set up a trial account for yourself. This trial account will be used to perform various exercises throughout this book. Data Engineering is a key aspect of data platform design and implementation. Chapter 10 covers some of the key features of Snowflake to implement data engineering pipelines. There are two universally used approaches to implement the data engineering aspects, namely **Extract, Transform, and Load (ETL)** and **Extract, Load, and Transform (ELT)**. ETL and ELT are the most common patterns used for data integration and transformation. This chapter covers the two most essential approaches, namely, ETL and ELT, used to design the data processing layer. This also helps to understand the implementation using Snowflake native services and features.

Structure

This chapter consists of the following topics:

- Understanding ETL and ELT

- ETL with Snowflake
- ELT with Snowflake
- ETL versus ELT
- Best practices and recommendations

Objectives

By the end of this chapter, you will be able to understand the ETL and ELT design patterns. You would also be able to learn and implement engineering workloads with Snowflake. This chapter also shares some of the best practices and recommendations to choose one design pattern over another: ETL vs ELT.

Understanding ETL and ELT

ETL is used as part of data integration and data warehousing. This process is used to collect data from heterogeneous sources and transform them on the fly to a consistent process or standards before loading to the target databases for any analytics purpose. The following are the components and processes involved as part of ETL:

- **Extract**: This is the process used to extract or read data from heterogeneous sources. This is also referred to as a process to gather data where data is read from multiple sources, like databases, file systems, APIs, or any other systems.

- **Transform**: This is the next phase in the process, once data is extracted, it undergoes transformations like joining, filtering, aggregations, data quality, or converting data in the required formats before being loaded into the database.

- **Load**: This is the last step in the process, where data is loaded to the target system. The transformed and cleaned data is loaded into the data warehouse or databases. Load may involve indexing or partitioning the data as well. The data loaded is further used to run the analytics, for reporting, or analysis.

There are various tools available in the market that enable users to implement the ETL approach. Informatica, DataStage, Ab-Initio, Pentaho, and a few others are famous ETL tools in the market used to connect to multiple sources, read data, transform on the fly, and load it to the target systems.

In contrast, ELT is an approach that enables users to extract the data and load it to the target system. Transformations are applied on top of the data that is loaded into the database. These transformations leverage the power of the data platform. Data platform capabilities are used to execute the transformations. The following are the processes involved in ELT implementation:

- **Extract**: Extract follows the same process as ETL to export the source data in raw format. ETL tools, libraries, and connectors can be used to extract the data to be loaded to the target systems.

- **Load**: As the name says, data is loaded in the target system in the form of RAW data in the original form and format.

- **Transform**: This is a transformation process to transform and clean data to be maintained in the target system. Data is processed, transformed, and stored to run the analytics, reporting, or analysis. With each transformation step, you can leverage the processing power and capabilities of the target system. In this case, the transformations can be written in the form of SQL or database scripts or any natively supported features like Snowpark, Stored Procedures, streams, tasks, Dynamic tables, etc.

There is also a set of integrators available to be used to implement the ELT approach. dbt can be used to orchestrate and set up the ETL scripts or pipelines to be executed as push-downs to leverage the Snowflake functionalities. In some cases, ETL tools are used to implement the ELT approach, also called push-down optimization. ETL and ELT can be implemented in different ways and can fit into any architectural pattern. In the following section, you will learn more about the implementation of ETL and ELT approaches with Snowflake.

ETL with Snowflake

Integrating data pipelines to connect to various sources using the ETL tool is the easiest to implement. Any ETL tool will have connectors to connect to Snowflake. You can configure the connector to connect to your Snowflake account with the account locator and login details. Some of the well-known ETL tools like Informatica, Pentaho, and DataStage can be configured to connect to Snowflake. Snowflake integrators like Matillion can be used to build ETL pipelines. Refer to *Figure 11.1*, which shares a typical ETL architecture:

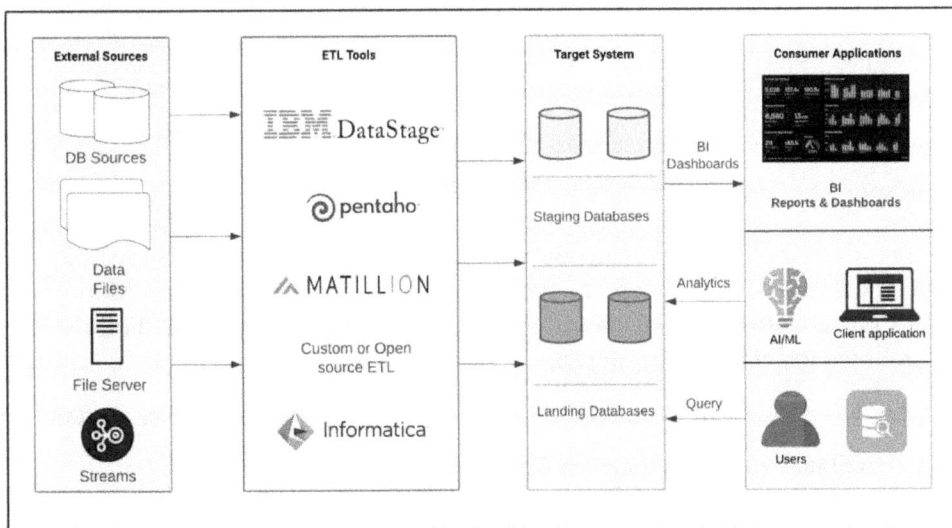

Figure 11.1: ETL reference architecture

As referenced in the ETL architecture, the first layer is sources where heterogeneous sources are mentioned, like files, databases, real-time streams, or databases. The middle layer is ETL, where ETL tools can be used to connect to these heterogeneous sources to pull data. Target systems here are connected and used to load the transformed data. Data analytics is run on top of Snowflake data. ETL plays a role in getting data, transforming it, and storing it in the target system.

Snowflake partner network also lists a bunch of ETL tools available to be used as data integrators. The existing data integrators are dbt, Fivetran, Matillion, Alteryx, Informatica, etc. Refer to *Figure 11.2* which shares the available data integrators:

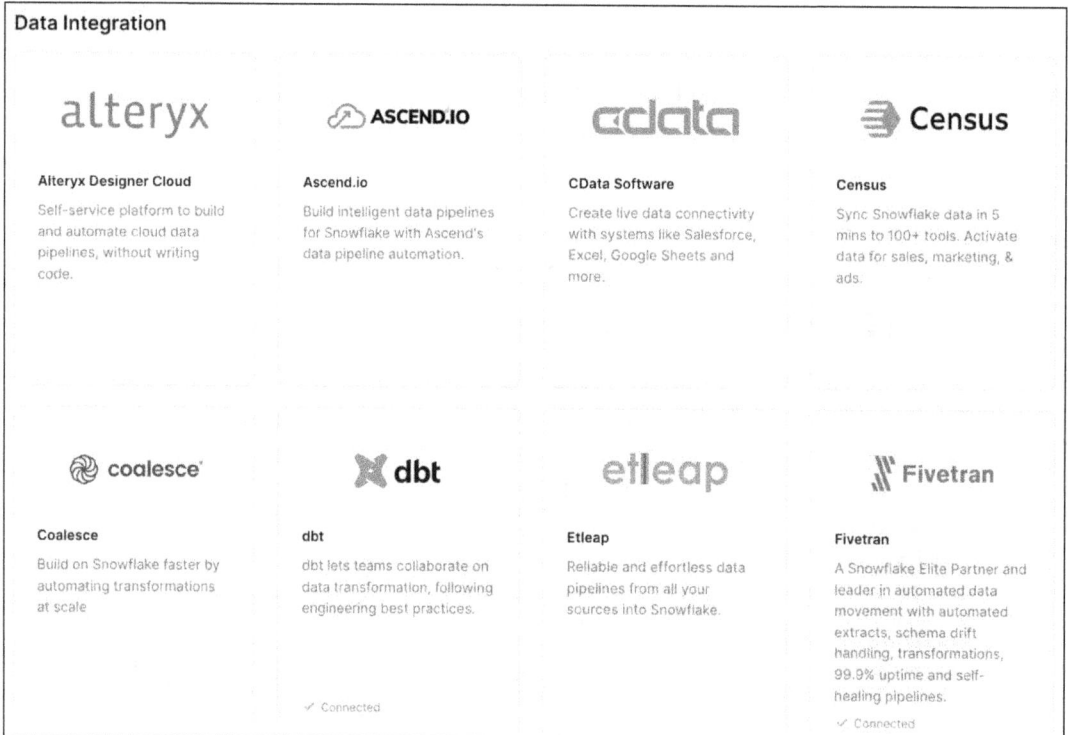

Data Integration

alteryx

Alteryx Designer Cloud

Self-service platform to build and automate cloud data pipelines, without writing code.

ASCEND.IO

Ascend.io

Build intelligent data pipelines for Snowflake with Ascend's data pipeline automation.

cdata

CData Software

Create live data connectivity with systems like Salesforce, Excel, Google Sheets and more.

Census

Census

Sync Snowflake data in 5 mins to 100+ tools. Activate data for sales, marketing, & ads.

coalesce

Coalesce

Build on Snowflake faster by automating transformations at scale

dbt

dbt

dbt lets teams collaborate on data transformation, following engineering best practices.

✓ Connected

etleap

Etleap

Reliable and effortless data pipelines from all your sources into Snowflake.

Fivetran

Fivetran

A Snowflake Elite Partner and leader in automated data movement with automated extracts, schema drift handling, transformations, 99.9% uptime and self-healing pipelines.

✓ Connected

Figure 11.2: Data integrator available with partner network

These integrators are easy to set up with a set of steps to create the Snowflake objects: warehouse, databases, and necessary tables. In this section, let us get a Matillion setup to run a **Proof of Concept (POC)** on integrating and implementing ETL. Follow the steps listed as follows to get Matillion setup:

1. Login to Snowflake as an ACCOUNTADMIN using **https://app.snowflake.com/**

2. Go to **Data Products | Partner Connect**.

3. Search for Data Integration. This page shares a list of available data integrators like dbt, Matillion, Fivetran.

4. Select **Matillion ETL**.

5. This opens a prompt and asks to create the db resources and warehouse required for Matillion. This also creates the partner account automatically. Once it is created, click **Launch** to launch the instance.

This process sets up the instance to be used to create ETL pipelines. Snowflake quickly starts to build a sample pipeline for the given use case. Once the instance is set, you can see it in the partner connect, as shown in *Figure 11.3*:

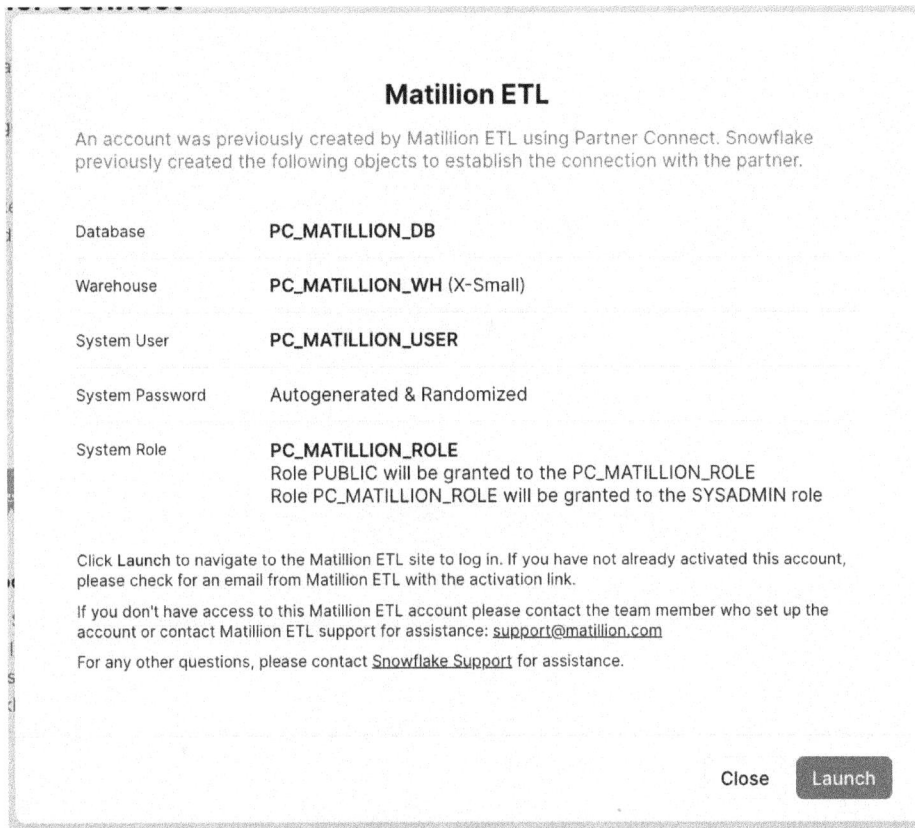

Matillion ETL

An account was previously created by Matillion ETL using Partner Connect. Snowflake previously created the following objects to establish the connection with the partner.

Database	**PC_MATILLION_DB**
Warehouse	**PC_MATILLION_WH** (X-Small)
System User	**PC_MATILLION_USER**
System Password	Autogenerated & Randomized
System Role	**PC_MATILLION_ROLE** Role PUBLIC will be granted to the PC_MATILLION_ROLE Role PC_MATILLION_ROLE will be granted to the SYSADMIN role

Click **Launch** to navigate to the Matillion ETL site to log in. If you have not already activated this account, please check for an email from Matillion ETL with the activation link.

If you don't have access to this Matillion ETL account please contact the team member who set up the account or contact Matillion ETL support for assistance: support@matillion.com

For any other questions, please contact Snowflake Support for assistance.

Close   Launch

Figure 11.3: Data integrator, Matillion

Refer to Snowflake use case to implement ETL quick starts **https://quickstarts.snowflake. com/guide/cloud_native_data_engineering_with_matillion_and_snowflake/index. html?index=..%2F..index#0** to start building a data pipeline using Matillion.

Similarly, Fivetran is another partner integrator widely known and used to set up the extract pipelines. This can be used in integration with dbt to implement the ELT approach. Fivetran is used to extract data, and dbt pipeline can be set to transform the data. In the following section, we will learn the ELT approach with partner integrators as well as Snowflake native integrations.

ELT with Snowflake

ELT can be implemented with partner integrators as well as native features. Refer to *Figure 11.4* which shares a reference architecture to implement the ELT approach. This architecture implementation may contain an additional layer to set up the export or extract process to store data within the storage layer.

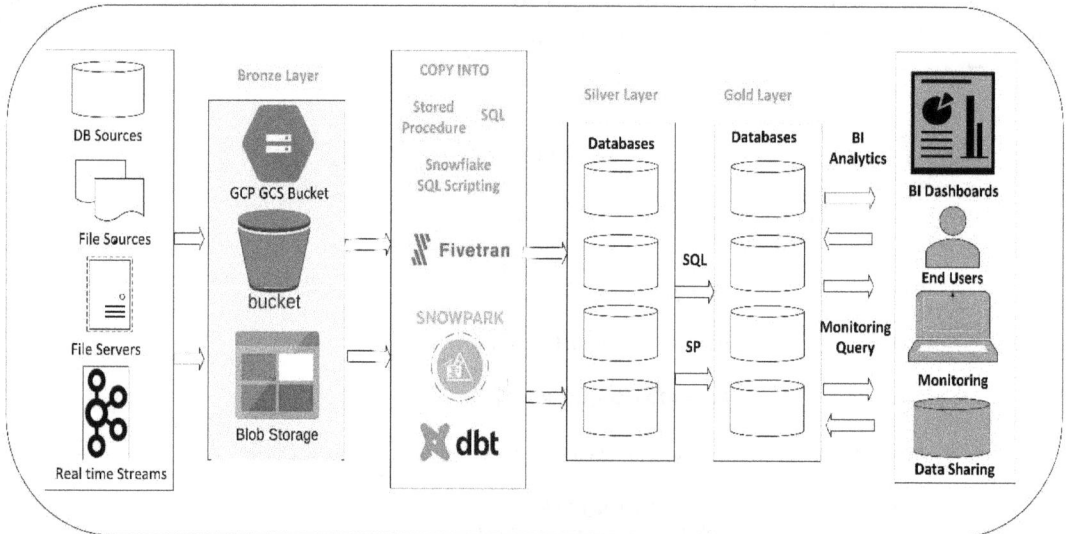

Figure 11.4: ELT reference architecture

As shown in *Figure 11.4*, there are separate extraction and tools used to load data to the landing layer. Source files can be pushed to the cloud storage buckets, and Snowflake native features are used to load data to the landing layer. Data transformations are built using Snowflake scripting and SQL features. Data is processed within the platform and stored in the transformed layer. BI reports and AI/ML use cases are run on top of the Snowflake transformed layer.

Snowflake offers various features and data integrators to implement the ELT approach. The following are the design options that can be considered:

- **Files as the source**: Set up the pipeline to pull files from the source system to cloud storage, or you can have the source files pushed to the storage buckets. These storage buckets can be integrated as external stages to read data.

- **Databases as source**: Setup extract job using ETL or ELT tool to connect and read data to be written to the target tables.

- **Streaming data**: Setup Snowpipe streaming jobs to connect to the streaming source to read data and write it to Snowflake tables. In case of near real-time data loads, Snowpipe can also be used to load data.

- **Data integrators:** Data integrator tools can be used to read files and load data to target tables. Fivetran is one of the tools used to extract the source data and load it into the bucket. Fivetran offers a variety of connectors to connect to diverse sources and allows users to set up data pipelines to export data.

- **Diverse source systems like ServiceNow or any other systems like databases, open-source systems, etc.:** Fivetran can be used to set the export pipelines. You can also use the ETL tool to read data and load it to the database.

Once data is loaded into the database, you can leverage Snowflake SQL features and native offerings to implement data transformations. You can use the following approaches to implement the transformations:

- **SQL**: Data transformations can be implemented using SQL functionalities like functions, stored procedures, and SQL queries set as jobs to be executed.

- **Scripting**: Snowflake scripting can be used to apply data transformations. Snowpark scripting can also be used in the case of ML engineering workloads. You can also set up the scripting jobs in the form of stored procedures and orchestrate them to apply the changes.

- **Snowflake native features**: Snowflake features like streams, tasks, dynamic tables, and materialized views can be used to implement the data changes in the form of transformations and operations.

After data transformations, the data is ready to be used to run any analytical functionality. Data is captured, processed, transformed, and stored for analytical purposes. ETL and ELT approaches can be used and applied to any data platform design. This can be applied to the data warehouse, data lake, data mesh, and any other architecture design pattern of the data platform.

ETL and ELT can be implemented with similar sets of tools and features. There are a few benefits to implementing one over another, which we will explore in the following section.

ETL versus ELT

ETL and ELT are engineering approaches to design and implement engineering pipelines to bring in data to be processed and prepare to run data analytics workloads. These approaches bring in the differences and allow users to compare them on the following aspects:

- **Performance**: This is one the most critical comparison measures to calculate and compare the performance of each approach. This is dependent on the type of approach, tool, compute available, size of the data, and transformations being applied. To compare the performance, you can design and implement the same pipeline to be tested with both approaches. Run them at the same time, same file, same compute, and level of transformations to capture the metrics. Once captured, you can compare the performance and identify the one that fits your existing tech stack or applications.

- **Scalability**: This is another comparison measure where we can evaluate the scalability of the pipelines to scale as per the data volumes. ETL tools can also offer scalability depending on the version and implementation on the cloud or on-premises. ELT with Snowflake native or data integrators enables users to design workloads to run them on Snowflake with *push-down*s to leverage the warehouse and platform capabilities.

- **Cost-efficiency:** This is a crucial aspect of designing the platform and architecting solutions. Often, the organizations run on a fixed set of tech stacks, and if you have the choice to leverage existing tools without adding an additional cost to the stack, then you can use those tools. In case you are open to choosing the stack while designing the Snowflake data platform and setting it up as part of migration, modernization, or from scratch, you can evaluate existing integrators and native services and perform a POC to calculate the cost projections.

- **Optimization**: Optimization is an essential aspect of engineering implementation. This is applicable to the pipelines being designed as well as pipelines that are already running as part of application workloads. Some of the ETL tools offer optimization techniques and best practices for designing the pipelines. However, in some cases, they recommend optimizing using **push-down**, which allows leveraging the power of the platform to optimize the pipelines. In this scenario, this gives benefits like ELT pipelines. ELT allows users to use various techniques offered by data platforms to optimize workloads. You can use native optimization techniques to optimize the engineering workloads.

- **Maintenance**: This is one of the pillars of architectural design applicable to all types of workloads. Users can choose any approach, ETL or ELT; pipelines should be easy to maintain, operate, and run operations once these are live in **Production (PROD)**. Operation ability is dependent on the operational logging and monitoring implemented with ETL or ELT. More standardized pipelines and a generic set of workloads ease the maintenance efforts and avoid additional complexities in managing the workloads.

While you compare the approaches to designing the pipelines, the next important thing to consider is the best practices and recommendations shared by the platform tools or integrators. Every platform or tool has its own limitations as well as preferences. We can understand them to design the workloads in a better fashion. The engineering approach should complement the data platform design instead of being an overhead to maintain the workloads or engineering aspects. The following section will share the best practices of Snowflake to help you design better engineering workloads.

Best practices and recommendations

There is a set of recommendations and best practices to be followed to implement the data engineering pipelines. Snowflake shares the best practices and recommendations for most of its features and enables users to use them effectively. Refer to *Figure 11.5*, which shares an overview of Snowflake native features that can be used as part of ingestion, transformation, and consumer processing:

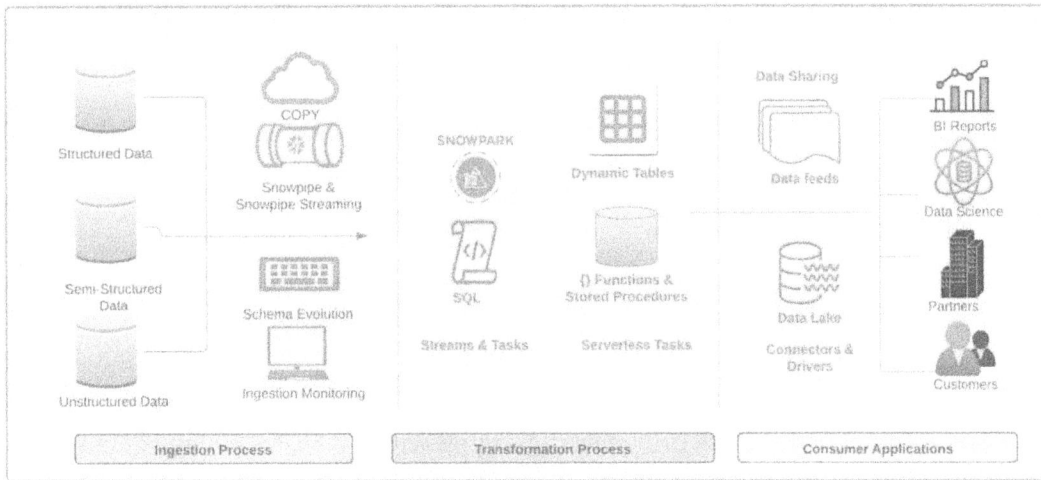

Figure 11.5: Snowflake engineering features

Snowflake's unified features allow users to integrate and implement engineering use cases to process structured, semi-structured, and unstructured data sources. Snowflake recommends using these features and best practices to use them. We have already learnt about the engineering patterns along with Snowflake services and features used to implement them. Refer to some of the best practices to handle data engineering workloads:

- Use the **COPY** command to load data in batches from named stages: internal and external. **COPY** enables users to apply some of the data transformations like casting, column omission, truncating, and re-ordering columns.

- Snowflake recommends loading files with a file size of not more than 5GB. It is recommended to divide larger files into smaller chunks and load these chunks in parallel to achieve better performance.

- **COPY** uses a customer-managed warehouse to execute the load. It is recommended to run the loads with different warehouses and capture the performance to derive the right-sized warehouse for data loads.

- **COPY** options allow users to customize the load by adding file patterns, error handling, allowing data loads with error limits, managing erroneous data files, and deleting files once data is loaded.

- Use Snowpipe to load data in near real-time and automate the data loads using auto-ingest Snowpipe in integration with cloud messaging service. Snowpipe wraps up **COPY** to load data into Snowflake tables.

- For Snowpipe, it is recommended to load files with a size of 10MB on average and a 100 to 250 MB range file size to achieve the best co-performance ratio.

- Data load with a larger file size takes time, and even if a single error is recorded, it can cause an entire load failure. The time taken to process larger files incurs compute cost to process files, though the load failed due to erroneous recording. It is recommended to use **ON_ERROR** while restarting the load to avoid additional costs.

- Recommended to use Snowflake native in integration with partner data integrators to perform ETL and ELT. For example, dbt can be used to orchestrate as well as implement data engineering pipelines.

- Snowflake's unified and extended SQL features enable users to implement error handling and capture using event tables, automate data transformations using Dynamic tables, implement notifications using notification integrations, and integrate with other cloud services with API integrations, etc.

- Recommended the use of dynamic masking with RBAC to manage data security and manage access of the users.

- As best practice to set up the development and test environments use Data cloning to make data available without copying the data and saving additional storage costs.

- It is recommended to consider Snowflake native features, integrators, and integrations to design the data engineering pipelines as part of ETL and ELT. You can choose one of the approaches to implement the engineering use case; however, based on the Snowflake architecture and performance efficiency with scalability, you can prefer to choose ELT over ETL.

- It is recommended to perform a quick POC to evaluate the approach, picking up the design of the engineering pipelines and overall platform architecture. Engineering plays an important role as a building block in designing the data architecture of any platform.

Snowflake shares best practices and recommendations for using most of its services as part of its documentation and resources. You can refer to **https://docs.snowflake.com/en/user-guide/data-load-considerations-prepare** to learn more about considerations to prepare files for data loading.

Conclusion

In this chapter, you have learned about the two most widely used engineering approaches, ETL and ELT. There are various tools, integrators, connectors, drivers, and native features available to implement ETL and ELT with Snowflake. As architects, we can design and choose the appropriate approach to implement data workloads. These workloads cater to the application as well as data needs. Data platforms are designed to source, process, and store data. There are various platform designs like a warehouse, data lake, data mesh, and Lakehouse that enable users to design the data capabilities. Engineering approaches may remain the same when implementing any of the data platform designs. However, the data storage and model may differ based on the platform design. You can also standardize the engineering workloads the same as operational or standard frameworks learned in earlier chapters, like logging, monitoring, error handling, audit control, etc.

The next step is to start designing the data architecture leveraging the various aspects of engineering, standards, and data architecture pillars learned till this chapter. The next series of chapters will guide you to start designing data architecture patterns. In the next chapter you will learn to design the warehouse, understand the capability of the warehouse, and implement the security and workloads leveraging the native features of Snowflake.

Points to remember

The following are some of the key takeaways from this chapter:

- Snowflake partner connect provides data integrators that enable users to integrate with tools like Matillion, Fivetran, dbt and many others to implement ETL as well as ELT.

- You can also leverage the commonly used or known ETL tools like Informatica, DataStage, Pentaho to build data pipelines to load data to Snowflake leveraging the ETL connectors to connect to Snowflake.

- Most of the BI tools in the market are also equipped to connect to Snowflake to run any BI workloads like Tableau, Power BI, etc.

- Recommended to perform a POC to design the pipelines and compare the performance as part of the data platform architecture design and implementations.

- As best practice, users can plan to use Snowflake native features like COPY INTO, Snowpipe, Streams, Tasks, and Dynamic tables to implement the ELT engineering approach.

Join our Discord space

Join our Discord workspace for latest updates, offers, tech happenings around the world, new releases, and sessions with the authors:

https://discord.bpbonline.com

CHAPTER 12
Architecting Data Warehouse

Introduction

Data warehouse (DW) is one of the widely used enterprise data platform architectures. This chapter covers the data warehouse architecture and implementation with Snowflake native services and features. This helps to understand the warehouse architecture, how to design a warehouse, how to share real-time use cases, and the best practices to implement a data warehouse using Snowflake.

This chapter focuses on guiding and sharing the best possible approaches to implementing the data warehouse design. This also shares a commonly used migration and modernization use case with Snowflake and monitors of usage and performance of the platform. This is the first chapter in the next phase of architecture design, where you will learn to design data platform systems.

Structure

This chapter consists of the following topics:

- Data warehousing with Snowflake
- Semi-structured data with Snowflake
- Migrating DW to Snowflake

- Usage and billing of DW
- Best practices and recommendations

Objectives

By the end of this chapter, you will be able to design data warehouse solution with Snowflake. You will also learn to handle structured and semi-structured data with this chapter. This chapter also shares various engineering options that can be considered while building any platform design with Snowflake. This chapter shares the typical migration process, steps, choices of tools, and recommendations for data platform migration.

Data warehousing with Snowflake

Data platform system architecture is designed as per the data needs to store, process, and consume data. Typically, the platforms are widely referred to as transactional and analytical. These are also referred to as **Online Transaction Processing (OLTP)** and **Online Analytical Processing (OLAP)**. OLTP systems deal with transactional operations and data platforms supporting transactional needs, referred to as database systems. These can be implemented by using some of the widely used platforms like Oracle, MySQL, etc. Snowflake also supports transactional processing.

Data warehouses are the systems that support analytical processing and meet the analytical needs of the data. Typically, these systems are used to perform data operations and prepare data to be consumed as part of analytical requirements for decision-making. Data warehouse design supports data integration with multiple sources and aggregates data to be used to provide a historical view of the data. This not only stores large volumes of data but also enables users to process complex queries to access data. In earlier eras with hardware and software procurement, there were multiple challenges to implementing data warehouse systems. Refer to *Figure 12.1*, showing a typical DW architecture that represents a typical data system:

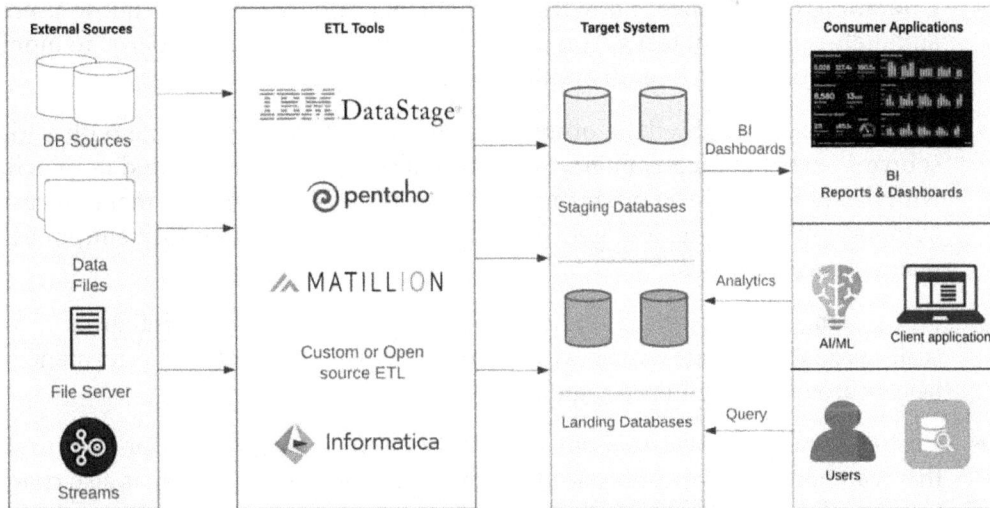

Figure 12.1: Typical DW architecture

These DW systems need to be over-provisioned to accommodate future workloads and data needs. The following were the typical challenges to implementing a data warehouse:

- **Elasticity**: Scaling needs to scale the resources, like computing and storage. This caters to scaling up and down based on the data needs.

- **Diversity**: Data needs to accommodate ever-evolving workloads, and data processing needs and support complex data processing needs.

- **Collaboration**: Sharing data with consumers requires additional data pipelines to maintain data consistency and refresh data shared with consumer teams.

These challenges can be overcome with cloud adoptions. Data implementation, integration, collaboration, and handling diversified data at scale. Cloud adoption allows users to design data platforms with seamless integrations and collaborations. As you learned, Snowflake is data on the cloud and offers features required to implement data warehouse design. This platform allows users to store large data volumes and scale storage irrespective of compute scaling. Snowflake compute provides the capability required to run large and complex queries to process the data. The compute can be scaled on demand to support query processing requirements.

You can refer to the data architecture pillars and tie them up with business requirements to design the data warehouse systems. Snowflake warehouse offers the following features:

- **Scalability**: Snowflake separates computing and storage. Each resource can be scaled up and down without impacting the other. Snowflake warehouses, aka compute resources, can be scaled and resized at any point during data processing. Storage also offers scalability, where storage is expanded based on the data storage requirements to meet growing data needs.

- **Operational excellence:** Snowflake's metadata and usage views allow users to automate operational tasks. You can implement alerts and dashboards to monitor the performance and overall application status.

- **Maintainability**: Snowflake offers diverse integrations to integrate with various source systems and consumers. Snowflake also lets users develop data pipelines with native features and programmatic approaches. One platform makes it easy to automate, standardize, and generalize the processes, which in turn simplifies the maintenance activities.

- **Performance efficiency**: Snowflake's parallel processing in integration with scaling capabilities allows users to implement efficient processes. Performance can be captured and monitored regularly.

- **Cost efficiency**: Snowflake's pay-as-you-use model charges only for the duration that warehouses or compute used to execute data processes. Storage is also charged based on the storage used and data protection used. Credit consumption is calculated based on the usage data available in metadata views. Snowflake offers cost-efficient solutions to implement data warehouse and other data platform solutions.

Snowflake data warehouse solution can be designed in both approaches, namely **Extract, Transform, and Load (ETL)** and **Extract, Load, and Transform (ELT)**. Snowflake's design allows users to implement the following warehouse features:

- **Vs of data**: This is one of the features referred to represent the data qualities like variety, velocity, veracity, value, and volume of the data. A variety of data caters to processing data in the form of structured, semi-structured, and unstructured data. Velocity refers to the data frequency, batch, and streaming loads of the data. Volume caters to the size of the data stored and processed within the data platform. Veracity caters to accuracy and data integrity. As you know, value caters to deriving data decisions and driving value from the data.

- **Supporting multiple languages**: Snowflake supports ANSI SQL standards, Snowflake scripting, and programming drivers and connectors. Users can use their choice of language from JavaScript, Java, Scala, SQL, and Python.

- **Variety of data formats**: Snowflake supports structured and semi-structured data formats like delimited files, CSVs, text files, XML, and JSONs, respectively. Snowflake also extends support to open file formats like ORC, Parquet, and Avro. Users can process any format of the data using Snowflake native features.

- **Extended support to open table formats**: Snowflake integrates with Apache Iceberg to implement open table format. This implementation can be done in two formats of tables, managed and unmanaged tables.

- **Integrations support:** Snowflake offers various integrations to integrate with data sources and data integrators to extract data from sources. Data integrators to implement ETL and ELT designs.

These data warehouse patterns can be implemented with various options depending on the business and application requirements. This section shares one of the use cases and design approaches to implement a data warehouse with Snowflake native features. Refer to *Figure 12.2*, which shares the data warehouse design approach:

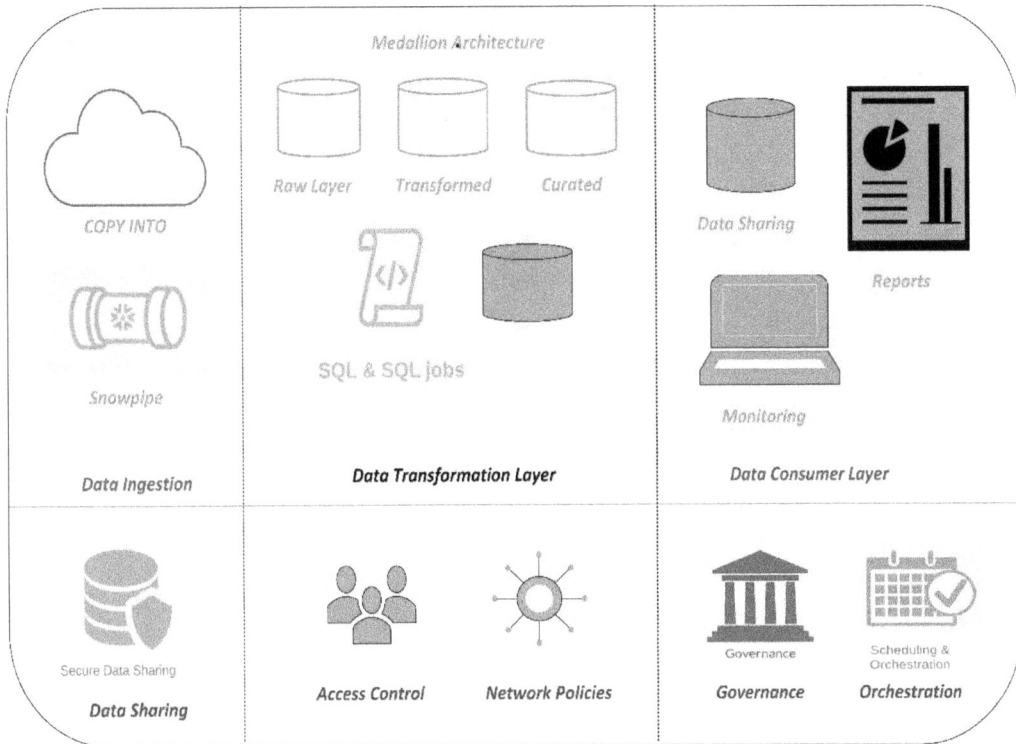

Figure 12.2: DW design solution

The following are the key features of data warehouse architecture:

- **Data source integrations**: Integrating with sources using data integrators.

- **Data processing**: Processing using Snowflake native SQL and Scripting.

- **Data layers**: Data is stored and processed within the data platform across data layers: Raw layer, transformed layer, and curated layer.

- **Data analytics**: Data analytics with BI tools and Snowflake native integrations to run data analytics.

Data engineering design is key when designing a warehouse platform. Data processing is defined and bucketed in the warehouse processing as follows:

- **Data ingestions**: Snowflake native features are used to load data into the raw layer.

- Source files from storage are integrated as an external stage and loaded to the raw layer with **COPY INTO**.

- Data loads are streamed using Snowpipe and automated using AWS SQS and SNS service.

- **Data processing**: Snowflake SQL objects and processes are used to load source data, as it is in raw format, to the raw layer. Once data is loaded to Raw, process it using SQL and stored procedures.

- **Raw loads**: Using **COPY INTO** and Snowpipe, the data is loaded to the raw tables in the raw database.

- **Transformed layer**: Setting up the following processes to process and transform data from the raw layer to the transformed layer. Intermediate data processing layer with transient, temporary, and permanent tables.

- **Change Data Capture (CDC)**: Implementing **Slowly Changing Dimensions (SCD)** Type II using Snowflake SQL **MERGE** command.

- **Data Quality checks (DQ)**: Automating the data checks using Snowflake stored procedures.

- **Data governance**: Data masking and implementing role-based masking to protect data from unauthorized access.

- **Data security:** Setting up network policies to whitelist IP addresses of the team connecting to the Snowflake account.

- **Data transformations**: Using Snowflake SQL and stored procedures to transform the data, implement data enrichment processes to prepare data for the curated layer.

- **Standard processes**: As you learned in *Chapter 9, Designing Data Solutions*, there are sets of standard processes to be implemented. Snowflake objects and integrations are used to implement error handling with notification integrations, monitoring warehouse usage with resource monitors.

- **Data curation layer**: Setting up views, materialized views, and tables to store the data in the curated layer. Data from this layer is used to run analytics.

- **Data aggregation**: Using Snowflake objects to set up the views for data analytics.

- **Scheduling and orchestration**: This is the top layer used to orchestrate the data pipelines and set the dependencies across data pipelines. Orchestration and scheduling can be implemented using airflow, astronomer, and Snowflake tasks for internal processes.

Now, we have learned the data warehouse architecture design, implementation strategy, and processes. You can refer to the previous chapters for sample loading, processing, and implementation of the standard process. You can also refer to the appendix for references and sample code snippets. The next section shares the processes used to handle semi-structured data and processing with Snowflake.

Semi-structured data with Snowflake

Snowflake offers **VARIANT** data types to store and process semi-structured data. Semi-structured data can be referenced as data stored in JSON or XML formats. **VARIANT** stores each row in one or multiple columns from the dataset and allows users to query the data with corresponding indexes and keys. You can also use **VARIANT** to store open format files like Avro, ORC, and Parquet. In this section, you will learn to load and process data using **VARIANT** followed by best practices and limitations of **VARIANT**.

Snowflake also supports **ARRAY** and **OBJECT** data types that allow users to load key-value pairs of the data, array format of the data, and hierarchical data.

Loading semi-structured data

You can use the **COPY INTO** command to load semi-structured data into the **VARIANT** column. **VARIANT** can store up to 16MB of data, and you can load data in one or more columns depending on the data format and size of the data. Refer to the following considerations while loading semi-structured data:

- If the data is in the form of key-value pairs, then the data can be loaded in column type of **OBJECT**.

- If the data is in the array format, then load the data to the **ARRAY** type column.

- Hierarchical data can be loaded by storing data in one or multiple columns:

    o Split the data into multiple columns by extracting and transforming the data columns into separate columns.

    o Snowflake can also run auto-detect to detect the schema and store the data in native tables, external tables, or views. Auto-detect enables users to store the data without defining the data format or type.

    o Store the data in the **SINGLE** column by explicitly specifying the data format and type. If you do not specify the format, Snowflake auto-detects to load into **VARIANT**, **ARRAY**, and **OBJECT** columns.

- With the preceding considerations, you can load semi-structured data using **COPY INTO** or **PARSE_JSON** commands. Refer to the following options to load semi-structured data:

    o Using **COPY INTO <table>** and specifying the format of the data feed. Define the table name, column, and data type while defining the **COPY** statement. Specify the file format or type of the format with **TYPE = <data_format>**:

```
/* LOAD using COPY INTO */
/* set context */
USE DATABASE DEMO_POC_DB;
USE SCHEMA POC;
/* define table DDL */
CREATE TABLE membership_info(info_variant_column VARIANT);
/* COPY INTO table */
COPY INTO membership_info
FROM @load_ext_stage/dataloading/members.json.gz
FILE_FORMAT = (TYPE = 'JSON')
;
```

Here, the column is defined explicitly to be a **VARIANT** data type, and the file format is also specified to JSON to identify the file type.

o   Create a file format for JSON files and use this to define an internal stage. Upload data files to the internal stage and load data to the target table:

```
/* Define JSON format to strips the outer array. */
CREATE OR REPLACE FILE FORMAT json_file_format
   TYPE = 'JSON'
   STRIP_OUTER_ARRAY = TRUE;

/* Define a stage with defined file format */
CREATE OR REPLACE STAGE data_load_stage
   FILE_FORMAT = json_format;

/* Copy load files to the stage */
PUT file:///load/members.json @data_load_stage AUTO_
COMPRESS=TRUE;

/* Load table for the JSON data. */
CREATE OR REPLACE TABLE membership(details VARIANT);

/* Load JSON data files into defined table. */
COPY INTO membership
   FROM @data_load_stage/members.json.gz;

/*select from table to view data loaded */
SELECT * FROM membership;
```

Here, a file format is defined and created in an internal stage. Files are uploaded to an internal stage to be loaded using the **COPY** command. Refer to the following sample records stored as sample data for JSON files:

```
/* sample JSON format records */
{
```

```
      "type": "Lifetime",
      "location": {
        "city": "North York",
        "zip": "140503"
      },
      "price": "999",
      "purchase_date": "2024-02-16",
      "members": "04"
    }
    {
      "type": "Short-term" ,
      "location": {
        "city": "Toronto",
        "zip": "194278"
      },
      "price": "99",
      "Purchase_date": "2024-04-02",
      "members": "02"
    }
    {
      "type": "Temporary" ,
      "location": {
        "city": "Winchester",
        "zip": "091420"
      },
      "price": "19",
      "Purchase_date": "2024-03-01",
      "members": "02"
    }
```

Semi-structured data can be loaded using **COPY** and **FILE FORMAT**. You can also load the data using **PARSE_JSON**.

o Specifying the input data format and data type by using data conversions with appropriate functions. Use the **PARSE_JSON** function to convert data to be loaded into a **VARIANT** column. The following is a sample load command used to insert data into a table using **PARSE_JSON**:

```
/* load using PARSE_JSON */
INSERT INTO membership(members) SELECT PARSE_JSON('{...}');
```

Data can be loaded with auto-detected schema as well as with defined file formats and data types. Like data loading, data can also be imported into these data formats. The following section covers the data unloading to semi-structured data formats.

Unloading data to semi-structured data

As you know, data unloading can be implemented using **COPY INTO**. Data can be loaded in structured and semi-structured data formats. Snowflake extended function, **OBJECT_CONSTRUCT** can be used to parse the relational table to JSON file format. This function converts each row of a table to the single **VARIANT** column. The following is the example used to export data:

```
/* copy command to unload data in JSON format */
COPY INTO @external_stage
FROM
(
SELECT OBJECT_CONSTRUCT('emp_id', eid, 'first_name', employee_fname,
'last_name', employee_lname, 'Location', city, 'Dateofjoining', DOJ,
'Status',status)
FROM employees
)
FILE_FORMAT = (TYPE = JSON);
```

As you observe here, the data is exported to an external stage, and relational data is converted to JSON format. Refer to the following sample records exported to the JSON file:

```
/*export create files on external stage */
/* File exported with data_0_0_0.json.gz in the stage */
{"emp_id":"123456","employee_fname":"Aryan","employee_lname":"Singh","Locat
ion":"Toronto","Dateofjoining":"2020-04-01","status":"Active"}
{"emp_id":"671260","employee_fname":"Andrew","employee_lname":"Jacob","Loca
tion":"Vancouver","Dateofjoining":"2002-03-10","status":"Active"}
```

Now, you have learned data loading and unloading for semi-structured data. You can also query the semi-structured data using a **SELECT** query. The following section covers the details of accessing and querying semi-structured data.

Accessing semi-structured data

As you know, the data can be stored in the form of **ARRAY**, **OBJECT**, and **VARIANT** data types. Data access queries are based on the data types and data formats. The following are the ways data can be accessed, along with reference queries:

- **Accessing data stored in ARRAY format**: **ARRAY** stores one type of data format and data type. The first element is referenced as 0, and the rest are all accessed with an INDEX number:

  ```
  /*sample SELECT query to access data stored in ARRAY format in a
  table */
  select acc_info[2] from accounts;
  ```

As you observe, the index here reads the data from an element present in the second place.

- **Accessing data in OBJECT format: OBJECT** can store data in the form of key pairs. **OBJECT** data can be accessed with the key name as follows:

```
/* query OBJECT format */
select customer_info['customer_id'] from customer;
```

Data can be accessed using key columns and retrieved data from the table. **SELECT** can be used with key columns to access data.

- **Access data in VARIANT format**: **VARIANT** data can be accessed with an element name and colon (:). Hierarchical data can also be used with the column name and first-level element. Refer to the following sample SQL that reads data from a **VARIANT** data type:

```
/* select data from VARIANT by accessing data with colon*/
SELECT brand:outlets
    FROM sales
    ORDER BY 1;

/* query result */
+--------------------------+
| SRC:DEALERSHIP           |
|--------------------------|
| "Macys"          |
| "HandM" |
+--------------------------+
```

Data can also be used with colon, dot, and bracket notifications. Each of these works is to scan and access the data from the **VARIANT** column.

Note: In any type of notation being used to access the data, the column name is case-insensitive. However, the element name is case-sensitive. Element names should follow the same naming convention and case as defined in table DDL.

In this section, you have learned to load, process, store, and access semi-structured data. Snowflake native features allow users to handle semi-structured data as well as open file formats like Avro, ORC, and Parquet. One of the typical use cases of data warehousing is the migration use case. You will learn about migration use cases and features used to migrate the data warehouse to Snowflake in the following section.

Migrating DW to Snowflake

Data and application migration is a process that involves multiple phases. There are two types of use cases: migration and modernization. Both processes involve five phases, as shown in *Figure 12.3*:

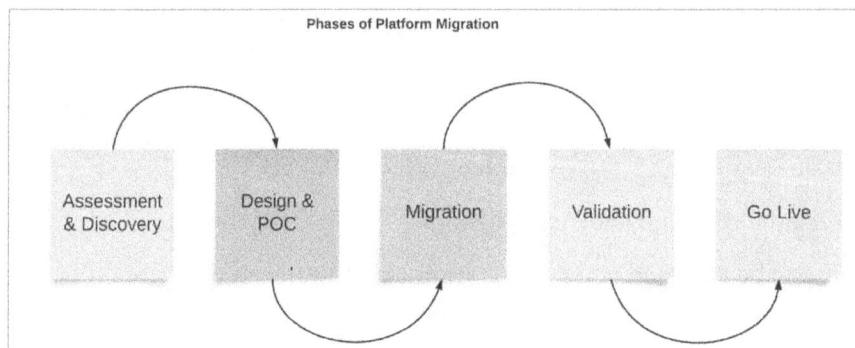

Figure 12.3: Migration phases

As you observe here, these five phases cater to migration requirements. Refer to the following details of each phase:

- **Assessment and discovery**: This is the very first step to initiate the migration journey. In this phase, an assessment of the existing platform is initiated to capture the details of data stored and processed, pipelines, and applications running on the platform. Discovery is part of the process where we typically gather information on data and engineering applications to prioritize the application migration.

- **Design and Proof Of Concept (POC)**: This is the next step where we work on the target design of the platform based on the discovery observations and considerations. A quick POC is performed to evaluate the target platform features. Develop a pilot application to test the platform's capabilities.

- **Migration**: This is the phase where actual data is migrated from the existing platform to the target platform. Identified applications and processes are migrated as per the priority and dependencies identified in earlier phases. Migration is never a big-bang approach and follows the agile method to build applications in phases.

- **Validation**: This is the next phase of migration, where data and processes migrated are validated. Data is validated post-historical migration to the target platform. Application pipelines and data processed as part of an application are validated to ensure the data matches with the source platform.

- **Go live**: This is the last phase of migration, where applications are staged and moved to the production environment. All converted and migrated applications are deployed in production and validated. Once processes are validated in production, then the Go Live date is planned. There can be various approaches to launch apps and processes as part of Go Live. In some cases, we prefer to implement and open for user testing as part of the soft launch, followed by going live based on user acceptance and business sign-off.

These phases are followed as part of data and platform migration. In the following section, let us understand the Snowflake migration considerations, guidelines, and benefits.

Reasons to migrate to Snowflake

Snowflake is data on the cloud with numerous benefits. Snowflake is not just a data platform, as this offers solutions to multiple workloads under one roof. This platform offers the following capabilities:

- Scalable computing and storage.

- Data processing with support to multiple languages, such as SQL, Python, Java, etc.

- Extended support to the data formats, such as open-source formats and open-table format.

- Support to AI and ML workloads and model implementations.

- Extended support to LLM capabilities with Snowflake Cortex.

- Support to all types of data platform patterns, data warehouse, data lake, data mesh, and data fabric.

- Native apps and Snowflake container service enable users to implement customized and containerized applications on Snowflake.

- Fully managed and cost-efficient platform.

- Data sharing and marketplace offerings.

- Near zero maintenance.

- Snowflake's ongoing enhancements and latest releases regularly enhance the platform. The preceding are just a few of the top features and reasons to migrate to Snowflake.

Snowflake also offers Snowconvert, a code conversion tool that helps users to migrate their existing workloads quickly and hassle-free to the Snowflake platform. Snowconvert has recently been made **generally available** (**GA**) to all users. We can now download Snowconvert and set it up to convert Data models, transformation jobs, scripts, and SQLs to Snowflake native. This tool currently supports Teradata, Oracle, SQL Server, and Azure Synpase migration to Snowflake. Refer to the following steps to start with Snowconvert:

1. Download Snowconvert from **https://docs.snowconvert.com/sc/general/getting-started/download-and-access**

2. Install Snowconvert tool from **https://docs.snowconvert.com/sc/general/user-guide/snowconvert/how-to-install-the-tool**

3. Understand the data migration considerations and supported features as part of automated conversions: **https://docs.snowconvert.com/sc/translation-references/translation-reference/data-migration-considerations**

4. Refer to the SQL translation guide to transform data types, data models, SQLs, native functions, built-in functions: **https://docs.snowconvert.com/sc/translation-references/translation-reference/sql-translation-reference**

Using Snowconvert can reduce considerable time to evaluate platform competencies as part of the assessment and initial POCs. Perform quick POCs to test the conversions and prepare estimations required to migrate data models, data workloads, and processes to the Snowflake platform.

Snowflake is relentlessly working on improving platform capabilities, enhancing features to support ever-evolving data use cases and needs. Snowflake offers simplified solutions to implement the most critical pillars of data platform design. Users can focus on solutions over infrastructure, maintenance, and management overhead. Refer to the following summary of design pillars and Snowflake offerings:

- **Data governance:** Easy RBAC controls to standardize, generalize, and automate users and objects management. Network policies and rules to protect platform accessibility. **Multi-factor authentication** (**MFA**) and federated authentication allow users to integrate connectivity and set up secure connections to the platform. Standard DQ functions with **data metric functions** (**DMF**) simplify DQ and data integrity checks. Dynamic masking allows the setup of tag-based as well as role-based masking policies to protect unwanted data access. Snowflake's built-in data lineage enables users to debug data from source to target easily.

- **Data engineering:** Simple yet powerful built-in features and services that cater to ELT workloads and easy maintenance. Storage, APIs, and notification integrations enable users to simplify integrations and use them as part of engineering processes. Dynamic tables are now in GA, which simplifies additional overhead to maintain engineering orchestration and pipelines for regular workloads. We have learnt various choices in *Chapter 10, Designing Data Engineering Pipelines.*

- **Data models and support to varying data**: Snowflake supports structured and semi-structured data. The platform also offers support to unstructured data in the form of directory tables and integration with OCR and Document AI for file processing. Recently, processing Word documents, presentation files (PPTx), and PDFs has been added to the document processing in preview. Snowflake supports Snowflake and Data Vault schema implementations. Users can control the data model designs and implementations with Snowflake's native capabilities.

- **Data platform maintenance and monitoring:** Snowflake maintains the platform infrastructure automatically. Users can manage required compute and storage on demand based on the workloads. Snowflake shares the USAGE schema with a bunch of metadata views that share usage details of Snowflake services and features. Automated tracking, monitoring, and implementing controls are easy with these USAGE views. You can refer to the following sections to implement monitoring dashboards and notifications.

Snowflake's ease of use and maintenance make it stand out in the world of ever-growing data and platform offerings. It takes no time to set up a Snowflake account and onboard workloads. Refer to the following sections that share the migration considerations and one use case of migration.

Migration considerations

There are several things to consider while choosing the migration path. If you are analyzing the data and pipelines for migration, then you need to review the following questions:

- **Workload analysis**: Analyze the workloads and data with the following questions:
    o How many processes and workloads can be migrated to Snowflake with minimal effort?

    o What processes are currently having issues and may benefit from the re-engineering approach?

    o Are there any workloads that are outdated and need to be redefined?

    o Do you have any future workloads planned for the target system? Would you like to add any future processes to the platform?

- **Data migration analysis**: Data migration is the most critical part of any migration. Data can be migrated as bulk transfer or follow a staged approach. The following is the set of considerations:
    o Bulk data transfer can be considered based on the data properties as follows:
        - Data is independent and has stand-alone data marts.

        - Well-designed processes and data with ANSI SQL standard.

        - Highly integrated data across the platform.

        - When you need to migrate from legacy systems quickly.

    o Staged data transfer can be considered based on the data properties as follows:
        - Existing warehouse with independent data marks and data applications that can be moved independently.

        - Any non-performing processes that need to be redefined and re-engineered.

        - Any new requirements cannot be addressed with legacy or existing platforms.

        - Upcoming changes to the existing platform to integrate new data, BI, and reporting needs.

The preceding are the considerations to evaluate the existing platform and design the target system architecture. Next, you will learn the migration use case and steps to migrate the Teradata platform to Snowflake.

Teradata to Snowflake migration use case

Teradata is a massively parallel processing data system that is widely used to implement enterprise data warehouse systems. Teradata is typically used to implement data platforms across domains like retail, banking, health care, entertainment, and many more. Teradata Vantage is Teradata's cloud solution used to implement DW that may address some of the challenges of typical DW systems. Snowflake is considered one of the best possible solutions to replace legacy data systems to achieve elasticity and performance efficiency. Snowflake offers features of OLTP as well as OLAP. Snowflake's parallel processing allows users to optimize workloads to achieve performance and cost efficiency. As you are aware, the data migration process follows a set of steps. The following are the steps and considerations for Teradata to Snowflake migration:

- **Data model migration**: Data model conversion is the very first step of data migration. If the existing platform uses a data modeling tool, then the same can be used to generate DDL scripts. Remember some of the Teradata-specific objects and DDL statements that are not supported in Snowflake. If there are no existing tools and scripts, then you can create new scripts. Remember the data types and object changes to be made to support the implementation of Snowflake.

- **Migrating existing data**: Once DDL scripts are ready, deploy them on the Snowflake platform to set up the data model. The next step is to migrate data from Teradata to the Snowflake platform. Teradata stores data in its supported format, and data needs to be exported using an ETL tool, third-party data migration tools, or custom manual scripts to export and load data. Teradata native utility TPT can be used to export the data from Teradata and push it to cloud storage. The exported data can be loaded to Snowflake using the COPY command.

- **Migrating existing workloads**: Data is migrated to Snowflake as part of the historical load. You can start working on the workload and query migration to Snowflake. As you know, both the data platforms support ANSI SQL standards, hence, the SQL scripts can be converted with minimal changes to make them run on Snowflake. If there are any ETL tools being used in the existing platform, then you can change the target connections and definitions to load data to Snowflake. Any third-party tools that can be converted to change the connection to Snowflake and can continue to be used as the target architecture. Any other Teradata native utilities can also be converted to equivalent Snowflake scripts. You can also use any supported tools for conversions.

- **Production and cutover**: Once data is migrated and workloads are converted to be executed on Snowflake. The following are the fundamental steps to be considered for production and going live:

o   Migrate historical data to Snowflake.

o   Set up and implement ongoing data catch-ups for incremental data loads.

o   Migrate, convert, and re-engineer workloads to run them on Snowflake.

o   Plan for cutover and inform all teams using the platform.

o   Run both platforms in parallel to validate the data and processes migrated.

o   Define the validation cycles to validate the data and processes between the two platforms.

o   Once data is validated, processes are tested and signed off by business users, then plan to go live.

o   Cut over the consumer applications to Snowflake and turn off the existing Teradata platform.

This is the most widely and commonly adopted use case to migrate data platforms from Teradata to Snowflake. Once the data platform is migrated the next critical part of the migration is to calculate the overall usage of the platform and monitor the Snowflake resources. You will learn to manage and monitor the billing and usage in the following section.

Usage and billing of data warehouse

Snowflake offers metadata views that capture the usages of Snowflake resources like warehouses, storage, Snowflake pipelines, queries, and serverless tasks. You have learned the utilization queries, monitoring, and optimizing them with *Chapter 6, Evaluating and Optimizing Snowflake's Performance,* and *Chapter 7, Unlocking Snowflake's Cost and Performance*. In this section, you will learn to use usage views to monitor the performance of the data warehouse.

This section shares some of the common use cases to implement billing and usage. There is a set of queries and options used to set up the monitoring and alerting:

- **Usage queries**: As we have learned, Snowflake metadata views are used to generate metrics and queries. The following are some of the reference queries:

  o   **Credit consumption for warehouse:** Use the following query to get warehouse consumption:

  ```
  /* credits used for warehouse without date filter*/
  SELECT warehouse_name as warehouse_name,
    SUM(credits_used_compute) AS credits_consumed
  FROM snowflake.account_usage.warehouse_metering_history
  GROUP BY 1
  ORDER BY 2 DESC;

  /* filter credit consumption on date */
  ```

```
SELECT warehouse_name as warehouse_name,
  SUM(credits_used_compute) AS credits_consumed
FROM snowflake.account_usage.warehouse_metering_history
WHERE start_time >= current_time()
GROUP BY 1
ORDER BY 2 DESC;
```

- o **Storage cost:** Use the following query to get storage details:

```
select date_trunc(month, usage_date) as usage_month
  , avg(storage_bytes + stage_bytes + failsafe_bytes) /
power(1024, 4) as billable_tb
from storage_usage
group by 1
order by 1;
```

The preceding is just a sample of queries used for usage tracking. Once you have defined the usage metrics, set up the alerts and monitoring.

- **Usage monitoring**: As you know, Snowsight can be used to develop dashboards to visualize usage. Snowsight is Snowflake's advanced UI with capabilities to build intuitive dashboards. Refer to *Chapter 7, Unlocking Snowflake's Cost and Performance* to implement Snowsight dashboards. *Figure 12.4* is a sample Snowsight dashboard that shares a view of computing and storage utilization:

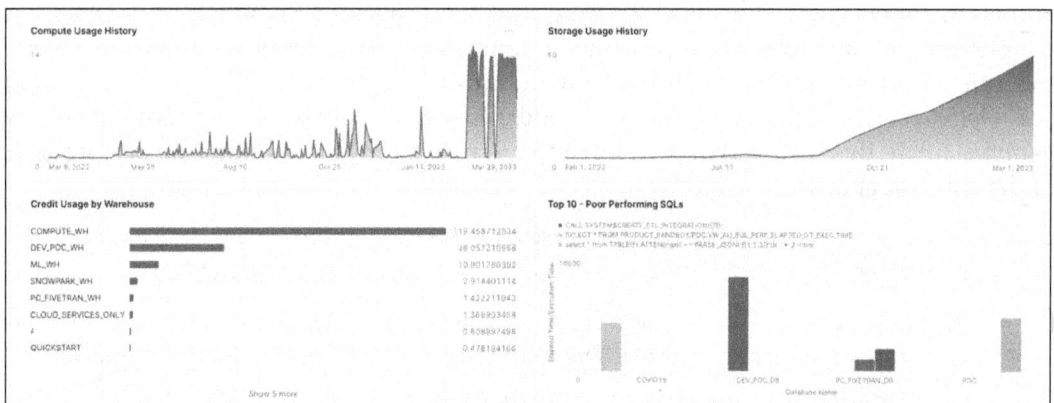

Figure 12.4: Snowsight dashboard

Snowsight dashboards can be shared with users for actions and tracking.

- **Usage alerting**: Snowflake resource monitoring and budgets are used to set up the threshold of the amount spent. Resource monitors are used to monitor and take action on warehouse spend. Budgets are used to set the limit on spending and set up notifications for it. Snowsight can be used to set up the budget. The following are examples of resource monitors:

```
/* create resource monitor */
USE ROLE ACCOUNTADMIN;

CREATE OR REPLACE RESOURCE MONITOR account_warehouse WITH CREDIT_
QUOTA=1000
TRIGGERS ON 100 PERCENT DO SUSPEND;
/* assign resource monitor to warehouse */
ALTER WAREHOUSE dev_poc_wh SET RESOURCE_MONITOR = account_warehouse;
```

- **Using Snowsight budget**: Change the role to **ACCOUNTADMIN** and navigate to **Admin** | **Cost Management** | **Budgets** to set up the budget limit. Refer to *Figure 12.5*, which shows the Snowsight page of the budget:

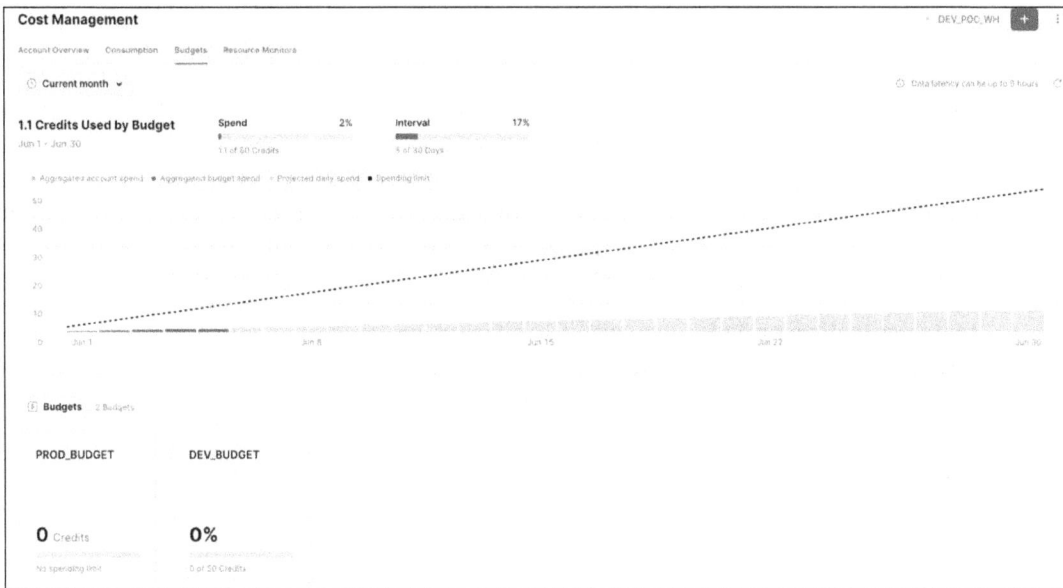

Figure 12.5: Snowsight budgets view

Snowsight cost management navigation gives a consolidated view of the cost spent on computing, storage, resource monitors, and consumption. You can follow the preceding steps to set up the monitoring of cost and overall usage. The next critical aspect of the designing platform is to understand the best practices and recommendations of the platform. The following section shares Snowflake's best practices and recommendations for implementing data warehouse systems.

Best practices and recommendations

Snowflake offers scalable, cost-effective, and performance-efficient solutions to implement data design patterns. This section shares some of the top best practices and recommendations to implement Snowflake data warehouse systems.

Best practices

Based on the Snowflake native features and capabilities of the platform, Snowflake shares some best practices and recommendations. The best practices are listed as follows:

- **Snowflake bulk data ingestion**: As part of the bulk data loads, use the **COPY** to get the data in raw format to staging or raw layer tables in Snowflake. One of the best practices as part of data ingestion is staging the data on named stages: external or internal stage.

- **Data storage**: Snowflake native tables store data and cater to the overall storage cost of the platform. As a best practice, loading the active or hot data is beneficial. As part of this implementation, bucket your data into hot, warm, and cold datasets. Hot data is frequently used data, and warm data is a moderately referenced and used dataset. Data that is not accessed often, however, needs to be maintained for historical references and can be categorized as cold data. You can plan to load hot data and the required dataset from warm data to Snowflake native tables. Next, you can set up the external tables to reference data from cold and warm data buckets based on their frequency of access and volume. Typically, an archival process can be set up to move the data from the native table to external stages or internal stages as part of the archival process to reduce the storage cost.

- **Data protection and storage cost**: Time-travel and Failsafe are used to protect data loss and recover data if needed. While we implement these features, this adds to the storage cost bucket. As design advice, it advised understanding the data and requirements to set up the time travel to avoid any additional storage cost. Plan to use transient tables as part of data processing, where data may not be required to persist for a longer duration.

- **Compute setup**: As you know, Snowflake warehouses, i.e., compute can be set up based on the application processes and requirements to set up the data workloads. You can plan and design to separate the compute allocated for data loading and data processing. Data loading compute may undergo resizing, and data processing needs auto scaling with clustered warehouses. Run the workloads with small to moderate sizes and monitor the performance before moving the workloads onto higher sizes.

- **Data pipelines**: There are two widely known approaches to implementing data workloads, ETL or ELT. As a best practice, you can plan to implement the data workloads and design pipelines in an ELT way. The ELT approach enables users to utilize the power of the platform and optimize workloads.

- **Observability design**: Snowflake offers a variety of metadata information that can be leveraged to design various metrics and measures to implement data observability. As part of the design best practice, implement resource monitoring, and set up the automated alerting, reporting, and stored procedures to push out required alerts to avoid any additional storage and compute costs.

These are some of the best practices based on the platform feature categories and widely used features. There are a few specific recommendations by Snowflake for choosing services and features over others. The following section shares some of the recommendations from Snowflake.

Recommendations

Snowflake is a platform rich in native features and integrations. This is not just a data platform, this is a platform that caters to all types of data patterns, workloads, AI workloads, and native apps with Snowflake container service. The following are some of the widely used recommendations:

- **Loading recommendations**: Snowflake recommends loading data in smaller batches and provides sizing recommendations to load data files with 100MB to 250MB. This will help to achieve parallel loads. Loading bigger files is not recommended. In case of bigger files, split them into smaller files and load them to the Snowflake table. The same is recommended even for Snowpipe data loading.

- **Load history monitoring**: Recommended to use Copy history to visualize the data loaded. Typically, the default history of seven days is shared for the data loads.

- **Streaming data load recommendations**: Snowflake recommends calling the API with Snowpipe Streaming clients to write more data per second. The client cost is charged only for the active clients. Snowpipe streaming opens multiple channels to send the data. However, the client can be used accordingly to control the cost. To reduce the lag in the streaming loads, it is recommended to use `MAX_CLIENT_LAG` to manage data flush latency.

- **Access control recommendations**: Snowflake recommends implementing **Role Based Access Control (RBAC)** and accessing the least granted privileges to the objects and users. Define the roles required for users and application groups. Grant only required permissions to the Snowflake resources.

- **Data unloading recommendations**: Recommended to use unloading when the data archival or data feeds are required to be shared with consumer applications and users. Unload only the required data and use `COPY` features to provide extensive file properties to manage exported datasets.

- **Snowflake cost recommendations**: Snowflake recommends implementing timely reports, alerting, and monitoring to identify any unattended resources that may end up with additional costs. Resource monitors are recommended to keep a tab on warehouse utilization across accounts within an organization.

These are some of the top recommendations shared by Snowflake. These can be used in consideration while designing data warehouse systems and engineering approaches. Snowflake platform is used to design, integrate, and implement data warehouse systems to address the data needs and applications.

Conclusion

In this chapter, you have learned about data warehouse systems. You learned the challenges with older data systems and how cloud adoption is helping to overcome the traditional challenges. You have also learned to design the data warehouse system using Snowflake native features and offerings.

A data warehouse is a data design pattern that allows users to address the challenges of storing, processing, and transforming data with traditional platforms. With this chapter, you have learned to design the data warehouse system and semi-structured data processing. This chapter also shared the engineering options to address data ingestion, data processing, and data transformation pipelines. Snowflake offers a variety of engineering options to implement engineering pipelines. Some of these pipelines may remain the same across data platform designs.

The next design pattern is a data lake, and the upcoming chapter shares details of the design, engineering approach, and pipeline design options to start designing the data lake leveraging Snowflake native features. The next chapter focuses on the data lake design with security, data governance, and programmatic implementation of data pipelines.

Points to remember

This chapter shares the following key takeaways:

- There can be various limitations with traditional warehouse systems, and the most critical limitations include elasticity, availability, operations, performance efficiency, and maintainability.

- Snowflake can process a variety of data and supports structured as well as semi-structured data feeds. Snowflake also supports open file formats like Avro, ORC, and Parquet data feeds.

- Snowflake VARIANT, OBJECT, and ARRAY data types are used to store, process, and implement semi-structured data feeds.

- Snowflake recommends implementing cost and usage monitoring. You can use Snowsight, Snowflake metadata information, and notifications to share the alert with users.

- Recommended to implement the ELT approach to design data warehouse pipelines and leverage Snowflake native features to optimize the workloads.

- As best practice, users can use Snowflake native features to build engineering approaches and design data warehouse systems. Data load unloads, performance, cost, and optimization techniques to design efficient systems.

CHAPTER 13
Implementing Data Lake Solutions

Introduction

A data lake is a data repository where data is stored in raw as well as original format to run any additional ad-hoc data analytics. Typically, these are built on top of large storage and store data in different formats and types. This chapter covers the data lake, the challenges with the data lake model, and how Snowflake can help to overcome the typical challenges. This chapter also covers the data lake architecture and reference use case to implement it with Snowflake native services and features. This chapter helps to understand the design of a data lake, choose the engineering approach, and share real-time use cases and best practices for implementing a data lake with Snowflake.

This chapter focuses on sharing the typical architecture and data needed to implement Lake with Snowflake. It also covers the guidelines and best practices to implement engineering approaches and optimizations as part of lake design. This chapter shares a commonly used modernization use case with Snowflake and the steps followed to migrate the data platform to Snowflake. This is the next chapter in the series of architecture design, where you will learn to design data platform systems.

Structure

This chapter consists of the following topics:

- Data lake with Snowflake
- Unstructured data with Snowflake
- Migrating data lake to Snowflake
- Data lake usage
- Best practices and recommendations

Objectives

By the end of this chapter, you will be able to understand the need for a data lake and design data architecture using Snowflake data platform. You will also learn about handling unstructured data in Snowflake. You can use the trial account setup to perform various exercises throughout this book.

Data lake with Snowflake

In the previous chapter, we learned about data warehouse systems and implementing them with Snowflake native features. In this section, we will learn about data lake systems and how they differ from data warehouse systems. We will explore the data lake capabilities and Snowflake features that can be leveraged to set up the data lake systems.

In data warehouse systems, data can be stored, processed, and maintained historically for analytical purposes. With data lake systems, data is present, stored, and preserved in raw format, along with processing it to support any enhanced analytical requirements. Typically, these systems are used to store and process data at a domain level and have various data marks supported for domain requirements. Each domain may have separate sources of data, need to integrate with heterogeneous datasets, and is required to design individual processes. Data lake supports extended data sizes and types of data formats in comparison with data warehouse systems. Refer to *Table 13.1*, which shares a feature comparison between data lake and data warehouse systems:

Feature	Data Lake	Data warehouse
Type of data (variety)	Structured, semi-structured, and unstructured data	Structured and semi-structured
Data volume	Can deal data up to Petabytes of volume	No strict limit as such, warehouses can also be expanded to support PBs of the data size

Feature	Data Lake	Data warehouse
Data velocity	High volume and high frequency data feeds	Supports high volume as well as low volume data feeds. Can support high and low frequency data feeds with extended capabilities
Data formats	Data is stored in raw format as well as processed format for analysis.	Data is processed, transformed, and stored for analytical purposes. Source raw data is not maintained for a long time.
Storage capabilities	Large storage capabilities, as data needs to be stored in raw format. Typically, storage objects are used to store the data, hence cheaper.	Small to moderate storage capabilities in integration with storage objects. Typically, the data is preferred to be loaded to native tables and queried. Storage is used only in the case of archival or source data retention for smaller durations.

Table 13.1: Data lake vs data warehouse feature comparison

These are just some of the key features compared, and there are many other aspects of the design differences. However, the engineering approach is not different in comparison with integrations, ingestions, processing, and curating data for analysis. Some of the processes may vary based on the extended support to handle unstructured data feeds. You might have worked on the Hadoop ecosystem. Hadoop is one of the tech stacks used to implement data lakes widely. This is used widely to implement data lakes. Refer to *Figure 13.1*, a typical data lake architecture that represents integration with data sources, storing data in storage for raw access, building data marts on top of the data layer, and implementing data analytics:

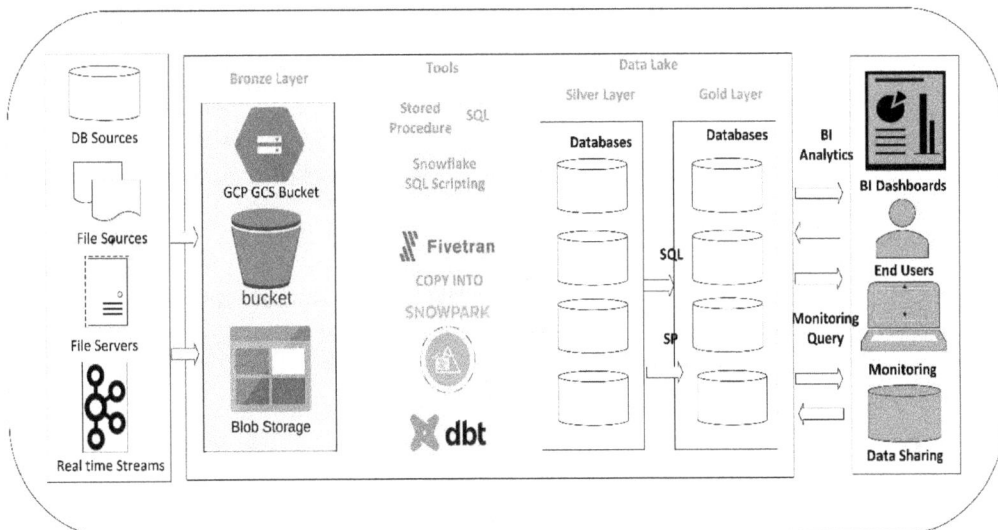

Figure 13.1: Typical Hadoop data lake architecture

Hadoop implementation was adopted across the industry to set up the data lake. A data lake can be set up as a legacy on-premises ecosystem, as well as set up on top of a private cloud. A private cloud can be set up leveraging commodity hardware and storage to implement a data lake. Usually, these systems are over-provisioned to accommodate a variety of data workloads and needs. The following are the features of the data lake:

- **Flexibility**: Data availability in raw format enables data scientists and analysts to build features for machine learning.

- **Accessibility**: Data is stored centrally in the storage layer and is accessible to all users in raw format whenever needed.

- **Affordability**: Storage is available at a cheaper cost to set up a storage layer to store data in raw format.

- **Compatibility**: Data lake platform is compatible for integration with other tools and open-source technologies.

- **Comprehensive**: Integrating various data sources to combine the data to set up a raw storage layer with the data platform.

These are some of the features offered by data lakes. Data platform setup on legacy, as well as private cloud, can impose challenges like elasticity, cost performance efficiency, and maintenance overhead. Snowflake can be used to address all challenges and design efficient data lake architecture. As you learned in the previous chapter, Snowflake offers the following features:

- **Scalability**: Snowflake warehouses can be set up to address several types of workloads with auto-scaling and resizing.

- **Operational excellence**: Notification integration can be used to implement alerting. Snowsight can be used to set up dashboards for operations and monitoring using metadata views.

- **Maintainability**: Snowflake is a data platform that allows users to integrate heterogeneous workloads and integrations with integrators. With one platform, it becomes easy to maintain and reduce the complexity of the workload's maintenance.

- **Performance and cost efficiency**: The Snowflake platform's parallelism allows users to achieve performance efficiency. Warehouse and serverless resource usage based on the utilization enables users to achieve cost efficiency.

Data formats and engineering design

Snowflake data solution allows users to implement, **Extract, Transform, and Load** (ETL) and **Extract, Load, and Transform (ELT)** engineering approaches. The following are some of the key data lake features that can be implemented using Snowflake:

- **Type of data:** Data lake needs to store data in raw format: structured, semi-structured, and unstructured data feeds. Snowflake integration with storage objects and buckets allows users to store the data in cloud storage.

- **Multi-lingual support:** Snowflake supports programmatic implementation of engineering pipelines using Snowflake scripting, Snowpark, and scripting with Python, Java, JavaScript, and Scala.

- **Data formats:** Snowflake supports open-source formats like ORC, Avro, and Parquet, which allow users to store and process files. Unstructured data can be uploaded to a storage bucket and create directory tables to access the data.

- **Open table formats**: Snowflake integration with Apache Iceberg allows users to create tables to access data in open table format.

- **Native and third-party integrations**: Snowflake native integrations and data integrators enable users to integrate with heterogeneous sources.

- **Data collaborations**: Snowflake data sharing allows users to set up the shares to be shared with consumer users. Data share can be set up to share the data in raw format for feature engineering and **machine learning** (**ML**) use cases.

- **Artificial intelligence (AI) and ML capabilities**: Snowflake cortex **large language model** (**LLM**) functions and container service allow users to implement AI/ML as well as LLM use cases. Snowflake offers a one-stop solution to implement data lake efficiently.

These features of a data lake can be implemented with distinct options depending on the business and application requirements. There are various engineering options to integrate, store, process, and transform data by leveraging Snowflake native features and services. This section shares a sample data lake design approach and engineering options to implement data pipelines with Snowflake native features. Refer to *Figure 13.2*, which shares a list of options and engineering approaches to implement data lake design:

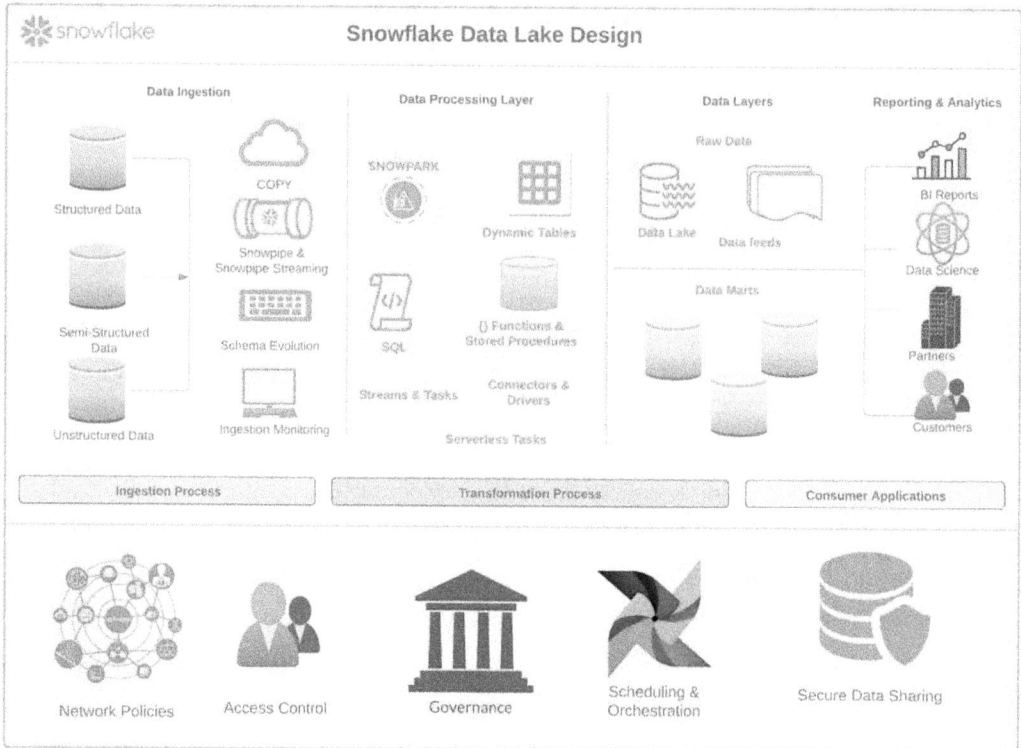

Figure 13.2: Data lake design solution

Here, *Figure 13.2* shares choices of the services and options used to set up the data lake design. The following are the choices available to set data lake architecture:

- **Source integrations**: Snowflake native integrations to integrate with sources. You can also use data integrators like Matillion and fivetran to bring in source data in raw format to named stages.

- **Data transformations**: Data processing using Snowflake native SQL, scripting, dynamic tables, streams, and tasks, programming approach with Snowpark, and other language support.

- **Data marts**: Data is stored and processed within the data platform across data layers: Raw layer, transformed layer, and curated layer. Setting up data marts to store the data based on the data domains. Data marts are set up using databases and objects.

- **Data analytics**: Data analytics with **business intelligence** (**BI**) tools and Snowflake native integrations to run data analytics. AI and LLM Support, implementing extended use cases with Snowflake cortex LLM functions. Snowflake also supports **bring your own model** (**BYOM**) and implementing using Snowflake container service.

Data engineering design is key when designing any data platform. Data processing can be designed with a variety of features available within the Snowflake platform. The following section shares the options available to develop engineering pipelines.

Data ingestions

There are diverse options available to integrate with source systems and get source data:

- Data integrators like Matillion and fivetran can be used to connect to any type of source to get data.

- Get the source data feed pushed to cloud storage buckets to integrate with the Snowflake platform.

- Streaming data loads using Snowpipe and automating data loads using cloud-native services.

- Snowpipe streaming to read data from Kafka streaming and load it to Snowflake tables.

- Creating external stages and tables to read data in an unstructured format using directory tables.

Data ingested is stored as part of the raw layer with the Snowflake database. Data is also stored at the stage level. There are two types of named stages used to store the source data: the internal stage and the external stage.

Data processing

Snowflake native features and integrators allow the implementation of data processing pipelines. Data transformations using Snowflake scripting and SQL jobs. Refer to the following processes and design approach to implement data pipelines:

- **Change data capture (CDC)**: Implementing SCD Type II using Snowflake streams and tasks.

- **Data governance:** Data masking and implementing role-based masking to protect data from unauthorized access. Setting up data masking policies to mask sensitive information.

- **Data transformations**: Setting up pipelines using debt and designing models to run data transformation logic. Data is processed and stored in the form of data marts.

Data processing is the core of the platform, where data is processed, transformed, and stored as data marts for consumers. Data pipelines are specific to the feeds, type of data, and complexity of the data processing. Apart from application and business logic, there is a set of standard processes and **nonfunctional requirements** (**NFRs**).

Refer to the following options to implement them:

- **Standard processes**: Error handling with notification integrations and generating alerts. Monitoring warehouse usage with resource monitors. Setting up operational observability with Snowsight.

- **Data quality checks (DQ):** Automating the data checks using Snowflake stored procedures.

- **Scheduling and orchestration**: This is the top layer used to orchestrate the data pipelines and set the dependencies across data pipelines. Orchestration and scheduling can be implemented using Astronomer airflow, Snowflake tasks for internal processes, and any other scheduling tools.

- **Performance and cost efficiency**: This is the layer used to set up the budgets and alerts. As part of performance efficiency and measurement, implementing processes to monitor the execution of workloads and reporting the long run queries or queued queries. Cost efficiency with monitoring metadata view information allows users to avoid any additional cost.

With the preceding sections, you have learned the data lake architecture design, implementation strategy, and processes. Refer to *Chapter 12, Architecting Data Warehouse* for sample loading, processing, and standard process implementation for structured and semi-structured data loads. The following section shares the processes used to handle unstructured data and processing with Snowflake.

Unstructured data with Snowflake

Unstructured data does not fit into any predefined format, like structured and semi-structured data formats. This data category includes data in the form of images, videos, and audio files. Snowflake extends support to handle unstructured data feeds. Snowflake allows the following processes for unstructured data feeds:

- Process unstructured data.

- Set up secure access URLs for unstructured data.

- Share file access URLs with collaborators.

- Load file access URLs and other details to the Snowflake tables.

This section shares details of accessing, processing, and sharing unstructured data within Snowflake. As you know, cloud storage buckets can store unstructured data. Cloud storage can be integrated as part of named internal and external stages with Snowflake. We will learn more about the processes in subsequent sections.

Setup secure access for unstructured data

Upload unstructured data to the cloud storage and integrate it to be accessed as a stage object. Snowflake offers diverse ways to set access to stage locations as URLs. Refer to the following ways to set the URL:

- **Scoped URL**: Setting up a scoped URL enables users to set up the stage access without granting access to the stage. This creates a URL with preauthorized access for 24 hours.

- **File URL**: This URL allows users to set access to the database, schema, stage, and file path. This needs to set the privileges to the role accessing stage.

- **Pre-signed URL**: As the name suggests, this allows users to set the pre-signed access token for files on stage. This is a simple HTTP URL path to access the files via the web browser. In this case, the access token can be set to grant access duration.

These URLs can be defined using SQL commands based on the use cases and usage. Refer to the following use cases and commands used to create a signed URL:

- **BUILD_SCOPED_FILE_URL:** This function is used to create the scoped URL, and admins can create these URLs to set access to the specific file. Create a signed URL with SQL command as shown:

```
/* Create Scoped URL */
SELECT BUILD_SCOPED_FILE_URL(@external_stage,'/source/images/home_new.jpg');
```

This command creates an https URL link to access the file, which is valid only for 24 hours.

- **BUILD_STAGE_FILE_URL**: This function is used to create a staged file name with two input parameters: stage name and relative path. This URL offers prolonged access to the file, which does not include. Refer to the following SQL command to create a URL:

```
/* create staged URL */
SELECT BUILD_STAGE_FILE_URL(@external_stage,'/source/images/home_new.jpg');
```

This creates a URL and allows users to access files in a stage. This sends a request to access the file via REST API for file support. Snowflakes perform a set of tasks to authenticate users, validate access privileges, and redirect users to the stage when users request to access a file URL.

- **GET_PRESIGNED_URL**: This function is used to generate pre-signed URLs, and this sets the URL access via one of the three methods. Snowflake sets access to staged files via pre-signed URL through a web browser, retrieves URLs via Snowsight, and sends URL requests through REST API file support. Refer to the following SQL command to create a URL:

```
/* create pre-signed URL */
SELECT GET_PRESIGNED_URL(@external_stage,'/source/images/home_new.
jpg',3600);
```

This sets up the URL to access the data via a pre-signed URL. You can also get the load metadata and load it to a table to generate the pre-signed URL. The metadata is available in JSON format, and this can be loaded into the table. Refer to the following set of commands:

```
/* Define a table to store the file metadata */
CREATE DATABASE POC_DB;
CREATE SCHEMA POC;
CREATE WAREHOUSE POC (Proof of concept) size = 'Small';
USE DATABASE POC_DB;
USE SCHEMA POC;
/* create table to store metadata information */
CREATE TABLE image_metadata_table
    (
        url string,
        format string,
        size number,
        tags array,
        details string,
        path string
    );
```

The preceding steps are used to set up the database and schema and create a table to load file metadata. Image metadata can be loaded to the table in JSON format using the **COPY** command:

```
/* load metadata to table using COPY */
COPY INTO image_metadata_table
    FROM
(SELECT $1:url::STRING, $1:format::STRING, $1:size::NUMBER, $1:tag,
$1:details::STRING, GET_RELATIVE_PATH(@external_stage, $1:url)
    FROM
    @external_stage/image_metadata.json)
    FILE_FORMAT = (type = json);
```

Once data is loaded to a table, then a view can be created on top of the table to access the images. Snowflake extended object directory tables are used to store catalogs of staged files in cloud storage. Role-based access control can be implemented for directory tables to set access to the table and retrieve file URLs.

Process unstructured data

Snowflake offers a directory table as an extended object that supports unstructured data processing. A directory table is conceptually the same as the external table that defines the implicit object layer on stage location. However, these objects do not have permissions of their own to be granted on tables. These tables can be created on internal and external stages. These tables can be defined on top of stages while defining stage using **CREATE STAGE**, as well as later using **ALTER STAGE**. Typically, directory tables are used to define implicit layers on top of unstructured data. The following are the use cases that can be implemented using directory tables:

- **Query unstructured data:** Like any other table objects in Snowflake, **SELECT** can be used to query the directory tables. Directory tables follow a predefined format and have a set of columns that store the metadata details of stage files.

```
/* Query Table*/
SELECT * FROM DIRECTORY(@external_stage);
```

- **Create objects on top of unstructured data:** View can be defined on top of a directory table that queries the metadata details stored as part of the directory tables. **CREATE VIEW** can be used to define the view, and directory tables can also be joined with any other objects within Snowflake. Consider a scenario where you want to analyze the e-newspapers to extract the required information. All newspapers are uploaded in PDF format to an external stage and a defined directory table on top of it. Define a view on the top directory table to access the details of the documents uploaded to the stage and join with metadata stored in a table.

```
/* create view */
CREATE VIEW newspaper_details AS
  SELECT
    file_url as paper_url,
    author,
    publish_date as publishing_date,
    approved_date as approval_date,
    geography,
    num_of_pages
  FROM directory(@newspaper_stage) p
  JOIN newspaper_metadata n
  ON p.file_url = n.file_url;
```

Directory tables are defined and can be set on automated refresh. This refresh can be set using a cloud-native messaging service. These are triggered as and when new files are added, files are updated, and files are removed from the external stage.

- **Setup file processing pipeline**: Directory tables are used to track the metadata information and details. Snowflake objects like streams and tasks can be used to track changes on directory tables and build pipelines. As you know, streams can be defined on a directory table that tracks changes in the table, and tasks can be configured to take an action. Refer to *Figure 13.3*, which represents the processing pipeline on the directory table:

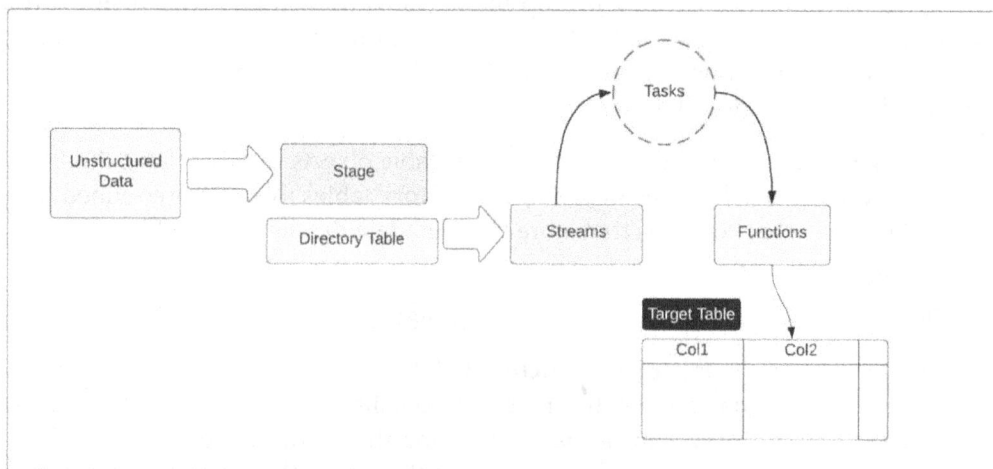

Figure 13.3: Data processing pipeline

As you observe here, unstructured data is uploaded to the stage that has a directory table defined. Streams defined capture the changes of the directory table, and tasks call functions that write to the table based on the changes. You can also refer to **https://docs.snowflake. com/en/user-guide/data-load-dirtables-pipeline** to implement a pipeline that processes unstructured data.

As you learned in this section, Snowflake's native features extend capabilities to store, define objects, and build data pipelines to handle unstructured data. Structured and semi-structured data processing follows the same pathway that leverages native capabilities of the platform. We have learnt structured and semi-structured data processing and options to develop engineering pipelines in *Chapter 12, Architecting Data Warehouse*. Data lake can be defined from scratch along with engineering pipelines. However, data platform migration is one of the widely known use cases of platform implementation. Snowflake is considered one of the efficient solutions to implement data lake design patterns. The following section shares one reference use case to migrate data lake platform to Snowflake.

Migrating data lake to Snowflake

In this section, we will learn about migrating the data lake platform to Snowflake. The migration process is a lifecycle with multiple phases and supports use cases where data and apps are migrated from one platform to another as lift and shift. Data modernization is a process of migrating data platforms from one ecosystem to another, where data and apps are modernized to improve performance and cost efficiency.

In this section, we will learn about a data modernization use case to migrate the Hadoop ecosystem data to the Snowflake data platform. Refer to *Figure 13.4*, which shares the reference architecture of data lake on Snowflake with engineering approaches:

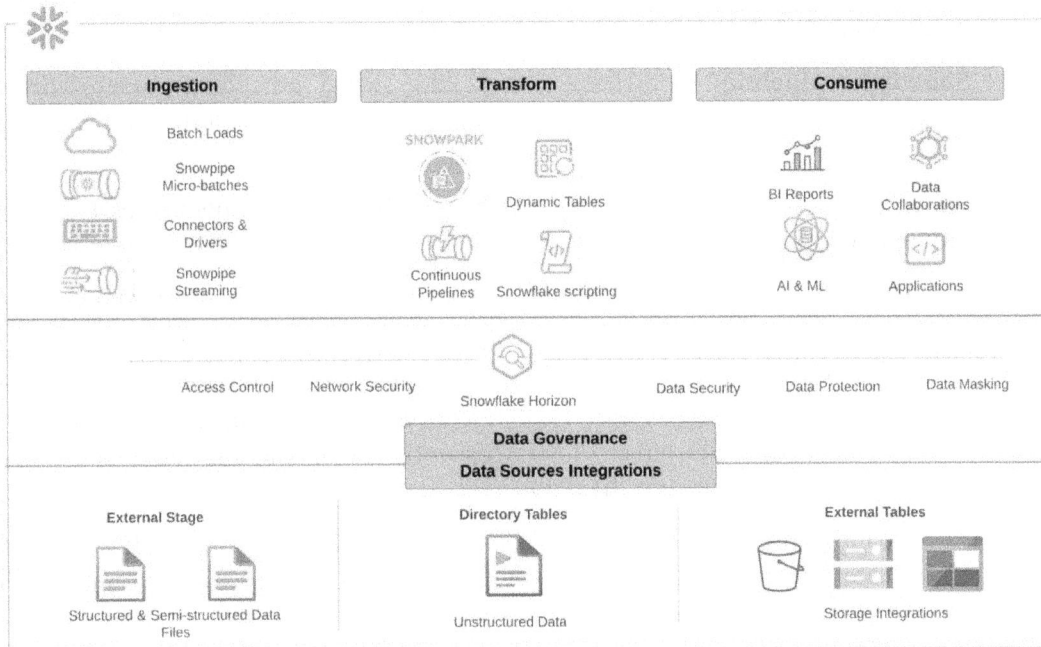

Figure 13.4: Data lake architecture

As represented in *Figure 13.4*, there are various engineering approaches to importing, ingesting, transforming, and storing data. The following are the load options to be considered based on the type and frequency of data:

- **Bulk load**: Structured as well as semi-structured data can be loaded as part of batch data loads using the **COPY** utility.

- **Near real-time streaming**: Data with low volume and low frequency can be loaded using Snowflake snowpipe. The data is loaded in the form of micro-batches.

- **Real-time Streaming loads**: Data with higher frequency and low volume can be loaded as part of streaming data. Snowpipe streaming can be integrated with Kafka to load data with real-time data loads.

- **Ad-hoc data loads**: Any type of data that needs to be loaded on an ad-hoc basis to Snowflake. These can be loaded using any native utility as well as using programming connectors and drivers.

Once the data is loaded to the Snowflake table, the data needs to undergo a transformation as well as an enrichment process to store data as part of the data lake processing. Data marts can be defined to store the data as per domain and run data pipelines within data marts. The following are the transform options, and these can be picked up based on the use case. One or more can be combined together to implement transformations:

- **Snowpark pipelines**: Snowpark is used to transform data using Snowpark dataframes. Transform the data and store it in a native table within the data mart.

- **Snowflake pipelines**: Snowflake objects like stored procedures, **user-defined functions** (**UDFs**), and UDFTs can be defined as Snowflake scripting pipelines to enrich the data and store it in DataMart.

- **Snowflake native pipelines using SQL**: Snowflake SQL scripts use SQL jobs to implement CDC, transformations, enriching data, and storing data into tables:

  o Snowflake native using streams to implement CDC and automate using tasks.

  o Snowflake extension with dynamic tables allows users to transform data and set it to automatic refresh. Dynamic tables refresh data within 60 seconds of the base table refresh. This does not need to maintain additional data pipelines to transform the data.

  o Data is transformed and stored in data marts for consumer processing. Data can be consumed in several ways with analytical requirements, BI reports and dashboards, AI/ML, and analytical functions. Migrating data workloads to Snowflake can also leverage the native services and features.

The migration use case is also an opportunity to evaluate existing workloads and design new workloads with target system architecture capabilities. Snowflake native features support the implementation of the following workloads:

- **Data transformations**: Snowflake supports custom functions to define the conversions to convert data from one binary format to another. Snowflake extended support to transform data in semi-structured formats like XML and JSON. Snowflake native features and extended support with Python libraries can define custom functionalities.

- **Data cleaning**: Snowflake features and custom functions with extended libraries can be used to define the functionality to validate the data format, data authenticity, data cleansing, removing data outliers, and data anomaly detection.

- **Data validation**: Define custom functionality to validate the data, and define data quality functions to validate the quality of the data. Custom functionality can also be defined to handle data augmentation for AI/ML use cases.

- **Data security**: Defining data security using data masking and dynamic functions to secure data. **Personal Identifiable Information** (**PII**) data can be masked using role-based or tag-based implementation to protect the data. Data requirements to support compliance implementations with HIPAA, CCPA, GDPR, etc.

- **Data sharing:** Snowflake native data sharing and cloning can be used to share the data with consumer users. Data shares can be created and shared with Snowflake as well as non-Snowflake users. This feature simplifies the data-sharing capabilities without maintaining additional pipelines for data consistency.

These are some of the common use cases and features used to implement data lake platforms. Let us learn about two of the data lake use cases and migration approaches to migrate workloads to Snowflake.

Hadoop migration use case

Consider the scenario of Hadoop data lake migration to Snowflake. Hadoop pipelines are developed using ecosystem services like Hive, **Hadoop Distributed File System** (**HDFS**), Sqoop, and Impala for consumer access. Data is exported and loaded to HDFS using Sqoop. There are a bunch of source files FTPed to HDFS. Hive scripts **Hive Query Language** (**HQL**) are used to transform the data from raw to the consumer layer. Data in the hive target layer is accessed via Impala for analytical queries. As part of data modernization, data lake use case 1 is to be migrated and refactored on the Snowflake data platform. Refer to *Figure 13.5*; this follows the same phases of migration as discussed in *Chapter 12, Architecting Data Warehouse*:

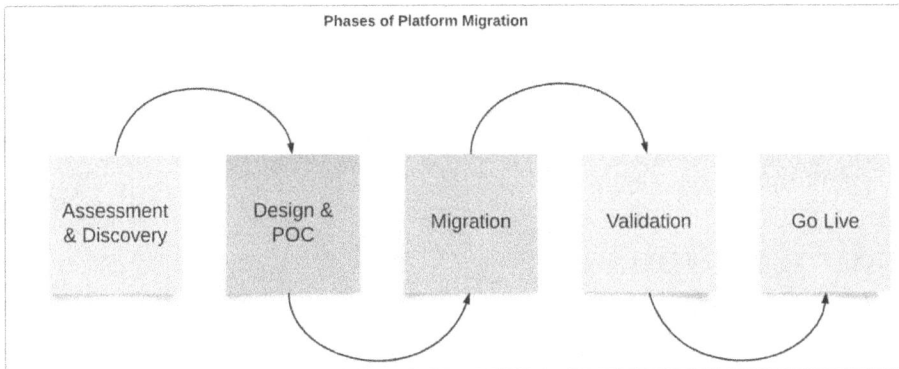

Figure 13.5: Data platform migration phases

The entire modernization journey follows the same path and phases to analyze, design, develop, validate, and implement in production. In the given scenario, data migration and pipeline conversions can follow the following options to migrate to Snowflake:

- **Data migration:** Hadoop data lake stores all the data on top of the HDFS file system. Data can be moved from HDFS to Cloud-native storage using cloud utilities or tools. Here, in this scenario, you can define the cloud storage buckets as a staging area and copy all HDFS files from Hadoop to storage. As you know, Snowflake supports open-source formats like Parquet, Avro, and ORC. These are also widely used file formats within the Hadoop ecosystem. You can plan to integrate this as external storage as well, depending on the existing cloud infra setup.

- **Data ingestion pipeline conversion**: The Hadoop ecosystem uses Sqoop to get source data from database or data systems and has a bunch of source feeds FTPed to HDFS. In this case, get all FTP jobs modified to push the source feeds to cloud storage buckets. Integrate these buckets as named stages to read source data. For data feeds, use data integrators like Fivetran or a programming approach to read from data systems and get data to Snowflake.

- **Data transform pipeline conversion**: Hadoop pipelines developed in HQL can be converted to Snowflake native SQL scripts. As you know, Snowflake supports ANSI SQL standards, hence convert all SQL queries to Snowflake. Hive-specific functions or custom functions defined using Java can be replaced by equivalent functions on Snowflake. Otherwise, convert the functions to custom functions on Snowflake using Java or JavaScript.

- **Impala queries**: Snowflake brings in capabilities of MPP systems and helps to achieve performance efficiency. Convert all impala queries, analytical jobs, and users to access data from the Snowflake data layer. Set up a target or consumer data layer to store the processed data and convert all queries, and set up user access to run queries on top of the consumer data layer. Define a dedicated warehouse to run converted impala queries.

This is one of the typical Hadoop data lake use case scenarios with native Hadoop ecosystem components. Apache Spark is also one of the widely used components to implement data transformation to achieve better performance over traditional hive or map-reduce jobs. Let us consider one more Hadoop use case with Spark pipelines to be modernized to the Snowflake platform.

Migration options

Hadoop data lake with HDFS, Hive, Sqoop, Impala, and Spark ecosystem components to integrate source data, transform, and create a curated layer on top of Hive and Impala for consumer queries and analytical workloads. You need to migrate this data lake to Snowflake for better performance and cost optimization with the best possible solution and approach. As part of migration, you can consider the following approaches to migrate data lake to Snowflake:

- **Lift and shift**: To consider this approach, you need to have an existing cloud adoption to integrate the data workloads. You can leverage the existing cloud platform capabilities to build a data lake using native or managed cloud services to set up the Hadoop ecosystem and move all data workloads to be run on these managed services. Store the data processed on Snowflake for better consumer integration. For example, consider that you have existing cloud adoption with **Amazon Web Services (AWS)** and can set up a data lake using AWS S3 and move all Spark workloads to EMR to process the data. All processed and transformed data can be stored on Snowflake for consumer queries and analytics.

- **Re-factor**: With this approach, all workloads are moved to Snowflake, and pipelines are converted to equivalent on Snowflake. All Spark workloads can be converted to equivalent Snowpark on Snowflake using Snowpark data frames. You can also consider converting all Spark workloads to SQL scripts or jobs, depending on the pipeline structure. Pipelines can be converted based on their structure if they are Spark SQL or native Spark with data frames.

Considering the two approaches discussed in the preceding section, the lift and shift is not a fully Snowflake-native solution. This is a hybrid solution with cloud-native and Snowflake implementation. To leverage the full potential of the Snowflake platform and lake capabilities with cloud storage integrations, convert all workloads to Snowflake native workloads. Nowadays, using a combination of Snowflake, Fivetran, and dbt is also considered one of the best solutions to design and implement data platforms with Snowflake. You will learn more about this in the next chapter, along with the data mesh design use case.

Data platform migration or modernization is one of the most common use cases across the industry. Snowflake's extended capabilities, like AI/ML workloads integration, Gen AI implementations, Native app, and container service integrations, enable users to adopt Snowflake as a one-stop solution for all data, app, and AI needs. Most of the customers are migrating to Snowflake to leverage the native capabilities to simplify data workloads. It is no longer a data warehouse solution; Snowflake is now data and AI on the cloud. Snowflake architecture and metadata information enable users to implement observability, monitoring, and tracking with simple native solutions over third-party tools. You will learn to implement usage observability and tracking in the next section.

Data lake usage

As you know, Snowflake offers **USAGE** and **INFORMATION** schema views to share the metadata information about storage, compute, and cloud services layer usage. We have learned about the utilization queries, monitoring, and optimizing them with *Chapter 6, Evaluating and Optimizing Snowflake's Performance*, and *Chapter 7, Unlocking Snowflake's Cost and Performance*. In this section, you will learn to set up the budgets and alerts using Snowflake Snowsight. Also, refer to *Chapter 12, Architecting Data Warehouse* to set up the usage queries to monitor the consumption. We will set up the monitoring using usage views to monitor the performance of the compute warehouses.

Snowflake budgets

Snowflake budgets allow users to set the threshold of the spend using Snowsight features as well as commands. Refer to *Figure 13.6,* which represents budget addition:

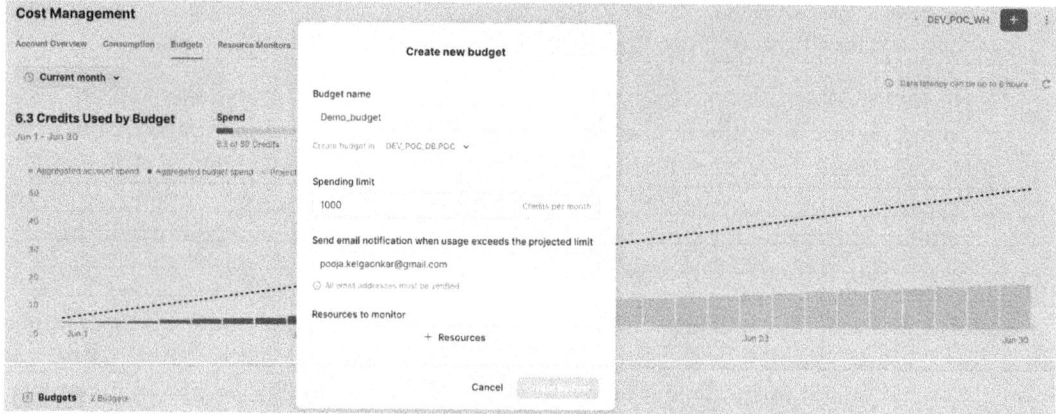

Figure 13.6: Snowsight budget setup

As you can observe here, you can define budgets as per your application needs, and multiple budgets can be set up for an account. Budgets can cover most of the Snowflake database objects. Refer to the following steps to implement budgets:

1. Login to Snowflake using **https://app.snowflake.com/**

2. Change the role to **ACCOUNTADMIN**.

3. Go to | **Admin** | **Cost Management**.

4. Click + on the top right corner to add a new budget.

5. Provide **Budget Name** and **Spending Limit**.

6. Add email notifications.

7. Add resources to monitor. Select all databases and warehouses to set the budget for monthly monitoring.

Once budgets are defined, they help to track the usage of the account and notify appropriate users to take required actions. This is a native feature of monitoring the overall usage apart from the resource monitors. You can also define the custom code leveraging metadata views to track the spending for a given application or integrations across the platforms.

Note: Snowflake accounts can have up to 100 custom budgets defined per account. The budget currently does not support hybrid tables and Snowpark container services. These cannot be replicated in the target accounts as well.

Custom usage queries

As we have learned in previous optimization *Chapters of optimization,* Snowflake metadata views are used to generate metrics and queries. There are various monitoring and observability tools available in the market that give additional plugins, blocks, or pre-built dashboards that share an account overview for the Snowflake account. You can also define custom functionality with native database objects and integrations to monitor the usage and push notifications to the messaging services.

Consider the data platform built on top of AWS with native services of AWS and Snowflake data lake setup, along with AWS S3, the storage service. AWS SQS is used to load micro batches of data to Snowflake databases using Snowpipe. AWS SNS is used to share alerts and notifications to the operations team. In this case, Snowflake metrics can be pushed to AWS CloudWatch to monitor if needed. You can also define a custom process to monitor using **stored procedure** (**SP**) and send an alert using SNS integration with Snowflake. Refer to the following sample code to send notifications to AWS SNS and a custom SP to monitor the usage:

- Setup the integration with AWS SNS.

- Like any other integrations in Snowflake, we can set up Snowflake SNS integration as a notification integration object. The following is the notification integration command to set up the SNS integration:

```
CREATE NOTIFICATION INTEGRATION aws_sns_int
   ENABLED = TRUE
   DIRECTION = OUTBOUND
   TYPE = QUEUE
   NOTIFICATION_PROVIDER = AWS_SNS
   AWS_SNS_TOPIC_ARN = 'arn:aws:sns:us-east-2:xxxxxxxxxxxx:sns_topic'
   AWS_SNS_ROLE_ARN = 'arn:aws:iam::xxxxxxxxxxxx:role/sns_role';
```

- Follow all steps from this documentation reference **https://docs.snowflake.com/ en/user-guide/notifications/creating-notification-integration-amazon-sns** to set up the integration.

- Define custom Snowflake SP to monitor the long-running queries to generate metrics. The following is a sample stored procedure that checks for queries that have run for an hour and captures the query ID and warehouse name:

```
CREATE OR REPLACE PROCEDURE SNOWFLAKE_LONG_RUNNING_QUERIES()
    RETURNS VARCHAR
    LANGUAGE JAVASCRIPT
    EXECUTE AS CALLER
    AS
```

```
$$
    result = '';
    try {
    var get_long_run_queries = `
       select query_id , total_elapsed_time , warehouse_name from
ACCOUNT_USAGE.QUERY_HISTORY where total_elapsed_time >= 3600000`;

         var long_run_queries = snowflake.execute( {sqlText: get_
long_run_queries} );

    while (long_run_queries.next()) {
    query_id_val = long_run_queries.getColumnValue(1);
    total_time_val = long_run_queries.getColumnValue(2);
    wh_name_val = long_run_queries.getColumnValue(3);
    var update_metrics_table =
`INSERT INTO LONG_RUNNING_QUERIES SELECT
            \'Total_Elapsed_Time\',` +
                total_time_val + `,
                \'Milliseconds\',\'`+
                 timestamp_val +`\',
                \'Snowflake\',
                \'[{\\\"Name\\\": \\\"Query_
ID\\\",\\\"Value\\\": \\\"`+query_id_val+`\\\"},{\\\"Name\\\":
\\\"Warehouse\\\",\\\"Value\\\":\\\"`+ wh_name_val+`\\\"}]\'
                )`;
    snowflake.execute( {sqlText: update_metrics_table } );
     result = 'Success';
            }
        }
        catch (err) {
            result = "Failed: Code: " + err.code + "\n  State: " +
err.state;
            result += "\n  Message: " + err.message;
            result += "\nStack Trace:\n" + err.stackTraceTxt;
        }
        return result;
    $$;
```

This is one of the sample pieces of code used to build custom features. You can also define it as a function and schedule it to be invoked every few hours using TASKs. Snowflake features let users define generalized, standardized functionality as per user requirements. You can follow the preceding steps to set up the custom monitoring of cost and overall usage. The next important aspect of designing the platform is to understand the best practices and recommendations of the platform. The following section shares Snowflake's best practices and recommendations for implementing data lake systems.

Best practices and recommendations

Snowflake offers scalable and efficient solutions to implement data lake systems. This section shares some of the best practices and recommendations to implement Snowflake data systems. The recommendations and best practices shared in the previous chapter, *Chapter 12, Architecting Data Warehouse,* can also be considered while designing the data pipelines to ingest the batch as well as real-time streaming data to the data lake systems. Apart from the engineering best practices shared in the previous chapter, this section shares some of the data lake features and best practices recommended by Snowflake.

Data lake systems follow their own standards and best practices. This section shares the corresponding recommendations to implement a data lake using Snowflake:

- **Data collaborations**: Data lake systems need to be well-integrated and open to storing the data from various applications. Data integration is key to sharing data with consumers as well as other applications. As the name suggests, data lake sets various data marts, and data needs to be shared between these marts as well as application teams. Snowflake data sharing allows users to share data in a seamless collaboration. There is no need to maintain additional pipelines to share the data, refresh, and maintain consistency across the platform. Recommended to use the sharing and cloning feature of Snowflake when applicable to set up the integrations.

- **Data governance**: As data resides centrally and is accessed via marts, governance plays a crucial role in maintaining data security and protection across the platform. Snowflake is rich in features to implement governance across the data platform. Recommended to use **Role Based Access Control** (**RBAC**) centrally to manage users, roles, and access to the platform. As a best practice, implement dynamic masking to protect sensitive information and access from unauthorized users. Recommended to use role-based policy control along with dynamic masking to protect data exposure. Define and manage the policies centrally.

- **Compute and storage cost**: As design advice, it advised us to understand the data and requirements to set up the time travel to avoid any additional storage costs. Plan to use transient tables as part of data processing, where data may not be required to persist for a longer duration. For compute costs, define the warehouses with optimum sizes and monitor the performance over a period before revisiting the warehouse configurations. Use the resize or redefine the cluster sizes based on the overall application usage across the platform.

- **Monitoring and operations design:** As a best practice, implement resource monitoring, and set up automated alerting, reporting, and stored procedures to push out required alerts to avoid any additional storage and compute costs. Set up budgets and track the overall platform usage.

- **Pipeline recommendations**: Snowflake recommends loading data in smaller chunks to achieve parallel loads. Recommended to use copy history to visualize the data loaded. Typically, the default history of seven days is shared for the data loads. Snowpipe and streaming loads can be implemented based on the requirements to load high-volume low-latency versus low-volume high-latency loads datasets.

- **Custom pipelines**: Snowflake's Snowpark can be used to replace the spark workloads and achieve better performance. Snowflake offers custom tools to help in migrating code as part of the Snowflake migration toolkit. It is recommended to check out the existing toolkit to support migration or modernization use cases. You can also leverage the programming connectors to define custom pipelines if needed.

- **Data integrators**: Snowflake integrators like dbt, fivetran, matillion can be used to define and orchestrate the data loads on top of Snowflake. Currently, the fivetran, dbt, and Snowflake design patterns are widely being used and adopted by many retail, healthcare, and other domain customers. It is recommended to use the integrators to orchestrate and optimize workloads on Snowflake if looking for custom solutions over Snowflake native solutions. These integrators can be used to integrate sources that are not part of the Snowflake or other cloud ecosystem, e.g., SAP data, Salesforce data sources, etc.

- **AI and ML workloads**: Snowflake supports and extends features to allow users to bring their own ML models to deploy within the platform. BYOM can be implemented using Snowpark container services. Recommended to leverage the native ML as well as LLM functions as part of Snowflake cortex to explore AI and ML capabilities without moving data to any other platform. Snowflake powers users to implement ML workloads without moving data outside your model and data resides within the same platform.

These are some of the recommendations to be considered while designing data lake systems and an engineering approach. Snowflake is a one-stop solution to all the data and AI needs.

Conclusion

In this chapter, we have learned about data lake systems and designing the data lake using Snowflake. We have also learned to design the data lake systems with two different use cases of migration and modernization using Snowflake native features and offerings.

Snowflake's architecture and variety of native features offer engineering options to implement engineering pipelines for any data system patterns. The next design pattern is data mesh, where we will learn how the mesh design reduces the data challenges and share details of the design approach. This will help start designing the data mesh systems by leveraging Snowflake native features and integrations. You will learn data mesh design patterns in the upcoming chapter.

Points to remember

Here are some of the key takeaways from this chapter:

- Snowflake supports open file formats like Avro, ORC, and Parquet data feeds. Data can be stored, processed, and accessed in these formats without any additional tools.

- Unstructured data can be stored on the cloud storage and integrated with the Snowflake platform as external stages and directory tables.

- Snowflake shares best practices and recommendations to design and implement data lake workloads.

- Data integrators can be used to design the data lake systems. Currently, fivetran and dbt are the commonly used data integrators to integrate heterogeneous sources as well as to define the data workloads on top of Snowflake. You can choose to use integrators over native features to do the heavy lifting of the workloads.

Join our Discord space

Join our Discord workspace for latest updates, offers, tech happenings around the world, new releases, and sessions with the authors:

https://discord.bpbonline.com

CHAPTER 14
Exploring Data Mesh Design Options

Introduction

The data mesh design pattern is an emerging data platform design to overcome challenges that are brought by **data warehouse (DW)** and data lake designs. Data mesh solves the data silos and integrates applications under one umbrella. This chapter covers designing data mesh solutions with Snowflake. This also covers the data mesh architecture pattern and explains how to implement data mesh using Snowflake services. This also covers the various design approaches to implement data mesh for your data using Snowflake.

This chapter helps to understand the design of a data mesh, choose the engineering approach, and share best practices to implement a data mesh with Snowflake. Snowflake native feature offers designing data mesh with a variety of design approaches. This is the next chapter in the series of architecture design, where you will learn to design data platform systems.

Structure

This chapter consists of the following topics:

- Data mesh features
- Knit your data mesh

- Data mesh with Snowflake
- Best practices and recommendations

Objectives

By the end of this chapter, you will be able to understand the mesh architecture and design data mesh with Snowflake. This chapter also shares various options to design data mesh along with engineering options. A Snowflake trial account can be used to perform various exercises in this chapter.

Data mesh features

Data mesh is not a technology; it is a design pattern that needs to be adopted in an organization. This needs responsibility and coordination across data products and teams within an organization. There is no single platform that can support and extend the need for data mesh architecture. However, Snowflake offers most of the capabilities with native features that can be used to design the data mesh design patterns. Snowflake's native capabilities, like data sharing, data cloning, data governance services, and many other features, enable users to implement self-service, governed, distributed, and domain-driven architecture that caters to the need to use data as a product. Data mesh design may add complexity to the design with heterogeneous requirements to process the data.

We have learned two unique design patterns, data warehouse and data lake, in the previous chapters. We have also learned the comparison between these data systems and their benefits over each other. There may be a few challenges imposed by the data designs discussed so far, and data mesh can solve some of these. Refer to the following major challenges that can be addressed with data mesh design:

- **Data silos**: Data applications running in silos often tend to have data ingested, stored, and processed independently. Data needs to be shared with the data consumers, data scientists, and domain experts to derive the business use cases to bring value.

- **Data consistency**: This is another challenge where data needs to be refreshed and pipelines to share the data across teams.

Data challenges can impact overall business use cases and may impose limitations on deriving the business value added. Data mesh architecture design pattern runs data applications as data products to store domain-wise data that needs to be shared across organizations. Here, the domain can be considered as a business entity that can be separated and needs individual processing or data platform requirements to separate the data ingestion, data engineering, and analytical workloads. Refer to the following benefits and features of data mesh design:

- **Faster access to fresh data**: Data mesh design allows users to share the data and data changes in real-time with consumers. A centralized data analyst and data scientist team can consume the domain data from data products. Data shared in real time removes the silos and consistency challenges.

- **Reduced complexities**: You can define the standards and guidelines for domains, data products, tools, tech stack, and products. Data products may have a distinctive design architecture. However, they use the tool, and the tech stack used is defined centrally. This helps to reduce further complexities that may be imposed due to technology and data needs.

- **Improved cost efficiency**: Mesh design reduces the cost complexity and allows users to use the resources efficiently as it defines the tech, infrastructure, data, metadata, and products with centralized repo. Infrastructure efficiency reduces the overall cost of the platform and applications.

- **Improved security and governance**: Like the data product centralized approach, mesh allows users to define the data governance, security, access controls, and protection policies centrally. Data policies defined at an organizational level set the guidelines for design implementations.

These are just some of the key features offered by mesh architecture. There are many other aspects of the design implementations. However, the engineering approach for each domain as a data product is not different in comparison with integrations, ingestions, processing, and curating data for analysis. Some of the processes may vary based on the extended support to handle data feeds and source integrations. Snowflake data platform is rich in native features and capabilities. You can leverage these features to design mesh architecture. We have learned various features of Snowflake from previous chapters. These Snowflake services and features help us design efficient data platform designs. Refer to some of the commonly used features to recap overall capabilities:

- **Scalability**: Snowflake warehouses can be set up to address diverse types of workloads with auto-scaling and resizing.

- **Type of data**: Snowflake integration with storage objects and buckets allows users to store the data on cloud storage. Structured, semi-structured, and unstructured data can be processed and stored within the Snowflake platform.

- **Multi-lingual support**: Snowflake supports programmatic implementation of engineering pipelines using Snowflake scripting, Snowpark, and scripting with Python, Java, JavaScript, and Scala.

- **Data processing**: Snowflake supports open-source formats like ORC, Avro, and Parquet, allowing users to store and process files. Unstructured data can be uploaded to a storage bucket and create directory tables to access the data. Snowflake integration with Apache Iceberg allows users to create tables to access data in an open table format. Snowflake native integrations and data integrators enable users to integrate with heterogeneous sources.

- **Data sharing**: Data sharing can be set up to share the data in raw format for feature engineering and ML use cases. Domain data can be shared with other domain users through data shares. This is a critical feature used to implement mesh architecture.

- **AI and ML capabilities**: Snowflake offers a one-stop solution to implement data lake efficiently. Data analysts and scientists get access to domain data to derive the business value.

With the preceding sections, you have learned the architecture design, features, and benefits. Designing the engineering workloads and approaches follows similar patterns discussed in earlier chapters. The following section shares the processes used to design data mesh architecture and the design options available with Snowflake.

Knit your data mesh

Every data platform system design follows the design architecture pillars and takes the architecture pillars as the base of the architecture. We have learned that the Snowflake platform extends the capabilities to design data systems. Data platforms allow users to implement the architecture pillars like efficiency, scalability, operability, and maintainability. Snowflake shares a few considerations for designing data mesh systems. We will learn about the considerations and design options in this section.

Snowflake considerations

Snowflake native features and capabilities allow users to design the data mesh with a variety of options. Refer to the following considerations before you start working on the data mesh design:

- The data mesh design is an org-wide implementation and needs IT changes across the organization to adapt to the mesh design. There are a bunch of non-technical, aka **non-functional requirements** (**NFRs**) to be considered along with the technical adoption of the technology across systems. For example, data process monitoring, alerting, error handling, notifications, etc.

- Being pragmatic is the choice to get started with the design over designing a perfect data mesh design architecture. Consider the pain points and challenges currently faced by the teams as well as systems, and consider them while designing the data mesh architecture.

- Adopt agile methodology, and start designing the small applications, systems, and domains over the big bang approach. Designing the applications and implementing the design helps to discover the tech challenges early and helps to improve the design approach for the next set of domain applications.

- Define the complexity of tools and integrations across domain designs. As you design the self-service data platform, defining the standard guidelines to use a set of tools to design domain architecture will help reduce the complexity of the platform and help control costs. For example, using Fivetran as a global integrator tool across to ingest data from various sources. Using a variety of integrators for each domain can lead to complex infrastructure and add overhead to maintenance overall.

- Define the success criteria in terms of metrics and **key performance indicators (KPIs)** to measure the performance of the domain, data maturity, sharing, and usage of the platform across the organization.

- Always remember that there is no one-stop solution or one design that fits into data design to address all data challenges. As you know, the type of data, frequency, complexity, and requirements to implement data systems vary, and hence, the target architecture fits into mesh requirements. You can define the standards, guidelines, processes, and tech stack to be used across data domains.

These are some of the critical considerations to be considered while designing the data mesh architecture. You have learned various Snowflake features and native capabilities to implement any data system design patterns. Refer to the following key features that are considered as well as essential to design data mesh:

- **Snowflake storage and compute**: As you know, Snowflake offers elasticity with scaling of compute and storage without impacting each other. Snowflake extends support to all types of data formats, i.e., structured, semi-structured, and unstructured data.

- **Snowflake parallelism**: Snowflake allows users to run the workloads in parallel with its massively parallel processing architecture. This helps to design the workloads to be executed in parallel without impacting the storage and compute requirements.

- **Snowflake data sharing:** Data sharing allows users to share data with other domains and applications. This is the critical feature used to design mesh that allows users to create shares for each domain and share it across when needed.

- **Centralized governance:** With native features to protect the data and secure data access, it becomes easy to define centralized governance and set up a design layer to cater to all governance needs.

- **Self-service platform:** Snowflake's seamless experience to build applications with ease. It is as good as a self-serve platform to design, develop, and test data applications.

- **Data products:** Data products can be defined as a combination of data, metadata, code, and infrastructure components. Snowflake architecture allows users to design data products with metadata views, information schema, easy-to-maintain code, and integrations with a variety of data sources.

These are some of the critical features of the platform that help users design the data domains to be part of the data mesh architecture design pattern. Snowflake's native offerings can be used to design the mesh effectively.

Snowflake design options

As you learned about the Snowflake features and considerations mentioned in the preceding sections, this section defines the possible design options that can be considered to implement data mesh architecture. Refer to the following options to design the data products per domain:

- **Define domain as Snowflake account**: Use multiple Snowflake accounts, one account to cater to one domain, and share the data between multiple accounts using data sharing. Set up accounts on multiple clouds within an organization to design the data products per domain.

- **Define domain as a Snowflake database**: Maintaining multiple accounts within an organization can be cumbersome, as you need to define the security, protection, control policies, and centralized governance at each account. Defining domain processes and data product setup at the database level can help to set up the data boundaries. Implementing data sharing, data governance, protection, and security can be centralized and easy to maintain with this approach. Domains at databases can manage separate computing and storage requirements to cater to their workloads.

- **Define domain as Snowflake schema:** Like the databases domain approach, domains can also be set up at the schema level. Though it is possible to separate the domain boundaries using schema, this can be the lowest isolation between domains. This can be challenging to maintain the different names in schema objects. This may be useful if you want to design the mesh within the domain and sub-domains.

As you observe, Snowflake accounts, databases, and schemas can be used to define the domain boundaries. Domain data products can be defined and designed using Snowflake native objects. Data sharing can be used to set up access across domains. Also, use the centralized control policies as well as define governance policies. Snowflake offers multiple choices to set up the architectural pattern. Each one of the design patterns may have different trade-offs between approaches. You will learn to design and implement the mesh pattern in the following section.

Data mesh with Snowflake

As we have learned in the previous section, data mesh can be implemented with three different approaches using the Snowflake data platform. This section covers the architecture design and implementation setup data mesh design pattern.

Data domain with Snowflake databases

This is the approach to designing data mesh by designing a data domain and product boundaries using Snowflake databases. The same approach can be applied to designing data mesh using Snowflake schema objects; however, managing data domains and products using schema might be a cumbersome task. This section talks about the design pattern, implementation steps, design approach, and strategies to implement data products. Refer to *Figure 14.1*, which represents the design approach using Snowflake databases:

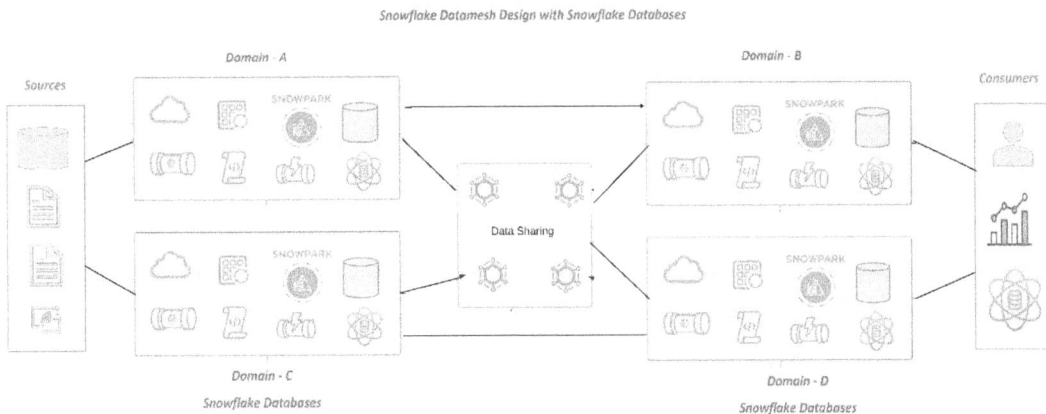

Figure 14.1: *Snowflake data mesh using databases*

As you observe here, each data domain is defined as a separate database, and data products used for each domain stay within the borders of the domain. As you are aware, Snowflake resources can be defined and set up for each data domain. These resources can include storage, databases, warehouses, access policies, etc. Refer to the following design considerations to implement data mesh with databases:

- One or more databases can be defined and combined to design a data domain. Database objects, processes, and resources can be used to set up data environments like development, **User Acceptance Testing** (**UAT**), and Production. Each environment can be set up with a database or schema. Compute can be defined as per the workload requirements for each data domain. Snowflake objects can be defined within databases, and usage monitoring can be implemented on top of each domain.

- Snowflake's self-service and data cloning can be used to set up the non-prod environments while developing data applications for each data domain.

- Define data ingestion pipelines specific to the domain that bring data from heterogeneous systems and types to the databases. Define schema to maintain the data layers and processing within databases.

- Use sharing to share the data between data domains as per the requirements to share data. Define a shared schema within the database to store objects to be shared. You can also define the share database that acts as a centralized repository or domain for data analysts and share the data from various domains with this common share database.

- Access control can be managed at the database, i.e., domain level. Define processes to request access to the domain databases and grant access to domain users.

- Compute and storage can be maintained separately for each domain in databases. Scaling up and down can be defined and managed in databases based on the workload patterns.

These are some of the key considerations to be considered while designing the data mesh with Snowflake databases. Snowflake resources can be used as objects to make it easier to define, design, and manage resources for each domain. This implementation brings a few benefits to the design, which are outlined as follows:

- **Access management**: Easy to manage and implement data access controls within an account. Access to data products can easily be set up by setting intra-database permissions.

- **Centralized governance**: Designing and defining the centralized network, security, and governance policy administration simplifies the overall management within an account.

- **Data availability:** Implementing **Disaster Recovery (DR)** for an account is simpler as it only requires one other account in another region or cloud to support it. One account can cater to the DR requirements for various domain data products designed using databases.

Implementing and managing resources at an account level can simplify the standards, guidelines, and processes. This is the simplest data mesh design approach with Snowflake. We can use Snowflake DDL and DML queries to create databases and maintain access privileges as part of data sharing.

Consider a use case where we implement a mesh architecture for an organization and want to separate the business units like finance, HR, operations, and IT. We can create these four databases and design corresponding engineering pipelines that have access to only those databases and schemas. Refer to the following queries:

```
/* Create databases for all business units */
CREATE DATABASE FIN_DB;   --database for Finance
CREATE DATABASE HR_DB;    --database for HR
CREATE DATABASE OPS_DB;   --database for OPS
CREATE DATABASE IT_DB;    --database for IT

/* create Schema for each database domain*/
CREATE SCHEMA FIN_DB.FIN;    --database schema for finance
CREATE SCHEMA FIN_DB.FIN_SHARE;    --database schema to share data with
other domains
CREATE SCHEMA HR_DB.HR;    --database schema for HR
CREATE SCHEMA OPS_DB.OPS;    --database schema for Operations
CREATE SCHEMA IT_DB.IT;    --database schema for IT

/*create roles  for FINANCE unit */
CREATE ROLE dw_fin_r;   --read only db role
CREATE ROLE dw_fin_rw;   --read and write role
CREATE ROLE dw_fin_admin;  --admin role
CREATE ROLE dw_fin_eng;    --engineering role
CREATE ROLE dw_fin_analysts;    --analyst role
CREATE ROLE dw_fin_reader;     --read-only account to share data
```

The next step is to grant permissions to the role and users to access and process data as part of the finance domain. In this case, finance is taken as one use case and other users that can access data from this database are added as read-only users of other domains:

```
/* grant permissions to the role */
-- Grant read-write permissions on database FIN to dw_fin_rw role.
GRANT USAGE ON DATABASE FIN_DB TO ROLE dw_fin_rw;
GRANT USAGE ON ALL SCHEMAS IN DATABASE FIN_DB TO ROLE dw_fin_rw;
GRANT SELECT,INSERT,UPDATE,DELETE ON ALL TABLES IN DATABASE  FIN_DB  TO
ROLE dw_fin_rw;

-- Grant read-only permissions on database FIN_DB  to dw_fin_reader role to
share read only data with other domain users
GRANT USAGE ON DATABASE FIN_DB TO ROLE dw_fin_reader;
GRANT USAGE ON SCHEMA FIN_SHARE IN DATABASE FIN_DB TO ROLE dw_fin_reader;
GRANT SELECT ON ALL VIEWS IN SCHEMA FIN_SHARE TO ROLE dw_fin_reader;
```

Like the finance domain, we can setup other domains and create roles to grant permissions to the required databases and objects. This implementation approach can be managed within the same account, and admin efforts can be reduced to manage multiple domains. The next option is to design a data mesh using Snowflake accounts. You will learn the design options and implementation considerations in the upcoming section.

Data domain with Snowflake accounts

Snowflake allows users to create multiple accounts on multiple clouds and multiple regions within an organization. These accounts can be set up on different clouds and regions depending on the application or business requirements. The design is very much like the database design. However, the data domains are defined as Snowflake accounts. Each domain has an individual account that ingests, processes, stores, and shares the data with centralized teams. The standards, guidelines, policies, and processes need to be defined and managed at an account for each domain. Each account will have its ingestion processes and data pipelines to transform data, storing the data ready for consumer applications. Store the data to be shared across domains and share the data using data sharing. Snowflake resources are defined and maintained at an account level independently for each domain to define the data products. Refer to *Figure 14.2*, which represents the data mesh design with Snowflake accounts:

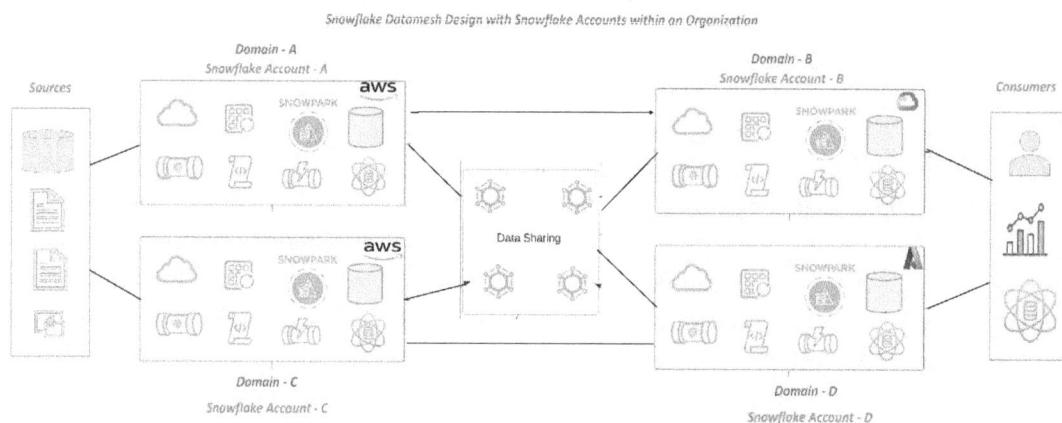

Figure 14.2: *Snowflake data mesh design with multiple accounts*

As you notice here, the Snowflake standard processes to ingest, transform, and store data remain the same across all domains. The data domains are products defined at an account level. Each domain can be a separate account on a different cloud and region. Here, four domains are defined: domains A, B, C, and D. Each domain has a set of pipelines to process the domain-specific information and create a data share to share data with other domains. Each domain can have different data consumers, such as BI, data analysts, data scientists, as well as data applications using AI/ML. All accounts can be defined within an organization. If you compare this design approach with the previous design approach with databases, then you will find some of the overhead in managing accounts. However, in some cases, companies want to adopt this implementation due to global presence and the need to maintain data within regional boundaries. Also, some of the organizations adopt multi-cloud strategies, and this will benefit the implementation of the data as a self-serve platform with a data mesh design approach.

With this approach, there are additional overheads to maintain the resources and some benefits over the database approach, as account level domain lets users define their namespace and processes. The following are some of the benefits of this approach:

- Snowflake data sharing and marketplace can be used to share data across domains and accounts.

- Global standards to define the naming conventions for resources can be maintained easily as each domain has a separate account. This helps to reduce the naming convention and namespace complexity with the database approach.

- These domains can be defined based on the business requirements to support specific regions and clouds.

- Instead of a centralized approach to standards, access control, and security policies, you can define separate policies independently for each account. This is a benefit and a challenge to maintain centralized governance. The standards need to be defined at an organizational level, and each domain should follow it with an account-level implementation.

- Resource monitoring and consumption policies can be set to an account and are easy to maintain. However, this needs to be set up as organizational policies to track each domain's usage and account to avoid additional spending.

These are some of the benefits of database approach implementation. Snowflake native resources and features allow us to define the standard practices across domains. Users can go with one of the approaches or a hybrid approach with a mix of both. Snowflake third-party tools and integrators can also be used in integration with native resources to maintain the data integrations as part of the source and consumer integrations. Snowflake shares some of the standard best practices and recommendations to set up the data platform. These are common across any data design, data warehouse, data lake, and data mesh. These are used to define the standards to reduce the overall complexity of the platform design. Refer to the following section to revisit some of the best practices shared by Snowflake.

Best practices and recommendations

Snowflake offers scalable and efficient solutions to implement data systems. Data engineering, data governance, and data integration are some of the critical aspects of data platform design. Snowflake recommends some of the best practices listed as follows for each of the design aspects:

- **Data engineering**: Snowflake recommends loading data in smaller chunks to achieve parallel loads. It is recommended to use **COPY** to load bulk data and Snowpipe to load micro batches to Snowflake databases. Snowpipe streaming can be used to bring in the streaming data to Snowflake. Use data integrators like fivetran, matillion, and others to bring in the source data to Snowflake. Snowflake's Snowpark can be used to replace spark workloads and achieve better performance. You can also leverage the programming connectors like Python -Snowflake connector to define custom pipelines if needed.

- **Data collaborations:** Data integration is key to sharing data with consumers and other applications. There is no need to maintain additional pipelines to share the data, refresh, and maintain consistency across the platform. It is recommended to use the data sharing and cloning feature of Snowflake, when applicable, to set up the integrations. Data sharing options like private listing, direct sharing can be used to share data across domains.

- **Data governance:** Snowflake is rich in features to implement governance across the data platform. Recommended to use **Role Based Access Control (RBAC)** centrally to manage users, roles, and access to the platform. As a best practice, implement dynamic masking to protect sensitive information and access to unauthorized users. It is recommended to use role-based policy control along with dynamic masking to protect data exposure. Define and manage the policies centrally.

- **Cost management**: As design advice, understanding the data and requirements to set up the time-travel to avoid any additional storage cost is advised. For compute cost, define the warehouses with optimum sizes and monitor the performance over a period. Use resize or redefine the cluster sizes based on the overall application usage across the platform.

- **Monitoring and operations design**: As a best practice, implement resource monitoring, and set up the automated alerting, reporting, and stored procedures to push out required alerts to avoid any additional storage and compute costs. Set up budgets and track the overall platform usage.

- **AI and ML workloads:** Snowflake supports and extends features to allow users to bring their own ML models to deploy within the platform. Snowflake powers users to implement ML workloads without moving data outside. We can run most types of ML models on top of underlying data in Snowflake platform. This benefits the overall process of having data and ML models reside within the same platform.

These are some of the recommendations to be considered while designing data lake systems and an engineering approach. Snowflake is a one-stop solution for all data and AI needs.

Conclusion

In this chapter, we have learned about data mesh systems and designing the data mesh platform using Snowflake. We have also learned to design the data mesh systems with two different approaches using Snowflake native features and offerings. Snowflake's native features and capabilities are used to design data mesh with multiple approaches.

The next design pattern is data Lakehouse, where we will learn how the Lakehouse design solves the challenges of data warehouse as well as data lake. This will help to start designing the data Lakehouse systems by leveraging Snowflake native features and integrations. You will learn Lakehouse design patterns in the next chapter.

Points to remember

The following are the key takeaways from this chapter:

- Data mesh design can be implemented with databases to set up the data products for each domain. Snowflake databases within an account can be used to design data mesh and allow users to share the data across data teams.

- Snowflake offers another option to implement a data mesh design with Snowflake accounts. Each data product can be defined as a data domain with an account. Data processes can be defined and implemented at an account for each domain. Data domains can be set up on multiple clouds and regions based on the business requirements to maintain regional data boundaries.

- Data integrators can be used to design data systems. Currently, fivetran and dbt are the commonly used data integrators to integrate heterogeneous sources as well as define the data workloads on top of Snowflake. You can choose to use integrators over native features to do the heavy lifting of the workloads.

Join our Discord space

Join our Discord workspace for latest updates, offers, tech happenings around the world, new releases, and sessions with the authors:

https://discord.bpbonline.com

CHAPTER 15
Building Data Lakehouses

Introduction

A Lakehouse is designed to have the capabilities of warehouses and a data lake. This chapter covers designing data Lakehouse solutions with Snowflake. This covers the data on Lakehouse architecture and the benefits of Lakehouse architecture patterns. This also covers the implementation of a Lakehouse use case using Snowflake services. Snowflake integration with Apache iceberg and open table formats allows users to design the lake house design platform. This chapter covers the integration and implementation of iceberg tables with Snowflake.

This chapter focuses on sharing the typical architecture and data needed to implement Lakehouse with Snowflake. This also covers the features, guidelines, and best practices to implement the features of Lakehouse design.

Structure

This chapter consists of the following topics:

- Unifying iceberg tables
- Implementing hybrid tables
- Data Lakehouse features
- Data Lakehouse with Snowflake

Objectives

By the end of this chapter, you will be able to understand the data Lakehouse and its design. You will also learn to design Lakehouses with Snowflake services and features. You can use the trial account setup earlier to perform various exercises throughout this book.

Unifying iceberg tables

Apache Iceberg and the iceberg open table format allow users to define the high-performance format of tables to implement analytical queries. Iceberg enables users to implement SQL-like features and operations on top of big data by simplifying the data format. Iceberg tables sit on top of the underlying data stored on storage buckets, enabling users to implement data lake and are powered with warehouse capabilities. Snowflake supports two types of iceberg tables, managed and unmanaged tables. The following are some of the workloads supported by the iceberg table:

- **Expressive SQL**: Supports flexible SQL commands to insert, update, delete, and apply changes to the target iceberg tables using SQL commands like **MERGE**. This also rewrites the files for read performance.

- **Schema evolution:** An iceberg table supports schema evolution without adding any extra steps to manage the table and underlying data. Column addition, deletion, and reordering can be done without rewriting the table with schema changes.

- **Partitioning**: Iceberg supports partitions and creates partitions automatically to improve the performance of data scans. The interesting fact about partitioning is handling dynamic partitioning based on the queries being executed or table layout changes.

- **Data protection**: The iceberg table supports time travel and rollback. Time travel allows users to query the data in past timestamps and access data from snapshots.

- **Data compaction**: This is used as an out-of-the-box solution to rewrite the data files by sorting or using any other strategies. This is used to improve performance by optimizing file layout and size.

These are some of the distinguishing features of iceberg tables. These tables are integrated with Snowflake and can be created as database objects. These types of tables are also considered as one of the table types supported in Snowflake. Let us learn about iceberg tables and use cases to implement these tables.

Snowflake iceberg tables

Snowflake iceberg tables act as an abstraction layer created on top of data files stored with open formats. Like iceberg tables, Snowflake iceberg tables support the following key features:

- ACID properties
- Schema evolution
- Data protection with time travel
- Hidden partitioning

These tables are defined on top of data feeds supported on the cloud storage. Snowflake iceberg table supports data feed stored in Parquet file formats. Let us understand how these iceberg tables work within Snowflake. Iceberg tables consume storage, metadata, and catalog information. The following are the components and resources consumed by iceberg tables:

- **Table storage**: Iceberg tables store data feeds on cloud storage, and metadata information files are also stored on external cloud storage. These data feeds are stored in external storage and need to be maintained externally by users. External storage can be configured as an external volume for iceberg tables, and these tables do not incur table storage costs.

- **External volume**: As you know, to integrate external storage buckets, we create external stages and integrate cloud storage buckets to read data from storage. For the iceberg table, we create external volumes, and these are defined as a Snowflake database object. Like an external stage, external volume can be used to define multiple iceberg tables. IAM is used to grant access and set up a secure connection to the external volume.

- **Iceberg catalog**: Catalog is the first architectural layer in the iceberg-specific tables. The catalog can be defined as an iceberg catalog as well as an external catalog. You can also define catalog integration as a database object used for multiple iceberg tables. Snowflakes can also be used to define the iceberg catalog.

- **Snowflake usage**: As you know, iceberg tables do not contribute to the storage cost as everything is set up on external volume and storage buckets. The Snowflake billing is incurred for using warehouses (compute) as well as the cloud services layer. The additional cost may add egress charges when the storage resides outside of the region where the Snowflake account is set up.

These are the key components and resources used to implement iceberg tables with Snowflake. As you have learned in this section, a catalog can be set up as an internal as well as an external catalog with catalog integration. Let us learn more about catalog design options in the following section.

Iceberg catalog design options

Snowflake's internal catalog and its external catalog can be defined using catalog integration. These two types of catalogs bring in their own benefits as well as challenges.

Snowflake's internal catalog allows users to perform read and write operations on the catalog. Snowflakes extends platform support and allows developers to work with iceberg catalog SDKs. Refer to *Figure 15.1,* which demonstrates the implementation of the Snowflake internal catalog and integration with external volume to get data and metadata information from the data feeds stored on external storage:

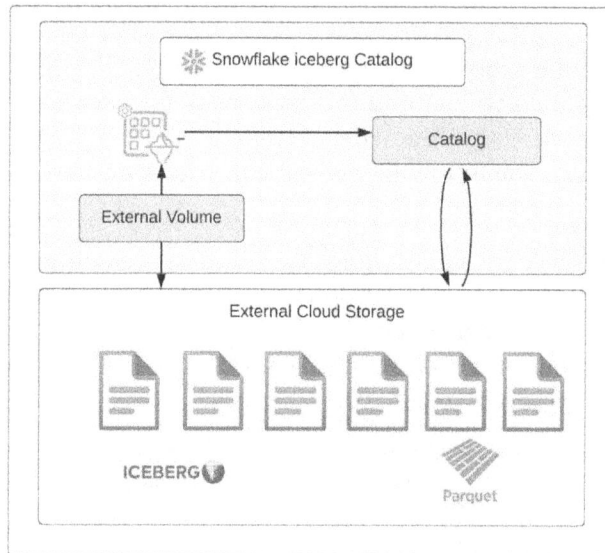

Figure 15.1: Snowflake internal catalog

As you can observe here, the catalog is defined within Snowflake, which pulls metadata details from the external data. Snowflake's internal catalog can be used to implement the managed iceberg tables, where data can be written back to iceberg tables. In this case, data will be written, and metadata information will be updated. Refer to the following steps and sample code to set up the external volume and Snowflake catalog and create an iceberg table:

1. Create a Snowflake database and warehouse to perform a demo of iceberg tables:

```
/* create Snowflake resources - database, warehouse*/
CREATE WAREHOUSE demo_iceberg_wh
  WAREHOUSE_TYPE = STANDARD
  WAREHOUSE_SIZE = XSMALL;

USE WAREHOUSE demo_iceberg_wh;
/* create database */
```

```
CREATE OR REPLACE DATABASE demo_iceberg_db;
CREATE SCHEMA poc;
USE DATABASE demo_iceberg_db;
USE SCHEMA poc;
```

2. Create an external volume:

    a. As you know, this is like an external stage that needs additional configuration, like the creation of an IAM role and setting up policies and rules to access the data from the given storage buckets. Follow the steps provided on the Snowflake documentation tutorial page to set the connectivity: **https://docs.snowflake.com/en/user-guide/tutorials/create-your-first-iceberg-table#create-an-external-volume**.

    b. Once you set the connectivity, use the **CREATE** statement to create the external volume as follows:

```
/* create external volume*/
CREATE OR REPLACE EXTERNAL VOLUME demo_external_volume
    STORAGE_LOCATIONS =
        (
            (
                NAME = 'demo-s3-us-west-2'
                STORAGE_PROVIDER = 'S3'
                STORAGE_BASE_URL = 's3://<demo_bucket>/'
                STORAGE_AWS_ROLE_ARN =
'<arn:aws:iam::xxxxxxxxxxxx:role/demorole>'
                STORAGE_AWS_EXTERNAL_ID = 'external_table_id'
            )
        );
```

Once volume is created, get the details, and allow traffic between **Amazon Web Services (AWS)** and Snowflake account by following up steps on the documentation link shared previously.

3. Create an iceberg table using the **CREATE** statement:

```
/* create table */
CREATE OR REPLACE ICEBERG TABLE account_demo_table (
    Account_id INTEGER,
    acc_name STRING,
    acc_address STRING,
    acc_zipcd STRING,
    acc_phone STRING,
    acc_bal NUMERIC,
```

```
      acc_status STRING,
      acc_comment STRING
)
      CATALOG = 'SNOWFLAKE'
      EXTERNAL_VOLUME = 'demo_external_volume'
      BASE_LOCATION = 'account_demo';
```

Here, the **demo_external_volume** points to an S3 bucket, and the base location is the folder location on the bucket where all corresponding Parquet files are stored. As this is a Snowflake-managed catalog, you can also define another iceberg table using the **CREATE TABLE AS** statement by selecting multiple columns from another iceberg table.

In contrast, the external catalog has restricted operations to be performed on metadata. Only read operations are allowed on the external catalog, and users cannot perform any write operations. Refer to *Figure 15.2*, which represents the use of an external catalog and integration with Snowflake using catalog integration. You can define the catalog using external cloud resources. Here, in this case, the AWS Glue catalog can be used to implement a metadata catalog for iceberg tables.

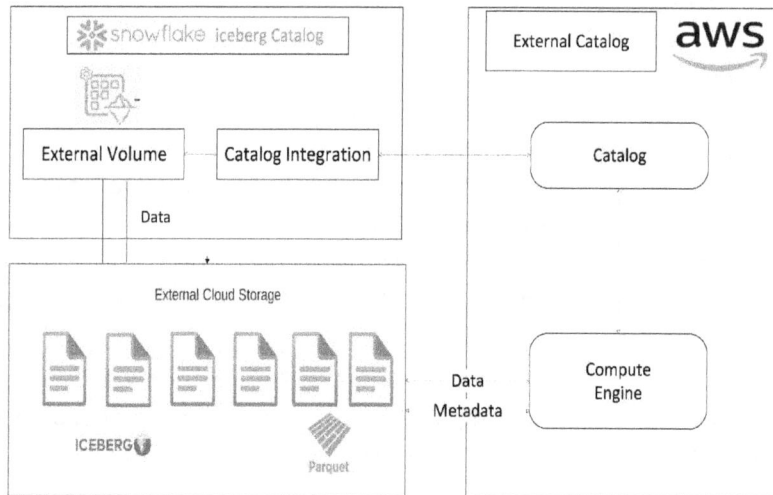

Figure 15.2: External iceberg catalog

The external storage stores the data in Parquet format and is integrated with Snowflake and the external cloud to maintain the catalog information. The data and metadata information are maintained at an external cloud using a compute engine. Cloud integration is created as an integration object within Snowflake to integrate with the catalog. Refer to the following steps and set of sample statements used to set up the catalog integration and external volume, and define the iceberg table.

1. **Setup the Snowflake database and warehouse for the demo:** Refer to the steps in the previous section to set up the context.

2. **Create external volume**: Follow the steps shared in the preceding section to create the external volume.

3. **Create a catalog integration:** As you know, the AWS Glue Data catalog needs to be integrated as a catalog integration before we create an iceberg table:

```
/* create catalog integration*/
CREATE CATALOG INTEGRATION aws_glue_int
  CATALOG_SOURCE=GLUE
  CATALOG_NAMESPACE='<catalog-namespace>'
  TABLE_FORMAT=ICEBERG
  GLUE_AWS_ROLE_ARN='<arn-for-aws-role-to-assume>'
  GLUE_CATALOG_ID='<catalog-id>'
  GLUE_REGION='<optional-aws-region-of-the-glue-catalog>'
  ENABLED=TRUE;
```

4. **Define table:** Once volume and catalog integration are defined, the next step is to define a table that uses an external catalog. For example, let us consider that we want to use the AWS Glue Data Catalog to set up the catalog for iceberg tables. The following is the **CREATE** statement to define the table with an external catalog:

```
/* create table */
CREATE ICEBERG TABLE demo_iceberg_table
  EXTERNAL_VOLUME='demo_glue_volume'
  CATALOG='aws_glue_int'
  CATALOG_TABLE_NAME='demo_Glue_Table';
```

Here, the catalog integration setup is for read-only access to the catalog and metadata information. These tables are used only to read data from storage. Snowflake users cannot write data back to these tables. We have learned to create and use iceberg tables in this section. Now, let us learn about the data platform design where we can implement transactional as well as analytical queries on the same table. Snowflake offers hybrid tables to extend support to transactional and operational operations same time. The following section covers the Lakehouse design features and benefits.

Implementing hybrid tables

Hybrid tables are tables that support operational as well as transactional workloads with low latency and high throughput. These tables support the enforcement of unique and referential integrity constraints, which are essential for transactional operations. Hybrid tables are integrated seamlessly with Snowflake architecture. These tables are accessed and queried in the same way as any other object within the Snowflake platform. Query executions follow the same path as other queries; these are compiled and optimized in the cloud services layer, which is later executed within virtual warehouses as a query engine. Implementation of hybrid tables brings several benefits of Snowflake architecture:

- Snowflake Data Governance features can be applied to hybrid tables.

- This supports hybrid workloads, i.e., operational and analytical queries.

- Hybrid tables are joined with other Snowflake tables.

- Queries with hybrid and native tables get executed natively and efficiently in the same query engine. There is no federation required.

You can use Snowflake native tables that offer support to workloads catering to analytical and transactional operations. Hybrid tables can be used to execute the following types of queries:

- Queries that have high concurrent reads over large reads

- High concurrent random writes over large sequential writes

- Queries accessing small numbers of records over narrow projected results

Hybrid tables are created using the **CREATE HYBRID TABLE** command. **CREATE** DDL can be used with DDL statements as well as with **CREATE TABLE AS** clauses. Refer to the following examples:

```
/* CREATE HYBRID table using DDL */
CREATE OR REPLACE HYBRID TABLE cust_info(
  cust_id NUMBER PRIMARY KEY AUTOINCREMENT START 1 INCREMENT 1,
  cust_addr VARCHAR NOT NULL,
  cust_email VARCHAR NOT NULL
  );

/* CTAS Hybrid table */
CREATE OR REPLACE HYBRID TABLE customer_demo(
  cust_id INT PRIMARY KEY,
  dept_id VARCHAR(200)
  )
AS SELECT * FROM customer_details;
```

Tables can be created using one of the preceding **CREATE** table methods. Data can be loaded using **COPY INTO** as well as using **INSERT SELECT** statement. Data loading can be slower for large data volumes. Like any other transactional tables, users can define indexes and constraints on top of hybrid tables. Indexes can be defined along with the **CREATE** DDL. Users can also add indexes using **CREATE INDEX** statements. Hybrid tables expect a unique primary key, and the data present in the table is ordered by primary key. Users can add nonprimary key columns as part of secondary indexes.

Hybrid tables consumption

The hybrid table cost is calculated based on the modes of consumption. The following are the modes of consumption and the cost incurred:

- **Storage cost**: Like any other table, hybrid table storage cost is associated with the data stored in these tables. Storage cost is calculated based on the flat monthly rate in GB.

- **Compute cost**: Virtual warehouse usage cost is the same as any other queries run on standard tables. The compute cost associated with hybrid tables is the same as queries executed on warehouses. Cost is based on the size of the warehouse and uptime.

- **Hybrid table request**: These tables consume additional credits to use serverless resources on the underlying row storage clusters. Consumption is based on read-and-write to the clusters.

Snowflake **USAGE** views are used to gather the consumption details of hybrid tables. The following views can be used to monitor the performance and consumption of hybrid tables:

- STORAGE_USAGE view
- DATABASE_STORAGE_USAGE_HISTORY view
- HYBRID_TABLES view
- HYRBID_TABLE_USAGE_HISTORY view

You can query these views to monitor the usage of hybrid tables. Transactions run on hybrid tables can be viewed using **SHOW TRANSACTIONS**, **DESCRIBE TRANSACTIONS**, **SHOW LOCKS**, etc. You can get started with hybrid tables with the tutorial **https://docs.snowflake. com/en/user-guide/tutorials/getting-started-with-hybrid-tables-tutorial**.

Hybrid tables allow users to design heterogeneous workloads within a single Snowflake platform. These tables can be used to implement a data warehouse, data lake, and Lakehouse systems. We will learn more about Lakehouse features in the following section.

Data Lakehouse features

Lakehouse is one of the widely adopted design patterns that can bring capabilities of both warehouse and lake design patterns. In previous eras, there was a choice to implement one design pattern or another. However, with cloud adoptions, the design patterns can also be combined. We have learned about the features of data warehouses and data lake systems. Now, let us understand the unified features of the Lakehouse design pattern and the benefits Snowflake offers:

- Independent storage and compute
- Scaling of data volumes as well as storage
- Handling heterogeneous types of data, structured, semi-structured, and unstructured
- Strong and centralized data governance

- Support to transactional operations with ACID

- Access to the raw as well as curated data

- Cost and performance efficiency

- Extended support to open table formats with iceberg integration

- Data sharing and cloning is easy with Snowflake

- Variety of data engineering design options with Snowflake

- **Artificial intelligence (AI)** and **machine learning (ML)** native support with Snowflake

- Data application development and support within Snowflake

These are some of the key features of Lakehouse and Snowflake native features that extend the platform capabilities for better data collaborations, security, engineering, enhancements, and availability. Snowflake native capabilities allow users to implement efficient, scalable data solutions that support any type of data. Platform benefits and features are common for any data system design pattern, data warehouse, data lake, data mesh, as well as Lakehouse. Refer to the following summarized list of features Snowflake offers to Lakehouse design:

- **Flexibility**: Data availability in raw format enables data scientists and analysts to build features for machine learning. Data can also be accessed from a curated layer for specific analytics and reporting use cases.

- **Compatibility**: Data lake platform is compatible to integrate with other tools and open-source technologies. This simplifies the integration with any source as well as consumer systems.

- **Elasticity**: Snowflake warehouses can be set up to address diverse types of workloads with auto-scaling and resizing.

- **Operational excellence**: Notification integration can be used to implement alerting. Snowsight can be used to set up dashboards for operations and monitoring using metadata views. We can use notification integration with cloud providers like AWS SNS and configure notifications to be sent over Teams, Slack, emails, etc. We can also use native **SYSTEM** function to send an email to the identified **distribution list (DL)**.

- **Maintainability**: Snowflake is a data platform that allows users to integrate heterogeneous workloads and integrations with integrators. With one platform, it becomes easy to maintain and reduce the complexity of the workload's maintenance.

- **Performance and cost efficiency**: The Snowflake platform's parallelism allows users to achieve performance efficiency. Warehouse and serverless resource usage based on the utilization enables users to achieve cost efficiency.

- **Engineering options:** The Snowflake platform offers a variety of tables and native tools that allow users to set up the data pipelines as per their needs to cater to business requirements. Dynamic tables can potentially replace the data pipelines used to transform the data. Iceberg is used to bring in open format data to Snowflake without loading data to native storage. Event tables allow users to log events and trace network issues. Hybrid tables allow users to define a single table for OLTP and OLAP operations.

These are some of the considerations, features, and benefits of implementing data Lakehouse with Snowflake. Data integrations and third-party tools are used to integrate with other data sources. Data processing pipelines can be implemented using SQL, SQL scripting, dynamic tables, and Snowpark. We will learn to design and implement data Lakehouse in the upcoming section.

Data Lakehouse with Snowflake

A data Lakehouse solution was adopted to extend the capabilities of the data platform beyond the warehouse and data lake. As you know, Snowflake data on the cloud offers a variety of features to handle heterogeneous data formats, types of data, real-time streaming, batches, and micro batches of data. Snowflake data solution allows users to implement, **Extract, Transform, and Load** (ETL) and **Extract, Load, and Transform** (ELT) engineering approaches. The following are some of the key considerations for designing a lakehouse:

- **Data layers**: Data is stored in raw format: structured, semi-structured, and unstructured data feeds. Data is also processed and stored as a curated layer for data analysts' use cases.

- **Data processing**: Snowflake supports the implementation of engineering pipelines using Snowflake SQL, scripting, Snowpark, and scripting with Python, Java, JavaScript, and Scala. Snowflake dynamic tables can be used to define and automate data transformation jobs. Snowflake streams and tasks can be used to implement **change data capture** (CDC).

- **Data formats:** Snowflake supports heterogeneous file formats, supported as part of structured, semi-structured, and open-source formats, like ORC, Avro, and Parquet allow users to store and process files. Unstructured data feeds are also supported with directory tables. Snowflake integration with Apache Iceberg allows users to create tables to access data in an open table format.

- **Data collaborations**: Snowflake data sharing allows users to set up the shares to be shared with consumer users. Data share can be set up to share the data in raw format for feature engineering and ML use cases.

- **AI and ML capabilities**: Snowflake cortex **large language model** (LLM) functions and container service allow users to implement AI/ML as well as LLM use cases. Snowflake offers a one-stop solution to implement data lake efficiently.

These features can be implemented with the right choice of tools and tech stack, depending on the business and application requirements. Refer to *Figure 15.3,* which shares a list of options and engineering approaches to implement data Lakehouse design:

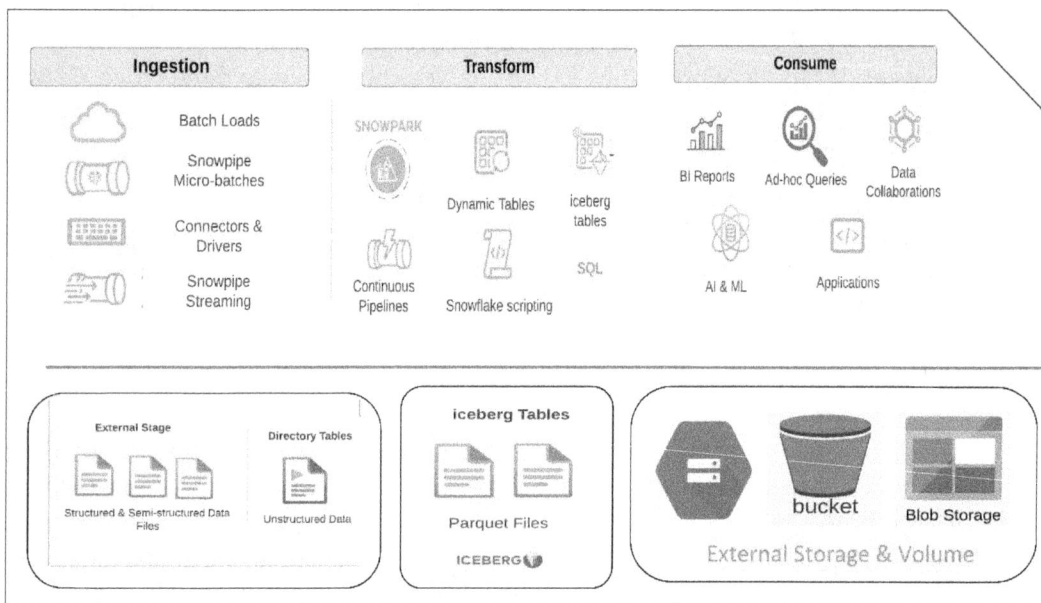

Figure 15.3: Data Lakehouse design solution

Here, *Figure 15.3* shares choices of the services and integrations that can be used to set up the data platform. The following are the choices available to set various aspects of Lakehouse design:

- **Data engineering:** Data engineering design is the core aspect of platform design. Data ingestion, data processing, data transformations, data aggregations, and data curation are the types of engineering workloads:

  o **Data ingestions:** There are distinct options available to integrate with source systems and get source data as part of ingestion processes. The following are some of the options for designing data ingestion pipelines:

    ▪ Get the source data feed pushed to cloud storage buckets to integrate with the Snowflake platform. Use COPY to bulk load data into Snowflake.

    ▪ Using data integrators like Matillion and fivetran can be used to connect to any type of source to get data.

    ▪ Micro batches or mini batches data load using Snowpipe and automating data loads using cloud-native services.

- Snowpipe streaming to read data from Kafka streaming and load it to Snowflake tables.

- Creating external stages or volumes to define integration with cloud storage. Define a table based on the underlying data stored in the storage buckets. You can create iceberg tables, external tables, and directory tables to get source data from external storage to Snowflake.

o **Data processing:** Data transformations using Snowflake scripting and SQL jobs. Refer to the following processes and design approach to implement data pipelines:

- **Change Data Capture (CDC):** Implementing SCD Type II using Snowflake streams and tasks.

- **Data transformations:** Setting up pipelines using dbt and designing models to run data transformation logic. Data is processed and stored in databases and tables. Designing native pipelines using SQL and SQL scripting can also be a choice for implementing transformation jobs.

- Dynamic tables and materialized views are the Snowflake serverless services that allow users to define the transformation logic, and data is refreshed in target tables automatically.

These are some of the engineering workloads and probable choices to implement the engineering pipelines on the data platform.

- **Data governance:** Governance is a critical part of data system design and sits on top of data architecture. Snowflake Horizon offers a bunch of services to implement data governance. The following are the features used to implement governance pillars:

o **Dynamic masking:** Sensitive data and personal information must be protected from unauthorized access. Dynamic data masking and implementing it for role-based or tag-based masking to protect data from unauthorized access. Setting up data masking policies to mask sensitive information.

o **Data protection:** Data can be protected from accidental drops and recovered using time-travel as well as failsafe. You can also recover the dropped objects like tables, schemas, and even databases. Failsafe is used in case of disaster recovery when the data cannot be recovered by the owners.

o **Data security:** Data security can be implemented with network policies, the right set of access control policies, and defining standards and guidelines on data sharing. Data is encrypted and stored within Snowflake native storage.

Row-level security can be implemented with the help of database objects like views and secure views.

o **Access control**: **Role-based access control (RBAC)** manages user access to the platform. It is recommended to manage the governance as a centralized layer; hence, implementing the roles and access as a centralized set of roles for each type of workload helps to implement better control over applications and processes.

Snowflake Horizon helps to define and implement centralized governance for the platform. Snowflake also supports compliance based on the data and compliance requirements for a given region.

- **Data processes and standards:** As you are aware, data architecture pillars cater to critical non-functional requirements and allow users to define a balanced, well-architected data architecture. This section shares the standard requirements of the platform. Refer to the following aspects of the design and define your processes accordingly:

o **Standard processes**: Error handling with notification integrations and generating alerts. Monitoring warehouse usage with resource monitors. Setting up operational observability with Snowsight.

o **Data Quality checks (DQ)**: Automating the data checks using Snowflake stored procedures. We can also use Snowflake's **data quality metrics (DQM)** and set them to run on a regular basis to report the DQ issues. These can also be configured using tasks to run regular interval.

o **Performance and cost efficiency**: This is the layer used to set up the budgets and alerts. As part of performance efficiency and measures, implement processes to monitor the execution of workloads and report the long run queries or queued queries. Cost efficiency with monitoring metadata view information to avoid any additional cost.

o **Operations and monitoring**: You can leverage Snowflake native features like budgets, resource monitors, and admin console options to monitor the overall spending for an account. You can also define custom solutions to monitor the usage of specific applications or workloads. Snowflake notification integrations can be used to generate custom notifications as part of operations and monitoring.

With the preceding sections, we have learned the Lakehouse architecture design, implementation strategy, and processes. You can also refer to the best practices and recommendations shared in earlier chapters, as these are applicable to engineering workloads and managing Snowflake resources across the platform.

Conclusion

In this chapter, we have learned about data Lakehouse systems and designing them using Snowflake. We have also learned about open file formats and iceberg implementation with Snowflake and external catalogs. Snowflake's architecture and variety of native features offer engineering options to implement any data system patterns. Snowflake introduced Snowpark and Snowpark-based warehouses to support memory-intensive workloads. Snowpark is also used to implement ML workloads. We will learn more about Snowpark and implementing ML workloads with Snowpark ML in the next chapter.

Points to remember

- Snowflake supports open file formats and creation of iceberg tables on top of the open file formats saved as data feeds on the external storage. Currently, it supports file feeds with parquet format only.

- Snowflake iceberg tables can be managed as well as unmanaged tables. Managed tables allow read and write operations, whereas unmanaged tables allow only read operations on the table.

- Data Lakehouse is an architecture pattern that enables users to implement data lake and warehouse capabilities. Snowflake native features and services can be used to implement Lakehouse.

Join our Discord space

Join our Discord workspace for latest updates, offers, tech happenings around the world, new releases, and sessions with the authors:

https://discord.bpbonline.com

CHAPTER 16
Embracing Snowpark and Snowpark ML

Introduction

Snowpark is one of the Snowflake offerings that is rich in programming support, data frames, and built-in libraries to support engineering as well as data science and ML needs. This chapter helps to understand Snowpark ML libraries and their use. This also helps to understand how Snowpark is different and used to design and develop engineering as well as ML pipelines. You will learn to implement ML lifecycle using Snowpark ML libraries and features.

This chapter focuses on sharing the typical architecture and data needed to implement Lake with Snowflake. This also covers the guidelines and best practices to implement engineering approaches and optimizations as part of lake design. This also shares a commonly used modernization use case with Snowflake and the steps followed to migrate the data platform to Snowflake. This is the next chapter in the series of architecture design, where you will learn to design data platform systems.

Structure

This chapter consists of the following topics:

- Distinguishing features of Snowpark
- Understand Snowflake ML lifecycle

- Build your ML use case with Snowflake
- Implementing existing ML use cases

Objectives

We will learn about the unified features of Snowflake Snowpark. This chapter also discusses the Snowflake features used to implement ML use cases and define the ML lifecycle. Snowpark ML libraries enable users to bring their custom models and integrate with the Snowflake platform. We will learn to implement new and existing ML use cases with Snowflake.

Distinguishing features of Snowpark

Snowflake provides Snowpark libraries in three languages: Java, Python, and Scala. This API provides a library that can be used to query and process data at scale. This is used to implement application code within Snowflake without moving data outside. Now, you can have your application code and data processed within the same platform.

Snowpark is different than Snowflake connector for spark, and this brings additional benefits, listed as follows:

- Snowpark offers libraries built for different languages that can be used to process data within Snowflake without compromising performance or functionality.

- Extended support to develop code using local tools such as Jupyter, VS Code, or IntelliJ.

- This offers extended support for pushdown for all operations along with Snowflake UDFs. Snowpark enables users to push down all heavy lifting to Snowflake data cloud, leveraging Snowflake performance efficiency to work with any size of data.

- Snowpark does not need any separate cluster within the platform to execute Snowpark workloads. Snowflake's Snowpark-designed warehouses bring all essential computing and scale.

- Snowpark also supports SQL statements to be incorporated into the code. You can define a dataframe that can read specified columns from a Snowflake table.

- Snowpark does not need to move data outside the data platform. Processing logic can read and process data using dataframe within Snowflake.

- Snowpark also supports user-defined functions that can be defined within application code.

Snowflake documentation shares a developer guide to help developers get started with Snowpark. Refer to the following links to get started:

- Snowpark developer guide for Python: https://docs.snowflake.com/en/developer-guide/snowpark/python/index

- Snowpark developer guide for Scala: https://docs.snowflake.com/en/developer-guide/snowpark/scala/index

- Snowpark developer for Java: https://docs.snowflake.com/en/developer-guide/snowpark/java/index

- Snowpark libraries can be downloaded from https://developers.snowflake.com/snowpark/

Snowflake platform enables users to maintain almost all types of workloads within the platform. Now, with Snowpark optimized warehouses and some of the extended features, the platform allows users to deploy ML workloads.

Understand Snowflake ML lifecycle

AI/ML is used to generate data insights from the underlying data processed as part of engineering processes. Typically, we have seen in the past where data is moved or copied over to other platforms for data analytics as well as AI/ML needs. Often, developing and managing data pipelines to refresh or replicate data over to other platforms is tedious as well as time-consuming. Though the pipelines are running and maintained, data consistency and availability are always questioned. Nowadays, with cloud adoptions and scalable data platform solutions, maintaining additional pipelines for analytics is no longer a challenge. However, with some cloud adoption use cases, data still needs to be pulled out of the data platform to be fed into AI platforms or services.

Snowflake has been working on making data platforms scalable and easier to implement in various data use cases. With Snowpark ML, Snowflake has made it easier to build and implement ML models. Snowpark ML offers Python libraries as well as the infrastructure required to build for end-to-end ML use cases. Snowpark ML allows data scientists to use Python-based frameworks to develop ML models on top of the underlying data stored in the same platform without moving data, creating data silos, and data governance trade-offs.

ML feature engineering and model training

Snowpark ML API enables data scientists to use the most used Python ML frameworks like XGBoost, scikit-learn, etc. We can work on feature engineering and model training within the same platform without moving data out of Snowflake. Refer to some of the benefits of ML modeling:

- **Improved performance**: With Snowpark ML, data pre-processing and feature engineering are easier with scalability and distributed processing of the Python-based learning functions.

- **Accelerated model training**: Snowpark ML helps to accelerate the model training without maintaining or creating the stored procedures or UDFs for machine learning programs like XGBoost or scikit-learn. Snowpark ML offers distributed hyperparameter optimization to accelerate training. Snowflake's scalable and distributed parallel processing helps to execute training processes in parallel.

Snowpark ML API offers various functions for performant and scalable solutions. This also provides built-in wrappers for classes to be executed in the Snowflake platform. This feature benefits data scientists and analysts by reducing overall development time by reducing the time to develop any custom stored procedures or user-defined functions to integrate these libraries into Snowflake for processing.

ML model operations and management

ML model development follows a similar path as any other development cycle, with a need to implement version control. As part of model management, model development is the first step, followed by training and maintaining the versions of the trained models to test and evaluate the performance of each improved version. Snowflake offers the ability to track versions and maintain the metadata of ML models in a scalable and governed fashion. Snowflake's Snowpark model registry allows users to secure, manage, and execute models within the platform. Refer to *Figure 16.1*, which represents the model registry:

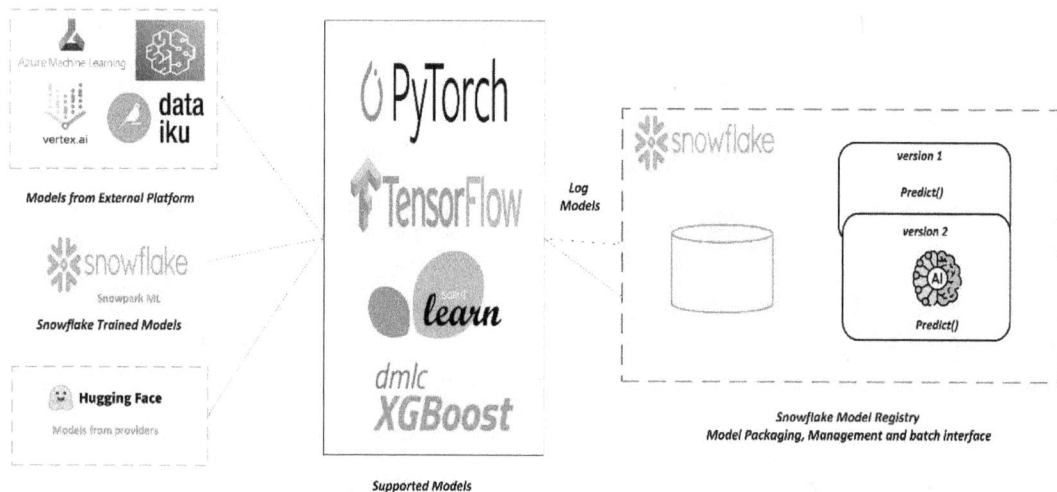

Figure 16.1: Snowpark Model Registry(Snowflake Documentation)

Snowpark Model Registry saves models as model entities and enables users to manage models created within or outside the Snowflake platform. The registry is managed as a Snowflake object that offers version-based containers for ML model artifacts, and these can be managed with **Role-Based Access Control (RBAC)**. Users can register several model types, including:

- Scikit-learn
- Snowpark ML modeling
- XGBoost
- Pytorch
- Tensorflow
- MLFlow
- HuggingFace pipelines

Snowpark's ML lifecycle has phases, and various ML components of Snowflake can be used to manage model lifecycle development. Refer to *Figure 16.2,* which represents a model development cycle:

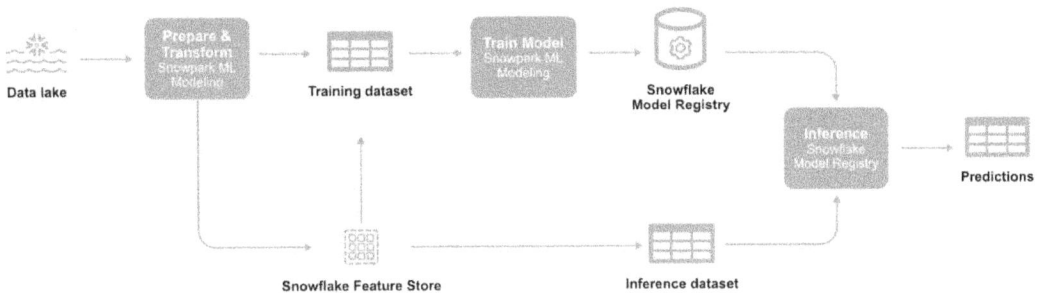

Figure 16.2: ML Model development cycle (Snowflake Documentation)

The following are the ML components that contribute to the overall cycle of ML development and management:

- **Snowflake Model Registry**: This allows users to manage deployed ML models within the Snowflake platform or outside.

- **Snowflake Feature Store**: This is an integrated solution to define, manage, store, and discover features that are derived from the data. Feature store supports automatic refresh based on the data refreshed in batch or streaming data sources. This helps to reduce the development and management of additional pipelines required for feature development or refresh.

- **Snowflake datasets:** This component provides immutable and versioned snapshots of the data required for machine learning models.

- **Snowflake notebooks**: This is like Jupyter Notebook and provides a seamless experience within the Snowflake platform. These are used to develop custom ML workloads.

Snowflake ML development uses defined components to build an end-to-end lifecycle. Snowflake also offers ML lineage to track the data flow and make it easy to debug the data flowing into models, just the same as data lineage. ML Lineage is a feature available in preview as of now and is available for all accounts with Enterprise and higher editions. Refer to *Figure 16.3*, which shares a view of ML lineage:

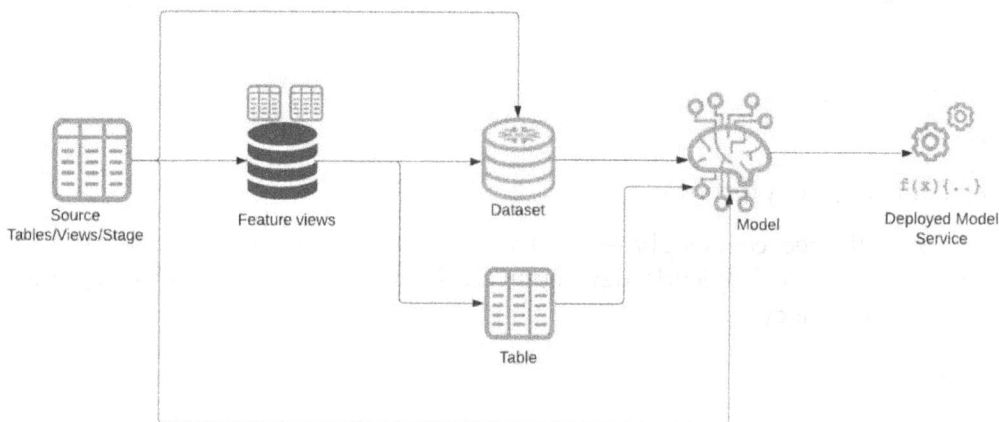

Figure 16.3: ML Lineage (Snowflake Documentation)

This lineage can be viewed using Snowsight lineage features and can query it using API along with ML workflows. Refer to **https://github.com/Snowflake-Labs/snowflake-demo-notebooks/blob/main/ML%20Lineage%20Workflows/ML%20Lineage%20Workflows. ipynb** ML lineage workflow notebook as reference examples.

Build your ML use case with Snowpark ML

In this section, we will learn to build ML use cases using Snowpark ML. As you know by now, there are various components involved in the ML lifecycle, and we can use Notebooks to start developing custom ML models. Before we start learning to build, the following are the prerequisites for the same:

- Snowflake Account

- Git installed, if you do not have it installed, you can download it from **https://git-scm.com/book/en/v2/Getting-Started-Installing-Git**

- Copy Snowflake reference Git Repo from **https://github.com/Snowflake-Labs/ sfguide-intro-to-machine-learning-with-snowflake-ml-for-python**

- Snowflake role with permissions to create databases, tables, functions, stored procedures, etc.

- Use a system-defined role or create one for the ML engineer along with the ML databases and warehouses for the **Proof Of Concept (POC)**.

We will take a reference from one of the Snowflake QuickStarts to get started with building a use case. This QuickStart includes the following steps:

1. Load and prepare data.

2. Features transformations using Snowpark ML transformers.

3. Train an XGBoost ML model using Snowpark ML estimators.

4. Log models and execute batch inference in Snowflake using the Snowflake Model Registry.

5. Apply a built-in explainability function to understand model performance.

6. Manage model metadata and trace machine learning artifacts via Snowflake Datasets and ML Lineage.

Refer to **https://quickstarts.snowflake.com/guide/intro_to_machine_learning_with_snowpark_ml_for_python/#0** for details. This QuickStart provides end-to-end steps and required code snippets to perform these operations. You can open the link and use the corresponding reference links for Git Repo and others as needed. Once you complete this lab, you will be able to complete an end-to-end ML workflow.

Implementing existing ML use cases

We have learned to develop and implement ML models with Snowflake ML Components. As you know, the ML model registry is used to register, maintain, and manage the versioning of the models. The same can be used to register any custom model that is pre-built on a different platform. Consider that you have a data platform and ML environment on-premise. There is a set of ML models running on legacy platforms or in your existing ecosystem. Your team has worked on migrating the data platform to Snowflake, and you are evaluating whether you can reuse the existing ML models within the Snowflake platform using Snowpark ML. You can follow these steps to start evaluating and planning to migrate existing models to Snowflake:

1. Analyze existing models, libraries, and packages being used.

2. Review existing models and packages supported by Snowpark ML.

3. Refer to Snowflake documentation to review the packages supported.

4. List down the packages and create a checklist of what is supported and what needs to be added to the Snowflake platform.

5. For prebuilt libraries available with Snowpark, validate the versions and classes available versus being used in the existing model.

6. For custom libraries to be added, create a list of libraries and gather the details required to start curating steps to create custom packages.

7. Develop and deploy custom packages.

8. Export the Jupyter Notebook to Snowflake notebooks.

9. Modify the existing notebooks to accommodate required changes as per platform specifics or syntax.

10. Register the custom model with model registry.

11. Train your model.

12. Start using the model as part of the SQL.

There are several references available to get started with the ML lifecycle steps. These steps are the same for new as well as existing models. You can refer to the previous section and quickstarts for ML lifecycle step reference. We can use the `snowflake.ml.model.CustomModel` class to log custom models to the Snowflake Model Registry and use them. You can also follow these steps and prerequisites before you get started.

We need the following setup to be done prior to starting with custom model registration:

- Snowflake trial account if needed
- Snowflake user logon
- Snowflake ML role
- Have the following tools installed on your local device:
  - Git
  - Anaconda
  - Python 3.10

Once we have this setup ready, follow the next steps to register a custom model. Refer to **https://quickstarts.snowflake.com/guide/deploying_custom_models_to_snowflake_model_registry/index.html#0** lab to register custom models.

We can use SQL DDL commands, the same as any other Snowflake database objects, to create and manage models. The following are the SQL commands used:

- CREATE MODEL
- DROP MODEL
- ALTER MODEL
- SHOW MODELS

Snowflake also offers a variety of SQL commands to manage versions, model functions, and model monitoring. Once an ML model is registered with the model registry, we can use this as a part of SQL, just like a function, and run predictions or get model results. Seamless integration and easier-to-follow steps set Snowflake as one of the preferred data platforms to implement ML within the same data platform.

Conclusion

We have learned about Snowpark ML in this chapter. We have also learned about the Snowflake ML lifecycle and how Snowpark can be used to define the lifecycle and implement ML models. Also, we have learned about the Snowflake ML components that are part of the lifecycle, including model registry, dataset, ML lineage, etc. This chapter also shares two use cases to build ML models within Snowflake, as well as bringing a custom model or package to the platform. We will learn more about architecting LLM solutions and using Snowflake Horizon and Cortex in upcoming chapters.

The next chapter shares insights on architecting LLM solutions, Streamlit, and native app framework implementation.

Points to remember

This chapter is the foundation of implementing AI/ML workloads within the Snowflake data platform. Refer to the following key takeaways from the chapter:

- Snowpark is a library-based framework supported by Snowflake in three different languages: Python, Java, and Scala.

- Snowpark data frames are an additional interface on top of underlying data in Snowflake. Internally, dataframes are converted to SQL and executed on the Snowflake SQL engine.

- Snowpark ML libraries offer a variety of built-in libraries and packages that can be used to define and implement ML models.

- ML lifecycle follows certain steps and components within the platform.

- Snowflake model registry is used to register the model and maintain versioning of the model. Snowflake ML lineage offers an end-to-end lineage of data sourced, processed, and fed into the ML models.

- Custom models can also be registered, and packages can be added in Snowflake.

Join our Discord space

Join our Discord workspace for latest updates, offers, tech happenings around the world, new releases, and sessions with the authors:

https://discord.bpbonline.com

Architecting LLM Solutions with Snowflake

Introduction

LLM, or large language models, are widely used these days to implement generative AI use cases. Snowflake offers a wide range of integrations and services to build applications with Snowflake. This chapter covers the most interesting offerings of Snowflake- native apps that support LLM capabilities and are used to implement most of the latest solutions with Snowflake. This helps to learn about the native apps, integrating the Open AI model with Snowpark and Streamlit to design and implement your first application with Snowflake.

This chapter focuses on sharing the typical architecture and data needed to implement Lake with Snowflake. This also covers the guidelines and best practices to implement engineering approaches and optimizations as part of lake design. This also shares a commonly used modernization use case with Snowflake and the steps followed to migrate the data platform to Snowflake. This is the next chapter in the series of architecture design, where you will learn to design data platform systems.

Structure

The chapter covers the following topics:

- Understand native apps and framework
- Integrating OpenAI with Streamlit
- Build and deploy your app with Streamlit

Understand native apps and framework

Snowflake native app framework is generally available for all accounts and regions, apart from government regions. Snowflake native app allows users to develop data applications that leverage the core capabilities of the platform. Refer to the following use cases that can be implemented with a native app framework:

- Applications that extend the capabilities of the platform with data sharing and implementing business logic with Streamlit app, stored procedures, and functions developed with Snowflake-supported languages like Snowpark API, JavaScript, and SQL.

- Build and make applications available as part of the Snowflake marketplace, where consumers can use these applications. There are a few apps available in the marketplace that are available for free, or some of them are available, like private listings, where consumers will be charged for the use.

- Streamlit applications with reporting integrations can be rich in dashboards and visualizations.

- Streamlit-based integrations with Snowflake native Cortex functions, as well as integration with Open AI, available foundation models for implementing a chatbot or interactive interfaces for users.

These are some of the widely used use cases to implement native apps with the Snowflake platform. There are various components of the Snowflake native app framework. Refer to *Figure 17.1*, which represents components of the Snowflake native app framework:

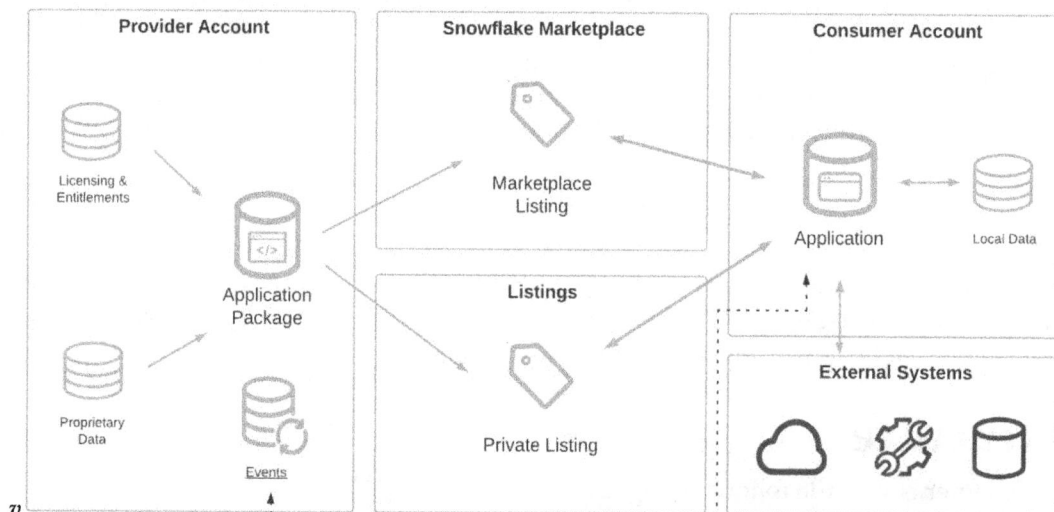

Figure 17.1: Native app framework components
(***Source:** Snowflake documentation*)

As you observe there, there are provider and consumer accounts. The native app framework is implemented around providers and consumers that use features of the Snowflake platform. Like data sharing, the providers and consumers here play a similar role in providing the data and app with business logic, and consumers are users who consume data applications.

Users can develop and test application packages before they are published. These application packages are published on the Snowflake marketplace and are listed as Marketplace as well as private listings. Once the application is published in the marketplace, users can install the app from the marketplace.

Benefits of native apps

Native apps developed and published on the marketplace as a provider bring a bunch of benefits. As a provider, designing, building, and implementing apps natively in the data platform makes it easy to deliver and manage apps to deliver value to the users. The following are some of the benefits as a provider:

- **Quicker dev cycle**: The native app framework allows users to develop apps with Snowflake native features, with data and objects. Snowflake native tools allow users to monitor and manage data applications.

- **Less or no need to manage infrastructure:** A native app framework is a native framework built within the platform and its functionalities. This is a managed service of Snowflake; hence, it does not need to manage any infrastructure within the platform.

- **Data management:** Native apps are deployed within the platform and use data stored in the consumer account. Data is read and written within the same consumer accounts; hence, it does not need to maintain any additional steps to manage data separately. The consumer account follows all security measures to secure the data and manage masking rules for sensitive data.

- **Availability for broader customers**: Native apps are published on the Snowflake marketplace and available to all consumers and users of Snowflake. Publishing on the marketplace allows providers to reach out to broader consumers and access the app to monetize it.

- **Maintaining data and freshness**: Native apps are deployed within the platform, which has access to data instantly. This helps to reduce as well as eliminate the need to define data pipelines to refresh the data to reduce data consistency issues. This extends the platform governance and security across the data platform.

These are a few benefits of implementing native apps as a provider as well as a consumer. Snowflake quickstart on native app will help you to get started with native app implementation. Refer to **https://quickstarts.snowflake.com/guide/getting_started_**

with_native_apps/#0 to get started with native apps. You can also refer to **https://docs. snowflake.com/en/developer-guide/native-apps/tutorials/getting-started-tutorial** for Snowflake native app tutorial to implement native apps. Streamlit is now part of the Snowflake family and allows users to implement various use cases with Streamlit. Streamlit can also be used to implement chatbots as well as interactive applications with generative AI. We will learn to integrate OpenAI with Streamlit in the following section.

Integrating OpenAI with Streamlit

As you know, OpenAI is a cloud-based service provided by Microsoft. This is an AI service that integrates OpenAI's large language models along with GPT-4. These are available and integrated into the Azure cloud platform to enable users to build and deploy AI applications that process applications with natural language processing. Open AI integration with Azure offers robust, secure, compliant features that can be used for enterprise applications for complex data processing and analytics. Along with the AI service, users can also use Azure's infrastructure to train the models, fine-tune models, and manage AI models. OpenAI simplifies the integration and implementation of LLM models. Refer to *Figure 17.2*, which represents the integration and workflow of request and response:

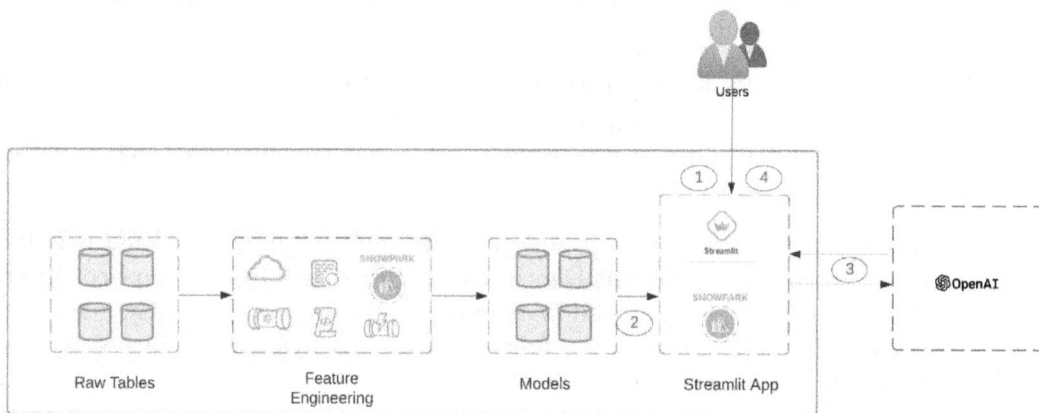

Figure 17.2: Open AI integration and implementation

Streamlit enables users to set up an interface to be used to interact with Snowflake and LLM models deployed. Streamlit accepts the prompts from users and converts them to be executed on Snowflake tables to gather the required data (context). Once data is gathered, this data, along with the prompt, is used to invoke the OpenAI model to generate the response. Based on the prompt and data, the OpenAI model prepares a response and sends it back to the Streamlit App. Later, Streamlit App prepares the response to be sent back to the user.

Implementation of Open AI and Streamlit requires the setup of the following components and access:

- Snowflake Account (existing or new).

- Access to create and manage resources (databases, functions, integrations, apps, etc.) Preferably a trial account with ACCOUNTADMIN privileges.

- Access to create an external function.

- Access to deploy the Streamlit App.

- Account or access to Open AI, existing or set a new one for integration testing.

- Azure Open AI can also be replaced with OpenAI endpoint access details if Azure Open AI is not available to be tested.

- Familiarity with Python programming to deploy the app and make necessary changes to the app before deploying it.

- SQL familiarity to set the required database, tables, and data within Snowflake.

- Snowflake experience or familiarity with setting up the external integration and functions.

You can use one of the Snowflake Quickstarts to get started with OpenAI integration and implement an app using Streamlit. Follow the steps of implementation shared in the lab **https://quickstarts.snowflake.com/guide/getting_started_with_azure_openai_streamlit_and_snowflake_for_image_use_cases/index.html#0**

With this exercise, you will learn to set up integration and deploy OpenAI models. Snowflake also has a bunch of LLM models available as part of Snowflake Cortex offerings. We will learn to use one of the models and deploy it using Streamlit in the next section.

Build and deploy your app with Streamlit

We have learned the integration of the Open AI model and using Streamlit to build an interface like a chatbot to query or interact with the underlying data. Streamlit is now part of the Snowflake ecosystem and can be used in the same way as the SQL workbook Snowsight feature. Snowflake has made this integration seamless and easy to implement with a few clicks. You can follow these steps to navigate through the features of Snowsight to get started with Streamlit:

1. Login to Snowflake.

2. Change your role to ACCOUNTADMIN or an equivalent role with permissions.

3. Navigate to the **Projects** menu.

4. Click on **Streamlit**.

All existing models are listed under this navigation page, as shown in *Figure 17.3*:

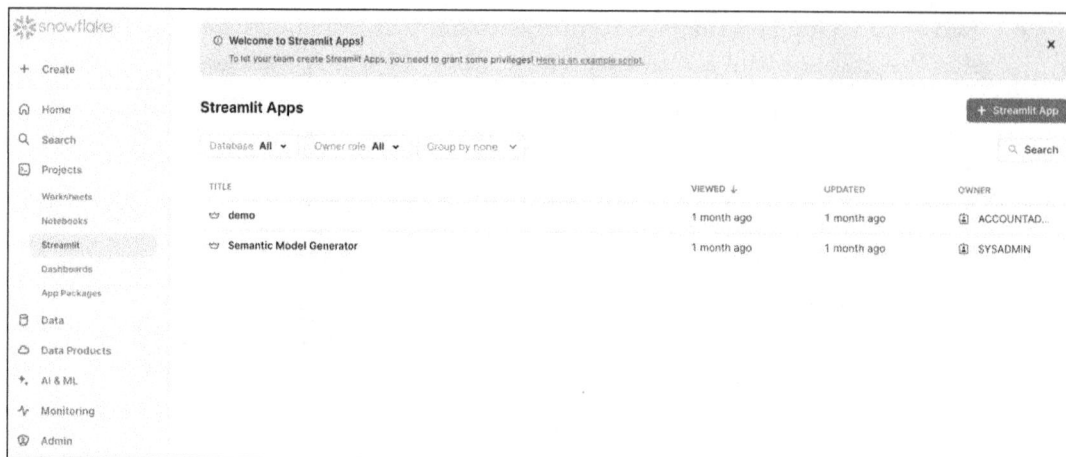

Figure 17.3: Snowsight Streamlit Navigation

Streamlit app can be created using the **+Streamlit App** button on the top right corner. Click the button, and a pop-up window will open, as shown in *Figure 17.4:*

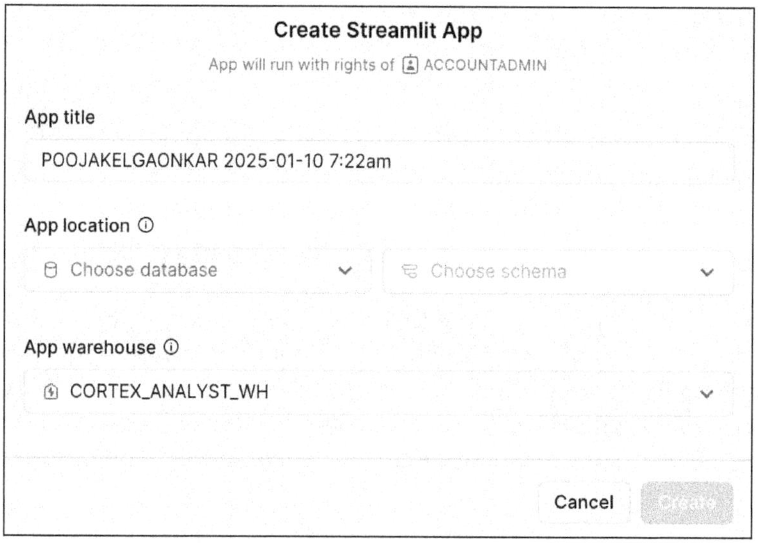

Figure 17.4: Create Streamlit app

To set up the Streamlit app, provide details as shown in the figure:

- **Title**: This is the title of the Streamlit app used to deploy the app and is seen on the Streamlit home page.

- **App location**: Select the database and Schema to store the streamlit app as part of the specific database. Streamlit is also treated as a database object and can be granted access using RBAC.

- **App warehouse**: Select the warehouse used to run the Streamlit app. Warehouse will be used to execute any queries used, as well as the app used to interact with the LLM model.

Along with the Snowsight features, we can also use SQL commands to create Streamlit as an SQL object. Refer to some of the following DDL SQL commands used to create and manage objects:

- CREATE STREAMLIT
- DROP STREAMLIT
- ALTER STREAMLIT
- DESCRIBE STREAMLIT
- SHOW STREAMLIT

Streamlit application integration and implementing it on top of the Snowflake warehouse has reduced the complexity of managing resources to set up and run Streamlit apps. The following are some of the reference SQLs to create and manage Streamlit apps:

- Create an app using the **CREATE** statement:

```
CREATE STREAMLIT demo_streamlit_app
ROOT_LOCATION = '@streamlit_demo.demo_schema.streamlit_stage'
MAIN_FILE = '/streamlit_main.py'
QUERY_WAREHOUSE = streamlit_demo_warehouse;
```

- **ALTER** command can be used to alter the Streamlit app. The changes made will not be reflected if the app is already running. We need to restart the app to reflect the changes made to it.

Streamlit app packages can also be added using the Streamlit navigation menu. There are some built-in packages available to be used while building a Streamlit app. You can use applications to build packages. Refer to the documentation page on **https://docs.snowflake.com/en/developer-guide/streamlit/create-streamlit-ui** to create an app using Snowsight. Also, refer to QuickStart to use public data available for the Finance domain and setup the Streamlit app **https://quickstarts.snowflake.com/guide/getting_started_with_streamlit_in_snowflake/index.html?index=..%2F..index#0**.

Along with Python, we can also leverage Snowpark Python modules and libraries to set up the Streamlit App. Snowpark ML APIs and libraries can be used to set up the app. Typically, these are used as part of Python libraries and packages while defining and developing the app. Refer to **https://quickstarts.snowflake.com/guide/getting_started_with_snowpark_for_python_streamlit/index.html#0** to get started with the Snowpark Python for streamlit app development.

Conclusion

We have learned about Streamlit apps and development using Snowflake features. We can integrate Open AI as well as other available LLM models using Snowflake integrations to design the LLM interface to interact with the data in natural language. Snowflake also introduced Snowflake Arctic as one of the LLM models that can be used in the same way as any other models, like Open AI or Hugging Face, etc. Snowflake also has Cortex offerings and LLM models implemented in the environment that can be used as functions. Snowflake Horizon offers a variety of services that are available at the fingertips of the users.

We will learn more about Snowflake horizon offerings, Cortex functions, use cases, and their implementation in the next chapter.

Points to remember

The following are the key takeaways from this chapter:

- Snowflake integration allows users to integrate with any available LLM offerings.

- Snowflake Streamlit feature allows users to set up the Streamlit app using SQL commands just like any other Snowflake object.

- Streamlit can also be set up using Snowsight console features and options.

- Python libraries and packages can be used and added if needed to implement specific applications.

- Snowflake Snowpark and Snowpark ML services can also be used in integration with Streamlit to implement the Chatbot or any other conversational interfaces.

Join our Discord space

Join our Discord workspace for latest updates, offers, tech happenings around the world, new releases, and sessions with the authors:

https://discord.bpbonline.com

CHAPTER 18
Unleashing Snowflake's Advanced Capabilities

Introduction

Snowflake is working on enhancing the platform to onboard advanced AI capabilities with a set of advanced features. Snowflake announced many features during SNOWDAY and Snowflake Summit last year. This chapter covers the latest and greatest offerings of Snowflake: Horizon and Cortex. This also helps to learn the usage of LLM functions to summarize, generate content, or translate the data on the fly. This chapter helps to learn the advanced features of Snowflake to deploy the LLM-based functionalities to improve the performance of applications or enhance application usability to derive new value adds with these LLM-based functions.

This chapter focuses on sharing the unified features of the Snowflake platform. This chapter shares various use cases to implement container service, Snowflake Horizon, Snowflake Cortex, Document AI, and universal search.

Structure

This chapter consists of the following topics:

- Understanding Snowflake Horizon and features
- Understanding Cortex-LLM functions
- Using Cortex-LLM functions

- Understanding and using Snowflake Copilot
- Using universal search
- Implementing use case with Document AI
- Using Snowpark container services

Objectives

By the end of this chapter, you will be able to understand the Snowflake LLM offerings and features used to implement the various use cases. You will also be able to use LLM functions, create LLM assistants, and set up a search service. You will be able to develop an understanding of the latest and greatest offerings of Snowflake.

Understanding Snowflake Horizon and features

Snowflake Horizon is the unified feature that allows users to implement governance, security, compliance, interoperability, and access capabilities. This feature is used as a unified solution to implement governance centrally across enterprises to meet organizational needs. Horizon offers data governance solutions, and data teams benefit.

Typically, data stewards are identified who work on defining standards and processes, and setting up rules to implement data governance. Data stewards can use Snowflake Horizon to effectively design governance solutions with predefined features. Snowflake Horizon allows users to govern the content, and content can include the following data objects:

- Database objects, apps, external tables, and iceberg tables
- AI/ML models across accounts within an organization
- Data sharing with private listings
- Stored and processed data within the platform using any third-party tools or connectors
- Public data feeds available on the Snowflake data marketplace

These are the objects that can be governed using Horizon. Typically, data stewards use features of Horizon to govern the data or content present in the objects listed above. Data stewards can run the following operations as part of data governance:

- Auditing data access history and dependency history.
- Review data quality metrics using built-in functions as well as custom functions.
- Review data lineage using the Horizon feature.
- Assess the security of an account using the Trust Centre.

- Using end-to-end encryption to prevent data breaches while data is stored at rest as well as in transit.

- Setting up an authentication method for the account using OAuth or federated authentication.

- Review granular access controls of the objects or content.

- Assess the data protection policies and implement row-level and column-level security measures.

- Review and track data using objects as well as classification tags.

- Extend the governance from Snowflake to the iceberg tables and capabilities with the partner ecosystem.

These are some of the widely executed operations on top of Snowflake Horizon. Snowflake Horizon caters to governance and can be accessed via Snowsight. Log on to Snowsight, go to Governance | Select warehouse to view the governed objects. Refer to *Figure 18.1*, which shares a view of Snowsight:

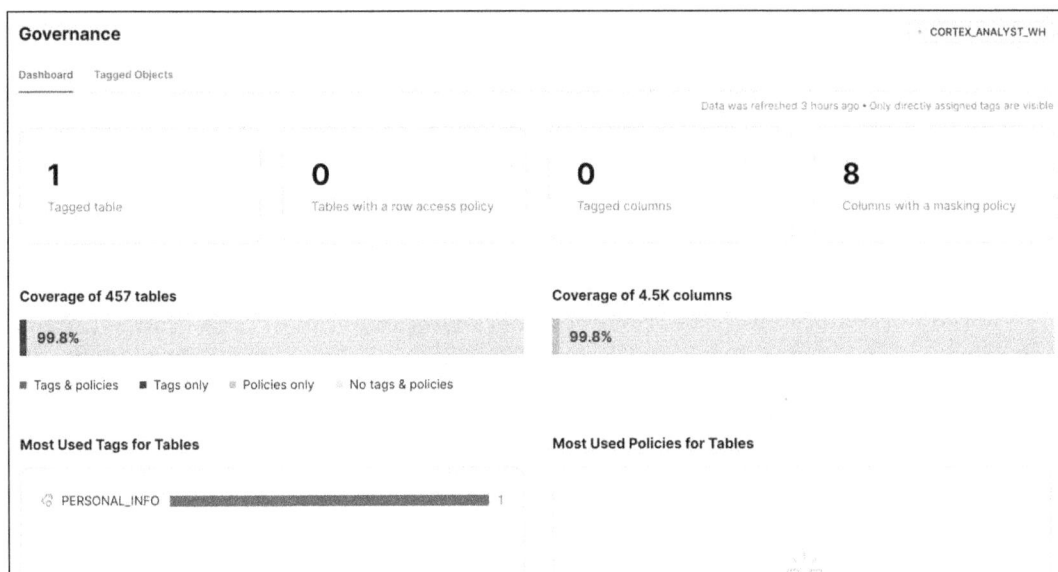

Figure 18.1: Snowsight governance

Here, as you observe, the dashboard shares a view of overall objects and governance implemented in an account. The tagged objects tab lists all the objects tagged in an account. The dashboard also lists the masking policies used, along with the number of columns they are applied to. Refer to *Figure 18.2*, which shares a view of masking policies and columns applied when you click on the masking policies from the dashboard:

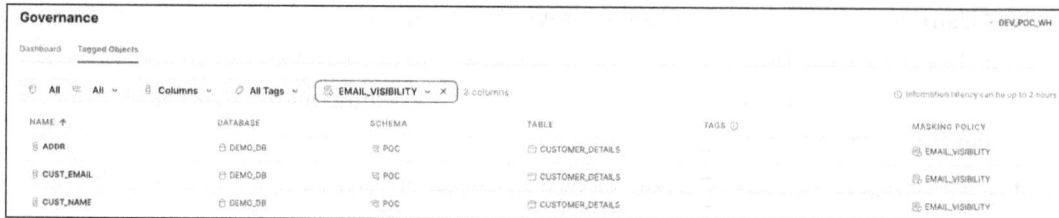

Figure 18.2: Governance masking policies

These governance features are useful for reviewing the policies and security of an account. Snowflake recently announced data quality and data metrics functions in preview to help data stewards implement data quality. We will learn more about these functions in the upcoming section.

Data quality and data metric functions

Snowflake announced the availability of data quality and metric functions to the enterprise and above accounts in preview. The **data metric functions** (**DMFs**) are used by data quality functions. Snowflake supports a set of pre-defined DMFs and allows users to create custom DMFs. DMFs are used to measure the key metrics to review the quality of the data. As you know, data quality is a critical aspect of data governance implementation. **Data quality** (**DQ**) implementation allows users to review the incoming and processed data. DQ identifies the records that do not meet the business and data requirements before it is used for any decision-making.

System defined functions

Snowflake shares a bunch of DMFs that can be used as system functions. Refer to the following set of functions available to review the quality of the data:

- **FRESHNESS**: Used to determine the freshness of the data.
- **NULL_COUNT**: Used to get a number of NULL values for a given column.
- **DUPLICATE_COUNT**: Gives the count of duplicate values for a given column, including NULL values.
- **UNIQUE_COUNT**: Used to get a count of unique non-NULL values of a given column.
- **ROW_COUNT**: Used to get a number of records from a table.

You can use these functions as SQL queries on top of table values. These are used as functions to read data from a given column and table. Following is one of the sample queries:

```
/* get number of null present in key column*/
SELECT SNOWFLAKE.CORE.NULL_COUNT(
```

```
SELECT account_num
FROM retail_poc_db.poc.account_info
);
```

Like **NULL_COUNT**, these system functions can be used to check the quality of the data present in tables. Users can also define custom metrics and functions used to review the quality of the data.

Custom functions

Custom DMF can be created using the **CREATE** statement, the same as **CREATE FUNCTION**, and define the metrics to review the quality of the data. Typically, data quality checks are implemented to review the quality of the data in terms of value, length, freshness, NULL records, unique records, etc. In some cases, the checks need to be implemented to design business requirements. For example, the account number needs to be 11 digits and cannot be NULL. In this case, the custom function can be defined to check the length of the column and validate if it matches the data requirements and standards. Refer to the following custom function:

```
/* Define custom function */
CREATE OR REPLACE DATA METRIC FUNCTION retail_poc_db.poc.validate_account_
number(
  arg_t TABLE(
    arg_acc_len NUMBER
  )
)
RETURNS STRING
AS
$$
  SELECT
    Case when Length(Account_number) = arg_acc_len then 'Valid Account' else
'Invalid Account' end as account_dq_indicator
  FROM account_info
$$;
```

As you observe here, the argument passed to the metric function is the generic argument that accepts the length of the account number. The custom DMF can be used to validate the account number length and mark the record as VALID or INVALID. You can also refer **to https://docs.snowflake.com/en/user-guide/tutorials/data-quality-tutorial-start** to implement the data quality and metrics function.

Snowflake Horizon is used to implement centralized governance across accounts and data objects. Snowflake announced many new features to implement AI and ML use cases along with data governance. We will learn about Snowflake's advanced and native features to implement Gen AI use cases.

Understanding Cortex-LLM functions

Snowflake offers native LLM functions to extend support for integrating generative AI features. Snowflake cortex LLM functions are part of the **STRING** functions. We will learn about the various functions available, the models available, and the limitations of the LLM functions. Cortex functions are pre-trained models with access to industry-leading models from companies like Google, Meta, Mistral, Reka, and Snowflake Arctic. These functions are fully managed and hosted functions on Snowflake that do not need any additional setup. These functions allow users to run LLM functions where data is stored without worrying about the infrastructure to achieve performance, scalability, and governance. Refer to the following LLM functions offered by Snowflake:

- **COMPLETE**
- **SENTIMENT**
- **SUMMARIZE**
- **TRANSLATE**
- **EXTRACT_ANSWER**

Snowflake recently announced helper functions as SQL functions in the preview. These functions are used to handle failures in case of function failure, as well as count the tokens provided as input prompts. The following are the functions:

- **COUNT_TOKENS**
- **TRY_COMPLETE**

These functions are used as SQL functions and call the choice of the model from the list of available models. Let us learn about the functions and access these functions as part of LLM use case implementation.

Accessing LLM functions

Snowflake has added **CORTEX_USER** as a database role that is granted to the public role by default. The **PUBLIC** role is the default role granted to all users onboarded to the Snowflake platform. This role can be managed and altered to avoid default allocation to the **PUBLIC** role using the **ALTER** command. This can also be used to define custom and user-managed role to assign LLM user roles to the users. The following is a set of sample commands:

```
/* remove access to cortex user role */
REVOKE DATABASE ROLE SNOWFLAKE.CORTEX_USER FROM ROLE PUBLIC;

/* create custom role and assign cortex role to the custom role */
USE ROLE ACCOUNTADMIN;
CREATE ROLE custom_cortex_role;
GRANT DATABASE ROLE SNOWFLAKE.CORTEX_USER TO ROLE custom_cortex_role;
```

```
/*grant access to user */
GRANT ROLE custom_cortex_role TO USER poojakelgaonkar;
```

These custom roles are used to manage access to the data as well as cortex functions. Snowflake cortex functions are now **generally available (GA)**. However, these are not available on all clouds and all regions. Refer to the **https://docs.snowflake.com/en/user-guide/snowflake-cortex/llm-functions** for the availability of specific functions and LLM models on AWS and Azure cloud.

Basics of LLM functions

In this section, we will learn the basics of Cortex LLM functions and use them to support extended generative AI use cases.

COMPLETE

This function is used to generate the response to the given prompt. This function accepts the model as an input parameter along with the input prompt. This function can be used for individual responses as well as on top of the table column. The following is the sample code to use the **COMPLETE** function:

```
/* run individual prompt using COMPLETE */
SELECT SNOWFLAKE.CORTEX.COMPLETE('snowflake-arctic', 'What are the use cases
to implement large language models?');
```

```
/* run on table column*/
SELECT SNOWFLAKE.CORTEX.COMPLETE(
    'mistral-large',
        CONCAT('Rate the movie review: <review>', content, '</review>')
) FROM movie_reviews LIMIT 10;
```

This sample code can be customized to be integrated with data use cases. **COMPLETE** is used to generate a prompt.

SENTIMENT

This function is used to get the sentiment score of the input prompt, and the prompt can be an English text. Refer to the following sample code to get the sentiment score:

```
/* get sentiment score */
SELECT SNOWFLAKE.CORTEX.SENTIMENT(review_comment), review_comment FROM
movie_reviews LIMIT 10;
```

Here, the sentiment is used to generate the sentiment score for **movie_reviews**. **Review_comment** is the **STRING** column where review comments are stored for movies.

SUMMARIZE

This is a summary function used to generate a summary of the given input text. This can be used to generate a short, crisp summary of the long paragraph or information. This can be run on top of a table as well. Consider a scenario where news data is stored, and the **summarize** function can be run to generate the summary of the column as follows:

```
/* generate summary of news column*/
SELECT SNOWFLAKE.CORTEX.SUMMARIZE(news_content) FROM daily_news LIMIT 10;
```

Here, the news content is the column that stores news details, and summaries can be used to generate a summary of the news.

TRANSLATE

This function is used to translate the input prompt from one language to another. This function supports only a given set of languages currently, and can be used as follows:

```
/* translate input prompt*/
SELECT SNOWFLAKE.CORTEX.TRANSLATE(news_content, 'en', 'fr') FROM daily_news
LIMIT 10;
```

Here, *en* is the source language, representing the input in English, and *fr* is the mnemonic of the target language, French, to convert the news from one language to another.

EXTRACT_ANSWER

This function is used to generate the answer from the input source document. This function accepts the source document as an input document to generate the answer to the question. The other parameter provided to the function is a question, as follows:

```
/* generate answer from input */
SELECT SNOWFLAKE.CORTEX.EXTRACT_ANSWER(movie_review,
    'What actors does this movie review mention?')
FROM movie_reviews LIMIT 10;
```

Here, the **extract_answer** function can be used to extract information from the input column. We will learn to implement these functions using sample review data.

Using Cortex-LLM functions

Snowflake pre-defined functions can be used on top of data stored within the Snowflake platform. We will create a table and load sample data to run the LLM functions. Refer to the following steps:

1. Create a sample movie reviews table to implement LLM functions:

```
/* create database for poc */
CREATE DATABASE LLM_POC;
CREATE SCHEMA POC;
USE DATABASE LLM_POC;
USE SCHEMA POC;

/* create movie reviews table */
CREATE TABLE MOVIE_REVIEWS
(
MOVIE_NM STRING,
MOVIE_REVIEWS STRING,
MOVIE_RATINGS float
);
```

2. Create a sample news table to implement LLM functions:

```
/* create news table */
CREATE TABLE NEWS_TBL
(
NEWS_NM STRING,
NEWS STRING,
NEWS_DT DATE,
NEWS_COMMENT STRING
);
```

Once you create the sample table to store **movie_reviews** and news details, you can run the following functions to perform POC.

3. Load sample data to the movie reviews table:

```
/* load sample row into movie reviews */
```

INSERT INTO MOVIE_REVIEWS VALUES('Arthur The King','Michael Light (Mark Wahlberg) has one last chance to win a championship and prove himself. Finding sponsorship and creating a team of four is challenging, given his washed-out career and a previous disastrous race. However, he assembles a team of an athlete and a social media star, Leo (Simu Liu), free climber Olivia (Nathalie Emmanuel), and Chik (Ali Sulaiman), who has a bad knee. During the race, he has a fifth and an unlikely teammate — an injured indie dog, Arthur.Director Simon Cellan Jones's offering is an account of companionship between man and dog. The story talks about loyalty, friendship, sacrifice, and survival. It also offers ample adventure through a jungle trek, rock climbing with bicycles, ziplining across a valley (a sequence that will have you on the edge of your seat), night runs, and more. Cinematographer Jacques Jouffret splendidly captures the Dominican terrains, forests, mountains, rivers, and valleys. The adventurous race also looks convincing and authentic. Writers Michael Brandt and Mikael Lindnord's narrative has all the ingredients you expect from this genre—friction amid friendship, obstacles, and the tough decisions the athletes must make. Although the story gets a tad too sappy, the narrative's even pacing prevents it from weighing you down. Mark Wahlberg delivers a powerful performance as the out-of-luck captain who wants to make a comeback no matter what. Nathalie Emmanuel, Simu Liu, and Ali Suliman are also worthy additions. Their banter and individual reasons for participating in the race add authenticity to the narrative. The movie's real star, however, is the dog. It's inspiring and incredulous to think this is a true story (of Michael Lindnord), and the narrative will tug at your heartstrings. The movie does not end with the race or whether the Broadrail team wins and goes beyond being an adventure sports drama. Whether you are an animal lover or an adventure sports enthusiast, Arthur the King will thrill you and warm your heart. Be warned: you may tear up at this endearing story of a dog and underdogs!',3.5);

4. Load sample data into the new table:

```
/* load news table */
```

```
INSERT INTO NEWS_TBL VALUES ('NEWYORK TIMES' , 'Researchers first discovered the link between heat and aggression by looking at crime data, finding that there are more murders, assaults and episodes of domestic violence on hot days. The connection applies to nonviolent acts, too: When temperatures rise, people are more likely to engage in hate speech and honk horn in traffic.  Lab studies back this up. In one experiment in 2019, people acted more spitefully toward others while playing a specially designed video game in a hot room than in a cool one.So-called reactive aggression tends to be especially sensitive to heat, most likely because people tend to interpret others' actions as more hostile on hot days, prompting them to respond in kind. Kimberly Meidenbauer, an assistant professor of psychology at Washington State University, thinks this increase in reactive aggression may be related to heat's effect on cognition, particularly the dip in self control. Your tendency to act without thinking, or not be able to stop yourself from acting a certain way, these things also appear to be affected by heat, she said.' , current_date, 'How Heat Affects the Brain. High temperatures can make us miserable. Research shows they also make us aggressive, impulsive and dull.');
```

5. Using functions to get the sample responses by processing review data from the table:

```
/* Using extract answer function */
SELECT SNOWFLAKE.CORTEX.EXTRACT_ANSWER(MOVIE_REVIEWS,
```

```
                'What movie does the review mention?')
FROM MOVIE_REVIEWS;
/* Using sentiment function */
SELECT SNOWFLAKE.CORTEX.SENTIMENT(MOVIE_REVIEWS), MOVIE_NAME FROM
MOVIE_REVIEWS;
/* using summarize function */
SELECT SNOWFLAKE.CORTEX.SUMMARIZE(MOVIE_REVIEWS) FROM MOVIE_REVIEWS;
/* using translate function */
SELECT SNOWFLAKE.CORTEX.TRANSLATE(MOVIE_REVIEWS, 'en', 'fr') FROM
MOVIE_REVIEWS;
```

As you observe here, these LLM functions can be used on top of review columns. Try out the same functions on top of the news table. This is the easiest way to implement LLM functions. The next Snowflake feature is Snowflake Copilot to help developers develop components. We will learn more about Copilot in the upcoming section.

Understanding Cortex Analyst

Cortex Analyst is Snowflake's fully managed LLM-powered offering that allows users to create applications to cater to their business queries on top of structured data. This feature allows us to set up conversational applications using which we can query using natural language, and answers will be returned along with SQL queries that are used to generate an answer. This feature is currently in preview. Some of the key features and use cases to use Cortex Analyst include:

- **Self-serve analytics**: This feature is used to build a self-serve platform for business users who can ask queries in natural language and get answers without writing SQL to generate the analytics. Data is stored in underlying tables in structured format and used to generate responses.

- **Enhancing existing applications by integrating as API**: Cortex analyst takes the API first approach that can be used to integrate into any existing business workflows to enhance the capabilities of the application.

- **Data governance**: Snowflake's privacy-first policies and security framework allow users to confidently explore AI-driven use cases. This ensures customer data is protected with the highest standards of privacy and governance. Some of the key aspects of using Cortex Analyst are:

    o Cortex Analysts do not get trained on the customer data. We provide the YAML file with the metadata information, and this information is used to prepare the SQL queries with the help of a semantic model.

    o Data stays within the governed boundaries of Snowflake. Snowflake-hosted LLM models are used for Cortex Analyst, and this ensures that data and metadata information do not leave Snowflake boundaries.

o Cortex Analysts adhere to RBAC and ensure that the queries generated and executed as part of the response follow the access control setup and execute queries as per the roles assigned.

- **Higher precision of accuracy**: Cortex Analyst uses a semantic model for higher precision, as using database name or table name is not useful to generate relevant queries as a conversational interface. Here, the semantic model contains the database, table, schema, column level details: data type, property, documentation, or description of the field. This model serves the purpose and helps the model to generate better results with higher precision of accuracy.

As a preview feature, Cortex Analyst is not available in all regions of all three clouds. The following are the regions where it is available. If you want to try this out, you can set up an enterprise edition in the AWS region as specified to implement the Cortex Analyst use case:

- AWS ap-northeast-1 (Tokyo)

- AWS ap-southeast-2 (Sydney)

- AWS us-east-1 (Virginia)

- AWS us-west-2 (Oregon)

- AWS eu-central-1 (Frankfurt)

- AWS eu-west-1 (Ireland)

- Azure East US 2 (Virginia)

- Azure West Europe (Netherlands)

We can follow certain steps to implement the Cortex Analyst feature. As we know by now, it needs a semantic model to be defined along with Streamlit Python to set up the app. The steps are as follows:

1. Create the semantic model as a YAML file.

2. Upload the YAML file or the semantic model to the stage.

3. Create a Streamlit app or upload the Streamlit app code to the stage.

4. Setup the Streamlit app and run the app.

5. Use the Streamlit app to interact with the data.

Refer to the QuickStart **https://quickstarts.snowflake.com/guide/getting_started_with_ cortex_analyst_in_snowflake/index.html?index=..%2F..index#0** to get started with the Cortex Analyst lab. You can set up the semantic model, modify the Python script of the Streamlit app to use the model defined, and create the Streamlit app. You can also use this as a baseline and create your use case/application with Cortex Analyst.

Using Cortex search

Cortex search is used to offer a search experience within the Snowflake platform. This allows users to run any search like a search on a search engine to provide the required information from Snowflake data. This can also be used with any **Retrieval Augmented Generation (RAG)** app. This is a low-latency fuzzy search within the Snowflake platform and on top of the underlying data.

Cortex search offers users a search engine that has hybrid search (vector and keyword) up and running without the need to maintain or create any embeddings and infrastructure, and fine-tuning for similarity searches. Cortex search can be used for enterprise searches as well as RAG-based LLM assistants (chatbots). Refer to *Figure 18.3*, which shares Cortex search implementation with RAG:

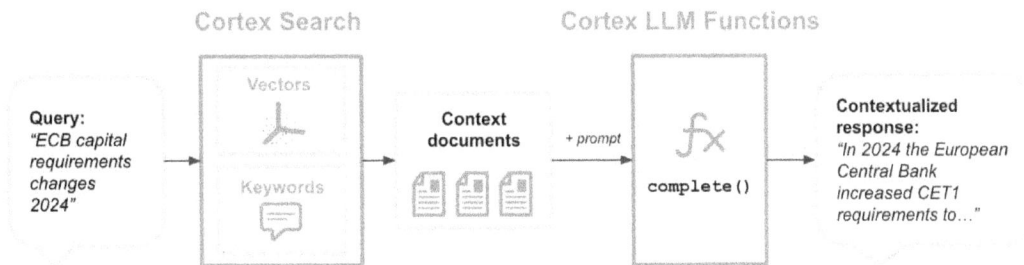

Figure 18.3: *Cortex search with RAG (Snowflake Documentation)*

Cortex search service can be created using DDL statements. Refer to the following sample reference code:

```
CREATE OR REPLACE CORTEX SEARCH SERVICE ticket_search_service_dev
  ON transcript_text
  ATTRIBUTES region
  WAREHOUSE = dev_cortex_search_wh
  TARGET_LAG = '1 day'
  EMBEDDING_MODEL = 'snowflake-arctic-embed-l-v2.0'
  AS (
    SELECT
        ticket_desc,
        Ticekt_id,
        Open_date,
         Status,
        agent_id
    FROM support_tickets
);
```

Here, **Target_lag** specifies the lag or duration this service would refresh. This will look for any changes or updates on the base table and refresh. Like any other Snowflake feature, Cortex search can also be set up using Snowsight web UI. Refer to *Figure 18.4*; this is the Snowflake AI & ML landing page that has a list of all services available as part of Snowflake Cortex features:

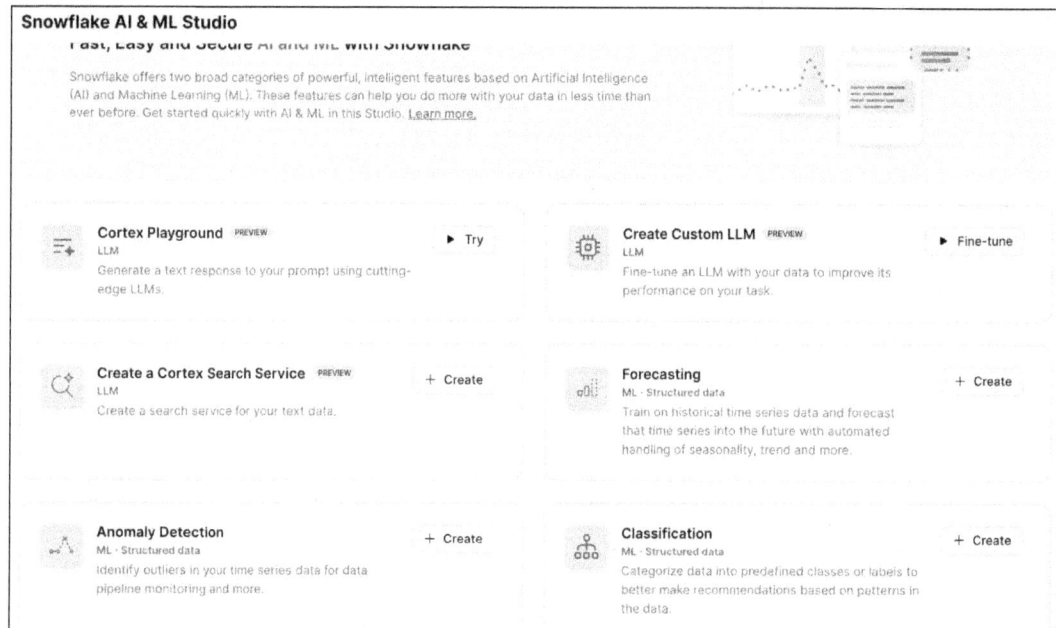

Figure 18.4: Snowflake AI &ML landing page in Snowsight

Next, follow the given steps to set up the service from the UI:

1. Login to Snowsight.
2. Select a role with permissions (cortex_user role should be granted to the role used).
3. Navigate to **AI & ML | Studio**.
4. Select role and warehouse.
5. Select the database and schema.
6. Provide the name of the service and click on **Let's go**.

Refer to *Figure 18.5*, which shares the service details and steps to be followed to set up the Cortex search service. Follow the steps as per Snowsight UI and provide the required details.

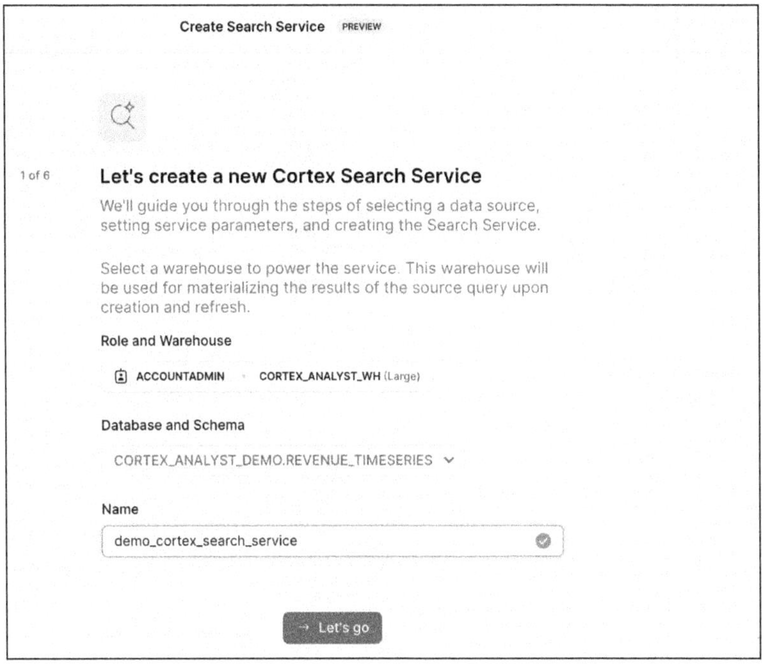

Figure 18.5: *Create cortex search service step 1 of 6*

The next step asks to select the table and data columns to create indexes, as shown in *Figure 18.6*:

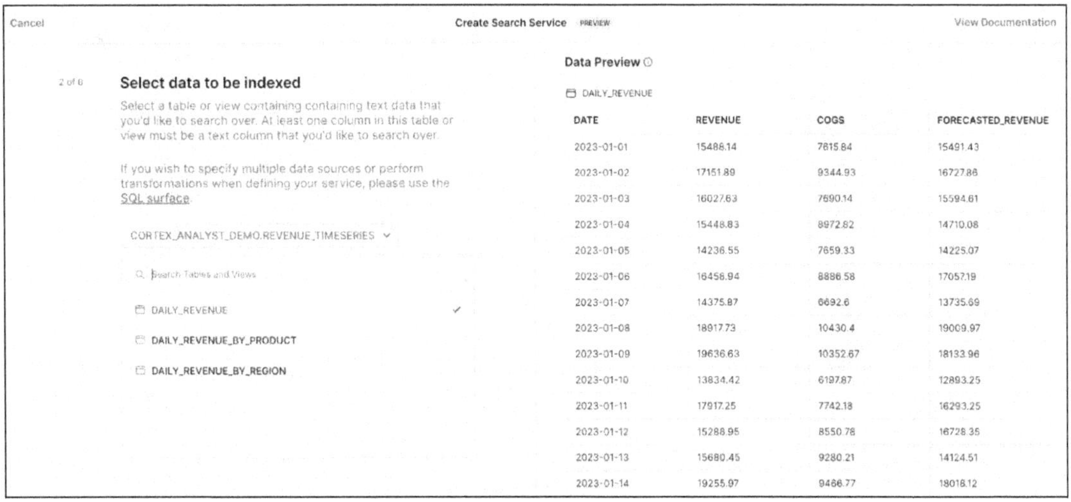

Figure 18.6: *Create cortex search service step 2 of 6*

On the next page, select the columns that are required for the service to be set, as shown in *Figure 18.7*:

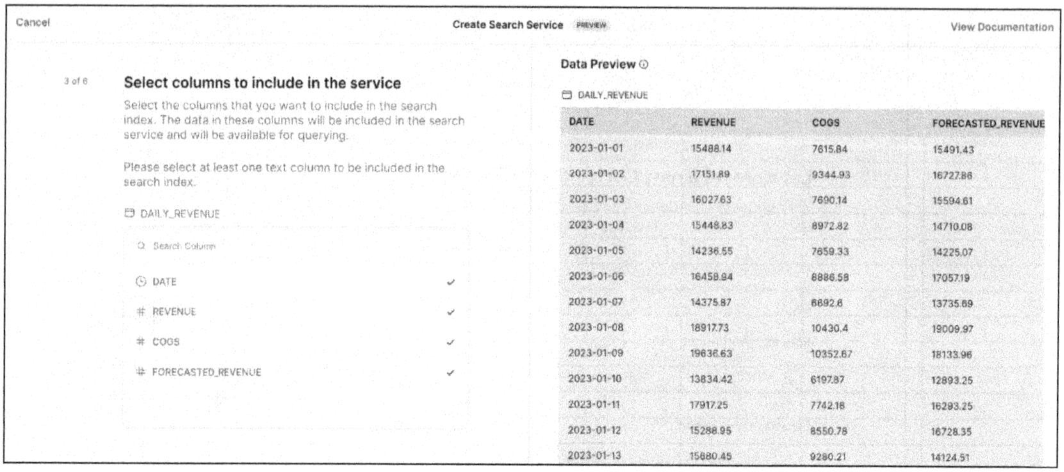

Figure 18.7: Create cortex search service steps 3 of 6

To set up the search, select a table or entity that has string data fields. The next step requires selecting the text column, as shown in *Figure 18.8*:

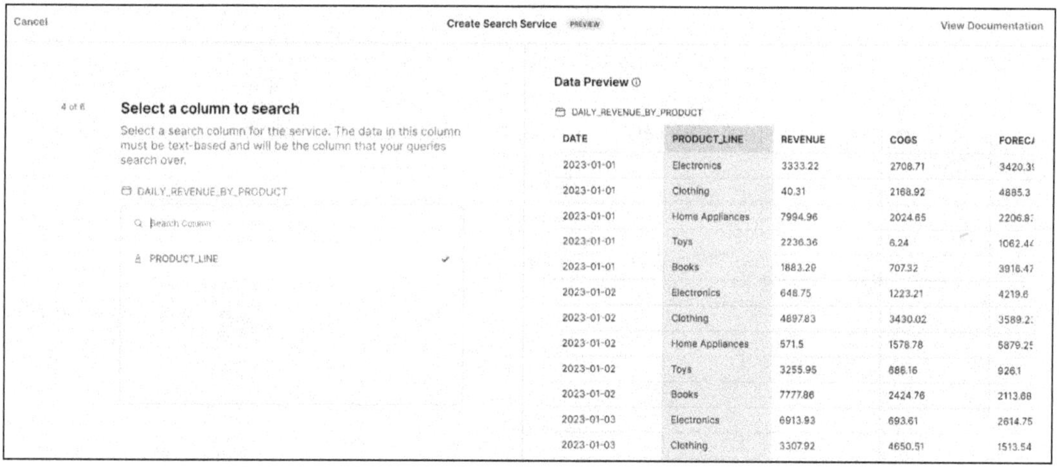

Figure 18.8: Create cortex search service step 4 of 6

The next step is to select the attributes; this can be optional if there are no attributes to be set up. Refer to *Figure 18.9*, which shares the option to skip the attribute selection if not required:

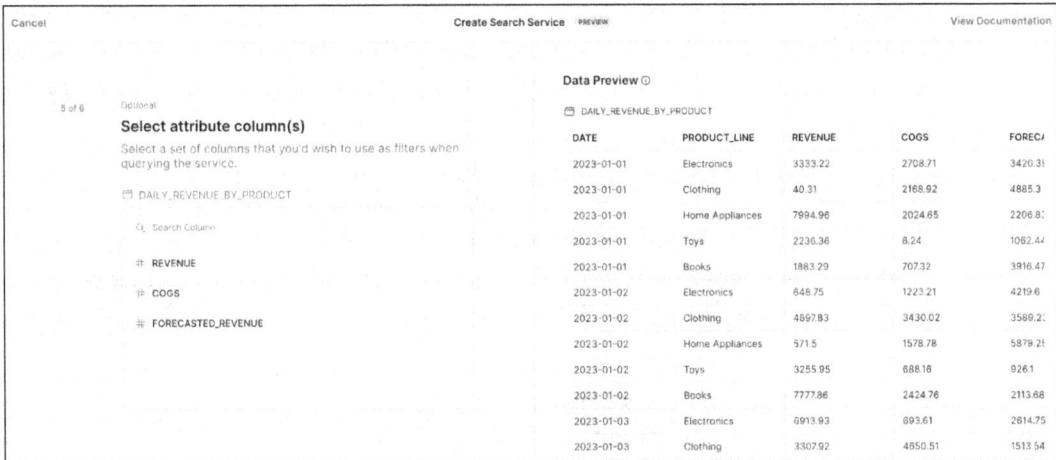

Figure 18.9: Create cortex search service step 5 of 6

The last step is to select the *lag*, and as we know, *lag* is one of the key parameters used to refresh the service based on the underlying table changes. Refer to *Figure 18.10* and select the LAG duration:

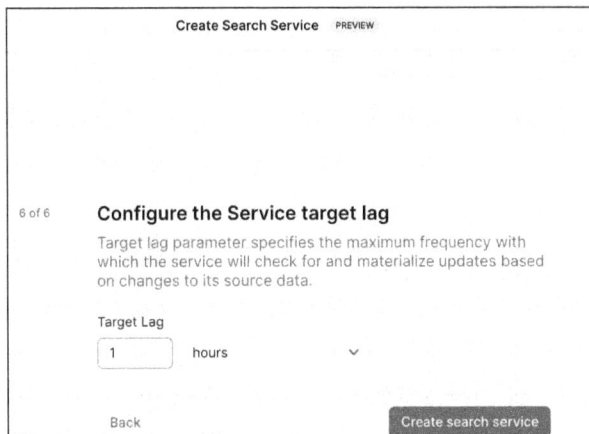

Figure 18.10: Create cortex search service step 6 of 6

Now, you can click on the Create search service button to create the service from the UI. We can also use the Cortex search service and query it. Refer to **https://docs.snowflake. com/en/user-guide/snowflake-cortex/cortex-search/query-cortex-search-service** for more details on querying the service.

As part of Snowflake labs, documentation shares three different labs as follows:

- **Build search using Cortex search:** Refer to **https://docs.snowflake.com/en/user-guide/snowflake-cortex/cortex-search/tutorials/cortex-search-tutorial-1-search** for detailed steps and the guide to setup the search.

- **Build chat application with Cortex search**: Refer to **https://docs.snowflake.com/ en/user-guide/snowflake-cortex/cortex-search/tutorials/cortex-search-tutorial-2-chat** to set up the chat-based application and the step-by-step guide to the implementation.

- **Build PDF chatbot cortex search**: As we know, Snowflake has a feature to access unstructured data stored on the storage buckets and process them. This lab uses PDF documents to set up the search and chat assistant on top of it. Refer to **https://docs.snowflake.com/en/user-guide/snowflake-cortex/cortex-search/ tutorials/cortex-search-tutorial-3-chat-advanced** as a step-by-step guide to the implementation.

Like any other services in Snowflake, there are cost components associated with and considerations while setting up the services. As you know, virtual warehouse, storage, and cloud services costs will be associated with it as we are creating it on top of the data and maintaining it to refresh automatically. Along with the traditional components, two of the AI components contribute to the cost of embedding creations and serving. AI services embedding cost and AI services-serving cost are two additional components associated with the traditional cost parameters.

There are some limitations associated with the service as well, which are as follows:

- This does not support replication and cloning as any other service of the platform.

- This service also does not support cross-cloud inference.

- The search service query follows the same restrictions that are there for dynamic table creation as well.

- The size of the base table, hence the result of the query, should not exceed 50 million rows as of now. If there are more rows, then it slows down the process and causes query formation errorouts. 50M rows are preferred for optimal performance of the service.

Now, we have learned about Snowflake cortex offerings like Cortex Analyst, Cortex Search, and Cortex LLM functions. There are a few more LLM features, as well as extended capabilities of the platform that can be leveraged along with Cortex offerings. We will learn about Snowflake Copilot, universal search, and implementing document AI in subsequent sections of the chapter.

Understanding and using Snowflake Copilot

A Copilot is an intelligent assistant that helps developers or users to develop code. Snowflake also offers Copilot, which is available in preview only for AWS-specific regions like AWS-us-east1, aws-us-west-2, and aws-eu-central-1. Copilot is an LLM-powered assistant that helps simplify data governance, data analysis, and integrations with Snowflake workflows.

This Copilot is a fine-tuned LLM model running securely inside the Snowflake cortex. Snowflake Cortex is Snowflake's intelligent AI service. This model is run securely within Snowflake with access to data and metadata within the Snowflake platform. Cortex can also be integrated with RBAC and provides additional suggestions based on the user role and access. Copilot supports natural language and questions asked by users. You can provide a database and schema, and ask the Copilot to generate a query to transform the data. Copilot can also be used to improve the performance of queries as well as workloads. Copilot can answer questions based on the documentation. Snowflake Copilot can be assessed from worksheets and notebooks. Once you log in to Snowsight, you can see Ask Copilot in the bottom right corner, as shown in *Figure 18.11*:

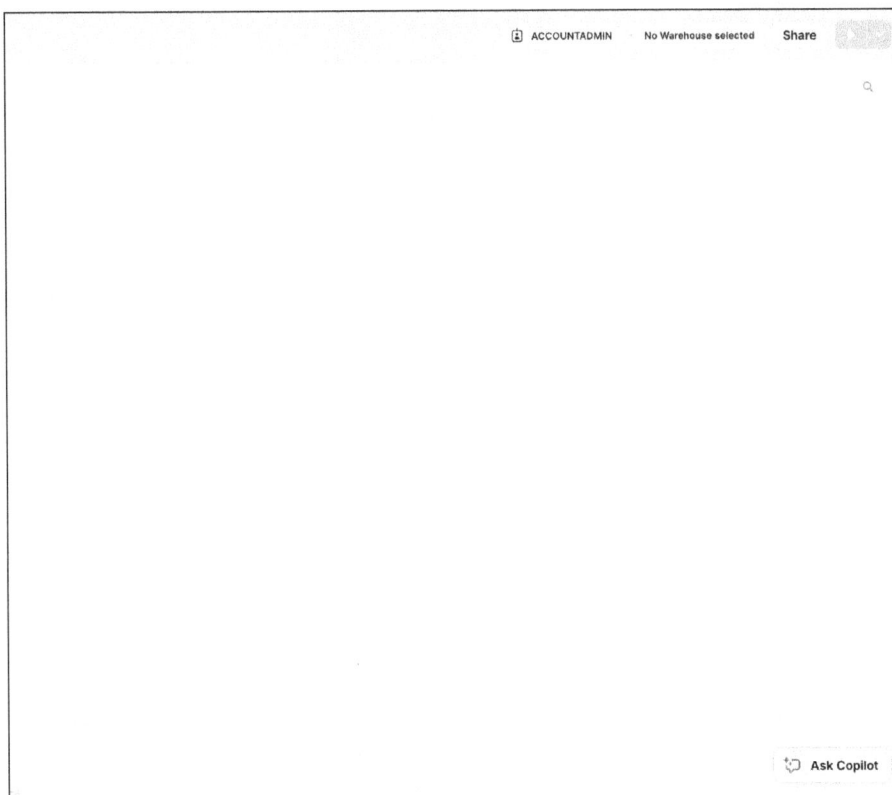

Figure 18.11: Ask Copilot on Snowsight

As you can see in the figure, you can click on the **Ask Copilot**, and a new sidebar will open where you can specify the database and schema and ask questions to analyze the data present. Refer to *Figure 18.12*, which represents the Copilot sidebar:

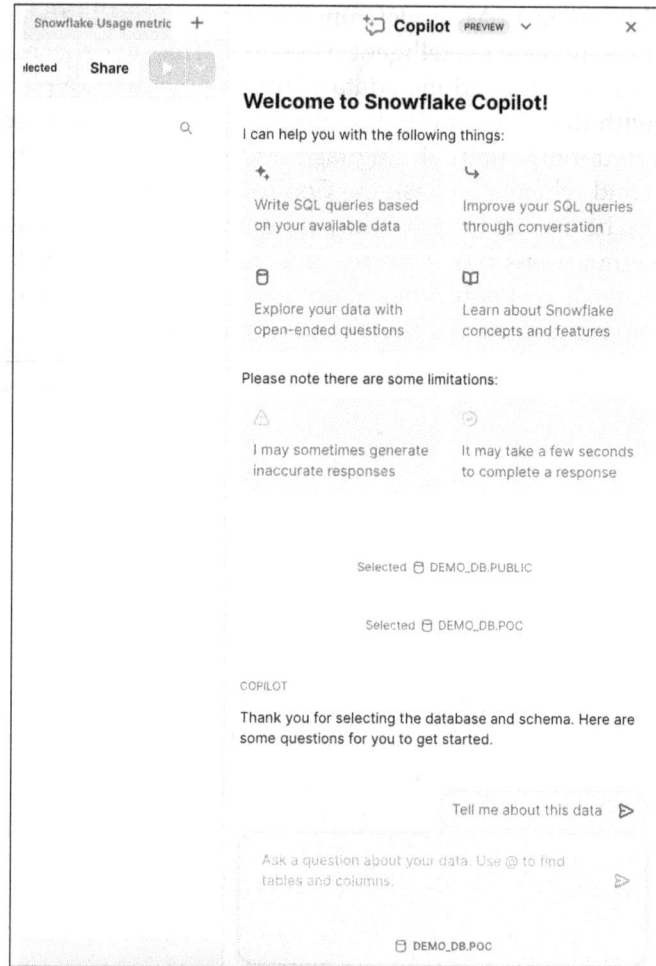

Figure 18.12: Copilot window

As you observe here, you can choose the options from the predefined list to write an SQL to analyze the data, improve the performance of queries, and ask questions on the underlying data. The following are some of the supported use cases with Copilot:

- **Query development**: Ask Copilot to develop queries for you, optimize queries, write complex queries, as well as try SQL queries.

- **Data analysis**: Ask questions to analyze the underlying table data by asking open-ended questions.

- **Learning:** Ask questions about Snowflake and its features to learn about the platform and possible use cases.

These are some of the categories of use cases that can be implemented with Copilot. Though these are great use cases to be implemented, there are a few limitations as well:

- **Multi-lingual support**: The current preview feature does not support multiple languages. This supports only English and SQL.

- **Accessing data**: Copilot can run on top of your data, but does not access data to filter out any specific portion of the data. You cannot run any questions with the where condition or any filter within a column.

- A limited number of tables and databases are supported to the query results. Copilot searches for the matching results, and relevant searches are ranked to share the top 10 results.

- Query Syntax might be an issue for a few queries. A few queries might give syntax that may not work in Snowflake.

These are the current limitations of the Copilot. Copilot can also be used to analyze queries and workloads. You can provide an SQL and ask a Copilot to explain it step-by-step. Copilot usage is free until June 2024; later, Copilot will be billed, and billing details will be shared on the Snowflake documentation soon. Refer to **https://docs.snowflake.com/en/user-guide/snowflake-copilot** for more details, as well as upcoming changes to Copilot. Like Copilot, Snowflake also announced a universal search to run searches across the platforms, and we will learn about it in the next section.

Using universal search

Snowflake announced a universal search to run a search within the Snowflake account to locate any data product available in the account, marketplace, documentation, knowledge base, Snowflake community, etc. Search accepts queries from the user and searches for the database objects. You can get results even if there are typos or spelling issues while searching a string or query using search. Refer to *Figure 18.13*, which shows the search pane:

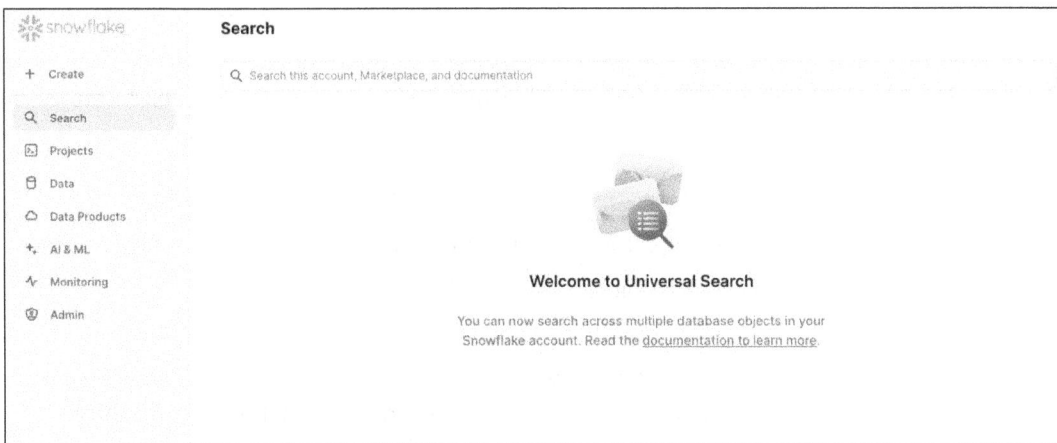

Figure 18.13: *Universal search*

Here, the search can be accessed by logging into Snowsight. Log on to Snowsight and click on Search from the left-side navigation menu. This opens a search window, where we can provide the input query or the name to be searched. You can search for any database object using search, as shown in *Figure 18.14*:

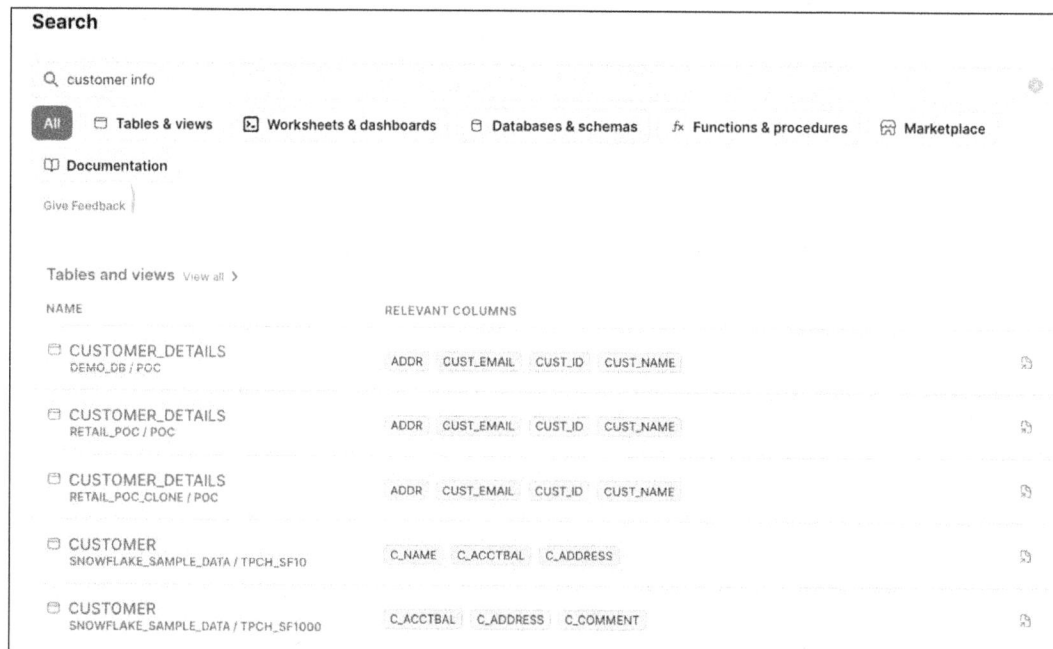

Search

Q customer info

[All] ▢ Tables & views   ▣ Worksheets & dashboards   ▤ Databases & schemas   *fx* Functions & procedures   ▨ Marketplace

▢ Documentation

Give Feedback

Tables and views View all >

NAME		RELEVANT COLUMNS			
CUSTOMER_DETAILS DEMO_DB / POC		ADDR	CUST_EMAIL	CUST_ID	CUST_NAME
CUSTOMER_DETAILS RETAIL_POC / POC		ADDR	CUST_EMAIL	CUST_ID	CUST_NAME
CUSTOMER_DETAILS RETAIL_POC_CLONE / POC		ADDR	CUST_EMAIL	CUST_ID	CUST_NAME
CUSTOMER SNOWFLAKE_SAMPLE_DATA / TPCH_SF10		C_NAME	C_ACCTBAL	C_ADDRESS	
CUSTOMER SNOWFLAKE_SAMPLE_DATA / TPCH_SF1000		C_ACCTBAL	C_ADDRESS	C_COMMENT	

Figure 18.14: Search results

As you observe here, the customer is one of the objects created as part of earlier **proof of concepts (POCs)**, and when we search for customer info, it lists down all the objects with details. Note that these objects are listed based on the role and access granted to the user running the search query.

The universal search results are limited to the Snowflake objects, marketplace, and documentation. Refer to *Table 18.1*, which lists the searchable objects and details from the resources:

Searchable object category	Resources
Database objects	Databases, Schema, Table, Views, UDFs, Stored Procedures
Snowsight features	Worksheets
Data marketplace	Data products listed on the Snowflake marketplace
Knowledge resources	Snowflake documentation https://docs.snowflake.com/ Knowledge documents from the Snowflake community https://community.snowflake.com/

Table 18.1: Search resources

As listed here, these are the objects and resources that can be searched using universal search in English. Any newly added objects may take a few hours to reflect in search results. Newly added, dropped, or deleted objects may take a few hours to reflect in search results. Search makes it easier to look for any objects, features, or documents. Like search, Snowflake has launched distinct LLM-based services and functions. One of the widely used LLM-based services is Document AI, which can be used to extract information and data from documents. We will learn more about document AI and using the service to implement a quick use case.

Implementing use case with Document AI

Document AI is Snowflake AI, offering to extract data from any type of document. This feature is based on Snowflake's Arctic-TILT proprietary LLM model. This is a preview feature and is available on AWS and Microsoft Azure accounts for most regions. This service can process any type of document and extract information in the form of data. This feature can be used to extract details from handwritten documents, PDFs, images, logos, or any graphical forms. This feature can be used to define pipelines that can process documents, extract information, feed into tables, train the models, or feed into any other models for future processing.

Document AI can be used for zero-shot extraction as well as fine-tuned usage. This can extract data from any type of new document that can be fed into it, which is called zero-shot extraction. This uses a predefined and pre-trained LLM model as a foundation model to extract the details. A fine-tuned model allows users to train the foundation model, Arctic-TILT, to process the specific documents. For example, in a healthcare use case, you can use DICOM files to train the model and use the trained model to extract required information as per the specific requirements of the healthcare use case. The trained model is specific to the account and available to the account users only. This will not be shared with any other customers of Snowflake.

There are specific use cases that can be implemented with Document AI. Refer to some of the following use cases of document AI:

- Converting unstructured data in the form of documents to structured data feeds that can be stored in the form of tables.

- Data pipelines that can process the incoming documents and generate the data feeds required for processing.

- Extracting details from the specific format of documents by training the foundation model and automating the extraction process for engineering needs.

These are some of the use cases that can be implemented with Document AI. You can also customize the solution based on your business requirements and application needs. Document AI can be used with a user interface as well as with SQL query processing.

Document AI implementation options

Like any other Snowflake features, Document AI can be used in the form of embedded SQL queries and using the Snowsight user interface to create models. The following are the options to implement use cases for Document AI:

- Document AI can be used with Snowsight as a user interface where users can define the model and validate it using natural language. Users can also fine-tune the models to improve the results of Document AI.

- **Using SQL method**: `<model_build_name>!PREDICT` to extract data from the documents. This can also be used as part of data pipelines to process incoming documents continuously using **streams** and **tasks**.

Note: **Documents processed through SQL method <model_build_name>!PREDICT must be stored on internal stage or external stage for processing.**

Users can use relevant options to set up the document processing. Both approaches consume compute and storage credits for processing. We will understand the usage components in the upcoming section.

Document AI usage

Document AI usage is calculated in terms of the storage and computing used to process the documents. The following are the usage components of the Document AI feature:

- **Compute usage**: There are two types of compute usage: AI service compute usage and warehouse usage. The AI compute is the usage required to execute the method to process the documents. Warehouse usage is the usage required to run the queries using the method as well as operations required to access, read, and process documents stored on the stage. The credit consumption is calculated based on the number of documents and pages processed.

- **Storage usage**: Documents need to be uploaded to the stage for extract method processing, which incurs storage costs. Also, the user interface approach needs to upload the documents from Snowsight that are stored in the user space for processing, which incurs storage costs.

Overall usage can be tracked and monitored using Snowflake usage metadata views. The compute cost can be identified by selecting the **ai_services** service type. These views are present in the organizational usage views and need appropriate permissions to run queries on top of organizational usage views. Usually, these views are refreshed. Refer to the following query to retrieve the usage details:

```
/* Metadata query to get document ai service compute*/
SELECT
ACCOUNT_NAME,
```

```
SUM(CREDITS_USED) AS TOTAL_CREDITS_USED,
SUM(CREDITS_USED_CLOUD_SERVICES) AS CLOUD_SERVICES_CREDITS,
SUM(CREDITS_USED_COMPUTE) AS COMPUTE_CREDITS
FROM SNOWFLAKE.ORGANIZATION_USAGE.METERING_DAILY_HISTORY
WHERE service_type ILIKE '%ai_services%' AND
start_time <= current_time
;
```

You can customize the query and set up a custom function or stored procedure to monitor the AI services spent.

Snowflake compute recommendations

Snowflake recommends using warehouses with X-small, Small, and Medium sizes for Document AI. Query processing takes its own time, and scaling up in this scenario might not help to process the documents faster. Instead, it will add to the cost of the warehouse. It is recommended to set up a separate warehouse for AI workloads from regular engineering workloads.

Now, you have learned about the service, usage, and monitoring of the overall spending for AI services. The next step is to learn to use the Document AI service. We will learn to implement a use case in the upcoming section.

Implementing Document AI

This section covers the Document AI use case along with its implementation steps. As you know, this can process documents stored on stages, and users can upload to Snowsight as part of interactive processing. Refer to the following steps to implement the use case:

- **Document readiness**: Snowflake supports documents in the form of PDF, DOCX, JPEG or JPF, TEXT or TXT, TIFF, PNG, EML, and HTML. Documents can be up to 125 pages long and not more than 50MB in size. Documents must be 1200 x 1200 mm in size, whereas images can be 50 x 50 and 10,000 x 10,000 pixels. It is recommended to obfuscate the sensitive or PII information present within documents until the service is in Preview.

- **Implementation using Snowsight:** Snowflake has a predefined role, **SNOWFLAKE. DOCUMENT_INTELLIGENCE_CREATOR** that can be used to grant to the user creating a model. Login to Snowsight | select the **Role** | go to **AI & ML** | **Document AI** | select warehouse | select **+Build** | select **Create**.

- **Implementation using SQL:** Snowflake has extracted the **PREDICT** method. Users can use this to query the documents. As you know, this needs documents uploaded to stage locations. Upload the required documents to the internal or external stage and run the following SQL query:

```
SELECT inspections!PREDICT(
GET_PRESIGNED_URL(@document_ai_stage, RELATIVE_PATH), 1)
FROM DIRECTORY(@document_ai_stage);
```

Here, the **document_ai_stage** is the stage defined to store the documents. Inspections is the model built, and 1 is the version of the model. You can build the model using Snowsight build and use it here to run as part of SQL.

Document AI can be added as part of data pipelines to extract information and process it as a data feed. Refer to **https://docs.snowflake.com/en/user-guide/snowflake-cortex/ document-ai/tutorials/create-processing-pipelines** to implement the data pipeline with Document AI. Snowflake also announced a managed service to allow users to implement the containerized applications that are native to the Snowflake platform with Snowpark Container Service. We will learn more about container service in the following section.

Using Snowpark container services

Snowflake container service is a preview feature available in all AWS regions, except in trial accounts. Snowflake container service is a fully managed service used to implement containerized applications within the Snowflake ecosystem. This service allows users to deploy and manage scalable applications with containerized workloads in the Snowflake ecosystem. This service allows users to implement applications without moving data from the Snowflake platform. These applications run in a containerized way that does not need to move data between applications and data platforms. With this service, applications can be brought to the data. Snowpark container service is a fully managed service that is integrated with Snowflake, and applications can perform the following operations:

- Running SQL queries on Snowflake with Snowflake virtual warehouses
- Access data files stored on the Snowflake stage
- Processing data with SQL queries

Snowpark container service can run and scale applications with container workloads across Snowflake regions and cloud platforms. This service allows users to implement long-running services, use GPUs to boost the speed and processing capabilities, write applications with a choice of languages, and use libraries with applications. This service is not available for implementation with a trial account. You can use the Snowflake platform, which are partner accounts or commercial accounts. Refer to **https://docs.snowflake. com/en/developer-guide/snowpark-container-services/overview-tutorials** to create Snowpark container service as well as job service.

Snowflake's Snowpark container service introduces a few additional objects like images, image registry, image repository, specification files, compute pools, services, and jobs. Refer to *Figure 18.15*, which shows the container service and integration with the Snowflake platform:

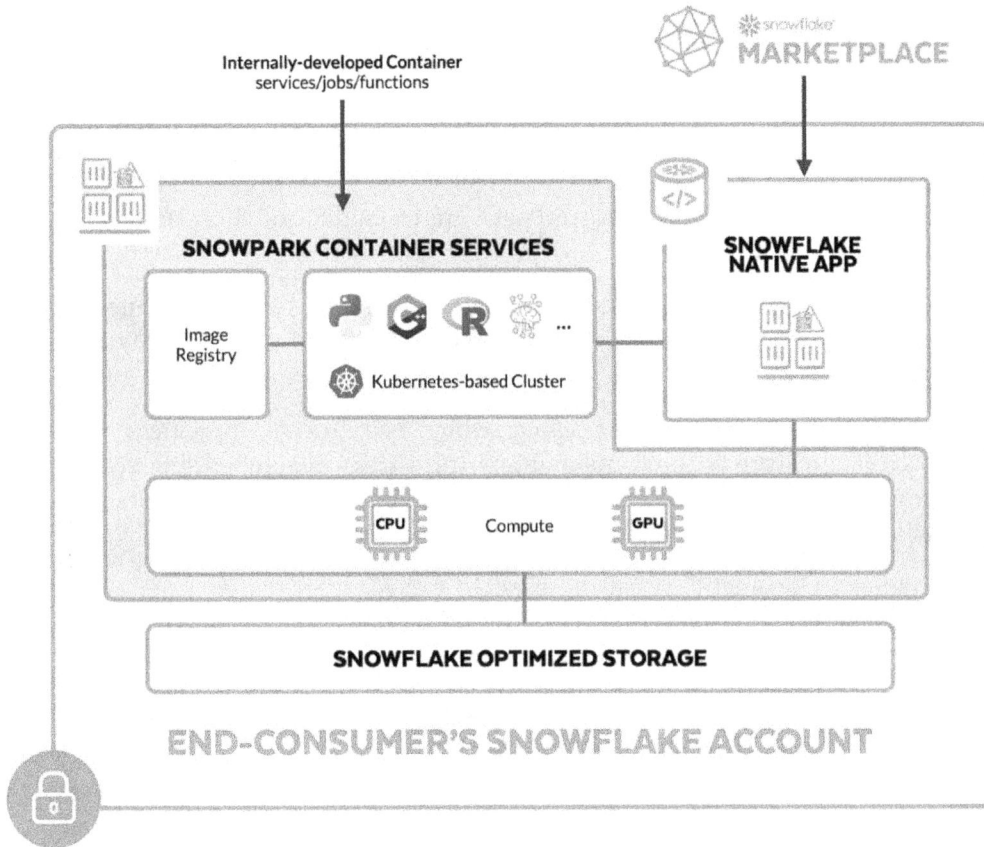

Figure 18.15: Snowpark container service (PC: Snowflake documentation)

Here, container services can be used to build and implement applications. You can build images using Docker and register with the image registry. You cannot implement a POC with a Snowflake trial account, as Snowpark container service is not available with trial accounts. Refer to **https://quickstarts.snowflake.com/guide/intro_to_snowpark_container_services/index.html#0** to implement container services. You can use partner accounts to implement POC.

Conclusion

Generative AI is the ask of the era, and most customers prefer to identify the Gen AI use case and start with a pilot to evaluate the business value adds. We have learned the most common use cases implementation with Snowflake native features, like Cortex LLM functions, Cortex Analyst, Cortex Search Service, Universal Search, and Copilot, and implementing various use cases with Streamlit. This chapter helps the reader understand and implement these features to start developing them on the Snowflake platform.

Points to remember

Here are some key takeaways from this chapter:

- Snowflake Cortex LLM offers a set of built-in functions to implement LLM functionalities like SUMMARIZATION, SENTIMENT, EXTRACT, and TRANSLATE. These functions support a pre-trained foundation model along with Snowflake ARTIC.

- Snowflake Cortex Analyst sets the easiest way and seamless integration to implement a chatbot or LLM assistant on top of the underlying data with the help of a semantic model.

- Snowflake also offers Cortex search, which helps users implement a semantic search-like feature without maintaining infrastructure, embedding creation, and using them to generate the response to the prompt. Cortex search does it all as a managed service of the platform.

- Snowflake Document AI can be used to extract information from any type of document, like PDF, DOCS, PPTX, TIFF, JPEG, PNG, etc. These documents can be stored on named stages to process as part of the document AI pipeline.

- Snowflake universal search is used to search the objects, features, and Snowflake knowledge base. Results are shown as per the Snowflake RBAC and the Role selected to run the search query.

- Snowflake Horizon allows users to implement unified Governance for the platform. Snowflake's native **data quality and metrics functions (DMFs)** can be used to validate the data quality.

- Snowflake's Snowpark container service is used to implement containerized applications within the Snowflake platform. This allows users to create and store images with a native image registry used to deploy applications.

Join our Discord space

Join our Discord workspace for latest updates, offers, tech happenings around the world, new releases, and sessions with the authors:

https://discord.bpbonline.com

Index

www.ingramcontent.com/pod-product-compliance
Lightning Source LLC
Chambersburg PA
CBHW061800210326

41599CB00034B/6820